The Colour of Sculpture 1840–1910

Ladies' Library Association.

The Colour of 1840–1910 Sculpture

Andreas Blühm

Wolfgang Drost
June Hargrove
Emmanuelle Héran
Philip Ward-Jackson
Alison Yarrington

Van Gogh Museum, Amsterdam
Henry Moore Institute, Leeds

Waanders Uitgevers, Zwolle

Contents

6 Lenders

7 Foreword

8 Acknowledgments

Andreas Blühm
11 **In living colour**
A short history of colour and sculpture in the 19th century

Wolfgang Drost
61 **Colour, sculpture, mimesis**
A 19th-century debate

Philip Ward-Jackson
73 **Sculpture colouring and the industries of art in the 19th century**

Alison Yarrington
83 **Under the spell of Madame Tussaud**
Aspects of 'high' and 'low' in 19th-century polychromed sculpture

Emmanuelle Héran
83 **Art for the sake of the soul**
Polychrome sculpture and literary Symbolism

June Hargrove
103 **Painter-sculptors and polychromy in the evolution of modernism**

117 Catalogue

241 Notes

257 Select bibliography

271 Index

Lenders

Musée d'Arras
Beauvais, Musée départemental de l'Oise
Kunsthalle Bremen
Brussels, Musées royaux de l'Art et de l'Histoire
Brussels, Musées royaux des Beaux-Arts de Belgique (Musée Meunier)
Caen, Musée des Beaux-Arts
Cardiff, The National Museum of Wales
Compiègne, Musée national du Château
Dijon, Musée des Beaux-Arts
Staatliche Kunstsammlungen Dresden, Skulpturensammlung
Frederikssund, J.F. Willumsens Museum
The Hague, Rijksdienst Beeldende Kunst
Hamburger Kunsthalle
Karlsruhe, Badisches Landesmuseum
Leeds Museums and Galleries
Liverpool, The Board of Trustees of the National Galleries and Museums on Merseyside
London, The Fine Art Society PLC
London, Royal Academy of Arts
London, Tate Gallery
London, The Trustees of the Victoria and Albert Museum
Lyons, Musée des Beaux-Arts
Marburger Universitätsmuseum für Kunst und Kulturgeschichte
Martigny (Switzerland), Collection Fondation Pierre Gianadda
Paris, Association des amis de Carlo Marochetti
Paris, Collection Lucile Audouy
Paris, courtesy of Brame & Lorenceau
Paris, Mme Rhodia Dufet Bourdelle (Musée Bourdelle)
Paris, Galerie Elstir
Paris, Galerie de France
Paris, Musée des arts décoratifs
Paris, Musée d'Orsay
Paris, Musée du Petit Palais
Paris, Musée Rodin
Roermond, St Christoffelparochie
Stedelijk Museum Roermond
Saint-Germain-en-Laye, Musée départemental Maurice Denis – Le Prieuré
A parish church in Scotland
Château d'Ussé
Vesoul, Musée municipal Georges Garret
Martin von Wagner-Museum der Universität Würzburg
Heirs of Dr. Roland Fleiner, courtesy Kunsthaus Zürich

and private owners who wish to remain anonymous

Foreword

An exhibition dedicated to the role of colour in 19th-century sculpture is, as far as we know, a novelty. When, in 1885, the Nationalgalerie in Berlin organised an exhibition of polychrome sculpture, it included all epochs and cultures, with the 19th century, of course, representing the 'modern.' Nonetheless, our enterprise should be seen within a certain context: the 1991 exhibition *Un âge d'or des arts décoratifs 1814-1848* in Paris, for example, provided an excellent overview of the variety and colour of the 19th century, as did *The Second Empire: art in France under Napoleon III*, organised by the Philadelphia Museum of Art in 1979. We are also indebted to the Musée d'Orsay which, since its opening, has striven to unify all aspects of 19th-century art, and has thus been a continual source of inspiration. For the Van Gogh Museum, *The colour of sculpture* is the logical successor to the 1995 exhibition *In perfect harmony: picture and frame, 1850-1920*, a presentation that also shed new light on a neglected subject.

There are probably not many museums which are so continuously reminded of the changing history of taste as the Van Gogh Museum, whose patron found so little recognition during his lifetime. His fate is both an exhortation and a sign of hope, and the staff regards it as a kind of duty to present not only the well-known and treasured to the general public, but also the unknown and forgotten. Over the last few years, sculpture, until recently under-represented in the collection, has gained a new status, one which is reflected in the present exhibition.

The Van Gogh Museum is pleased to have found a partner in the Henry Moore Institute, which also offers much more than its name implies. Devoted to the study and display of sculpture, it was the institution most capable of supporting this endeavour. Although mainly concerned with modern and contemporary work, the Henry Moore Institute greeted the idea spontaneously and with great enthusiasm. In fact, recent art production in particular offers enough links with the past to merit a renewed interest in 19th-century polychrome sculpture. This should not be taken to mean those neo-realist sculptors who employ traditional methods, thereby merely reheating an old debate, but rather those who use new materials and media in order to call art itself, its appearance and reception, into question. From Marcel Duchamp to Joseph Beuys, artists have overcome the limits of sculpture and in so doing retrospectively transformed the use of colour into a sanctioned means of expression.

When speaking of Duchamp and Beuys, it is difficult not to think of the unusual substances employed by 20th-century sculptors, but the list for the works in this exhibition is no less heterogeneous: marble from different parts of the world, bronze in various patinas, onyx, granite and alabaster, plaster, terracotta and mortar, limewood and mahogany, porcelain, *gessoduro*, glass paste and stoneware, amber, semi-precious stones such as opals and agates, lapis lazuli, silver and ivory, even textiles, wrought iron, wax, mother-of-pearl, cameos, a scarab, glass, and a light bulb. One should never forget, however, that these materials were not thought of as an end in themselves but rather as a means of expressing an idea or a formal concept.

The many different materials listed here are found in a great variety of sculpture which is eloquent proof of the generosity of their owners in lending to this exhibition, and so ensuring its success. Such an undertaking would not have been possible without their cooperation and, above all, trust. We would like to express our gratitude to the directors and staffs of the various museums and galleries, as well as to numerous private collectors: Norman Adams, David Alston, Guillaume Ambroise, Pierre Arizzoli-Clémentel, Lucile, Paul and Aude Audouy, Pierre Baudson, Casimir de Blacas, Alan Borg, Antonia Boström, Annemieke Broeke, Thérèse Burollet, Agnès Delannoy, Eliane De Wilde, Rhodia Dufet Bourdelle, Philippe Durey, Josette Galiègue, Sabine Gangi, Léonard Gianadda, Ralph Grossmann, Julian Hartnoll, Carl Hedengren, Brigitte Herrbach-Schmidt, Wulf Herzogenrath, Christian Klemm, Andreas Kreul, Leila Krogh,

Antoinette Le Normand-Romain, Bernard Lorenceau, Henri Loyrette, Françoise Maison, Hélène Meyer, Edward Morris, Jean-Luc Olivié, Gisèle Ollinger-Zinque, Andrew McIntosh Patrick, Anne Pingeot, Evelyne Possémé, Heiner Protzmann, Marie-José Salmon, Nicholas Serota, Uwe M. Schneede, Harald Siebenmorgen, Evelyn Silber, Ulrich Sinn, Peyton Skipwith, Emmanuel Starcky, Bärbel Stephan, MaryAnne Stevens, Georg Syamken, Alain Tapié, Catherine Thieck, H.Ph.A. Tillie, Julian Treuherz, Helen Valentine, Francis Van Noten, Jacques Vilain, Irma Wehgartner, Alistair Wilson, Jürgen Wittstock and E.M. Younie.

We also wish to thank the conservators and technical assistants behind the scenes, whose work was made all the more difficult by the fragile state of so many pieces. The authors of the catalogue have succeeded in shedding light on what was once unknown material. The translators have helped make their facts and ideas available to a large audience. Photographing these three-dimensional *and* coloured works – and reproducing them – was also a challenge to be mastered.

In addition to the lenders and helpers, we would also like to express our thanks to our colleagues at both institutions: in Amsterdam, Andreas Blühm, who conceived the exhibition, as well as Aly Noordermeer and Sandra Sihan, responsible respectively for the coordination and administrative assistance. In Leeds, Penelope Curtis worked with Andreas Blühm to clarify the nature of our project and was responsible for bringing the show to Britain. Stephen Feeke and Helen Pearson provided the administrative support. Jackie Heuman was responsible for the conservation of the exhibits. Pieter Roozen designed the catalogue and, in association with Jan Hofstra, the installation in Amsterdam.

Charles Baudelaire's condemnation of sculpture – as expressed in his critique *Pourquoi la sculpture est ennuyeuse* – still haunts the memory. The time has finally come to abandon this prejudice. *The colour of sculpture 1840-1910* will, we hope, be a decisive step in this direction.

Ronald de Leeuw *Robert Hopper*
Director *Director*
Van Gogh Museum *Henry Moore Institute*

Acknowledgments

The announcement that we were busy preparing an exhibition of 19th-century coloured sculpture was generally greeted with a puzzled frown. Usually, however, this scepticism quickly turned to interest and then to enthusiasm. The circle of colleagues on the lookout for works grew by leaps and bounds, and in a short time new discoveries were arriving every day. All the information I received is contained in two metres worth of files, and can only be dimly reflected in the present book. Often, it was the curators from the lending institutions mentioned above who gave the decisive clues in the search. I am especially grateful to them, and all the others named here who supplied both inspiration and criticism. First and foremost I would like to thank my co-authors and, practically, co-editors, Wolfgang Drost, June Hargrove, Emmanuelle Héran, Philip Ward-Jackson and Alison Yarrington. Nathalie Bondil spent many hours at the Service de Documentation of the Musée d'Orsay and brought numerous interesting facts to light. The Service de Documentation itself proved once again to be an absolutely indispensable source of knowledge. Donald Myers contributed his as yet unpublished ideas on the British New Sculpture movement to the relevant catalogue entries. Nienke Blom assisted in the last phases of editing and production.

Many other colleagues have given their time and advice to this project. I am particularly indebted to Anne Pingeot, whose enthusiasm and knowledge were invaluable. I would also like to mention Victor Arwas, Jean Aubert, Joanna R. Barnes, Albert Benamou, Sigrid Braunfels, Jacques de Caso, Catherine Chevillot, Michel Draguet, Annick Fix-Masseau, Tom Flynn, Anne Birgitte Fonsmark, Patricia Foujols, Albert Gallichan, Christopher Gow, Michael Hall, Julian Hartnoll, Waring Hopkins, R.S. Hunsucker, Daniel Imbert, Gaëlle Jacques, Gerlof Janzen, Robert Kashey, Kordelia Knoll, Walter Krause, John H. Larson, Francine Legrand-Kapferer, Mary L. Levkoff, Elena di Majo, Ulrike Maltschew, Laure de Margerie, Corinna Pertschi, Ulrich Pietsch, Mathieu Pinette, Stuart Pivar, Klaus-D. Pohl, Liz Prettejohn, Rodolphe Rapetti, Jacqueline Rapmund, Benedict Read, Patrik Reuterswärd, Patrick Roger-Binet, Peter Rose, Chantal Rouquet, Susann Schaal, Ulrich Schießl, Stephan Seeliger, Timothy Stevens, Alain Tarika, Karina Türr and Jörg Zutter.

We believe that the present catalogue goes beyond what has been published to date, although it only presents a small proportion of the polychrome sculptures in existence. We are more than aware of what still needs to be done and particularly regret that the geographical scope was limited to works from western and central Europe. Artists from southern and eastern Europe, as well as North America, all made important and original contributions to polychrome sculpture, works which could not be included due to purely logistical considerations. The list of sculptors who combined colour and volume given in the index clearly demonstrates that the phenomenon discussed in this book was in no way marginal to the history of art. Anyone desiring more information is welcome to examine the papers now in the Van Gogh Museum. This book cannot give a complete picture of the epoch, but if it draws attention to colour in sculpture, inspires the public and stimulates further research then it will have already achieved its aim.

Andreas Blühm
Head of Exhibitions
Van Gogh Museum

Note to the reader: **[00]** refers to catalogue nos., [00] refers to illustrations

Andreas Blühm

In living colour

A short history of colour in sculpture in the 19th century

There does not exist in the world a single object which has not both form and colour. Alexander Archipenko[1]

The Italian sculptor Giovanni Dupré was on his way to London in 1859 to present his model for a monument to the Duke of Wellington when a catastrophe occurred: 'The ship had sprung a leak and water had got into the crates, the plaster figures had softened and separated from the base; body parts rolled about in the cases: heads were severed from their torsos, hands were broken and disfigured, hawk-noses had become pug-noses, helmets had lost their crests and plumes, everything was a mess. And, as if this was not enough, I had wrapped my work in linen and packing paper and the salt water had caused a chemical reaction which gave the model a fantastic coloration. Dark blue, red and yellow had mixed to create a bizarre effect. It would have been impossible to treat my poor opus with more contempt.'[2]

1   The Egyptian Court in the Crystal Palace, stereo photograph, c. 1860, Amsterdam, Rijksmuseum

The sculptor's dismay is understandable: a freak of nature had spoiled his model and dashed his hopes of obtaining a lucrative commission. Even had he added colour on purpose, however, enriching the three dimensions of his statue with a fourth, his chances still would have been slight. Experiments with colour had only been conducted occasionally before 1859, and were almost always subjected to severe criticism or even open hostility. European sculpture had been 'colourless' for decades so that to most viewers anything else seemed almost improper. When seen within a broader geographical and temporal context, however, this voluntary restriction is exceptional: Mesopotamians, Egyptians, Aztecs and Incas, Africans, Indians, Chinese, Japanese and Oceanians – as a rule the majority of cultures produced coloured sculpture. From this perspective, the renunciation of colour no longer seems normal.

It is also contrary to human nature. This becomes particularly clear when the loss of colour perception is involuntary, as in the case of a New York painter who became colour-blind after an accident. The effect his condition had on the way he perceived those around him was even more disturbing than what it did to his professional practice: people suddenly seemed to him 'like animated grey statues.'[3] Perceptual limitations, however, are only seldom pathological. On the contrary, human beings rarely use their senses at full capacity: a built-in censor protects us from a confusing flood of external visual, acoustic and tactile stimuli. Selective perception is thus not necessarily crippling; it can also serve a protective physiological and psychological function: we see what we choose to see and only what is good for us.

Physical and mental factors alone do not determine perception, culture is also important; and it has its own history. The human beings who flocked to the cities from the woods and fields eventually lost certain sensibilities they had once needed to survive. On the other hand, they had to learn to recognise completely new signals. The history of art can help us better understand some of the finer points of such transformations.

One of the interesting aspects of this chronicle of vision and blindness is the perception of colour in space. Although colour was employed differently and to varying degrees in European sculpture, there are no overarching descriptions of either its history or implications. This book aims to shed some light on the phenomenon in the 19th century, a period in which the fight to reinstate colour was fought on a broad front. A single volume can hardly do justice to the course of this struggle and the incredible variety of artworks it produced. The enormous number of works and texts stands in glaring contrast to the lack of knowledge on the subject among both art historians and the public so that the first step must be a rehabilitation of polychrome sculpture in general.

Why this 'colour-blindness' with regard to sculpture? I believe it has three fundamental causes: 1. the power of convention; 2. the retrospective 'correction' of history due to changes in taste; and 3. the complacency of art history.

1. Our definition of sculpture as artistically formed volume in black (bronze) or white (marble) is based on the canon of the 18th century. Johann Joachim Winckelmann's descriptions of ancient statuary set the standards by which both old and new sculptures were to be judged. The works Winckelmann had available to him were, however, either black or white, so that these norms were themselves the result of visual 'restrictions' – despite the fact that rumours of antique polychromy were already in circulation. Further, Winckelmann did not regard history with a neutral eye; he was searching for guidance in the present or, still better, for ratification of a (preconceived) ideal of beauty. One of his aesthetic principles was clarity of plastic form, which, of course, can be endangered by the use of colour. Because it 'reflected the largest number of rays of light,' there was no question in Winckelmann's mind that white was the best possible colour for sculpture.[4]

Most other 18th-century archaeologists also either ignored or decried antique polychromy. Even the great Phidias was not spared the scholars' contempt: his colossal statues in gold and ivory, known only from written sources, were condemned as tasteless.[5] Newly acquired collections of ancient sculpture both reflected and confirmed Neo-classicism's 'white' ideology. Johann Zoffany's portrait of Charles Townley in his Park Street gallery may be said to illustrate contemporary opinion: Townley is depicted amid a forest of splendid marble bodies, contemplating the grandeur of the art of the past; his dog Kam cowers at his feet, mistrustfully eyeing his own compositional counterpart, a two-toned bust of Minerva. Placed in this lowly position, the dog and the bust seem to signify the abasement of both nature and art. [2]

Not long after its establishment, Winckelmann's aesthetic was challenged by the first indisputable traces of antique polychromy.

2 Johann Zoffany, *Charles Townley and friends in the Park Street Gallery, Westminster*, 1781-83, Burnley, Towneley Hall Art Gallery and Museums

It was only in the 19th century, however, that these archaeological discoveries became the subject of serious scholarly consideration. Due to the intensity of the controversy that soon arose, as well as to a tenacious opposition to the evidence, perceptual mechanisms changed only slowly. The champions of polychromy realised their greatest enemy was habit: people were simply more used to seeing sculpture in white marble.[6]

2. The struggle to re-establish colour in sculpture was not always rewarded with success. On the contrary: in general it was the forces of resistance that triumphed. As far as actual works are concerned, a statistical compilation is hampered by the fact that many early attempts were later destroyed. The desire to 'restore' monuments to their (supposed) original state had particularly terrible consequences, often causing irreversible damage to the historical substance as colour was added or subtracted at random.[7] Purism effected architecture and sculpture equally. Churches like the cathedral at Limburg an der Lahn and St Elizabeth's at Marburg, for example, were completely robbed of their characteristic decoration; they had been, as one contemporary put it 'washed, brushed and shaved.'[8] In an endeavour to make the aesthetics of the past conform to those of the present, the intentions of the medieval artisans were actively misinterpreted and many sculptures were stripped to the core in order to

reveal the material. The structure of the wood and the marks of the carving tools, carefully hidden so as to give the work a perfect appearance and flawless character, were forced to light.[9] Even as late as 1888, the art historian Louis Courajod could note that an important statue of the Madonna, at first rejected by the Louvre, had finally come into the collection after the owner had washed away all the colour, thereby demonstrating the 'purity' of its sculptural qualities.[10]

Contemporaries fared no better. The polychrome interior of the neo-gothic church Sainte-Clotilde in Paris, built around the middle of the century by Franz Christian Gau and Théodore Ballu, was repainted a monochrome stone colour only shortly after its completion. John Gibson, advocate of neo-classical polychromy, saw his statues of *Queen Victoria* and *Countess Beauchamp*, as well as his *Pandora*, deprived of their coloration.[11] In 1873, Henri de Triqueti's plans for a gold and enamel cenotaph for Prince Albert were rejected.[12] Carlo Marochetti's bust of *Dalip Singh* in the British royal collection in Osborne now gleams in brilliant white, and it is only thanks to the relative 'neglect' of the artist's heirs that their version has retained its polychromy. [46] The painting on Jean-Léon Gérôme's monumental seated nude *Tanagra* (1890) is now practically invisible. [112] A similar striving for 'immaculacy' led to the cleaning of his *Pygmalion and the statue* (1892) – from the point of view of both form and content comparable to complete destruction. [46]

3 August Allebé, *The museum attendant*, 1870, The Hague, Museum Mesdag

Immeasurable damage was done to bronzes, with patinas rubbed off or additionally manipulated, procedures that border on forgery. These examples more than prove that it is not only works from Antiquity or the Middle Ages that can be deceptive about their original appearances.

3. Scholarship, too, is to blame for the lack of knowledge about polychromy and the resulting clumsy, even barbaric, treatment of both older and more recent art. Sculpture, in any case, has always been a kind of step-child of the discipline. Since at least the 18th century, it has been generally recognised that the public has more difficulty with this genre than with painting, a fact much lamented by sculptors. As recently as 1973, Horst W. Janson described 19th-century production as 'unexamined, poorly recorded and unphotographed, hence inaccessible.'[13] This inaccessibility – the result of difficulties with both transport and reproduction – as well as its reputation for weightiness, have kept the medium from making more friends.

One would naturally think that at least the problems involved in reproduction had now been solved. It was photography itself, however, which was originally responsible for the scholarly conventions that eventually led to the neglect of colour. Because its immobility and whiteness helped to overcome various weaknesses in the new technology, the early champions and pioneers of photography – from François Arago to William Henry Fox Talbot – recommended sculpture as a subject.[14] On the other hand, black and white photography has painted the past century in shades of grey.[15] Just as binoculars allow us to see into the distance at the cost of what is directly in front of us, so the enrichment of our vision through photographic reproduction has had its price.

Next to these 'objective' reasons for the disregard of colour in sculpture due to photography, aesthetics also played a role. As reproductions became increasingly exact – as well as more suggestive as slide projections in a darkened room – originals became less and less important in the practice of art history. One cannot, of course, hold Heinrich Wölfflin personally responsible for this development, but already in his influential book *Principles of art history*, first published in German in 1915, one gets the sense that he privileges the photograph over the original. Elsewhere, Wölfflin also made extensive comments on the photography of sculpture, suggesting ways of perfecting it; it goes without saying that colour had no part here or in the discussion about the medium in the *Principles*.[16] Wölfflin's ideas, like those of the 20th century as a whole, were formed by the ideology of truth to materials, a concept which, although a blessing in many regards, has often prejudiced scholarship. The perseverance of purist academic conventions made it impossible for either Wölfflin, or later Rudolf Wittkower, to give the role of colour the

4   View of the London International Exhibition, 1862, hand-coloured stereo photograph, Amsterdam, Rijksmuseum

attention it deserved.[17] Even such an open-minded scholar as Janson felt that one learned more about 19th-century sculpture 'by viewing it in relation to the sculpture of the preceding centuries than [...] by trying to correlate it with the evolution of nineteenth-century painting.'[18] The 19th-century notion of artistic unity had come to be neglected, even by the experts. They consciously ignored the common ground of time and space, and continued to isolate painting and sculpture from one another.

Only the reevaluation of Historicism and the inclusion of 19th-century monuments in preservation projects has reawakened an interest in polychromy.[19] Nonetheless, the majority of even the most recent scholarly publications are still under Winckelmann's spell. A true acceptance of colour in 19th-century sculpture still lies ahead. Although many works are now being restored, others are being destroyed, and the purists of the 20th century are as ruthless as their predecessors. The aim of this book is to deepen our knowledge of polychrome sculpture from the period 1840 to 1910, the era of its most rapid development and success: knowledge precedes appreciation. Neither this book nor the exhibition are meant as an apology for colour in sculpture. They are designed to make us aware of the great variety of artistic expression, to inspire us to look at and protect the original works, and to develop criteria for their examination.

The hierarchy of the arts

Why is it, when colour is so effective in painting, that a statue coloured according to nature is ugly rather than beautiful? Because colour is not form, because it is invisible to closed eyes and cannot be known by touch, because when seen it actually hides the beauty of form.
Johann Gottfried Herder[20]

The more art came to be seen as something independent of specific uses, the more it became a field of study for those who had never touched either a brush or chisel. The humanists made art a subject for non-professionals, soon academies were established and finally, in the 18th century, art criticism was born. One of the consequences of this scholarly and pedagogical approach was the creation of theoretical categories and the division of art into genres, which became new points of reference for artistic practice. The measure of a work's value was no longer the degree to which it fulfilled a certain task, but the extent to which it conformed to a specific set of rules.

In the Middle Ages, painting and sculpture were defined simply by tools and materials. Colouring sculpture for church interiors was not only completely natural, it was also an essential means of communicating the message. Painters were not restricted to the planar surface but were required to decorate figures, and sculptors had to take the painting of their statues into account from the very beginning.[21]

In the wake of humanist enthusiasm for the (supposedly) colourless works of Antiquity, painted statuary began to decline during the Renaissance. Nonetheless, a large number of all sculptures were still polychrome, in any case many more than today's disregard for colour would lead one to believe. Because history rewards the conquerors, and because in the Renaissance marble and bronze were considered the most important mediums for sculpture, Donatello's coloured works are now thought of as 'lapses' and Della Robbia's placed in the 'lower' category of decorative art. [122] In many ways, artists had only themselves to blame: the power of archaeologists and their faded artifacts, the wish to compete with science – all this led to an increased need for definition and differentiation among the arts.

Which art, painting or sculpture, was superior? This soon became the most absorbing question. The fruitless *paragone* debate came to occupy artists and theoreticians over the course of centuries. The arguments of Leone Battista Alberti and Leonardo da Vinci, repeated *ad nauseam*, devolved around the issue of mimesis. Painting, with the help of colour, could create the illusion of reality on a flat surface. Sculpture, on the other hand, was something spatial; it could achieve mimesis through volume

5   Young woman painting a statue of the Virgin, 15th century, miniature on parchement from the *Livre des femmes renommées de Jehan Boccace*, Paris, Bibliothèque nationale de France

alone, without colour. Obviously, each party defined these capabilities to their own advantage, thereby underlining the superiority of the genre they themselves favoured.[22]

During the Baroque period, with its love of the painterly, polychrome decoration once more became fashionable: one need only think of the papal tombs in St Peter's, with their masterly handling of colourful body parts, clothing and attributes. By employing an enormous assortment of coloured marble, Baroque artists were in fact appealing to an ancient tradition. Their aesthetic ideals changed the way Antiquity itself was seen, even altering its physical evidence, as demonstrated by the very freely-invented additions to older sculptures.[23] [124]

In general, it was the church which tended to favour polychrome sculpture. Particularly Spanish religious sculpture developed a kind of realism (*verdad*) which remained paradigmatic until far into the 19th century. [67] Here, classical modelling was combined not only with naturalistic painting, but also with real hair, teeth and glass eyes.[24] The lesser degree of coloration in courtly (as opposed to religious) sculpture may be the result of the higher level of education of its audience. This experienced public demanded more than superficial naturalism. One of the motivating factors behind the renewed dominance of white in the 18th century was certainly the desire to distinguish 'high' art from votive statues and other forms of colourful devotionalia. Those classes for whom art theory was not an everyday topic remained, however, receptive to all kinds of illusionism.

Once Neo-classicism became the dominant style, coloured sculpture seemed destined to die out completely. The *philosophes* preferred the brightness of white marble, which they saw as a symbol of their triumph over unenlightened mysticism; clarity of contour was to prevail over the sensuality of polychromy. Diderot was only one among many who spoke out against the use of colour. Etienne-Maurice Falconet, whom the philosopher so admired, for example, formulated his rejection of polychromy with great precision: 'Each art has its own means of imitation; in sculpture, colour is not one of them.'[25] Diderot had praised Falconet's marble group *Pygmalion and the statue* at the Salon of 1763. [7] The myth had long been a subject for painters, who could show the statue coming to life only by giving her white legs and red cheeks. [6] According to Diderot, Falconet was the first to have accomplished this through pose alone.

New perceptions

Already in 1762, while Winckelmann was still busy writing his *Geschichte der Kunst des Altertums*, empirical evidence began to challenge the premises of 'white' Neo-classicism. In that year, John Stuart and Nicholas Revett published their *Antiquities of Athens*, which included a discussion on the monumental gold and ivory statue of *Athena Parthenos*.[26] The excavations at Pompeii and Herculaneum brought wall paintings to light that further supported the notion that ancient sculpture had been painted.[27] Since the 1780s, the French archaeologist Antoine-Chrysostome Quatremère de Quincy had been conducting systematic research into antique polychromy.[28] The focus of his investigations were Phidias's monumental chryselephantine statues, the *Athena Parthenos* and the *Olympian Zeus*.

6   Jean Raoux, *Pygmalion and the statue*, 1717, Montpellier, Musée Fabre

7   Etienne-Maurice Falconet, *Pygmalion and the statue*, 1763, marble, Baltimore, Walters Art Gallery

In relation to his studies, the archaeologist was particularly interested in the experiences of contemporary sculptors. He often discussed Phidias's complex procedures, described in the literature, with his friend Antonio Canova. The sculptor was fascinated by Quatremère's findings, even endeavouring to colour the marble of his own statues.[29] Canova also experimented with combinations of marble and bronze. In his group *Daedalus and Icarus* (1777-79), the father is shown binding his son's wing-feathers together with a real piece of wire (Venice, Museo Correr).[30] Canova's *Hebe* was somewhat more controversial, not only because she holds a gold-bronze amphora, but also because the sculptor tinted her lips and cheeks a light red.[31] [10] Canova's idea had been to give her more expression, more life, but in the end he was forced to wash away the colour. *Hebe* now exists only in pure white, 'color da morto,' as her creator once said.[32] The time was not yet ripe for such experiments.

Due to inadequate techniques and negative criticism these early, fairly timid essays were usually failures. In painting, however, things were quite different and polychrome statues soon found their way into the antique interiors of neo-classical paintings. In 1789, for example, Jacques-Louis David set his *Brutus* in a environment that could have developed out of a conversation with Quatremère. At the back of the sombre room, David depicted a statuette of the goddess Roma which, despite being in shadow, is clearly coloured.[33] [11] Ten years earlier, David had travelled to Paestum with Quatremère de Quincy, and it was on this trip that the archaeologist developed his interest in polychromy.[34]

During the Empire, artisans often combined numerous materials and contrasting metallic patinas. Around the turn of the century, this trend moved from decorative to monumental sculpture. In 1806, Antoine-Denis Chaudet's *Peace* was shown in the Salon de la Paix in the Tuileries. [110] The gold and silver came

9   Head of the *Apollo* from the Villa del Citarista, Pompeii, bronze, Naples, Museo Archeologico Nazionale

from the receptacles that had once held the hearts of Louis XIII and Louis XIV, but the charm of the work allows one to forget these somewhat macabre origins. Charles Percier's Arc du Triomphe du Carrousel (1806-08) is also a combination of colourful stones and was originally crowned by the bronze horses from San Marco in Venice. In Berlin, Gottfried Schadow began experimenting with polychromy as early as 1812. He asked the director of the academy, Friedrich Georg Weitsch, to colour a relief he had made, based on a drawing by Karl Friedrich Schinkel: 'I want to have it painted! The whole should look antique, gothic, barbaric – these days that's *grand mode*!'[35]

Quatremère was not interested in such superficialities, but rather carried out his research with the utmost conscientiousness. This was probably the reason why his epoch-making treatise *Le Jupiter Olympien* was only ready for publication in 1814.[36] This beautifully illustrated book contained all that was known about polychrome sculpture at the time and convincingly proved that Phidias, one of the unchallenged masters, had practised it. [12] It soon became obvious that even the Greeks, in the period of their greatest creativity, had broken the rules of good taste. Cherished ideas suddenly began to founder.

8   Johann Joachim Kändler, *Huntsman*, c. 1760, porcelain, Staatliche Kunstsammlungen Dresden, Porzellansammlung

10 Antonio Canova, *Hebe*, 1817, marble, Forlì, Pinacoteca Communale

11 Jacques-Louis David, *Brutus*, 1789, Paris, Musée du Louvre (detail)

One of the first to appreciate Quatremère's apologia for polychromy was the archaeologist Martin von Wagner, who worked as an agent for the Bavarian crown prince, later King Ludwig I. In 1817, he published his description of the figures from the Temple of Aegina, recently purchased for the Glyptothek in Munich. On the subject of the traces of colour he wrote: 'We are puzzled by this apparently bizarre taste, and judge it as a barbaric practice, left over from earlier, less civilised times. This attitude, it seems to me, is comparable to the man in the Gospels who wanted to pull the splinter from his brother's eye without realising he had a beam in his own. If our eyes were pure and unprejudiced and, at the same time, we were lucky enough to see one of these Greek temples in its original perfection, I wager [that we] would change our minds and praise what we now condemn.'[37] Friedrich Schelling praised Wagner's exposition, expanding the latter's thoughts into a more general reflection and bitterly complaining of the 'complete division among the arts' and the decadence which had resulted from it.[38]

This acceptance of Greek polychromy opened the floodgates. New finds were made continually, providing archaeologists with fresh ammunition against the defenders of white Neo-classicism. Should the controversy at any time have threatened to die down, a new excavation would ensure that it was quickly rekindled. The end of Winckelmann's 'noble simplicity and quiet grandeur' came with the detection of hints of colour on the fragments of the Parthenon purchased by the British government,[39] and in the 1820s and 30s there was suddenly 'an undignified rush to win the polychrome honours.'[40] Researchers from all over Europe flocked to southern Italy and Greece, hunting for remnants of colour on statues and temples.[41] For many archaeologists, however, the discovery that the art of Antiquity had been both diverse and colourful came as a shock. Nonetheless, one could also hear an occasional sigh of relief amid all the defiant cries of resistance: polychromy seemed to prove once again that the riches of Greek art were limitless.

Leo von Klenze – 'his majesty's minister of polychromy' – was one of the first to move from theory to practice. The Bavarian crown prince had contemplated asking Klenze to erect a coloured temple in the Englischer Garten as early as 1822.[42] Only the Monopteros (1836), however, was finally built. The architect's major work, the Walhalla near Regensburg (1830-42), was also originally conceived in colour. Klenze's influence soon spread far

12 Frontispiece from Quatremère de Quincy, *Le Jupiter Olympien*, Paris 1814

13 Illustration from Franz Kugler, *Über die Polychromie der griechischen Architektur und Sculptur und ihre Grenzen*, Stuttgart 1835, Amsterdam, Rijksmuseum

beyond the borders of Germany. He sent his plans to the Royal Institute of British Architects, site of an ongoing and lively dispute about colour, and the sculptor John Gibson freely admitted that his interest in polychromy derived from the ideas of the circle around Ludwig I. Gibson was acquainted with the Walhalla and thus with Ludwig von Schwanthaler's polychrome Valkyrie-caryatids.[43] [16] Later, Klenze distanced himself from the polychrome debate, afraid that 'the art of our age may be suffocated by the pressure of art history' – a fear that proved only too justified.[44]

Finding 'elements suitable to aid in the practice of architecture' was also the goal of Klenze's competitor, the Cologne-born architect Jakob Ignaz Hittorff, who worked in Paris.[45] His Cirque d'Eté (1838) and the church Saint-Vincent-de-Paul (1844) were already completed when he began preparations for the final publication of his *Restitution du temple d'Empédocle à Sélinonte*, a compilation of his archaeological research of the 1820s and 30s. Hittorff's reconstructions, although scientifically founded, contained highly controversial assertions. [13] Resistance to them was inevitable, and the enemies of polychromy were not to be underestimated, neither in number nor influence. Hittorff's most prolific opponent was the Frenchman Raoul-Rochette, who flatly denied the authenticity of coloured remains, claiming they were of medieval origin. Most critics were capable only of accepting the hardest evidence, and clung to the idea of colourlessness until remains had been found on every last inch of the marble surface.

Like its adversaries, the champions of polychromy could be divided into camps: realists and radicals. Patrik Reuterswärd called the former, influenced by Franz Kugler, the 'party of the cautious,' and the latter, including Semper and Hittorff, the 'party of total painting.'[46] In *Über die Polychromie der griechischen Architektur und Sculptur und ihre Grenzen*, published in 1835, Kugler recounted all that was then known about polychromy in Antiquity. He refused, however, to recognise that statues had been fully painted, claiming that this would have been 'incompatible with the seriousness of high art.'[47] [14]

This allegation angered Gottfried Semper, who had already disagreed with Leo von Klenze's findings.[48] At the very beginning of his *Vier Elemente der Baukunst* (1851), Semper referred to

14 Illustration from Jakob Ignaz Hittorff, *Restitution du temple d'Empédocle à Sélinonte*, Paris 1851, Amsterdam, Rijksmuseum

15 Adèle Chavassieu d'Audebert, *Count Sommariva visiting Anne-Louis Girodet painting his* Pygmalion *in artificial light*, c. 1819, Milan, Civica Galleria d'Arte Moderna

Quatremère de Quincy's treatise on the *Olympian Zeus*, calling it 'one of the most important works of art history and the triumph of our century.' He disapproved of many of the first efforts at practical imitation, referring to them derogatorily as 'Marzipan- und Fleischerstil.'[49] For Semper, polychromy was not an end in itself: just as in Greek art and architecture, it should be part of a larger harmony, created from an independent but closely associated 'combination of equal elements' – a kind of 'democracy in the arts.'[50] The essence of Greek polychromy lay in the ordering of the ancient community, as well as in its climate and morals. To merely copy the Antique was thus of no value for the present.[51]

Semper enlarged the architectural vocabulary, basing his creations – as did his comrade-in-arms Owen Jones – on a great variety of stylistic models. The wave of enthusiasm for polychromy had reached England by the mid-1830s. Jones was one of the pioneers of the movement, and in the 1850s he created a global compendium of coloured architecture for the Crystal Palace. [1] Stylistic pluralism and 'colour pluralism' went hand-in-hand, reaching new heights in this historical 'polychromania.'[52] The Assyrian, Egyptian, Old English and other 'period rooms' were the expression of a new desire to reunite the arts, and gave an important impulse to the reintroduction of colour in sculpture.[53]

As the examples given above demonstrate, in the beginning, considerations on polychromy were inseparable from architectural theory. Contributions by sculptors were rare. This is a little surprising, despite the technical difficulties inherent in making coloured statues: Quatremère's standard work was, after all, dedicated to sculpture and not to architecture. The reconstructions of builders like Klenze, Hittorff, Semper and Jones, however, make clear that for them sculpture was the servant of architecture, and thus also coloured.

It was not only during the preparations for his book that Quatremère had sought a dialogue with artists; he remained in contact with them even after its completion, and influenced them both directly and indirectly. Antonio Canova, for example, is said to have had the *Jupiter Olympien* read aloud to him while he worked. Canova, in turn, played a role in the creation of Anne- Louis Girodet's painting *Pygmalion and the statue*, a controversial late masterpiece exhibited at the Salon of 1819. Commissioned by the Count Sommariva, it was designed as an homage to

16 Caryatids by Ludwig von Schwanthaler in the Walhalla, before 1842

17 Jean-Auguste-Dominique Ingres, *Antiochus and Stratonice*, 1840, Chantilly, Musée Condé

18 Charles Gleyre, *Bacchanal*, 1846-49, Lausanne, Musée cantonal des Beaux-Arts

the sculptor.[54] [15] Although already a well-known convention, the critics were appalled by Girodet's use of red cheeks to indicate the statue's coming to life. There is no proof that this was intended as a reference to Canova's experiments. It is, however, interesting to note that the work was bought by Honoré-Théoderic-Paul-Joseph d'Albert, Duc de Luynes, in 1839 for his castle in Dampierre. As the sponsor of Charles Simart's three-dimensional reconstruction of the *Athena Parthenos*, it was this amateur archaeologist who finally put Quatremère's theory of antique polychromy into practice.

The Duc de Luynes's profound influence on the fine arts in France in the 1830s and 40s has not yet begun to be understood. Only the rather sad incident involving the Swiss painter Charles Gleyre is well known. In 1838, the artist executed a series of frescos for the stairwell at Dampierre, but the paint was barely dry before – at Ingres's insistence – they were covered over.[55] A year later, the Frenchman himself painted his monumental *Golden Age* for the same patron. Ingres not only frequented the duke's residence, he was also a good friend of Hittorff's. In 1840, the artist set his *Antiochus and Stratonice* in a remarkably colourful, carefully detailed Roman interior. [17] Despite his mistreatment, even Gleyre must have recalled the conversations at the château, for he included a bright-red Bacchus in his *Bacchanal* of 1846-49. [18]

The Duc de Luynes's enthusiasm for polychromy reached its culmination in 1846: in that year, he commissioned the sculptor Charles Simart to reconstruct Phidias's *Athena Parthenos*.[56] [19] This is the first modern work to use the Greek chryselephantine technique and stands permanently in front of Ingres's *Golden Age*. Using ancient sources, as well as casts and coins from the duke's collection, and aided by various kinds of craftsmen, Simart was eventually able to create a figure nearly three metres high. The sculptor had unlimited resources at his disposal: in addition to marble and bronze, he also employed ivory and precious stones, tinted the face and patinated the armour and garments.

The work was presented to an astonished public in 1855 at the Exposition Universelle in Paris. The critics' reactions were mixed. No one could be sure if what they were looking at was a modern work of art or a scientific experiment. The arguments were particularly fierce among archaeologists. The statue's most vocal detractor was Charles-Ernest Beulé. He compared the *Athena* with the staging of a lost play by Sophocles based on nothing but a few sentences, and regarded the whole enterprise as a kind of intellectual sham, designed only to trick the public into accepting coloured sculpture. 'M. Simart,' he wrote, 'is a conservative entrusted with a revolution.'[57] Others, however, including Théophile Gautier, admired Simart's illusionism. All the reviewers not only discussed sculptural polychromy in the Antique, but also drew consequences from it for contemporary sculpture.[58]

While Simart was still busy with the *Athena*, the Swiss sculptor James Pradier was preparing his *Phryne* (Musée de Grenoble) and *Light verse* (Nîmes, Musée d'Art et d'Histoire), exhibited at the Salons of 1845 and 1846 respectively. Both were a contribution to sculptural polychromy in a new style. As Canova before him, Pradier was quite moderate in his use of colour, doing little more than painting the hems of the garments. Some doubt has been expressed as to whether or not these trials can even be considered relevant to the rebirth of polychrome sculpture,[59] but contemporary criticism tells a different story. The chryselephantine *Leda*, executed a short time later (1849), gives further evidence that Pradier was one of the few sculptors in the 1840s to have taken a decisive stand with regard to polychromy.[60] [21]

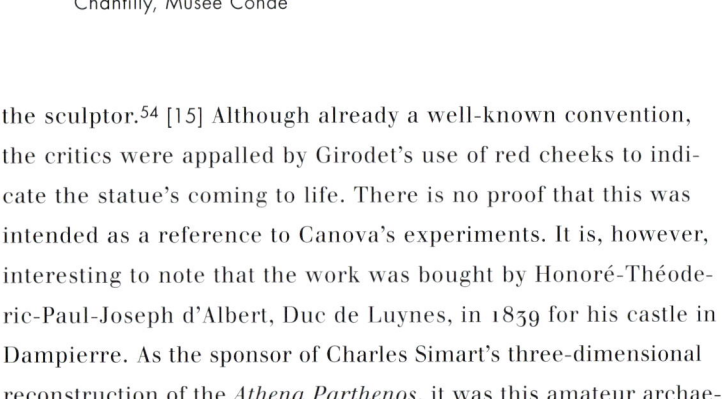

19 Charles Simart, *Athena Parthenos*, c. 1846-55, marble, bronze, ivory, precious stones, Château de Dampierre

Pradier knew his *Leda* was something both sensational and controversial: 'Mouths will fall open in ecstasy, but I won't get anything from it but the envy of my fellow artists.'[61] The statuette was exhibited at the Great Exhibition in London in 1851. Placed in the class of decorative arts, it was registered under the name of Pradier's assistant, the goldsmith Froment-Meurice. The execution of some of the technical details had proven extremely difficult and the sculptor, like Simart, had required the help of craftsmen: the combination of ivory, gold, silver and turquoise succeeded only after two tries.

Tinting the Venus

Whatever the Greeks did was right – that ought to be our law in art, in sculpture. John Gibson[63]

Since Simart's *Athena* was more or less a scientific experiment, and Canova's and Pradier's works little more than decorative beginnings, the honour must go to Gibson for having re-established polychrome sculpture in the 19th century. After a long period of apprenticeship in Rome with, among others, Canova, Gibson had become a rather dry Neo-classicist. In his own country, he was considered one of the leading academic sculptors, and had numerous commissions.[64] Already in the 1820s, following Canova's example, he had gilded Psyche's headband and wings in *Psyche borne on the shoulders of two zephyrs* (Rome, Galleria Nazionale d'Arte Antica, Palazzo Corsini). Around the middle of the century, he became the first to paint a statue's entire body, not merely its garments and accessories.

Although Gibson himself once attributed this idea to heavenly inspiration,[65] it is more likely to have resulted from his contacts with his German colleagues. We do not know precisely what he discussed with Klenze in Rome or everything he saw in Bavaria in the early 1840s: either his topographical indications are wrong or the works he describes have been lost. There can be no doubt, however, that he knew both the Walhalla and Klenze's decorations at the Munich Residenz. He described the new ballroom with great enthusiasm: 'statues large as life of Cariatedes with the skin of very faint flesh colour, the hair gold, the eyes painted, tunic white upper dress purple gray and ornaments at the edge of their draperies. The bassirilieve around the room & by Shawnthaler [sic] all painted, the ground blue flesh colour skin and draperies all coloured but so delicate & harmonious is the effect of the whole, you have no idea […].'[66]

20 Caryatids for the Salle des Sept Cheminées in the Louvre, designed by Félix Duban, 1848-51

21 James Pradier and Emile Froment-Meurice, *Leda*, 1849, ivory, silver, gold and turquoise, Geneva, Musée d'art et d'histoire

Surprisingly, the sculptor's first practical application of polychromy came not in the representation of a mythological theme but in a portrait of his sovereign, Queen Victoria (London, Buckingham Palace). The portrait was commissioned in 1844, but it seems that only after his trip to Bavaria did he dare to carry it out in colour. The few touches that are now left give little idea of how the marble figure once looked. Elizabeth Darby, drawing on contemporary descriptions, concluded that '[…] red and blue were introduced into the decorative border of the classical robe, and that the diadem and sandals, and the acorns hanging from the dress, were tinted with yellow.'[67]

In 1854, Gibson exhibited his famous marble statue of Aphrodite, later known as the *Tinted Venus,* in Rome. [7] It was also shown in London in 1862 at the International Exhibition, displayed in a templelike pavilion designed by Owen Jones. [65 109] The *Tinted Venus* leaves the experiments of Canova and Pradier far behind. The *Queen Victoria* was still largely indebted to these predecessors and closely followed the 'moderate' theories of Franz Kugler, theories we know the artist was acquainted with. The *Tinted Venus*, on the other hand, approaches the concepts of the 'radical' protagonists of Greek polychromy, who believed that the Ancients had not only painted the eyes, lips and hair of their figures, but also the bare skin. The initial appearance of Gibson's *Venus*, which exists in a number of versions, can best be judged by the restored original in the Walker Art Gallery in Liverpool.[68] The sculptor based his painting technique on antique recipes, applying the paint mixed with hot wax.

For the sculptor, colour was the equivalent of life; with it he could, like Pygmalion, create living form: 'yes – yes indeed she seems an ethereal being with her blue eyes fixed upon me!'[69] Gibson's interest soon took on an almost obsessive character: '[...] my eyes have now become so depraved that I cannot bear to see a statue without colouring.'[70] The sculptor, still impressed by Klenze's Residenz, could no longer imagine white statues in a coloured room: '[...] if you see a white statue in a room that is hung with coloured curtains and furniture, and surrounded by objects all having colour in them, how poor, and cold, and lifeless it looks; but if you introduce a faint tint on the flesh and drapery, it then becomes a part of the suit, adds to the harmony of the whole room, and is more consonant with our habits and feelings, who make our rooms places of elegant comfort, and not like the atrium or public rooms of the Greeks or Romans.'[71] His passion, however, was not shared by all his patrons. The Duke of Wellington, for example, refused to allow Gibson to paint the *Pandora* he had ordered.[72] Most of the visitors to the 1862 International Exhibition also had great difficulties accepting the notion of colour in sculpture. Looking at the *Tinted Venus*, the French critic Paul Mantz was reminded of the rosy, semi-erotic porcelain figurines sold on the Paris boulevards. He felt Gibson's attempt had not succeeded and predicted a speedy end to the new movement.[73]

The stream of treatises on polychrome architecture and sculpture (both pro and con) did not, however, abate. Despite the indisputable evidence of polychromy in ancient art, and the quite convincing reintroductions of the practice in the present, the subject remained controversial. Nonetheless, by the middle of the century a first reckoning could be made. In 1856, Beulé asked the critical question: 'Is [polychrome sculpture] worth reviving or should it remain forgotten?'[74] For him, the answer was clear: if contemporary sculptors dared to try and resuscitate Greek conventions but failed in their endeavours, then this was not the fault of the Greeks but of the moderns.[75]

Gibson's compatriot Richard Westmacott, a connoisseur of Antiquity and a sculptor himself, spoke out firmly against the polychrome revival.[76] In the *Archaeological Journal* of 1855 he asked the movement's advocates a perceptive question – what precisely did they expect to gain by colouring their sculptures, or rather, what did they feel was missing from 'colourless' sculpture: 'Do we feel that the Theseus and Ilyssus, the Venus of Melos, the Apollo of the Belvedere, and others, show a deficiency that colour could supply? [...] or believe they would be improved by receiving it?'[77] For him, the fact that the Greeks had coloured their statues was not a good enough reason; after all, he wrote, contemporary actors no longer hid their faces behind hideous masks, as had been customary in ancient times. He skilfully placed his opponents in the conservative camp and represented himself as a champion of modernity: 'What hope can there be of ever succeeding in making art the expression of real sentiment and living thought, if we are systematically to ignore our own age and its wants, and only to put forward mechanically – in short as the academic expression of factitious Greek sentiment – in such classic guise as museums and galleries of ancient sculpture suggest?'[78]

The cleft between the factions was even deeper when it came to the question of how (and how much) one should imitate the past. Here, the use of colour had touched the raw nerve of Neoclassicism. Westmacott, like Winckelmann before him, understood the principle of 'imitation' not as mere copying, but as recreation 'in the spirit of.' The aesthetician Charles Lock Eastlake pointed out that the Greek use of colour had nothing to do with mimesis: 'A statue coloured to the life might deceive the spectator for a moment, but he would presently discover that life and motion were wanting; and the imitation would be consequently pronounced to be incomplete.'[79] Imitation of life meant precisely the absence of colour: 'To conclude: it appears that, of all the Fine Arts (except perhaps theatrical representation), sculpture is most liable to be partially confounded with reality. Of the attributes of material objects, it first possesses substance and form; and when in addition to these qualities it happens to have colour and surface in common with nature, it is evidently in danger of sacrificing its general consistency, and the illusion which art proposes. Again, in consequence of the absence of colour, identity with nature is impossible in the chief object of imitation, the living figure.'[80]

Intellectual and 'colourless' abstraction found eloquent defenders in these authors. The question remains whether Eastlake's and Westmacott's theses are merely backward-looking or already point to the future. It is, however, difficult to divide the advocates and adversaries of polychromy into either progressives or conservatives. Westmacott, at least, was absolutely convinced that the era of coloured sculpture would soon be at an end: 'We have not now to learn that contemporary favour or popularity is no security for future fame; and it is remarkable how surely, sooner or later, false taste meets its fate.'[81] Whether the product of bad taste or not, Westmacott did not live to see the end of *polychromania*: while the Neo-classicists were still haranguing over the Greek legacy, coloured sculpture had already set out on a new path.

Style and colour:
Gothic and Renaissance in a new look

Au retour de la croisade, la couleur triompha...
Ludovic Vitet[82]

When Charles-Ernest Beulé condemned Simart's *Athena* – and with it polychrome sculpture as whole – he was also forced to ascertain that there were already coloured statues everywhere: 'polychrome sculpture [...] exists, it has never ceased to exist.'[83] The reader needed only to look around, he wrote, for proof that Christianity had also brought pagan elements to the west, foremost among them the painted statues of the orient. Not only in southern Italy but in the middle of Paris, in the area around Saint-Sulpice, were dozens of dealers in vulgar devotional objects supplied by failed sculptors, who thus contributed to the downfall of a great art – 'it is polychromy fallen back into its childhood.'[84] Why, Beulé asked desperately, were academically-trained sculptors incapable of supplying churches with high-quality works? In that context at least polychrome sculpture could have served a purpose.

While the Neo-classicists continued to believe in the 'lifeless imitation of Antiquity,'[85] and while they were still busy debating whether or not polychromy could be incorporated into their ideology, the Romantics had already begun to free themselves from the rules of academia. The 'anti-Enlightenment' brought with it not only a religious reawakening but also a national one, and many countries became interested in their own art-historical past. Beginning in the 1830s, a wave of restoration swept over all of Europe. This phenomenon has only just begun to be explored and it is difficult to achieve an overview, particularly where the restoration of medieval polychromy is concerned. There can be no doubt, however, that the more general issue of colour in architecture and sculpture was central to the discussions. As early as 1797, Friedrich Gilly had noted traces of decorative colour in the Marienburg in East Prussia.[86] In 1825, Robert Smirke commenced the restoration work on the Temple Church in London. Medieval polychromy could be easily studied both here and in Westminster Abbey. In 1828 and 1834 respectively the cathedrals of Regensburg and Bamberg began to undergo a process of 're-medievalisation.' In 1833, Tilman Riemenschneider's *Münnerstadt Altar* was re-coloured, as were the pillar statues in the choir of the cathedral in Cologne in 1840.[87]

In France, the Revolution was followed by a period of political and cultural restoration. Already during the Reign of Terror, in 1792, Alexandre Lenoir had founded the Musée des Monuments Français as a means of rescuing the country's threatened heritage. In the course of time, the collection of original remnants developed into a plaster compendium of French sculpture, but

22 The Cheminée des Preuses, Château de Pierrefonds, designed by Viollet-le-Duc, c. 1860-70

was plagued by the lack of a permanent residence and limited access. An obvious disadvantage was, of course, that the casts could not give any indication of the colours of the originals. Nonetheless, the museum was at least partially responsible for the renewed interest in medieval art and architecture characteristic of Romanticism.

The Catholic revivalists around Charles de Montalembert called for the use of the building style that best represented the triumph of the church of Rome, namely the Gothic. They rejected attempts to rescue Classicism for religious architecture, such as Hittorff's Saint-Vincent-de-Paul, consecrated in 1844 and based on the form of a colourful antique temple – for the architect the ancestor of the early Christian basilica. One of the pioneers of the neo-gothic movement was Eugène-Emmanuel Viollet-le-Duc. This great conservator was well-acquainted with medieval sculptural painting: he had studied and described it at the cathedrals of Paris, Chartres, Amiens and Rheims.[88] He was, however, quite modest when it came to applying this formal vocabulary in modern times. The *Heroine frieze* over the fireplace in the Salle des Preuses at Pierrefonds is one of the few examples of polychrome sculpture he allowed into his restorations. [22]

23 Project for the restoration of the Sainte-Chapelle in Paris by Félix Duban and Jean-Baptiste Lassus, 1847, Paris, Musée d'Orsay

24 Detail of the interior of the Sainte-Chapelle

Viollet-le-Duc's contemporaries, particularly Jean-Baptiste Lassus, were considerably more daring. Lassus was in charge of the restoration of the Sainte-Chapelle, one of the most important projects of the whole 19th century. The plans for the renovation and reconsecration of the chapel originated in 1836, and the work was carried out between 1840 and 1856 by Lassus and Duban.[89] Together, they turned the royal chapel into a colourful jewel-box, where old and new were harmoniously combined: every element, even the highly-coloured reliefs and pillar figures, is subordinated to the overwhelming effect of the whole. [23–25]

Lassus was an acquaintance of both Victor Hugo and Montalembert. Despite these prominent advocates, the critical success of the Sainte-Chapelle was in no way guaranteed. This is not surprising, considering that each political faction within French society sought out a different style with which to identify. The criticism was so harsh, however, that Lassus felt compelled to publish a defence of the project in 1846.[90] Many enemies of the Neo-gothic, particularly in Germany, turned against medieval polychromy as a whole, challenging it with arguments borrowed from the pamphlets of the adversaries of colour in the Antique.[91]

25 Illustration from Decloux and Doury, *Histoire archéologique, déscriptive et graphique de la Sainte-Chapelle du Palais*, Paris 1857, Amsterdam, Rijksmuseum

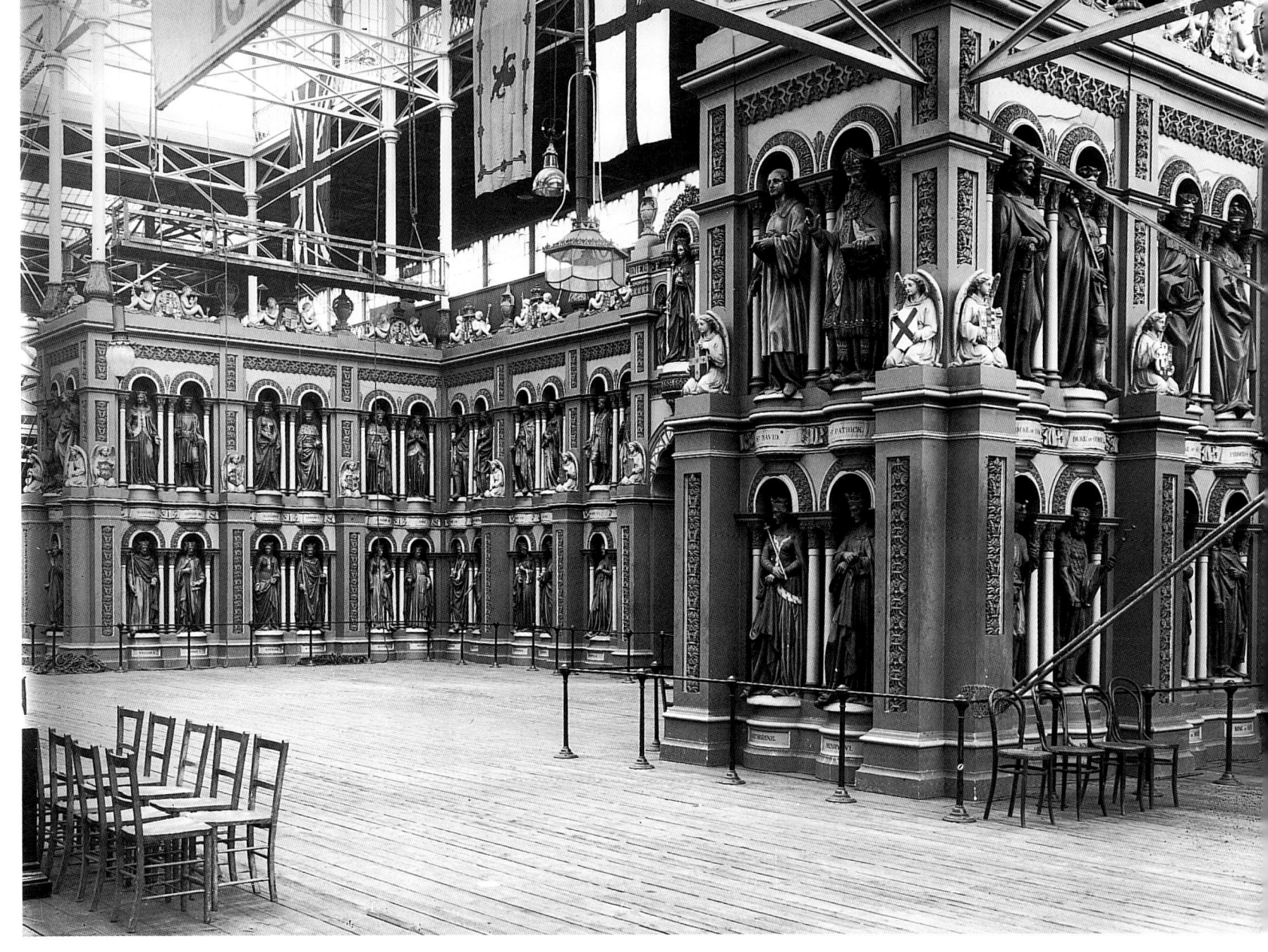

26 John Thomas, Original models for the statues at the Houses of Parliament, Crystal Palace at Sydenham, photograph, c. 1860

The philosopher Friedrich Theodor Vischer saw no reason for the existence of gothicising Madonnas in the age of the railway, and the archaeologist Anselm Feuerbach ascertained a loss of respect for the past in the contemporary urge to give everything a fresh coat of paint: 'The venerable grey hair of Age is covered up by a blond wig [...] or a spotted fool's cap.'[92]

The works chosen and the ways in which the restoration was carried out had much less to do with the supposed intentions of artists of the past than with the taste of those in the present. The debate among practitioners gave rise to two schools of thought. On the one hand, there were the partisans of architectural polychromy, who were particularly interested in optical emphasis and thus in using colour for the structural differentiation of individual elements. On the other, there were the representatives of decorative polychromy, who dreamed of sumptuous symphonies of colour. To achieve their goals, conservational efforts ranged from radical exposure of the object's core to complete repainting. Some projects were not even given time to develop a patina of their own before becoming the object of renewal.[93] Occasionally, this zeal for the Middle Ages could be quite capricious, and the border between a restoration and a completely new work of art is often unclear. A typical example is the tomb of King John in the cathedral at Worcester, reproduced in its original, medieval colours as a bone china inkwell in the first half of the 1840s (London, Victoria and Albert Museum). In 1873, as the result of an equally enthusiastic and patriotic 'will to colour,' the tomb itself was deprived of its coloration by being gilded.[94]

We have already spoken of the painted decoration of Sainte-Clotilde: today, only the side-altars bear witness to the original colour scheme. Sometimes the arrival of a new priest was

27 Franz Schneider, *Margrave Konrad von Wettin*, 1879, limewood, painted, Meissen, Albrechtsburg

28 Figures from the central domed hall of the parliament building in Budapest, c. 1885-1904

29 Prosper d'Epinay, *Joan of Arc*, 1902, marble, ivory and lapis lazuli, Rheims, Cathedral

30 St Margaret of Scotland, c. 1900, marbles, London, Farm Street, Church of the Immaculate Conception

31 Francesco Laurana, *Bust of a young woman (Isabella d'Aragon?)*, c. 1483-98, marble, painted, Vienna, Kunsthistorisches Museum

32 Richard Cockle Lucas, *Flora*, c. 1846, wax, Staatliche Museen zu Berlin, Preußischer Kulturbesitz, Skulpturengalerie

enough to decide the fate of a sculpture or interior. The sculptor Victor-Edouard Le Harivel-Durocher must have been shocked to discover that his 1863 relief in the Chapelle de l'Immaculée Conception at Sées (Orne) had been coloured on the order of the clergy.[95] In 1884, another priest is reported to have told one of the visitors to his newly renovated church that if it had been up to him, he would have simply left it grey.[96]

The men of the cloth were apparently very heterogeneous patrons, and this is perhaps one of the reasons for the lack of a high-ranking school of neo-gothic sculpture.[97] In general, one can also say that it was theologians, and not artists, who promoted the new style: Montalembert in France, August Reichensperger in Germany, and Jean-Baptiste Bethune in Belgium. There are other explanations as well. Increased demand meant that quantity was often more important than quality. In addition, the renaissance of builders' and painters' workshops in the 19th century left little room for the development of individual talent. Given this, trying to discriminate among neo-gothic sculptors seems futile. Romanticism's internal contradiction – a *retardataire* ideology combined with modern artistic solutions – characterises neo-gothic artistic production. The art forms of a period long past, fresco painting, mosaics, stained glass and polychrome sculpture, were revivified under the banner of the workshop, but in truth with a kind of early industrial division of labour. The Neo-gothic subordinated all genres to the decorative and evocative *gesamtkunstwerk* 'church.'[98]

Independent romantic sculpture, a somewhat vague and rarely-used term, consists mostly of small-size decorative pieces for the private household. The most appropriate medium for such works was bronze, so that polychromy plays only a limited role. Many fashionable chivalric motifs were, however, silverplated, increasing the value of these historical or invented medieval figures. An early example is François-Joseph Bosio's (life-size) *Henri IV as a boy* of 1824 (Paris, Musée du Louvre). The precious metal gives the young king a sensitive appearance appropriate to the romantic idea of the French hero. A similar feeling inspired Christian Daniel Rauch's *Lorenzen of Tangermünde* (1832) and its follower, *Innocence* by Albert Wolff (1836) – judging by the number of versions an enormously popular work. Only Marie d'Orléans's *Joan of Arc in prayer* (1840) was more successful. It is uncertain whether this silverplating was a conscious reversion to medieval techniques, such as those used for figurative reliquaries. On the other hand, these examples were certainly designed to attract buyers of small-scale sculpture with a new and costly surface, unlike the usual bronze.

There is only a narrow border between this type of sculpture and decorative art.[99] The larger the number of substances used the more 'decorative' the effect, and thus the more likely a work will be attributed not to a museum's sculpture department but to the applied arts. One of the consequences is that the oeuvre of one and the same artist becomes dispersed throughout the institution; another is that the artist is often consigned to oblivion. This is the case with Félicie de Fauveau, one of the most important practitioners of troubadour-style sculpture.[100] Her combination of medieval subject matter and polychrome sculpture was almost unparalleled in her time. A Legitimist, she was imprisoned in 1830 and later went into exile. Supported by her like-minded aristocratic friends, Fauveau received numerous lucrative commissions until the middle of the century. In her works, she evoked the pre-Revolutionary era, a period when the nobility and the king had no need of a constitution. Although she used polychromy only sparingly – limiting herself to the application of colour on the hems of garments and for ornaments – her works precede the experiments of Simart, Pradier and Gibson. [24]

Félicie de Fauveau chose Florence as her adopted home. This Renaissance city became increasingly popular as Rome's star began to sink. Quattrocento sculpture, however, had little influence on the development of polychromy in the 19th century – for the simple reason that it was in this period that colour was first systematically banned. Still, it is unfair that the Neo-renaissance as an independent movement has been given so little attention.[101] Renaissance monochromy is, after all, only part of the truth: in addition to his delicately manipulated marbles, Donatello also left behind numerous polychrome works. Portrait sculptures, too, were for the most part coloured and, thanks to their protective glaze, the brilliant coloration of the Della Robbia family's ceramic reliefs has survived the centuries.

Close imitations of polychrome Quattrocento sculptures are rare.[102] A 19th-century coloured bust directly inspired by the Renaissance did – however ingloriously – once make history: the Berlin *Flora*. [32] This wax pastiche, executed in 1845 by the British sculptor Richard Cockle Lucas, was bought by Wilhelm von Bode in 1909 as a work by Leonardo or his circle, a purchase which caused a great deal of turmoil. Unfortunately, the strife over the work's authenticity soon became political, and only recently has a certain consensus been reached. Even at the time of purchase, however, there was enough evidence to suggest that the work was of much more recent origin than it appeared.[103] The *Flora* case is interesting in connection with the history of polychrome sculpture for two reasons. For one, Bode's purchase once again proves that a clever imitation can fool even the most experienced connoisseur, particularly when certain (visual) expectations help to abet the mistake. The acceptance of colour in sculpture was greatest at the turn of the century, and only then could such an unusual work have been attributed to the Renais-

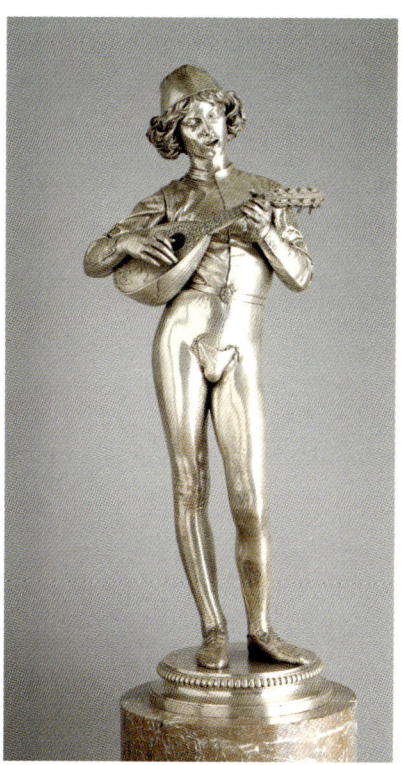

33 Paul Dubois, *Florentine singer*, 1865, bronze, silvered, Paris, Musée d'Orsay

sance itself. Also telling is the fact that a practitioner, the sculptor Martin Schauss, who had himself made polychrome works and thus understood all the technical aspects, exposed the bust as a 'fake' as early as 1910.[104]

This reference raises a second interesting question, this time about the character of the bust itself. Lucas had gained a certain amount of respect for his reconstructions of antique statues. Even Charles Simart had made use of some of his findings.[105] To criminalise the sculptor is therefore unjust. Until proven otherwise, one must assume that Lucas was not intending to make a forgery. On the other hand, the *Flora* is certainly not a mere interpretation of Renaissance art. Judging by his meticulous working method, one is forced to conclude that the artist sought not only to revive the style and spirit of the Renaissance, but also its sculptural techniques. His specific knowledge, the continuing tradition of wax sculpture, and the current discussions about polychromy must have encouraged him to work in colour. The *Flora* is in a sense applied art history, and thus an outstanding example of scholarly historicism.

The Bode/Lucas case is symptomatic, but singular. It does not allow any conclusions about Neo-renaissance sculpture in general. If such a sculpture ever existed, it would include mainly those works in which 19th-century sculptors used the Quattrocento as a source for historical genre or freely interpreted its formal vocabulary – ideally both at the same time. Until the end of the century, when clay and ceramic became permissable mediums for sculpture, and artists from Adolf von Hildebrand [41] to Robert Anning Bell [43 44] drew inspiration from the reliefs of Donatello and Della Robbia, polychrome sculptures in this style were rare. The most famous example, Paul Dubois's silverplated *Florentine singer of the 15th century* of 1865, is not actually coloured. [33] Antonin Mercié's *David* of 1872 might be considered another example. Like the even more popular *Gloria victis* of the same year, it exists in numerous casts and variations with differently-worked patinas. With such meagre evidence, however, it is difficult to speak of polychrome Neo-renaissance sculpture before the end of the century.

Fantasy and reality

Although coloured sculptures made up only a fraction of production at the middle of the century, they could no longer be overlooked and quickly gained a permanent place in the artistic repertoire. By reintroducing colour into their works, neo-classical and neo-gothic sculptors aimed to resurrect the past and to test whether its values were appropriate to their own time, a period of astonishingly rapid transformation. Still, every touch of colour was the cause for damning criticism and words like 'banal,' 'vulgar' and 'unchaste' were bandied about indiscriminately.

Despite the fact that the partisans of colour were not Realists *per se* – nor the Realists necessarily supporters of polychromy[106] – most critics could not resist comparing coloured sculptures with wax figures. Beulé had set a precedent with his remarks about Simart's *Athena*, as had Baudelaire with his criticism of Auguste Clésinger's *Sappho*,[107] and the analogy soon became a standard weapon in the critics' arsenal. Wax itself, however, had been a respected medium for portrait sculpture for centuries, falling into oblivion only with Neo-classicism.[108] A genre once considered worthy of sovereigns was now frowned upon, exiled to the fairgrounds. To this day, these works produce a feeling of discomfort, but in fact this is only a relatively recent phenomenon. It was Schopenhauer who first turned this emotional response into an aesthetic judgment. For him, the task of a work of art was to 'give us knowledge of the (Platonic) idea,' and this was only possible when form and substance were not identical. He continued: 'It is thus intrinsic to the work of art that it should represent form alone, independent of the material, and it should do this openly and conspicuously. This is the real reason why wax figures make no aesthetic impression and are therefore not works of art (in the aesthetic sense) although, if well-made, they are a hundred times more convincing than the best painting or statue; thus, if pure illusionism were the purpose of art, they would have to be put in the highest rank.'[109] According to this theory, a work becomes Art when something is missing from the depiction of what is seen or imagined: in painting volume, and in sculpture colour.

Every attempt to overcome such limitations, even the most tenuous, was branded a 'curiosité vulgaire.'[110] Particularly the critics for the *Gazette des Beaux-Arts* railed against polychromy at every opportunity. Charles Blanc, the magazine's founder and first editor, was one of those who persisted in denying the existence of coloured Greek sculpture. From his comments it becomes clear that for him only barbarians, savages and the insane could feel drawn to painted statues – both in the past and the present.[111] The real issue here, however, was the academy's fear of the general populace and their traditional culture. The enemies of polychromy saw the achievements of the 18th century threatened by concessions to popular taste. By rejecting colour, Neo-classicism had finalised the divorce between high and applied art, and this new order had to be defended. There were, nonetheless, dissenters: for some, the constant appeal to Antiquity by the self-declared arbiters of good taste was misleading. Anselm Feuerbach, for example, wrote that 'many Greeks, as well as those Romans who had enjoyed a Greek education, were not nearly as concerned with purity of taste as we are in their name. One need only look at the figurines of actors in the Vatican Museum. What art lover today would tolerate these ivory and wood shepherds and bagpipe players in his collection [...]?'[112]

It was precisely the enormous gap between abstract white statues and votive images and mascots that made success so difficult for the polychrome party. According to the guardians of taste, realism in colour could mean only one thing: caricature. This assumption was not completely unjustified, as Honoré Daumier's *Celebrities of the Juste Milieu* demonstrate. [34] These unbaked clay busts, commissioned in 1830 by Charles Philipon, publisher of the satirical journal *La Caricature*, are the artist's first sculptures. Jeanne Wasserman has suggested that the 36 remaining portraits, today in the Musée d'Orsay, were contingent excercises, not meant to outlive a quite limited function.[113] As caricatures, Daumier's parliamentarians do not fall within the usual critical categories. Colour serves, among other things, to exaggerate the character of the person represented. Almost more interesting than the busts themselves is the history of their reception: only decades after they were produced, in the wake of Impressionism, did it become possible to declare them full-fledged works of art.

A true revolution in portraiture was accomplished only around 1850-60 with the work of Carlo Marochetti, a sculptor of Italian origins raised in France, but who had become famous in England. He had participated in the decoration of Napoleon's

34 Honoré Daumier, *Philipon*, from the series of the *Celebrities of the Juste Milieu*, 1831, unbaked potter's clay, Paris, Musée d'Orsay

tomb together with Simart, Pradier and Triqueti, but, in fact, he had been interested in the more painterly aspects of sculpture even earlier. Around 1856 he produced two busts of members of the Indian nobility, which fortunately have retained their original coloration. One, the *Princess Gauramma of Coorg*, is painted terracotta, the other, *Dalip Singh*, is painted marble. [45 46] Little is known of the circumstances of the commissions; the sitters, however, were celebrities at the time.[114]

The extraordinary care Marochetti took with all the details in these busts is quite novel in the depiction of dark-skinned foreigners. In order to understand why these works look as they do, one must go far afield. In addition to the ongoing altercation about polychromy, their appearance was certainly determined by the change in European attitudes towards other races, a phenomenon inadequately described by the term 'Orientalism.'[115] Obviously, these portraits are a consequence of the incorporation of India into the British Empire: members of the Indian nobility travelled to England, where they were introduced to the 'blessings' of western culture. One may presume that these aristocrats were looked upon with curiosity, but certainly not with the same condecension as the legions of Arab snake-charmers and bazaar traders depicted in innumerable Salon paintings. One should not automatically equate this kind of cheap exoticism with the multifaceted artistic analysis of non-European culture: in many cases,

In living colour 35

an interest in the Orient stemmed from real enthusiasm for its languages and philosophies. Due to their skin colour, the Indian princes certainly stood out; they were not, however, 'types' but rather historically significant individuals, worthy of portrayal.

In these works by Marochetti the painting of the faces and clothing is more than just an artistic experiment. He took portraiture's fundamental concept – similarity – at face value, and in so doing paid tribute to a kind of beauty that could not be justly reproduced in marble or bronze. In the eyes of some Europeans, such splendid representations of persons of colour made the portraits of their own compatriots (literally) pale in comparison. One of these was Oscar Wilde, after seeing the monument to the Maharajah of Kolhapur, Rajaram Chuttraputti, in Florence. [123] The maharajah had died there on his way back to India, and the monument was erected in 1874 by the American Charles Francis Fuller on the spot where the Brahmanic funeral had taken place. Wilde yearned for a similar polychrome work on the grave of John Keats, writing: 'Keats's delicate features and rich colour could not be conveyed I think in plain white marble.'[116]

The work of Charles Cordier, the orientalist sculptor *par excellence*, combines scientific with aesthetic interest.[117] [47–49] His busts of African and Mediterranean peoples are different from Marochetti's, not only in the anonymity of the persons depicted but also in technique. Cordier did not paint his works, achieving his polychrome effects instead through the use of various coloured materials. In 1856, during a trip to North Africa, the sculptor had discovered the fascinating veined structure of Algerian onyx, and since that time employed it for the drapery of his figures. His historical precedents were the ancient Romans, who had similarly exploited the marble quarries in their colonies.[118] [124] By combining contrasting elements in this way, Cordier gave new life to a tradition that had existed from Roman times into the 18th century.[119] Of course, the rediscovery of the onyx quarries had only been possible with the conquest of Algeria and art and commerce could sometimes even be united in one person. This was the case with the Marseilles entrepreneur Jules Cantini: he was the owner of quarries in Italy and North Africa and, as a supplier to large-scale construction projects, not only made decorative designs, but actually occasionally took up the hammer and chisel himself.[120] [35]

In 1848, the year in which Cordier exhibited his first – bronze – portraits of an African couple in the Salon, slavery was abolished in the French colonies. The catalogue gives the name of the man represented: 'Saïd Abdalla de la tribu de Mayac, royaume de Darfour.' Less than two years later, Saïd Abdalla lost his name, becoming a mere 'Nègre de Tombouctou' – a geographical designation some 3000 kilometres from his actual birthplace. As Hugh Honour pointed out, this change of title also transformed the portrait from that of an individual to the depiction of a racial type.[121] The female pendant was shown at the Great Exhibition in London in 1851 under the title 'Vénus africaine,' and from there entered the collection of the queen of England.[122]

Such anonymity was attractive to a potentially large circle of clients. Success convinced Cordier to cease giving the names of the people he represented and instead mention only their tribe of origin. There may have been another reason as well: many of the busts were products of official commissions for the new *Galerie anthropologique* in the Muséum national d'histoire naturelle. In 1858 and 1860 two photographic compendiums of Cordier's works were published; in them, the busts are referred to specifically as 'sculpture ethnographique.'[123] At the same time, the leap from empirical anthropology to racial theory was often a short one – Gobineau's *Essai sur l'inégalité des races humaines* had appeared in 1853. Cordier, however, was an abolitionist, and thus above all suspicion, as his group *Love one another* demonstrates: two children, one white, the other black – made of white and black marble – are represented moving towards one another in order to embrace (private collection).[124]

The question of whether Cordier turned to science as a means of legitimising his efforts is probably futile. The history of the reception of the busts, exhibited first in the Salon, then in a museum of natural history, and then later again in the Salon does, however, show that in the 19th century there was still often only a fine line between an artwork created for pure aesthetic enjoyment and one made for the purposes of science. The sculptor Giovanni Dupré's eye-witness account of his visit to the Crystal Palace certainly confirms the impression that the medieval *kunstkammer* lived on as the panopticon, and that polychrome sculpture could have any number of subjects: 'In addition to animals and plants from all parts of the world, from the far north to the tropics, one can also see people represented in living colour: Cretans, Eskimos, savages, Tartars, Mongolians, cannibals, all very natural-looking, in their native dress. One sees strikingly authentic reproductions of Egyptian, Indian, Assyrian, Mongolian, and Moorish architecture; part of the Alhambra, rooms from Pompeii, minarets and Chinese temples, the best sculptures from Egypt, India, Greece, Rome, from the Middle Ages, the doors of Ghiberti, the equestrian portraits of Colleoni, Gattamelata, Marcus Aurelius, and some more contemporary statues, including my Abel.'[125]

Imperial polychromy

If Charles Cordier had to defend himself against any accusation during his lifetime, it was that his works were too full of bravura: 'If the progress of polychromy depended on multiplying the numbers and kinds of precious materials, than M. Cordier would cer-

35 View of the section of foundries, steel factories, forges and blast furnaces at the Exposition Universelle Paris, 1889. To the left a statue by Jules Cantini.

36 Paul-Charles Galbrunner after Henri-Frédéric Iselin, *Napoleon III*, 1866, chalcedony, porphyry, marble and gilt bronze, Paris, Musée d'Orsay

37 The Grand Salon of the Château de Ferrières with atlantes and caryatids by Charles Cordier, 1861-62, bronze, marble and onyx

39 Charles Garnier, *Section of the temple of Jupiter at Aegina*, reconstruction of 1852-53, Paris, Ecole nationale supérieure des Beaux-Arts

tainly be in the lead.'[126] Although the majority of contemporary critics were opposed to colour in sculpture, they could not prevent its eventual triumph and in France it reached a new apogee during the Second Empire. Napoleon III had already followed Hittorff's research with great interest and the fragments of the frieze from the mausoleum at Halicarnassus, unearthed in 1856, and the discovery of the *Prima Porta Augustus* in 1863 kept the polychrome debate alive.[127] A visit to Greece was necessary for all young architects, and every year their studies flooded the Ecole des Beaux-Arts. A comparison of the *envois* over a longer period of time shows that the reconstructions of the Acropolis and other famous sites became increasingly liberal in their use of colour. [39 40]

The love of luxury which characterises the Second Empire created an excellent climate for polychrome sculpture. An artist like Cordier was assured of high ranking patrons. He found a loyal ally in the Comte de Nieuwerkerke, Intendant des Beaux-Arts de la Maison de l'Empéreur. The sculptor participated in all of the era's most influential decorative projects: the Paris Opéra, the Rothschilds' Château de Ferrières [37], and the Hôtel de la Païva on the Champs-Elysées. The latter still gives the best idea of a French Neo-baroque interior. It was built using the apparently unlimited funds of the Silesian steel magnate Count Guido Henkel von Donnersmarck, married to the Russian lady of the house, better known by the name of her first – Portuguese – hus-

38 View of the Grand Escalier in the Garnier Opera in Paris with a *torchère* by Albert-Ernest Carrier-Belleuse and Gabriel-Jules Thomas's caryatids representing Drama and Music in the background, 1866-73

band. The house is furnished with such extravagances as an onyx stairwell and figurative table decorations by Albert-Ernest Carrier-Belleuse and Emile Froment-Meurice, described by the Goncourts with a mixture of admiration and disgust.[128]

Carrier-Belleuse had submitted a polychrome *Sappho* to the Salon of 1859, an 'essai curieux, mais discutable,' as Paul Mantz wrote.[129] His best-known works, however, are the so-called *torchères* at the foot of the grand staircase in Garnier's Opéra. [38] These twisting bronze female figures carry lamps, combining a dark medium with a source of light that reflected back on them and on the colourful surroundings – the effect being completed by the rustle of gala dresses. Such candelabras became enormously popular: illuminated first by gas and later by electricity, these imaginative figures came to populate bourgeois interiors throughout the world.

Charles Garnier, architect of the Opéra, was Hittorff's spiritual heir. Sometime between 1852 and 1853, he had sent an interesting and very colourful reconstruction drawing of the Acropolis in Athens to the Ecole des Beaux-Arts.[130] [39] This love of colour became an integral part of the program of the Opéra: 'I have conceived the central opening of the staircase as a joyous space which, with its coloured substances, will form a glittering focal point within the glittering ensemble of which it is part.' Garnier's explicit aim was to revive the polychrome sculpture of Baroque Rome, and his instrument was to be Gabriel-Jules Thomas. To flank the entrance to the auditorium, Garnier commissioned the sculptor to make caryatids representing Drama and Music, using several kinds of marble. [38] At first, the sculptor was appalled by the architect's request: 'But this poor Thomas, a conscientious and chaste talent, was afraid of the violence he might thereby do to the tradition of *grand art*, and he tried to convince me to let him make the caryatids in white marble. Now it was my turn to be troubled. No matter how lovely the figures he modelled would surely have been, they would still have the appearance of two icy phantoms, and my first-rate polychrome contrivance would die before it was even born.'[131] Garnier then stated clearly what he wanted, challenging Thomas to make him 'Bernin de mauvais goût!' According to Garnier, the sculptor felt like an honest man who had been asked to join a band of robbers. Naturally, however, he allowed himself to be convinced; but it was only when a large number of interested viewers came to his studio to admire the works that he was finally truly converted.

By strictly subordinating all the decorative elements to the effect of the whole, Garnier went a small but decisive step further than either the previous generation or most of his contemporaries. Even such a 'colourful' architect as Theophil Hansen did not dare to have the statues in his otherwise polychrome chambers of the Viennese parliament painted, so that they now gleam like white pearls. It is no coincidence, and certainly not a question of quality, that neither Thomas's caryatids nor Carrier-Belleuse's monumental lamps were able to make a name for their creators. These sculptures were interchangeable props, absorbed into the *gesamtkunstwerk* Opéra.[132] The sculptors who worked on the *grand projets* of the 19th century were little more than interior decorators, a fate they serenely accepted.

'Should we paint our statues?'

As long as principles dictated that modern methods of production were to be hidden, Neo-classicism remained unchallenged. Sculptors were necessary in order to clothe novel construction techniques in expensive materials and classical myths. Polychrome sculpture, too, continued to receive its most important impulses from archaeology. In the 1880s, Georg Treu, excavator of Olympia and director of the Königlich Sächsische Antiken- und Abgußsammlungen, touched off a new phase in the polychrome dispute. Treu belonged to the generation of archaeologists who had already learned about antique polychromy in the course of their studies.[133] Recent discoveries confirmed and deepened what they already knew, which by this time was part of general knowledge and had at last silenced the advocates of white marble.

On 5 November 1883, Treu gave a lecture in the auditorium of the Königliches Polytechnikum in Dresden entitled *Sollen wir unsere Statuen bemalen?*[134] Although his theses were neither particularly original nor radical, they were extremely important: unlike anyone before him, Treu emphasised the ways in which knowledge of the past could become relevant for present practice. In his role as curator, Treu always combined his interest in Antiquity with a great concern for contemporary art. For him, buying coloured sculptures for the Dresden collection from both 3rd-century B.C. Etruria and 19th-century France was merely logical.

Treu became director in Dresden in 1882. Only one year later, he organised two exhibitions of historical and contemporary polychrome sculpture, one in his own museum and one in the Nationalgalerie in Berlin.[135] Like Quatremère de Quincy before him, the archaeologist sought to establish connections with living artists. Among other things, he obtained them commissions for reconstruction and restoration of the antique originals that opened the Berlin exhibition. These coloured casts were to serve as a kind of preparatory exercise for the general public: 'As far as sculpture is concerned, most of us are like someone who has seen only cartoons and engravings his whole life and who is suddenly, at the age of 60, confronted with an oil painting: we are frightened by its illusionism and cry bloody murder.'[136] One of the aims of the exhibition was to attract to art those 'less high-standing members of society' who found 'pure white marble and plaster figures' incomprehensible.[137] Academic sculpture was simply unpopular; as Alfred Lichtwark, the director of the Hamburger Kunsthalle, put it: 'It is pretty difficult to pray to a white Madonna.'[138]

We do not know if the public reacted as the organisers hoped, but for once the art critics were capable of balanced commentary. Slating reviews were rare: only Max Schasler mourned the loss of 'the ideal of pure, that is, colourless, form.'[139] It is surprising to discover that some reviewers were even a little disappointed that the works were not more colourful; one even spoke of an 'almost inexplicable timidity,'[140] an assessment which today can be neither confirmed nor denied: most of the contemporary sculptures recorded in the catalogue have since disappeared and their creators are forgotten. Judging by the list, it would seem that more emphasis was placed on quantity than on quality. Another major disadvantage was that Treu almost only included German sculptors among contemporary artists, so that his enterprise got little recognition abroad.

To be for or against polychromy did not necessarily place a critic in the camp of either the academy or the avant-garde. Theodor Alt and Jules Laforgue, the former a radical opponent of Impressionism, the latter one of its greatest champions, could both speak in favour of coloured sculpture. Laforgue reviewed the Berlin exhibition for the *Gazette des Beaux-Arts* and he had planned to translate and publish Treu's lecture in French.[141] As a friend of Henry Cros and a connoisseur of the works of Cordier, Jean-Désiré Ringel d'Illzach and others, Laforgue had been well aware of the coloured sculpture phenomenon long before coming

40 Benoit Loviot, *Section of the Parthenon*, reconstruction of 1879-81, Paris, Ecole nationale supérieure des Beaux-Arts

to Berlin. He felt the new movement was somewhat belated, claiming that in Germany (unlike in France) artists felt compelled to read a professor's treatise before getting down to work.[142] From his detailed description, one gets the sense that the exhibition was a conglomeration of heterogeneous works of varying quality, and also that the author's initial sympathy for the undertaking eventually waned. Laforgue did not, however, abandon his basically positive attitude: sculptural polychromy was successful and appropriate when colour was not merely applied to the form, but when both were conceived together.[143]

Treu himself never made a secret of his own moderate position. He was particularly interested in enriching interior decoration and did not want to see public spaces filled with polychrome sculpture: 'In general, our unfriendly climate means that we should never try to create a southern atmosphere outside the home. But inside, in the rooms where we celebrate, the eye can feast on colour with impunity and refresh itself from the grey of the outside world – what should stop us here from drenching our

41 Leon Pohle, *Portrait of Georg Treu*, 1901, Staatliche Kunstsammlungen Dresden

sculptures in colour?'[144] Some critics felt this did not go far enough. Because 'the people get little from the way a rich man decorates his rooms,' Martin Feddersen, in an article in the *Kunstchronik*, called for the immediate introduction of coloured statuary in the marketplace and on the streets.[145] In general however, both authors wanted the same thing: a 'truly popular art, such as existed in Antiquity and in the Middle Ages.' According to Treu, this was only possible if sculpture 'completely gives in to the contemporary desire for truth, life and colour.'[146] Gottfried Semper had believed a revival of a democracy in art, like that known in ancient Greece, was a utopian wish. By reconciling the academy and popular art through polychromy, Georg Treu at least wanted to attempt it.

Symptomatic for the new acceptance of Treu's ideas is the re-evaluation of wax figures, once the bogey of the polychrome debate. He and his followers claimed that wax figures had been rejected because of low quality and not because they were coloured; such sub-standard works should not be considered representative of polychrome sculpture 'any more than an inn sign is representative of oil painting.'[147] Renowned sculptors had already begun collaborating with waxworks in the 1880s: Ringel d'Illzach, for example, worked for the Musée Grevin in Paris. Wax figures were also used in panoramas, another mixture of fine art and popular entertainment.[148] Even the avant-garde could not resist this soft substance. Medardo Rosso created his most important wax pieces in the 1880s and 90s, among them the relief-like head *The flesh of others (Carne altrui)*. [76] Its title summons up associations with flesh, thereby once again equating the modelling of form with the divine act of creation.

In 1881, Edgar Degas startled the public with his *Little dancer of 14 years*, a work which broke any number of taboos.[149] [68 69] Creating a 'monument' to a living ballet student was daring in itself; more so was the fact that it was made of wax and yet not a study but a finished piece. Most disconcerting was certainly that she was dressed in real clothes – a shirt and skirt, with shoes and a hair ribbon. Degas had taken up the technique of the waxworks, but none of its illusionism. The author and critic Joris-Karl Huysmans wrote: 'The terrible reality of this statuette makes one distinctly uneasy; all one's ideas about sculpture; about these inanimate whitenesses, about these memorable clichés copied down the centuries, all are overturned.'[150] Degas had returned to the methods of the Old Masters of Spain, where the tradition of combining classically modelled figures with realistic colour and attributes had survived.[151] [67] This kind of *verismo* had always been looked upon with distaste by visitors from outside the Iberian peninsula or southern Italy, and it was only in the late 19th century that art history began to regard the phenomenon with any interest. In 1888, the English writer Samuel Butler published his description of Gaudenzio Ferrari's *Calvary* in Varallo under the title *Ex voto*: 'We cannot dismiss such works with cheap commonplaces about Madame Tussaud's – and for aught I know there may be some very good stuff at Madame Tussaud's.'[152]

The *Little dancer*, which Huysmans called the first truly modern sculpture,[153] was an aesthetic revolution. Schopenhauer's dictum had lost its credibility. The reasons for its disappearance from the arguments against polychrome sculpture are manifold, and many of them are worth examining in more detail. It is remarkable, for example, how often both supporters and opponents call upon childhood memories to support their opinions. Franz Kugler and Paul Mantz both recalled their first encounters with wax figures with horror.[154] A generation later, this had all changed. For G. Schäfer and Theodor Alt childhood traumas were no longer associated with coloured statues but with the white of marble and plaster: 'One often speaks of a "white lady," but no one has ever heard of coloured ghosts.'[155]

> *Whether colour be really an added grace to sculpture in its highest development, is for the thought and practice of the sculptor to determine.* Matthew Webb[156]

Even if only a small number of the works exhibited in Berlin satisfied the expectations of the critics, Georg Treu must be credited with establishing polychrome sculpture as a legitimate form. He found a kindred spirit in the painter-sculptor Max Klinger. The scholar and the artist were in close contact, and their correspondence reveals both their enthusiasm for 'the cause' and the ways in which they influenced one another.[157]

The sculptor is one of the few to have revealed the motivations behind his work. Reading his notes, it immediately becomes clear that Klinger, inspired by Richard Wagner, sought to regenerate interior decoration by treating it as a total work of art: 'It is [here] that coloured sculpture – which everyone seems so strangely afraid of – belongs. We continually seek sculptural works in the lower and purely architectural zones of every monumental space, in order to strengthen the room's character; they form groups that mediate between this area and the more fantastical works in the upper reaches. Since there can be no doubt that our first impression of such rooms is one of colour, the sculptures themselves must never be monochrome; this would make them appear like silhouettes and contradict both their purpose and essence.'[158] John Gibson had expressed it similarly, but was never given the opportunity to put his ideas into practice.

Klinger demanded further: 'Colour must come into its own here, must structure, fit, speak. It is wrong to see in these coloured sculptures the encroachment of realism. Certainly, they can become merely realist or purely gratuitous when they have

42 Max Klinger, *New Salome*, 1893, plaster and amber, Staatliche Kunstsammlungen Dresden, Skulpturensammlung

43 Max Klinger, *New Salome*, 1893-1903, marbles, partially painted, Leipzig, Museum der bildenden Künste

not been conceived for coloured rooms. If, however, one takes colour into account from the beginning and uses the right materials, a whole other effect will be achieved. In contrast to what is generally feared, there will be a return to simplicity, the sculptural form will be emphasised, and each part of the composition carefully balanced. This will open up the way for a new style, one that rejects the inessential and the naturalistic [...].'[159] According to Klinger, colour had always been the link between architecture, painting and sculpture; this connection, which had existed until the Rococo, was now in the process of disintegration: 'Nowadays we have the art of architecture and the art of sculpture, painting and the so-called reproductive arts, and further decorative art and crafts. What we are missing is a collective expression of our philosophy of life. We have arts, but no Art.'[160]

Since 1884 Klinger had been involved in the decoration of the Villa Albers in Berlin. Here, he had not only the opportunity to hear a reprise of Treu's lecture, but also to see his exhibition. The villa was a meeting place for art historians and writers and one of the visitors was Jules Laforgue, who shared Klinger's basic beliefs about polychrome sculpture. Before beginning to sculpt himself, Klinger had tested his abilities by painting plaster models of marble busts by Artur Volkmann. His own sculptures, made up of various kinds of stone, were worked out in careful studies. Using painted plaster models, the artist included colour in his concept from the start. Klinger's methods were different

44 Standing woman, Tanagra, 325-300 B.C., painted clay, Staatliche Museen zu Berlin, Preußischer Kulturbesitz, Antikensammlung

from Charles Cordier's, in whose work body parts and garments are distinguished by the naturalistic association of substances. Klinger chose instead to emphasise the painterly quality of his marbles.

Following his work at the Villa Albers, Klinger began making studies for his first polylithic sculpture, the *New Salome*, completed only in 1893. [42 43] For this piece, the sculptor used not only marble from Pentelikon, Hymettus, Carrara and Tuscany, but also included amber and shells. The black socle, made of Belgian limestone, and the dark polished wooden plinth enhance the polychromy, as does the large cube of coloured chalk from the Pyrenees upon which the sculpture rests. Klinger went still further, tinting the skin and accentuating the hair, eyebrows and lips with paint. Success was guaranteed as the completed marble version travelled to a number of German museums. It was thanks to Klinger's example that – ten years after Georg Treu's lecture – polychrome sculpture finally achieved the status it deserved. Colour and sculpture, form and idea now corresponded to the tenor of the times.

There were few artists in Germany who dared to follow Klinger down this difficult path. In the broader European context, however, there were a number of sculptors who worked in a similar manner, that is, using distinct types of marble or combining stone and bronze. In Great Britain, Edward Onslow Ford's *Shelley Memorial* in Oxford, completed in 1894, with the prone figure in white making an impressive contrast to the coloured socle, must be seen as an answer to the comparatively dry, neo-classical *Shelley Monument* by Ford's adversary Henry Weekes in the Priory in Christchurch, Hampshire. In 1880, in his *Lectures on art*, Weekes had spoken out against sculptural polychromy, calling it vulgar and immorally sensual.[161] In England we also find the masterpieces of Désiré-Maurice Ferrary, who explored combinations of materials in the 1890s. His *Leda* of 1898 **[59]** and the life-size *Salammbô* from 1899 [91], both in the Lady Lever Art Gallery in Port Sunlight, are in fact characterised by a certain superficial eroticism. The female figures are white, while their respective partners – a swan and a snake – are made of black bronze.

Klinger's *Cassandra* was shown in France in 1895. [114] French sculptors were acquainted with Treu's theories not only through Jules Laforgue but also through the critics Edmond Pottier and Maxime Collignon.[162] Here, it was Théodore Rivière who developed this type of mixed-media figure to the fullest. His greatest success was the small-scale bronze and ivory group *Salammbô at the house of Mathô* (1895). [90] There was hardly another subject of the period more popular or more appropriate

45 Jean-Léon Gérôme, *Painting breathes life into sculpture*, 1893, Toronto, The Art Gallery of Ontario, Gift from the Junior Women's Committee Fund, 1969

for translation into precious materials. Flaubert's novel, which had appeared in 1862, had given a public schooled in Orientalism the chance to feel transported to other times and countries. It is not certain whether the minute and highly colourful descriptions of the heroine's clothing and jewellery were the result of Flaubert's encounter with the first wave of polychrome sculpture, more specifically with the works of Pradier, as has been recently suggested.[163] The influence of the novel on sculptural production is, however, unquestionable, more, though, as a result of the operatic version by Ernest Reyer, which premiered in Brussels in 1890, than of the book. While Rivière limited himself to a small format and an anecdotal treatment, Denys Puech came closer to Klinger's manner in his life-size figure *La pensée* of 1890 (Paris, Musée du Petit Palais). Barrias's *Nature revealing herself to science* (1899) is also important in this context, although the choice of materials is more like that of Cordier than of Klinger. [129]

Tanagra

It was, however, an artist a generation older than Klinger who played the most decisive role in the history of polychrome sculpture in France, a painter who only later turned to sculpture: Jean-Léon Gérôme. As a rule, Gérôme preferred to paint directly on the white marble. The artist, who had become both rich and famous with his orientalising genre paintings, was inspired to transpose his academic, highly detailed realism into a third dimension by a sensational archaeological find: the discovery in 1873 of thousands of small terracotta figurines in and around the Boeotian village Tanagra. [44] The daily life of the Greeks suddenly appeared in a new – and colourful – light. The reports of the excavation spread like wildfire. Museums and private collectors hurried to purchase the statuettes, and soon workshops began producing forgeries. Particularly the representations of

46 Jean-Léon Gérôme, *Pygmalion and the statue*, 1892, marble, San Simeon, California, Hearst San Simeon State Historical Monument

47 Jean-Léon Gérôme, *Pygmalion and the statue*, 1890, New York, The Metropolitan Museum of Art

women, revealing the details of ancient Greek clothing, enjoyed great popularity. In 1878, Reinhard Kekulé published an opulent volume entitled *Griechische Thonfiguren aus Tanagra*, which included illustrations in colour.[164] Kekulé, head of the collection of ancient art in Berlin, had planned a complete *catalogue raisonné*, which would have raised the status of these doll-like objects to that of real works of art. The discovery of the figurines may have been accidental, but their immediate and unqualified acceptance was the result of a new attitude towards the delicate and playful forms of the Rococo. For the advocates of polychromy, they were the last piece of evidence that their theories had always been correct. For the sculptors themselves they were a new source of inspiration, one which spoke to them far more directly than the faded hints of colour on known works or all attempts at reconstruction.

No other artist remained as fascinated by the Tanagra phenomenon as Jean-Léon Gérôme. As a painter, he had always been dedicated to the exact reproduction of historical detail – some critics had even called him a slave to archaeology.[165] After well-known sculptors like Falguière and Mercié had translated isolated motifs from his paintings into sculpture in the 1860s, the artist himself took up the idea.[166] One of his first works was the monumental seated female nude *Tanagra* (1890), now largely deprived of most of its coloration. [112] Gérôme did not actually tint the skin, but rather accented the lips, eyes and hair. *Tanagra* is naturally an allegory of the Boeotian village and the school of sculpture named after it. In her left hand the figure holds a polychrome hoop dancer, reminiscent of the terracotta figurines but actually Gérôme's own invention. The artist also had an independent version of this tiny figure reproduced in bronze. In his vision of the workshops of ancient Tanagra, such figures were produced in series. In *Painting breathes life into sculpture* of 1893, an artist is shown painting the statuettes, while her fashionable customers inspect the works for sale.[167] [45]

The painting's Latin title, 'Sculpturae vitam insufflat pictura,' as pretentious as it might seem considering the homeliness of the young woman's activity, summarises Gérôme's beliefs. By combining colour and sculpture in a naive and naturalistic style, he sought to resurrect the past, to make his creations truly speak. Gérôme did not hesitate to compare himself with Pygmalion, the mythical sculptor who brought life to one of his own figures, and in 1892 he completed and polychromed a marble group of the subject. Its original colour is now unfortunately lost. The artist's own copies after his oil-on-canvas version give a good impression of what the original piece must have looked like. [46 47] Pygmalion himself is a somewhat flattering portrait of the artist as a young man. The painter followed the usual custom and depicted the moment when the statue's blood begins to circulate. Contradicting all the laws of nature, it appears to move progressively downward from the head – a bit of artistic licence that had enraged doctors when used by Girodet in 1819.[168] Whether Gérôme's sculpture thus succeeded in giving the illusion of life is doubtful; the public, then as now, was probably more impressed by the artist's technical skill. By this period, mimetic works of art were already on the decline, soon to be completely overtaken by photography and film. To gain and hold the audience's attention, other means were now needed.

Auguste Rodin's version of the Pygmalion myth proves that colour was not necessary to convincingly indicate the statue's coming to life.[169] [48] In his variations on the subject, in both marble and bronze, he rejected illusionism almost completely, leaving parts of the bodies unfinished. Pygmalion's facial features are barely distinguishable, and the statue is bound to the block in a way that mocks all conventions. One can only speculate whether Rodin's group, produced a few years before Gérôme's, was the inspiration for the latter's very dissimilar interpretation. There can be no question, however, that Gérôme and Rodin, as the main representatives of two irreconcilable directions in late-19th-century art, knew of each other's work and ideas.

Pygmalion was not the only subject they had in common. Other comparisons seem to point to a kind of artistic disputation between the two. One such theme was Bellona – beginning with François Rude's relief *La Marseillaise* on the Arc de Triomphe (1836), a symbol of valiant France and a particularly popular motif after the Franco-Prussian War. Rodin's 1879 *Bellona* was his contribution to the competition for a bust of the Republic.[170] [132] Rodin himself consciously used colour as a means of expression in this militant female figure: the bronze of the helmet and armour has a black patina, while her grimly determined face is green. This distinctive contrast between the skin and the rest of the bust cannot be disregarded; it not only increases the painterly effect, but also emphasises Bellona's martial character. What makes this early, still somewhat neo-baroque Rodin so effective is not the use of contrasting colours or precious materials, but

48   Auguste Rodin, *Pygmalion and the statue*, 1889, marble, Copenhagen, Ny Carlsberg Glyptotek

rather the subtle appeal of the surface. The polychromy is not added to the sculpture, but is an integral part of it.

Gérôme's *Bellona*, on the other hand, created around a decade later, is a mere conglomeration. [54] For both the head and the full-length version, which now stands in a hotel lobby in Canada, the artist received the advice and help of craftsmen. Moreau-Vauthier and Clovis Delacour assisted with the parts in ivory, while Emile Gallé and René Lalique aided in the execution of the Medusa's head that decorates the breastplate.[171] The result is a pastiche, concealing its weakness as sculpture behind a mass of attributes.

Rodin and Gérôme could be said to stand for two contrasting ways of working and seeing. Both included colour in the conception and execution of their sculptures. Rodin's *Bellona*, however, has withstood changes in taste because it unites colour and form. Apart from a retrospective evaluation, one conclusion can be drawn from the comparison of the two works: the combination of colour and sculpture was not the exclusive right of one artistic direction any more than the combination of paint and canvas.

Patina

Long before Barye and Rodin, sculptors had sought to influence the patina – the word for all discolorations due to age – of their bronzes. Pliny reports that Aristonidas mixed copper with iron in order to make one of his figures look like it was blushing.[172] Leonardo praised the variety of colours of bronze, Pomponius Gauricus collected the different recipes for his treatise *De sculptura* (1504), and Vasari commented on their successful use.[173] Although the Neo-classicists preferred a uniform coloration, the technique of polychrome patina was revived in the decorative arts after 1800. In the course of the 19th century, industrialisation led to a tremendous increase in the number of metal alloys that could be employed by artists. Cheaper materials such as zinc could be transformed to resemble bronze, with colours ranging from the classic black, brown and green tones to red and gold.[174] The colour gold played a particularly important role in the sculpture of the Neo-baroque. From Friedrich Drake's *Victory*, atop the Siegessäule in Berlin (1872) to Augustus Saint-Gaudens's *General Shearman* (1903) [49], this precious metal (or imitations of it) was used for every imaginable kind of sculpture.

Since the middle of the century, newly introduced metal alloys from Japan had had a great influence on European production. These alloys were previously more or less unknown, and the word 'bronze' does not even begin to describe them adequately. In the Meiji period, Japan had experienced not only an opening to the west, but also the unemployment of an army of swordmakers, who were forced to turn their talents to more decorative uses after the Samurai were banned from carrying weapons. The first exhibition of Japanese art took place in 1854 in London, and a few years later the English diplomat Rutherford Alcock presented his collection in the same city.[175] Finally, Japan itself displayed its superior products to the world at the Exposition Universelle in 1867. These exotic and fascinating works had a profound effect on sculptors such as Alfred Gilbert.[176] [75] **[69]**

Over the course of time, independent and decorative sculpture became increasingly entwined. A critical factor for artists was that since the 1840s foundries had begun to close contracts on the number of editions, a practice already well-known from porcelain manufacturing. Many sculptors, such Antoine-Louis Barye and Emmanuel Fremiet, who had his own booth at the world's fair of 1900, were entrepreneurs who managed their own production.[177] Inventions like the pantograph (a machine used to enlarge or reduce sculptures), galvanoplasty, or photographic sculpture were further steps on the way to a total mechanisation of production.

The influence of these new reproductive techniques should not be underestimated.[178] The German art theorist Theodor Alt

49 Augustus Saint-Gaudens, *Monument to General William Tecumseh Shearman*, 1903, bronze, New York

believed that industrialised polychrome sculpture was a means of conquering new markets: 'May the nation secure for itself such an important source of income and take its place at the head of the world market, achieving great wealth through its decorative objects. The introduction of colour in sculpture will prove fruitful, and with it will come both a new flowering of the art and an economic triumph.'[179] The result of all these developments was a new arbitrariness in subject matter, format, material and colour. One and the same figure could exist in various patinations – one need only think of the work of Barye. With the help of chemicals, the artist varied the colours of his bronze menagerie from traditional brown-black to a saturated green.[180] [61] [74] The sculptors paid for their use of semi-industrial methods of production with the loss of their hard-earned status. They became nameless, disappearing into the industrial sections of the world's fairs, where their art bronzes were displayed next to canons.[181]

The partisans of an autonomous art looked upon this downfall of sculptors with disgust. The social history of 19th-century sculpture has yet to be written, but Jules Laforgue, friend of the Impressionists, has left us a good picture of the depths to which the art had sunk. He described what he saw in the stores of Berlin: 'One cannot imagine the types of places the public is drawn to: [full of] furniture made by the dozen, and bronzes and other trinkets produced using the rasp of mechanical banality. [...] there are four vast stores, none of which could survive in Paris, promoting a whole industry of copies [...] of the most banal antiquities, Canova's affectations and pieces by all the other modern sculptors whose work aims for *le gemüth*.'[182]

An inner light – Impressionism in sculpture

It was not only 'industrial' artists, however, who profited from the possibilities offered by the new metalworking techniques. The cooperation between sculptor and caster had always been one of the fascinating aspects of working in bronze. Already Christian Daniel Rauch, inspired by the crusty patina on antique works, had sometimes consciously avoided an overly smooth surface.[183] Some artists used the accidental deformations that continued to result from casting for their own purposes. Finally, in the second half of the 19th century, patina became a means of individual artistic expression.

Rodin's bronzes best illustrate the – conscious or accidental – use of patina. In general, Rodin is not considered a sculptor who was particularly interested in polychromy: 'Colour! Try to give your work colour! This is an expression a sculptor should never use!'[184] This would appear to be self-deception, or perhaps the artist did not consider patina to be colour. In fact, however, Rodin not only varied the colours of his bronzes from deep black to bright green, but also had his casters combine several tones in the same work. While in the *Bellona* this helped to distinguish fundamentally distinct parts, Rodin later gave larger, connected areas an uneven coloration. [70] Just as he no longer smoothed the clay in order to leave the marks of his genius untouched, he allowed his sculptures to retain a quasi-natural surface structure. These effects do not serve to strengthen an illusion, but rather allow the viewer to re-experience the moment of creation.

In earlier times, too, modelling had seemed to 'flicker.' This was the result of unstable lighting conditions and, as a way of making statues seem alive, the effect was sometimes heightened by the use of torches. Advances in technology revolutionised perception. As we have seen in the stairwell of the Paris Opéra, such progress was mostly celebrated with pompous figural decoration. [38] Light, once so ephemeral, was imprisoned and became static. Rodin reacted to this blinding illumination by breaking up the surface. Camille Claudel followed his lead and even intensified the effect. In *Lost in thought*, which represents a young girl kneeling before a fireplace, she not only combined bronze and onyx in a very painterly manner but also included an electric bulb. The veined stone filters the light source, making the fire seem to glow and dance. [82] Rodin himself never went this far, and with good reason: additives such as these or the actual application of colour (as in Gérôme) were unacceptable to him. He was satisfied to replace classical smoothness with broken modelling. For him, the natural incidence of light was sufficient to create colour and life.

Rodin's 'handwriting' has given him the reputation of an Impressionist among sculptors. This concept has been rejected by many art historians, who feel that a term designed to characterise painting cannot be applied to sculpture.[185] By using a painterly, even draughtsmanlike, method and proclaiming the sketchy as finished, Rodin is in some sense himself responsible for this linguistic inaccuracy. His most 'impressionist' bronzes are of course those which have long stood outdoors and now show bizarre traces of weathering. [70] Whether or not these changes were calculated from the beginning, or at least condoned by the artist, must remain an open question.[186] One thing, however, is certain: Rodin did not take his own words very seriously, and experimented with polychromy much more than one would assume from the quotation cited above. Art history has allowed itself to be deceived by photography and later solid-black casts, and has trusted the artist's statements more than the appearance of the originals.

Rodin's wife, Rose Beuret, had probably already been the model for *Bellona*. [132] The portraits he made of her between 1880 and 1911 are particularly conspicuous examples of his interest in colour. The series begins with bronzes and continues with a marble version, carved by Antoine Bourdelle in 1898, and one in *pâte de verre* by Jean Cros.[187] [71-74] Rodin's 'palette' ranged here from black and green (bronze) to white (marble) to full polychromy (glass paste). In direct comparison, it becomes obvious that the colour, determined by the material, completely changes the work's general appearance. The incidence of light on black or green in one case shows the contours to advantage, in another the internal structure. Perhaps, oddly enough, it is the white marble which calls our attention to the overall colourfulness of Rodin's oeuvre. Thanks to the modelling, it reflects light in all its nuances, and since this particular medium does not distract the viewer with 'real' colour, it helps make him aware of this phenomenon. Rodin's figures allow even marble and bronze to appear polychrome. In any case, they give the role of colour in sculpture a new dimension.

Rodin was not averse to true polychromy either, as his cooperations with the ceramicists Paul Jeanneney and Jean Cros prove. The regularity with which he ventured into the realm of colour demonstrates a serious artistic interest in the subject and that such works were not simply deviations from the norm. These collaborations had some remarkable results. Paul Jeanne-

50 Paul Gauguin, *The singer (Valérie Roumi)*, 1880, mahogany and plaster, partially painted, Copenhagen, Ny Carlsberg Glyptotek

ney turned a number of Rodin's compositions into large-scale, fire and earth coloured sculptures, among others his studies for the *Burghers of Calais* and the *Colossal head of Balzac*. [**79**] This earthenware head exists in three variations and the blotchy colour adds an original aspect to the deeply furrowed volumes, corresponding to the form and increasing the expressive intensity. Jean Cros was not only the creator of the life-like mask of *Rose Beuret* [**74**], but also of at least four other portraits, made either after or in association with Rodin himself. His father, Henry Cros, had rediscovered coloured glass paste as an artistic medium and was much admired by Rodin, who even wrote the introduction to the catalogue of the retrospective exhibition of his work at the Galerie Hébrard in 1908.[188]

In living colour

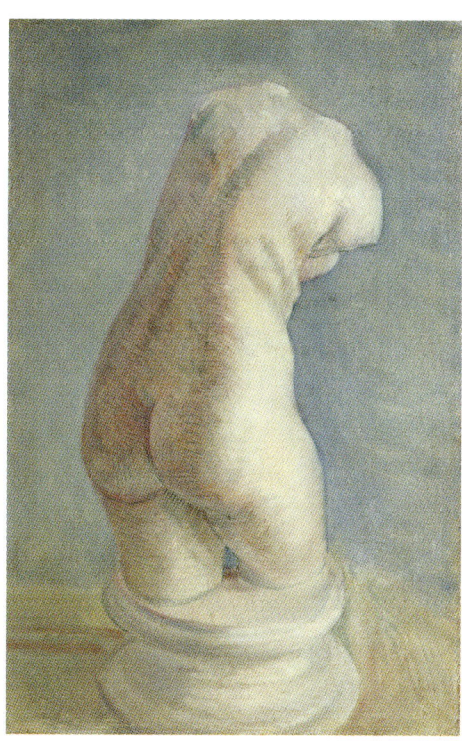

51 52 Vincent van Gogh, *Studies of a plaster cast*, 1886, both Amsterdam, Van Gogh Museum (Vincent van Gogh Foundation)

The techniques used by Jeanneney and Jean Cros, although similar in principle, yielded very different results. Important for both was that colour was an integral part of the sculpture, a result of the medium and working methods employed, and not merely added afterwards. This aspect is characteristic of Rodin's approach as well and corresponds to the demands of Jules Laforgue and Georg Treu. It had been said of the latter that his defence of colour in sculpture had opened the way for kitsch.

Already in 1894, it was this same Georg Treu who bought the first works by Rodin for a public collection in Germany.

Defining Impressionism in sculpture is not only a problem in the case of Rodin. Renoir and Degas, even the young Matisse and Picasso, made sculptures that one could call Impressionist. [83 85] Contemporaries, too, had trouble labelling them. In this context, the critic Edmond Claris asked artists and connoisseurs in 1901: 'Can and should sculpture compete with painting?'[189] This bid to rekindle the *paragone* debate of the Renaissance backfired: the answers he received were spiritless, if not frankly disinterested. One may assume that no one wanted to endanger the freshly re-established unity of the arts by insisting on retrograde distinctions. Further, the avant-garde was moving in a completely new direction, one which could be neither satisfactorily defined nor described according to the usual criteria.

There are, however, more similarities between 'Salon sculpture' and the sculptures of the Impressionists and Post-Impressionists – particularly with regard to the use of colour – than is generally assumed. The path taken by Cordier, Barrias and Klinger had helped to break certain, more general taboos. The avant-garde, however, used colour and modern techniques not to resuscitate a dying academic tradition, but rather as an aid in their search for new means of expression. Paul Gauguin's early portrait of the singer *Valérie Roumi* marks a transition.[190] [50] One of his first works in wood, it was executed in 1880 and exhibited a year later with the Impressionists. Although a *chanteuse* from a Parisian café is a perfect avant-garde motif, stylistically speaking the work is still indebted to Carrier-Belleuse. Gauguin exploited the reddish tone of the mahogany in a very decorative way, colouring the background gold and the hair ornaments red. The bouquet of flowers was added in plaster, whether due to the artist's inexperience with carving or as a conscious mixing of materials is unknown. The medallion's impact should not be underestimated: it defined the genre anew, not only in terms of subject matter, but also because of the way in which it obscured the border between 'high' and applied art.

A few years later, in 1886, the Belgian sculptor Constantin Meunier created an intimate portrait of his daughter *Charlotte*, with a patina that seems to shimmer in all the colours of the rainbow.[191] [66] Even Aristide Maillol was more interested in polychromy at the beginning of his career than he was later willing to admit. According to his own statements, he had little feeling for colour in sculpture and knew almost nothing about it. He even referred to it as 'non-sens,'[192] forgetting both his early ceramic work and his relief *The wave* (c. 1895).[193] Henri Matisse's statuette *The serf* from the turn of the century, on the other hand, as well as Picasso's *Head of a jester* of 1905, were clearly inspired by Rodin's bronzes. [85] In the case of both artists, the relationship between their paintings and sculptures is complex. Matisse often included his figurines, reproduced in brilliant local colour, in his canvases, and Picasso's *Jester* has a painted pendant as well (private collection). The latter not only went further than Rodin in furrowing the clay, he also sprinkled the bronze with paint.[194] If Françoise Gilot's reports are true, then Picasso took a great interest in the patina of his bronzes. According to her, a worker had recommended the artist urinate on the piece in order to achieve the desired effect – a somewhat unorthodox technique, but one which had enjoyed some success in Antiquity.[195]

Ceramic, gesso, ivory

The same *kunstwollen* that sanctioned the unpredictable in bronze patination was also responsible for the technical experiments of those sculptors interested in ceramic and related substances, the most important among them Henry Cros and Jean Carriès. Despite their innovative contributions, neither has received the attention he deserves: their work is difficult to categorise and their cooperation with ceramic manufacturers has given them the reputation of (mere) 'decorative' artists. Such collaborations had, however, a long and respectable tradition. Already in the 18th century, Etienne-Maurice Falconet, then director of the Sèvres manufactory, had his marble groups reproduced in series.

While Falconet considered matte-white bisque appropriate to his early neo-classical figures, later generations often cared little for such 'truth to materials' (or even coherence of colour) and allowed porcelain reproductions of bronze statues and vice versa. Manufacturers were always anxious to secure the rights to make reduced and painted versions of popular sculptures. Contemporary critics even thought they recognised national peculiarities in the choice of colours: Germany, for example, in contrast to England and France, appeared to prefer particularly strong shades.[196] The rather unflattering terms 'patisserie allemande' and 'Bilderbäcker' demonstrate that these ceramic products were held in very low esteem.[197]

Sculptors, of course, dreamed of popularity, but did not want to be associated with popular taste, a tendency we have already observed in relation to Impressionist bronzes. Ceramics and glazes were to these artists what patina was to sculptors like Rodin. New kilns allowed for a greater spectrum of colour, and earthenware was the preferred medium. Both these factors made it possible for artists to reproduce their ideas, borrowed from Asian or Near Eastern art, in a very personal way. The actual combinations used were extremely complex, and in many cases are still not completely understood.

53   Henry Cros, *The history of water*, 1904, glass paste, Paris, Musée d'Orsay

Henry Cros had become known in the 1880s for his wax portraits and troubadour scenes.[198] [94] Descended from a family of scientists and inventors, and well versed in the classics, Cros carefully studied the recipes of the Ancients, using them as the foundation for his reinvention of *pâte de verre*. The production of works in glass paste resembles that for ceramics in its main procedures, namely firing and glazing. Here, pigments are mixed into the raw medium and the final result is dependent on the temperature at which the piece is fired. The process was difficult to control, but with a little experience the artist could separate the colours fairly precisely, although no two objects would ever look exactly the same.[199]

In 1893, Cros was given a studio at Sèvres, which allowed him to perfect his process, developing glass paste into a full-fledged artistic medium. [12-16] [53] Despite his interest in technical questions, the sculptor never neglected his art. As Jean-Luc Olivié has pointed out, Cros did not consider himself a craftsman; he saw his pieces as sculpture in the truest sense. It was not, however, recognised as such, and the artist continually saw his work shuffled about between art and craft. His flat reliefs with their delicate coloration, the elegiac character of his scenes of life in the ancient world, earned him the reputation of the Puvis de Chavannes of sculpture. Cros did not, however, merely follow in Puvis's footsteps; he actually returned to the sources. For him, polychromy was not an end in itself but a means of approaching the essence of the ancient world.[200]

What Antiquity was to Henry Cros, Japan was to Jean Carriès. His admiration for Japanese ceramics began at the Exposition Universelle of 1878.[201] It would be hard to find a greater contrast to Cros's classical clarity. While the latter employed subtle and clearly delineated pastel tones, the surfaces of Carriès's sculptures are bathed in streams of unidentifiable earthy colours. While Cros took his subject matter from the more harmless myths of the Antique, Carriès drew from a bizarre world of fauns, knights and fantastic creatures. [86] Forms he had been unable to achieve in either bronze or plaster became possible in earthenware, and he compiled a fabulous repertoire of figures unlike any since the mannerist period. After working for some of the large manufactories in the Saarland, Carriès opened his own studio in 1888. Legends soon grew up around his recipes, myths a chemist friend waved off with the words: 'il fallait ne rien savoir pour oser cela [...].'[202]

The discovery of new materials and the love of colour unleashed a storm which quickly swept through Europe. Ceramic sculpture was almost always polychrome. Modernist artists could finally produce 'popular' art, without being accused of creating mere kitsch. From Camille Alaphilippe to Aristide Maillol, from Alexandre Charpentier to Paul Gauguin, from Isidore De Rudder, Richard Luksch, Franz Metzner to Michael Powolny, Ernst Barlach and Niels Hansen Jacobsen, almost everywhere artists experimented with decorative sculpture. Alaphilippe and Charpentier even attempted works on a monumental scale. Both used a kind of builder's technique, composing their figures or reliefs out of moulded bricks. Alaphilippe developed a 'ceramic stone inlay' process, which he used to reconstruct the courtly world of the Middle Ages.[203] [54] Charpentier turned to still older, oriental methods. He was inspired by the *Archers frieze* from Susa, which came to the Louvre around 1886.[204] His major work is *The bakers* (1897): one version stands in the Square Scipion in Paris and another is preserved in the Skulpturengalerie in Dresden, purchased by Georg Treu as part of his collection of contemporary polychrome sculpture.

New processes using combinations of clay, plaster and ceramic also became popular in Great Britain. Artists remained faithful to their medieval subject matter – in fact it would seem that here the Gothic had survived the centuries. The Houses of Parliament were a profane monument to the Middle Ages, decorated in glorious colours in the 1840s by A.W.N. Pugin and his assistant John Thomas. [26] A new vogue for the period, which

54 Camille Alaphilippe, *Woman with a monkey*, 1908, stoneware and bronze, Paris, Musée du Petit Palais

55 Edward Burne-Jones, *The hand refrains (Pygmalion and the image II)*, 1868, Birmingham Museum and Art Gallery

56 Edward Burne-Jones, *The soul attains (Pygmalion and the image IV)*, 1868, Birmingham Museum and Art Gallery

fed both literature and the art of the Pre-Raphaelites, resulted in a number of interesting coloured sculptures around the end of the century.[205]

Coloured ceramic had re-established itself in England – see, for example, the Della Robbia Pottery in Birkenhead – but the renewed enthusiasm for medieval *gessopainting* was still more important. Artists like Robert Anning Bell, Henry Fehr, George Frampton, Gerald Moira and Frank Lynn Jenkins used it to create large-scale reliefs depicting episodes from British history for the decoration of town halls and other public buildings. Scenes from the War of the Roses or the Legend of King Arthur were very much *en vogue*.[206] Some critics praised this 'midway between painting and sculpture' (Walter Crane)[207] in the highest tones, and likened these artists to the masters of the Renaissance. *The Studio* even went so far as to compare Henry Fehr's frieze in Wakefield with the choir stalls in the cathedral at Amiens.[208] [57] Others were more modest, recognising in the coloured reliefs a way for poorer communities to afford appealing public decoration and a means of giving second-rate talents a chance at self-expression and income.[209] With *gessopainting*, artists like Bell and Frampton, who were close to the Arts & Crafts Movement, were able to realise their ideal of an 'all-over' decoration and achieve the unification of painterly and sculptural techniques.[210]

Symbolist polychromy and fin-de-siècle decadence

This turn-of-the century medievalism was not limited to England, but was rather an international phenomenon, which encompassed everything from Cardiff Castle (1868-81) to the Albrechtsburg in Meissen (c. 1870) and the Parliament in Budapest (1885-1904). [27 28] It was also responsible for a veritable army of coloured statues. In France, the cult around Joan of Arc had kept interest in the Middle Ages alive, and there was no church in the entire country without its figure of this patriotic warrior.[211] Ingres's monumental painting of 1854 (Paris, Musée du Louvre) was one of the earliest depictions of the young heroine based on actual sources. The colours in the painting encouraged a number of sculptors to give their figures an historically correct appearance with the help of polychromy.[212] [29]

In Belgium, the second neo-gothic movement was already Symbolism. Fernand Khnopff's visions of Bruges are the most

57 Charles Henry Fehr, *The Wars of the Roses*, 1898, *gessoduro*, painted, Wakefield County Hall (detail)

58 View of the Congo exhibition of 1897 in Brussels-Tervuren with sculpture groups representing scenes of African life, photograph, Brussels, Musée royal de l'Afrique centrale

famous examples. The 'classical' Neo-gothic of the 1840s and 50s had already achieved a great deal in this new state, which sought to construct its identity by turning to the past. A local speciality within 19th-century polychrome sculpture was the rebirth of ivory carving. This was the result of the intensive exploitation of the Congo, which until 1908 was the private property of King Leopold II. At the enormous Congo exhibitions of 1894 (Antwerp) and 1897 (Brussels-Tervuren), ivory was extolled as an export product. The exhibition in Tervuren was an unparalleled act of state and more than one million visitors saw the 'white treasure' displayed in specially-designed cases in the so-called *Salon d'Honneur*, making a startling contrast to the painted plaster groups of natives, executed from life. [58 136]

Sculptors and craftsmen, regardless of ideology, were encouraged to use ivory. After the tusks had been used only to make billiard balls, piano keys and all kinds of other trinkets, the material experienced a true artistic renaissance.[213] The strategy of Leopold and his ministers quickly showed results.[214] The elite among Belgian's sculptors – De Rudder, Julien Dillens, Josuë Dupon and Charles Van der Stappen – participated in the Antwerp and Tervuren exhibitions and sold well. Hardly any of them had worked in this soft substance before. Most of the sculptures were chryselephantine female nudes, with the bodies made of ivory and the decorative attributes of metal and stones. [88 89] These applications were designed to increase the impression of delicacy and fragility.

The love of exquisite materials was characteristic of the fin de siècle.[215] During the height of the Art Nouveau movement, fantasy was given free rein and many artists, such as René Lalique, Wilhelm von Cranach, the Vever brothers or Philippe Wolfers could hardly be distinguished from goldsmiths. Even Alphonse Mucha, better known as a painter and illustrator, created a polychrome *gesamtkunstwerk* with his decorations for the jewellery store Fouquet, and one of the most decorative sculptures of the period was his bust *La nature*. [139] [92]

The *femmes fatales*, who hid their true characters under a mantle of jewels or fabrics, soon became art products. Here colour no longer symbolised the origination or illusion of life, but rather concealed the threat of death. Jane's make-up in Georges Rodenbach's novel *Bruges-la-Morte* (1892) is reminiscent of corpselike wax figures, and numerous polychrome Gorgons populated the exhibitions, warning male visitors of the dangers of women. One of the most important works created in this genre is Charles Van der Stappen's *Secretive sphinx*, with her hand held mysteriously in front of her mouth. The gleaming silver of the helmet makes an elegant contrast to the matte surface of the ivory. [138]

Fernand Khnopff also took part in the ivory revival and praised its continuing progress in a review that appeared in *The Studio*.[216] As a frequent participant in exhibitions abroad, Khnopff helped spread symbolist doctrines. The Vienna Secession in particular was a meeting place for the international avant-garde. In addition to Khnopff its foreign members included such sculptors and painter-sculptors as Jean Dampt, Alexandre Charpentier, Constantin Meunier, Ville Vallgren, Max Klinger, Franz von Stuck and Charles Van der Stappen. Polychrome sculptures could be found with extraordinary regularity in Vienna, some of the most interesting by Khnopff himself. In 1898 he exhibited the life-size coloured torso *Vivien*, a representation of the thieving witch from Tennyson's *Idylls of the king*. Werner Hofmann has placed her among the 'votive figures of the cult of Eros practised at the turn of the century,' and in her polychromy recognised 'Pygmalion's creation apparently come to life.'[217] [99] Also on display were two versions of the *Bust of a young English woman*, one in delicately tinted *gessoduro* [59],[218] a technique Khnopff had become acquainted with in Great Britain, and the other in tinted marble.

An 'iconic' principle is at work not only in Khnopff's images of women, as suggested by Michel Draguet, but also in his use of polychromy.[219] Like no other artist, Khnopff exploited the magical qualities inherent in coloured sculpture. Primordial memories from the pagan past and the iconoclasts' fear of idols play an important role in Khnopff's pictorial strategy. The artist becomes a demiurge, using mysterious methods to create living, or at least lifelike, beings – without, however, resorting to naturalism. The icon can be extremely truncated, as in the *Bust of a young English woman*, without losing any of its power. Khnopff's sculptures are thus closely related to the masks of 'primitive' peoples which, despite their highly abstracted form, nonetheless have an immediate and unmediated impact on the viewer. In his own coloured

59 Fernand Khnopff, *Bust of a young English woman*, 1891, *gessoduro*, painted, Brussels, Musées royaux des Beaux-Arts de Belgique

masks, the Symbolist played with levels of reality, and an uncertainty about truth characterises his art. [90]

Just as Khnopff was influenced by the renaissance of *gessoduro* in England, the English sculptor George Frampton looked to the ivory movement in Belgium for inspiration. His major work is the bust of *Lamia*, 'one of the most truly symbolist sculptures in western art.'[220] We know a great deal about the creation of this hieratic bust. Working on a clay model, Frampton produced the face and upper body in ivory, while the fabrics and seams were to be made of silver with mother-of-pearl and gold. According to Susan Beattie, financial considerations finally forced the artist to use less expensive materials like bronze and opals instead. [91]

Frampton took as his subject a modern Ovidian metamorphosis, John Keats's *Lamia*. In the poem, the author revels in listing all the colours which accompany the apparent transformation of the snake-woman (in reality only an illusion). Frampton's bust transports a *femme fatale* of the Romantic into the era of Symbolism. Lamia is represented in her purest state; the colour that went before, and that which is to come, is scarcely indicated. A visitor to the Academy Exhibition of 1900 saw her and wrote:

'As you gaze, a faint colour comes to the lips – the loveliest, most sensitive of mouths – the eyelids quiver a very little, and her expression changes, but never loses its mystery or sadness. She makes an absolute silence in the room; whoever turns his head in passing stops and remains as one enchanted.'[221] The principles of life and death are united in this symbolist masterpiece: colour vivifies dead matter and the living bust turns the viewer to stone; Pygmalion's statue and Medusa become one.

The appearance of so many sphinxes, Medusas, and other fabulous creatures – interestingly enough drawn from the same antique sources used by academic artists in the earlier part of the century – was a product of contemporary taste. These works document the striving of a group of artists to provide their well-situated urban clients with refined fetishes. These sculptors were uninterested in either questioning or criticising the general state of humanity, and so their endeavours to unify the arts in polychrome sculpture remained superficial, a mere episode. Their opponents accused them of decadence and instead sought contact with an unspoiled world, whether in the countryside of Europe or further afield.

Paul Gauguin fled to Tahiti, where he hoped to purify his art of sated civilisation and find new inspiration. His 'primitivism' had a liberating effect on art in general, and opened up new perspectives for polychrome sculpture. Colour in sculpture had never been a matter of strife in non-European cultures; it was available everywhere. Even until recently, but particularly in the 19th century, 'primitive' art was held up as a negative example, used as proof of the superiority of western production, and obstinate opponents of polychromy like Charles Blanc had always used it as their final argument. In choosing precisely this art as his model, Gauguin accomplished a revolution which opened the eyes of his contemporaries. His Tahitian figurines and reliefs are proof of his striving for unity in colour and volume; in them, sculpture and the painting of sculpture are one, and out of this synthesis Gauguin believed he could conquer new artistic terrain. [100–102]

The colourfully glazed earthenware statuette *Oviri* is the most radical of Gauguin's sculptures.[222] [95] The title, the Tahitian word for 'savage,' is incised in large letters on the plinth. *Oviri* is a standing female nude, carrying on her left hip an unidentified animal, sometimes thought to be a puppy or a cub of some kind. At her feet is a wolflike creature with its mouth open, lying in what appears to be a pool of blood. The wolf is Gauguin's personal symbol of unbridled freedom or perhaps, as Susan Taylor has suggested, the artist himself, 'victimized by forces personified by a menacing female.'[223] According to this interpretation *Oviri*, too, would be a *femme fatale*. Is she Gauguin's earthy answer to all the Salon Salammbôs and Nanas, an avant-garde reaction to the elegant temptresses of the Belle Epoque? In this rough and badly proportioned figure, the artist has united a fashionable motif with the magical powers of a coloured idol. By forming the work in clay, Gauguin made a conscious reference to the myth of the demiurge, the sculptor-god, and perhaps even to the story of creation itself. *Oviri*, however, is not only a threat, the harbinger of death: the vaginal opening at the back indicates that she is also the source of life.

Gauguin seems to have been almost possessed by his figure. Not only do *Oviri* and related creatures appear as idols and spirits in many of his paintings, he also meant to have the ceramic sculpture placed on his grave. According to Taylor, the statuette was a symbol 'of the very essence of his self-constructed savage and creative identity.'[224] Gauguin's *Oviri* moves towards a new form of artistic self-expression which, despite its appeal to the oldest sculptural traditions, was absolutely modern. With *Oviri*, colour in sculpture, so often accused of banal illusionism, became the strongest weapon in the fight against Naturalism.

Gauguin's example inspired Maurice Denis, Jens Ferdinand Willumsen and Georges Lacombe, all of whom tried their hand at polychrome sculpture. Denis made only one coloured relief [93]; the Dane Willumsen, however, remained true to polychromy until well into the 1920s.[225] [94] Lacombe could particularly be said to have developed a sculptural language tied to the ideas of the Nabis. Whereas in the *Isis* of 1893-94 (Paris, Musée d'Orsay) he had given the demonic aspects of a strange cult a highly vivid form, in the polychrome plaster *Mary Magdalene* of 1896 he created a balance between colour and volume. [96] His forms are even more simplified than Gauguin's; contours and lines abstract the details and underline the impression of the whole rather than distracting from it. Turning inward on herself, the *Mary Magdalene* is reminiscent of romanesque sculpture.[226]

Later generations, the Cubists and Expressionists, were also indebted to Gauguin. The avant-garde figurines of the early 20th century are all children of *Oviri*. The use of colour became a characteristic declaration of opposition to tradition. For Jacques Lipchitz colour and volume were one and polychromy was 'the inner light' of sculpture.[227] Paul Klee called all sculptors who still resisted the new trend 'bores and idiots.'[228] Whether figurative or constructive, abstract or expressionistic, the modernists continued to create scandals with their rough-looking coloured sculptures. Picasso, Laurens, Archipenko or Zadkine, Brancusi, Arp or Schlemmer, Kandinsky, Kirchner, Kokoschka or Rouault, not one could have done without colour. The story of their efforts on behalf of polychromy would, however, be the subject of another essay.

60 Lawrence Alma-Tadema, *The golden hour*, 1908, present location unknown

61 Gustav Klimt, *Pallas Athena*, 1898, Vienna, Historisches Museum der Stadt Wien

The end of a dream

A lot was lost when colour was abandoned in sculpture.
Quentin Bell[229]

In a letter to Clemens Brentano, Philipp Otto Runge mourned the disunity among the arts. He complained that architects, painters and sculptors were so alienated from one another 'that one is forced to conclude that they have no need of each other, and that it would now be impossible to get a number of competent people together to carry out a large-scale project, one which goes beyond the strength of any given individual.' For Runge, this was a sign of chaos, and his dream was to bring all the arts together once again.[230] Polychrome sculpture, revived at the beginning of the century and eventually developing into a permanent part of art production, was an important milestone on the way towards fulfilling this aspiration. By the mid-1880s, many contemporaries believed that the triumphal march of polychromy could no longer be stopped.[231] Neo-classicists and Orientalists, Symbolists, Impressionists and Post-Impressionists, the representatives of all the 'neo'-styles and particularly the eclecticists, turned to polychromy as a means of realising their aesthetic ideals. Praise or censure of a polychrome sculpture was no longer dependent on whether or not a critic was for or against colour in general, but was based on the individual artistic achievement: 'Examinons donc les monuments sans parti pris.'[232]

The unprejudiced judgment of polychrome sculpture had just begun when a new end threatened. In 1908, Lawrence Alma-Tadema painted *The golden hour*.[233] [60] In it, a young Englishwoman is shown admiring Gérôme's *Hoop dancer*; behind her is a repository from the Hildesheim treasury: an antique original and an imitation are confronted with one another. How much longer – one imagines the young lady thinking – can Greece remain the model for civilisation?

On the eve of the First World War, the previously unchallenged values of European culture seemed to be disintegrating. In 1906, Carl Kundmann's monumental marble and gilt *Athena* was installed in front of the Vienna Parliament. For some, the figure was a logical form for the self-expression of a community; for others, it was absurdly archaic. Eight years before, Gustav Klimt had already painted an *Athena*, which aimed to destroy the last remnants of Classicism. Here, there is no sign of either calm grandeur or noble simplicity: the goddess appears out of the misty background like a ghost. For Klimt, the little Nike she holds is no longer the symbol of the abstract state but a sign of the triumph of the individual.[234] [61]

The colourful interiors of the Makart era suddenly seemed oppressive and affected. Even Klinger had to submit to the new trend towards light and air: his *Beethoven* was displayed at the Vienna Secession in 1902 in one of Josef Hoffmann's sober rooms, where it surely looked more than a little out of place. [62 63] Ekkehard Mai has called the sculpture – respectively its presentation – the 'swan-song [...] of the total work of art.'²³⁵ Worlds collided here and the conflict was only just beginning. No reconciliation seemed possible between the partisans of academic illusionism and this latest generation of reformers. 'Truth to materials' was now the battle cry.

Pure material, which had lost its identity and expressive force in the course of the 19th century through industrialisation and chemical manipulation, became the new fetish. Its partisans, too, looked to the past for legitimation, forgetting, however, that in previous centuries the imitation of a material was often considered more valuable than the material itself. It was the sublimation inherent in imitation that was admirable, or at the very least the technical skill required, and not the substance alone.²³⁶ Nor was this ideology actually very new. The Bauhaus's ancestors range from Gustav Pazaurek and John Ruskin to Emperor Joseph II, who decreed in 1784 that 'a statue must consist only of the material it is made of.' For all of them, coloured sculpture was something alien.²³⁷ The strict formalists no longer relied on the precepts of Winckelmann, but on those of Adolf von Hildebrand, who soon forgot his own 'polychrome' past. His influential treatise of 1893, *Das Problem der Form in der bildenden Kunst*, barely mentions colour, admitting it only in a subordinate function.²³⁸ The young discipline of art history quickly took up this newly proclaimed division of the arts. In the eyes of the triumphant Modernists, 19th-century polychrome sculpture was a purely historical phenomenon or merely kitsch.²³⁹ As the art of the 20th century has shown, however, many sculptors rejected purist doctrine and continued to work in living colour.

62 Max Klinger, *Beethoven*, 1902, marbles, Leipzig, Museum der bildenden Künste

63 Max Klinger's *Beethoven* in the Vienna Secession, 1902, photograph, Leipzig, Museum der bildenden Künste

Wolfgang Drost

Colour, sculpture, mimesis

A 19th-century debate

Nous avons trop oublié la polychromie. André Michel[1]

'The notion of adding colour to form is as old as the world itself, and will certainly last as long,' so the French critic Paul Mantz in 1859.[2] This realisation, and the prophecy that followed, were more controversial at the time than one can imagine at the end of the 20th century, with polychrome sculpture an integral part of art production. By the middle of the 19th century, as a result of the archaeological research of the previous decades,[3] there was a general awareness that, as Mantz wrote, Egyptians, Assyrians and Greeks had coloured their statues, and that even the Byzantines had not been opposed to this custom.

Nonetheless, despite the evidence, Mantz was not yet completely convinced, and his condemnation of medieval sculpture indicates that his conception of the use of colour in the Antique was in fact somewhat limited. To his mind, the artists of the Middle Ages had abused ancient practice: by adding 'the brutal reality of actual garments' to their coloured statues they had exaggerated it to an unacceptable degree.[4]

This was the position of an open-minded theorist among the French art critics, one which was to be found, with various nuances, all over Europe. By the 1850s, it had become impossible to deny the use of colour in the Antique; its scope, intensity and artistic intention, however, were still a matter of debate, and critics continued to react sceptically towards those contemporary sculptors who employed it. The history of the aesthetic controversy over colour and its introduction into sculpture begins in classical antiquity. In the 19th century, discussions on the subject formed not only the basis of neo-classical aesthetics, but also to a large extent those of Realism, the Neo-baroque and Symbolism.

Antiquity to the Renaissance

Since the beginning of western culture, art had aimed to recreate reality. However, *what* aspects of the real world should be represented, and more particularly *how*, was already a question among the Greeks. The concept of 'mimesis,' the exact meaning of which was always subject to interpretation, was formulated in the Antique. Sceptical about the fine arts, Plato banned artists (as well as poets) from his ideal state because he felt they reproduced the *appearance* of the world and not its *essence*. He particularly objected to colour, which he thought distracted from the 'philosophical knowledge of the truth' – the *idea* beneath the visible surface – of the object. The Roman sculptures unearthed during the Renaissance (generally copies of Greek originals), having received a surface cleaning, shone in a brilliant white that made them seem like incarnations of Plato's philosophy. The white dematerialised the stone and gave the figures a sublime and noble appearance – notions which became an integral part of the idea of Greek art in western thought from this point onwards. The white of the marble disassociated the statues from reality, making them 'philosophically pure' and beautiful in a way that seemed to correspond to the Platonic theory of ideas.[5] Temporal and local factors, the base, ugly, prosaic and contingent were excluded; in the depiction of reality, ideal beauty, believed to represent the universal, was emphasised.

According to Plato, form and proportion were the main criteria for beauty; colour was lacking in his definition. The Ancients, however, were not as rigid in their theories as the Neo-classicists. Although he was indeed suspicious of its seductive power, Plato did in fact recognise colour as an additional quality: 'colours in correct combination' could, as it were, give the sculptural contours 'clarity.'[6] It is surprising how openly the philosophers admitted their dilemma. For both Plato and Aristotle, the goal of art was mimetic representation: in this sense, colour could be an aid to the artist, but at the same time it could also be an impediment. The sculptor, working in three dimensions, gives nature a concrete and tactile form. The painter, on the other hand, merely gives the viewer the *illusion* of reality. Painting, like poetry, was believed to be fundamentally mendacious, and this is the reason so many philosophers were opposed to colour in art. They were, however, perceptive and self-critical enough to realise that it was precisely this aspect that made a work appealing: as Plutarch argued, colour was more convincing and closer to life than line, gave the viewer more pleasure, and was also more stimulating. Cicero even went so far as to proclaim colour on a par with form, recognising in it an equal element of physical beauty.[7]

In reality Greek sculpture did not correspond to Platonic philosophy; it was indeed almost garishly colourful. The aim of the painting, however, was not to make the works more realistic. The painters who collaborated with sculptors, like these highly respected artists, employed four basic colours: red, blue, yellow and green, applying them to figures on the pediments and metopes in sharp contrast. In a painting of 1868, Lawrence Alma-Tadema depicted Phidias revealing the Parthenon frieze to the Athenians: historically accurate (as far as we know), he envisioned the sculptures in red against a blue background. [64]

Renaissance sculptors, particularly in Italy (for example, Donatello and Della Robbia), did not hesitate to work in colour, and the opposing positions outlined above were reiterated, in more pointed form, in many treatises of the period. The numerous and often very subtle discussions of the Cinquecento are important in this context, as they laid the foundations for the art-theoretical debates about polychrome sculpture in the 19th century. The *dialoghi* of the Renaissance focused attention once again on the age-old dilemma: mimesis, that is, the depiction of the essential and universal, stood in contrast to the unmediated registration of reality and its sensual rendering through colour. Citing Michelangelo, the Florentine sculptor Benvenuto Cellini referred to colour in his treatise on sculpture of 1568 as a seductive sham: *disegno*, i.e. the linear expression of the artistic idea, was to come first.[8] Francisco de Hollanda, another of Michelangelo's circle, took a more moderate view: although colour was incidental, it was nonetheless necessary to mimesis.[9] For Lodovico Dolce, colour and line were more or less equals: he did not consider the former accidental, something that obscured the idea embodied in the *disegno*; on the contrary, it gave form the finishing touch. The famous anecdote of Zeuxis's grapes and the story of Parrhasius, who painted a curtain so realistically that even Zeuxis himself was deceived, served as his examples.[10] It is here that we find the source for the wide-spread association of colour and naturalism that lasted until the late 19th century.

Appealing instead to the theory of *divina proporzione*, proposed by Fra Luca Pacioli in Venice in the early years of the 16th century, the artists of the neo-classical movements returned to immaculate white marble, eventually developing the notion of the *beau idéal* championed by Winckelmann. A normative aesthetic, founded on the false assumption that Greek sculpture had originally been white was born, and was to remain dominant – although not unchallenged – until at least the middle of the 19th century.

The history of the revision of these views in both theory and practice is one of resistance to ever-increasing factual evidence, reinterpretation and even wilful misinterpretation. It is connected to the ongoing history of white neo-classical sculpture and its qualified acceptance of polychromy in the form of coloured marble as well as ivory and gold, so-called chryselephantine sculpture. The Neo-classicists' resistance to polychromy was part of their struggle against Realism, whose proximity to nature was felt to threaten the idealist principles of 'high' art. This, too, was a misunderstanding: neither the painting on Greek sculpture nor all 19th-century coloured sculptures can be subsumed under the banner of Naturalism.[11]

A shocking discovery: antique polychromy

According to Winckelmann, who published his *Geschichte der Kunst des Altertums* in 1764, 'a body is all the more beautiful the whiter it is.' White emphasised the 'unity and simplicity' through which 'all beauty becomes sublime.'[12] This notion did not, however, remain unchallenged for long: although suppressed by Winckelmann, the existence of antique polychromy could soon no longer be denied. This phenomenon seemed to break all conventions; it disturbed traditional ways of seeing, and reactions ranged from irritated surprise and disbelief to fanatical rejection of the data. Polychromy violated deeply engrained sentiments about the purity and ideality of marble, as expressed in Théophile Gautier's programmatic poem *L'art*, which appeared in *L'Artiste* in 1857. That the Greeks had disregarded the intrinsic beauty of the stone was thought strange, incomprehensible and even barbaric until it became clear that they had exploited its whiteness within a whole polychrome system. Most often, the hair and beards of the figures, as well as the reins of the horses were painted red or red-brown, while the faces (with the exception of the eyes and eyebrows), arms, legs and animals' bodies remained uncoloured, allowing the marble to work to full effect.

A first breakthrough for polychrome sculpture came in 1814, with the publication of Quatremère de Quincy's treatise *Le Jupiter Olympien, ou l'art de la sculpture antique considéré sous un nouveau point de vue*, a folio volume with numerous hand-coloured illustrations.[13] [12] The archaeologist convincingly demonstrated that the Greek sculpture of all periods had been painted (to a greater or lesser degree) or diversified by employing colour.[14] He argued against the positions of the Neo-classicists, who continued to insist that Greek art had been monochrome. With remarkable open-mindedness he noted that the Greeks hardly 'distinguished [...] between the pleasures of the eye and the pleasures of the mind,' claiming that for them the 'variety and beauty of materials' was in no way a contradiction of

64 Lawrence Alma-Tadema, *Phidias and the frieze of the Parthenon, Athens*, 1868, Birmingham Museum and Art Gallery

'essential beauty.'[15] Three years later, Sir William Gell put it still more explicitly: 'No nation ever exhibited a greater passion for gaudy colours' than the Greeks.[16]

A modern *querelle*: arguments against the colourists

A truly self-contained and binding theory of polychrome sculpture was apparently never constituted, and it is only in the second half of the 19th century that one encounters an increasing number of apologies. The advocates of colour in sculpture were generally on the defensive, and could do nothing but distance themselves from firmly-established conventions and the preeminence of white marble sculpture in order to arrive – *ex negativo* – at a definition of their aesthetic goals. Nonetheless, by this time, a change in favour of polychromy had taken place. A hundred years earlier, disapproval had been greater: in the neo-classical period in France, the use of colour in sculpture had been considered an attack on the *beau idéal*. Etienne-Maurice Falconet had taken this position in a speech at the Parisian Académie Royale de Peinture et de Sculpture in 1760.[17] According to the sculptor, an artwork should be 'the summary of the beauty of nature,' combining its best elements to create 'essential beauty.'[18] For him, art was a matter of 'correct proportions and beautiful forms,' of 'grace and nobility,' which made 'the most perfect representation of the human body' possible.[19] There was no room for colour in this system. Falconet concluded – perhaps with some regret but without any hesitation – that the sculptor must do without the 'seductive charm of colour.'[20]

Similar views were expressed in Germany. In his early years, Johann Gottfried Herder – a disciple of Rousseau's who was open to anti-rationalist aesthetics – described 'sculptures coloured after nature' as ugly and 'deform[ed].' In *Kritische Wälder*, published in 1769, he spoke in favour of 'uninterrupted' white form; colour, he wrote, is that which 'impedes form and is not part of it.'[21] The 25-year-old Herder's formulations prevailed until far into the 19th century: pure form, volume, and particularly contour, were thought to be masked by the use of colour. These opinions were founded on the belief that painting, by employing aerial perspective, had introduced a way of seeing that was contrary to the concrete character of sculpture, which created perspective through volume alone. The two systems were incompatible, and any undertaking to join them could only have negative effects on sculpture.

At around the same time, in his *Salon de 1765*, Denis Diderot, who disapproved of the imitation of the Antique to a certain extent,[22] introduced another argument against colour, one which we have already encountered among the Greek philosophers: colour did nothing but simulate reality. Diderot took this suggestion somewhat further, declaring outright that sculpture, which embodied Truth in all its substantiality, and colour were completely at odds: 'nothing is so unpleasant as the contrast between the true and the false, and the truth of colour will never correspond to the truth of an object; the object – that is, the statue – is something independent, isolated, solid, always ready to move.'[23] Diderot thus entered upon the terrain mapped out by Abbé du Bos in his influential *Réflexions critiques sur la poésie et la peinture* (1719): what is important is no longer the determination of a canon of proportions but rather the *effect* the work of art has on the viewer. Contemporary feeling, even in the case of so sensitive a critic as Diderot, could not accept the coupling of colour and form, which for him violated the laws of art. An almost ethical question about truth and illusion in works of art thus arose: sculpture could make a claim to truth, whereas colour could not. For Falconet, the real weight of Du Bos's aesthetic lay in the idea of *goût*, that is, the good taste of an aristocratic society. A painted statue could appeal only to the uncultivated masses and was therefore trivial: 'The gleam of gilding, the dissonance of different marbles, will fool the eyes of the mob, addicted to mere externals, and the man of the world will be outraged.'[24]

At the beginning of the 19th century, little had changed. Antiquity remained the model, and the notion of *style* still carried with it a specific philosophical meaning. As Goethe wrote: 'Style rests on the deepest foundations of the perception of truth, on the essence of things – insofar as we are able to recognise it in visible and comprehensible figures.'[25] For Hegel, sculpture was 'the true art of the classical ideal as such.'[26] The philosopher was strictly against polychromy, appealing to the Greeks themselves for confirmation. Although he was well aware of Greek examples of multicoloured sculptures, he attributed these – mistakenly – to the post-classical period, making a qualitative differentiation between these works and those of the 'great' epochs of Greek art. According to Hegel, the human figure was 'the real existence of the spirit.' He argued against the idea that sculpture, a spatial totality, would be more perfect when complemented by the 'advantages of painting.' An artist's refusal of such an alliance was neither 'arbitrary' nor a sign of 'clumsiness,' but rather a voluntary restriction that was part of creating 'true art.' The aim of sculpture was to reproduce 'an abstract side of the human body,' and this meant that 'all particularising colours and movements' had to be left aside.[27] Hegel wrote: 'This is not a shortcoming but an established limitation on material and means that arises from the concept of Art itself. For a work of art is a product of the spirit, that is, the most noble, thinking spirit, and as such must take upon itself not only a certain content, but also a certain abstract means of realisation.'[28] According to Hegel, the sculptor represented 'the spiritual individual,' but not as something 'living, that is something which always returns to the singularity of the body.' The human form is conceived as the '*real* existence of the spirit.'[29] In this sense, colour could only detract from sculpture, since it exists without colour harmony or colour contrast – is 'so to speak clotted light.'[30]

In France it was Charles Blanc, founder of the *Gazette des Beaux-Arts* and spokesman of a more or less pan-European aesthetic, who set the tone. With one important exception (discussed below) he remained dedicated to the classical mimesis throughout his life. According to Blanc, the true artist imitated reality with the explicit goal of 'finding the ideal.'[31] White marble was 'ideal life,'[32] it embodied the *beau idéal* and encompassed truth, beauty and goodness – as these had been formulated by Victor Cousin in 1853.[33] The pure material and its white colour, its remove from lowly reality, were guarantees of moral integrity; moreover, they represented an exemplary ethos. Colour, on the other hand, was ephemeral; it 'imitates life by puerile means,' thereby violating the rules of the Absolute. By employing it, sculpture abandoned its claim to universality and thus its essence.[34]

For the critic and poet Théophile Gautier, too, the fascination of white marble sculpture lay in its paradoxical combination of solidity and abstraction, which 'gives form eternity.'[35] This latter idea proved particularly tenacious and we find it again 30 years later in Henri Jouin's *Le génie de l'art plastique*: in a work of art, the sculptor gives form to the 'soul,' 'that immaterial being inside the marble.'[36] The 18th-century opposition between white marble sculpture, thought to represent a universal and philosophically purified reality, and polychrome sculpture, believed to be capable only of reproducing material reality, remained essential to the neo-classical doctrine throughout the 19th century.

The ancient *querelle des dessinateurs et des coloristes*, that is, between the followers of Poussin and Rubens respectively, found its echo in the debate on polychromy. The advocates of traditional painting took the same position as the defenders of white marble: line and contour corresponded to the ideal, whereas colour represented nothing but base sensualism. As late as 1862, Eugène Véron still stressed this clichéed opposition: the colourists were more interested in the 'play and movement of light than in the soul, [and] one cannot deny that their paintings have something more physical and sensual about them than those of their rivals.'[37] The academic aversion to the colourists was expressed in France by the complete rejection of the art of Bernini and his followers. In a lecture at the Ecole du Louvre, Louis Courajod condemned the Italian master and bemoaned his influence on the students at the Villa Médicis.[38] He railed against the 'operatic phantasmagoria' of Michel-Ange Slodtz's tomb of Languet de Gergy in St Sulpice in Paris (1753), and the staged agony of the blessed Stanislaus Kostka in the monastery of Sant'Andrea al Quirinale in Rome (1702-03). The resistance to polychromy in France can be explained in part by this neo-classical dislike for the Baroque, a period that experienced such a revival during the second half of the 19th century that one can even speak of a 'neo-baroque' movement, within which a number of polychrome sculptures should be situated.[39]

Revitalising sculpture through colour: Owen Jones and John Gibson

The cooperative efforts of archaeologists and sculptors in England to revive polychrome sculpture was an interesting aspect of the movement's development, and was in many ways influential throughout Europe. The sensational Crystal Palace, re-opened at Sydenham in 1854, marked a turning point. Despite protests from the citizenry and thanks to the efforts of Prince Albert, Owen Jones, 'superintendent of the works' for the Crystal Palace, had been able to carry out his project for a multicoloured Greek Court. In the centre of a room adorned with columns in yellow, red and blue, Jones placed plaster casts of the Elgin Marbles, restored to their original – colourful – state.[40] Such an enterprise, and in a such a place, could not help but cause a sensation, and was to find its reflection decades later in similar exhibitions in Dresden (1885), Berlin (1885) and New York (1892). It demonstrates how broad the interest in the polychrome debate actually was,[41] how deeply it had penetrated the minds of the educated, and how, through newspaper reports, it came to awaken the curiosity of the people at large. The Crystal Palace experiment had been preceded by public deliberations on the role of polychromy in Greek architecture between Owen Jones, Jakob Ignaz Hittorff and Gottfried Semper at the Royal Institute of British Architects in London, as well as by the publication of a series of essays by Semper and other archaeologists. These were printed in the first volume of E. Falkener's *Museum of Classical Antiquities*, and the title of Semper's contribution made explicit reference to contemporary practice: 'On the study of polychromy and its revival.'[42]

'Colour is used to assist the development of form and to distinguish objects, or parts of objects, one from another.'[43] Owen Jones's thesis corresponded as a whole with those of the moderate champions of colour in the Antique and in the Renaissance, such as Lodovico Dolce. Nonetheless, the controversy over polychromy in general, and the Greek Court at the Crystal Palace in particular, was so great that Jones eventually found it necessary to write *An apology for the colouring of the Greek Court*, which he published together with Semper's *On the origin of polychromy in architecture* in 1854.[44] The architect bravely defended his position, and at the International Exhibition of 1862 he built a kind of coloured temple, adding to it three inscriptions, the first of which John Gage has justly referred to as a symbol of the 'death of [the] Renaissance and neo-classical aesthetic':[45] NEC VITA NEC SANITAS NEC PVLCRITVDO NEC SINE COLORE JVVENTVS (Without colour there is neither life, nor health, nor beauty, nor youth). [65 109] By introducing the word 'health,' Jones effectively dismissed the position, first introduced in Antiquity, that the aim of art was to capture the universal, and in doing so turned sculpture towards the realm of the purely human. The rupture with the ideals of the Antique – as conceived in the Renaissance and Neo-classicism – was complete. The inscription on the temple pediment was programmatic: FORMAS RERVM OBSCVRAS ILLVSTRAT CONFVSAS DISTINGVIT OMNES ORNAT COLORVM DIVERSITAS SVAVIS (The sweet variety of colours enhances the dark form of things, differentiates what is confused and ornaments everything).

It was naturally no accident that this temple was designed to house a coloured marble statue, namely John Gibson's famous *Tinted Venus*, commissioned by Robert Preston in 1851.[46] [7]

65 Owen Jones, Design for a pavilion to house John Gibson's *Tinted Venus*, c. 1860, London, Victoria and Albert Museum

Gibson, a long-time resident of Italy, had the work shipped from Rome, where it had been completed in 1856. The sculptor had applied the colour as an extremely subtle layer, thus allowing the marble to shine through and giving the whole an almost porcelain-like sheen. Nonetheless, this attempt to revitalise Neo-classicism using an ancient technique was greeted with hostility in both England and on the continent. In a review entitled 'Notabilia of the International Exhibition,' an anonymous critic for the *Art Journal* wrote on Gibson's 'Tinted sculpture': 'It has either been carried too far, or not far enough; it is neither flesh nor marble. We consider the adjunct of colour, thus applied, as a departure from the original high purpose of sculpture, which never aimed at more than an abstract type of the subject represented in form and expression; its end being to idealise rather than to realise. This attempt at *too palpable flesh* not only destroys the very essence of the sculptor's art, but violates the delicacy that attaches to pure material.'[47] This defender of neo-classical ideals even went so far as to use the word 'repulsive.'[48] The sculptor John Bell expressed 'admiration for his [Gibson's] work,' but had no intention of becoming himself 'a convert to this practice.'[49]

The French critic Paul Mantz's review was even more slating. He compared the *Tinted Venus* and the *Pandora* (also exhibited in 1862) with the tasteless neo-rococo porcelain figurines sold in the boutiques of the Paris boulevards, which he called examples of 'le sentiment le plus bourgeois.'[50] Mantz gleaned his criteria mainly from the neo-classical doctrines discussed above, but brought an additional argument to bear – one that was used often and with almost disagreeable insistence in the decades to come – namely that of the moral duties of high art. The critic complained that works like Gibson's were missing a decisive element of true sculpture, namely chastity. The pinkish complexion, vaguely imitating the colour of flesh, made the figure 'immodest.' Gibson was doomed to failure, as Carlo Marochetti and Auguste Clésinger were before him. For Mantz, there was only one conclusion: 'the defeat is total, and it is no longer possible today to make sculpture in colour.'[51] Thus, the condemnation of polychrome sculpture came to be based on criteria that had little to do with the art itself.

The discussions among French art critics and the statements of the artists themselves show certain parallels with regard to the rejuvenation of classical sculpture. Clésinger, for example, had sought to emphasise the erotically-charged white marble body of his *Woman bitten by a snake* (Paris, Musée d'Orsay) – his great success at the Salon of 1847 – by painting the flowerbed blue and pink, colours which have now disappeared. In 1859, he exhibited his *Sappho polychrome*, reviewed by Théophile Gautier in sympathetic if somewhat condescending tones: 'M. Clésinger has given into a whim and has created a polychrome statue as if he were an Athenian. There is nothing wrong with this and we are even willing to admit that this painted Sappho has managed to seduce us entirely.'[52] Gautier, however, regarded the coloration – lightly tinted skin, blue and pink tones for her garment and gold for the meander pattern on the hem – merely as a decorative addition. He remarked nonchalantly to the reader: 'If the polychromy bothers you, you can eliminate it, and you will then have before you a charming statue of perfect delicacy and purity.'[53] Given the fact that this somewhat blasphemous statement came from the pen of a sensitive critic, founder of the doctrine of *l'art pour l'art* and an authority in the French art world, one cannot be completely sure that it was not taken literally by some owners of polychrome sculpture.... Whatever the case, the notion that in sculpture colour and form could be conceived together still lay in the future.[54]

Clésinger's work should be seen as an effort to lead neo-classical sculpture out of a period of crisis with the help of polychromy. In 1855, Charles Simart had exhibited his 2.6 metre high reconstruction of Phidias's *Athena Parthenos* at the Exposition Universelle. [19] Simart used ivory for the face and arms, gilded silver for the dress, and bronze for the chased shield; he painted the lips and eyebrows and used semi-precious stones for the eyes. This revival of the chryselephantine technique was the result of a purely archaeological interest, fed by a fascination with Phidias's lost work. Simart created the *Athena* for the château at Dampierre, where it was placed in front of Ingres's large-scale wall painting *The Golden Age*. Although Gautier greeted the 'cool serenity' of the figure with some hesitation, he was captivated by the 'bizarrerie inquiétante' of the azurite pupils, which gave the goddess's glance a 'strange glimmer.'[55] What Gautier admired about the figure was not the ideality intended by the artist and his patron, the Duc de Luynes, but rather a certain mental ambiguity, which in many ways points to the decadence of the fin de siècle.

The majority of critics, however, saw this monumental work as the perfection of Neo-classicism. In his book with the telling title *Le spiritualisme dans l'art*, Charles Lévêque, professor of philosophy at the Collège de France and director of the Académie des Beaux-Arts since 1867, quoted the orthodox Neo-classicist Etienne Delécluze's statement that the head was 'of calm and chaste expression.'[56] Lévêque saw in Simart a 'spiritualised sculptor' (the title of a chapter dedicated to him) and dismissed all accusations of academicism. The *Athena* was the embodiment of pure spirituality: 'I am convinced that the work accomplished by M. de Luynes and M. Simart was useful; it not only gave us an idea of the splendour of Greek art at its apex, it did much more: it reminded our artists that the greatest sculptor who ever lived was committed to expressing that which is most invisible in the world, the purity of divine thought.'[57]

A new canon: 'natural polychromy'

The endeavours to give neo-classical sculpture a fresh lease of life through colour are reflected in the aesthetic considerations of so-called natural polychromy, referring to the Roman technique of combining various sorts of coloured marbles and other stones, revived around 1860. Even Falconet had made an exception for polylithic statues, feeling they had a 'painterly effect' and in certain cases could be pleasing to the viewer.[58] Charles Blanc was to take this somewhat further in *La sculpture*, published in 1888. He created a clear distinction between 'natural polychromy' – in which the artist accomplished his effects by joining substances like gold, ivory and coloured marbles – and the 'artificial polychromy' achieved by painting. He rejected this latter on the grounds that pigment was ephemeral; since it could easily be washed away, it covered the sculpture like a second skin.[59] The materials of polylithic sculpture, on the other hand, were real and could thus make a claim to truth and universality.

Statements such as these opened the way for polychrome statues to be considered great sculpture. Despite this one can still read between the lines Blanc's discomfort with coloured sculpture, which, in the final analysis, was for him somehow always in conflict with the *beau idéal*. In the *Grammaire des arts du dessin* he had described polychrome sculpture as a sign of the 'decadence of Roman art': 'It was in the time of the emperors that sculpture [...] used and misused polychromy.'[60] The Neo-classicists' main objection was that in coloured sculpture there was a lack of harmony: polychromy impeded sculpture's striving for unity. As late as 1897, René de Saint-Marceaux condemned the heterogeneity of coloured works and the shocking contrasts that arose from it.[61] Blanc, however, was open enough not to let his aesthetic ideology check his appreciation of artistic quality. He could, for example, praise Charles Cordier's famous coloured busts of Africans and Arabs, although without mentioning the artist's name.[62] [47–49] The 'discovery' of such 'types' had given Gautier hope for the regeneration of the exhausted antique ideal: according to him, these 'virginal natures, archetypes, [and] strange and proud models' from unknown continents could give art renewed inspiration.[63]

The most outstanding example of natural polychromy is Louis-Ernest Barrias's allegorical female figure *Nature revealing herself to science* (1899). [129] The analyses of this somewhat over-life-size figure indicate the dilemma in which the critics of polychromy found themselves. Paul Desjardins was one of the most reserved: he regarded the statue as a mere 'essay' and a 'caprice pittoresque.'[64] For him, it disregarded the rule of the sublimity of gesture, exemplified by Chaplain's medal for Albert Dumont entitled *History lifts its veil*, which the critic admired.

His main objection, however, was its patent, if subdued, eroticism: 'she is a *coquette* who provokes with her smile.'[65] According to Maxime Collignon, the work was nonetheless pleasing because Barrias had respected the basic laws of harmony and subordinated colour to form. He had thus managed to stay aloof from both slavish *imitatio naturae* and pure fantasy, which – in contrast to the truly creative and unifying imagination – led to disorderliness and 'incoherence.'[66] Within this meandering and somewhat contradictory argument, the critic recognised Barrias's *Nature* as a new canon: 'She has the value of an art theory' that 'eloquently pleads the case for polychrome sculpture.'[67]

Another provocation: polychrome wax sculpture

The sketch, which in the course of the 19th century came to be regarded as an independent form worthy of exhibition, also became acceptable in wax sculpture. In a three-part article outlining the history of *Les modeleurs en cire* published in the *Gazette des Beaux-Arts*, Spire Blondel remarked that for some time – thanks to the skill of a number of artists – monochrome wax sculpture could be seen in the Paris Salon. He mentioned Géricault's *Cheval écorché* (Washington, National Gallery of Art), as well as the study for his *Emperor Alexander of Russia* on a rearing horse as precursors and, as one of the first works of its kind in the later period, Pierre-Jules Mênes's *Derby winner*[68] (Salon of 1883, Oxford, Ashmolean Museum). This latter work contradicted all classical conventions, depicting a jockey pouring champagne into his horse's mouth. An original kind of representation, drawn from the realities of modern life, had become acceptable as art.

Fully realised busts and reliefs in wax also enjoyed great popularity, particularly those by Henry Cros. His relief *Tournament prize* (1873) [94] was referred to as 'full of feeling and charm' and received, as Blondel wrote, 'warranted praise': 'The public was pleased to see the revival of an art so rightfully enjoyed by our ancestors.'[69] Henri Bouchot, in his review of the Salon of 1893, was impressed, indeed almost haunted, by the 'virtuosity' of the 'works in painted wax' on display.[70] It became fashionable to reject the ideals of Neo-classicism, which now seemed – literally – pale, and critics soon recognised that another venerable tradition had now become the model, namely the Italian Renaissance. Philippe Burty noted that the wax revival had in part been inspired by an anonymous wax bust from the Wicar collection, preserved in the museum in Lille. [66] This 'strange and mysterious work,'[71] whose ambiguous facial expression reminded contemporaries of the Mona Lisa, was copied by Henry Cros for Alexandre Dumas *fils* and enjoyed a popularity that is surprising to us today.[72]

Large-scale polychrome figures in wax, although they aroused interest, were still controversial. In his review of the Salon of 1879, Eugène Guillaume remarked on the growing number of 'increasingly interesting trials' in this genre.[73] Jean-Désiré Ringel d'Illzach's life-size *Demi-monde* – according to Spire Blondel much admired[74] – caused a scandal, and it was supposed to be destroyed during the course of the exhibition.[75] The problem lay not in the artistic quality of the work but rather – as in the case of Manet's *Olympia* – in the subject matter. Baudelaire's celebrated vision of *la modernité* appeared to have invaded the realm of sculpture, a medium whose task traditionally had been to represent noble concepts like 'Nation' and 'Family.' Guillaume recognised the young artist's talent and even accepted polychromy, but, surprisingly, felt that colour and naturalism were incompatible. 'Judging by this attempt, it appears that in the art of sculpture colour can only be combined with ideal forms and noble characters, or be used in portraiture. When simple reality is incorporated, the work becomes insipid, even morbid, and in this particular case it invokes a mental association with anatomical galleries.'[76] Depicting a subject from one's immediate surroundings in colour ran the risk of becoming merely inartistic duplication. Guillaume also reiterated another accusation continually made against wax sculpture: the handling of the surface, he wrote, left the viewer cold. He assumed that the figures were cast and missed the personal mark of the artist, his *facture*. The critic's principles were founded on the methods of the painter: 'Is it not a large part of the charm of this complex art, having many kinds of wax available (as a painter has his palette), to form and mix them to achieve different tones at will, feeling how shape and colour are born under the fingers!'[77]

This discussion reached a climax with the controversy surrounding Edgar Degas's *Little dancer of 14 years* (1880-81). [68 69] A number of issues were involved here: the choice of subject matter, which was drawn from prosaic, artistically unworthy reality; the introduction of science into art; the presumed proximity of the figure to waxworks; and particularly the presumed immorality of the girl represented. As in the case of Millet's *Gleaners* (1857, Paris, Musée d'Orsay) and *Woman pasturing her cow* (1859, Bourg-en-Bresse, Musée de l'Ain), which many critics rejected on the grounds that the women depicted were morally degenerate, both the public and the critics found the ballet-dancer somehow repugnant. The associations that led to this indignant condemnation can be reconstructed with great precision from the reviews. Charles Ephrussi and his colleagues claimed that Degas had made use of the 'exact science' of criminology,[78] and, indeed, the statue can be seen in relation to the two pastels of *Physionomies de criminels* the artist exhibited in the same Salon. The sculptor thus captured unprettified reality in

66   Attributed to François Duquesnoy, *Head of a girl (Tête Wicar)*, c. 1630-40, wax, Lille, Musée des Beaux-Arts

67   Pedro de Mena, *St Magdalene*, 1664, wood and diverse materials, Madrid, Museo del Prado

a way that went far beyond ethnographic sculpture. The later bronze cast, too, was seen as a paradigm of Naturalism and compared with figures from Madame Tussaud's. As demonstrated by Anthea Callen, however, the figure's naturalism derives not from an exact representation of the model, the young Belgian dancer Marie Van Goethem, but from Degas's deformations of her face, which he manipulated to bring into line with the physiognomic research on facial forms and angles by Petrus Camper and others.

In this way, the little girl came to be seen as the precocious embodiment of the *classe ouvrière* and thus of the *classe dangereuse*. According to the codes of the day, her – putative – ugliness was a sign of immorality. For the critics she was the sister of the cold-blooded murderer Abadie, born corrupt and with a 'store of bad instincts and sinful passions.'[79] Her nose was described as a 'vicious snout' and she herself as the 'essence of horror and bestiality.' Only Nina de Villard spoke of 'the promise of future beauty.'[80] Degas's art was seen as the counterpart of the novels of the naturalist Emile Zola, who had based his work on Claude Bernard's *Médecine expérimentale*, and the figure was even referred to as 'a little Nana,'[81] a young example of the sexual power capable of destroying society.

The critics saw their moralising, extra-artistic judgments confirmed by the similarities of the *Little dancer* to studio mannequins.[82] As the articles by Spire Blondel demonstrate, they were well aware of the polychrome wax figure tradition that had flowered in the 18th century: Henri IV with real hair and a beard, dressed in clothing copied from originals; or the portrait of the Polish king Stanislas Leczinski's dwarf, *Bébé*, kept in the library of the Ecole de Médecine in Paris.[83] Works such as these were considered mere 'curiosities,' 'soulless copies' of reality; they did not belong to the category Art. This type of strict hierarchy among the genres blinded the critics to the innovative aspects of Degas's *Little dancer*.

For many viewers, the figure triggered memories of the Exposition Universelle of 1878: there, in the Mexican section, polychrome wax figures representing traders in their picturesque folk-costumes, modelled by Montanari, had been displayed and admired.[84] [84] It was thus also the addition of real attributes that made it so difficult to accept the statue as a work of art: the real hair (which Degas covered with wax in order to make the bronze cast), the coloured garments – the ribbon, bodice, and skirt which, in contrast to the pseudo-reconstructions, were originally much less elegantly arranged – as well as the ballet shoes. Although Degas, in contrast to traditional nativity figurines,[85] had actually modelled his *Little dancer* in wax, many critics still felt he had dressed the sculpture as if it were a doll.

For most of his contemporaries, this meant that Degas had relinquished artistic imagination. More than 100 years earlier,

68 Edgar Degas, *Little dancer of 14 years*, 1880-81 (cast of 1922), bronze and textiles, New York, The Metropolitan Museum of Art, Bequest of Mrs. H.O. Havemeyer

Herder had claimed that if one were to put a hide on Myron's cow it would 'no longer be a work of art but rather a sack stuffed with hair [....] too much like a cow and yet not one – that is affectation.'[86] The public in 1881 felt similarly. Degas's way of imitating nature broke with the classical doctrine of mimesis, which was established on the distinction of the ideal human being from the multitude of individuals. The *beau idéal*, however, was no longer the ruling paradigm: attention had now shifted to an investigation of the human type as formed by heritage and environment. The novelty of this conception often blinded the critics to more specific artistic issues. Degas's interest lay not in creating a hyper-realistic figure, but in exploring the tension between the objective reality of clothing and hair on the one hand, and the artistic *facture* in the formation of the body and face on the other.

The case for polychromy: Georg Treu and Jules Laforgue

In 1883, two years after the *Little dancer* scandal, Georg Treu, professor and director of the Königlich Sächsische Antiken- und Abgußsammlungen in Dresden, organised an exhibition of both antique and modern polychrome sculpture. In so doing, he took up the tradition initiated by Owen Jones, carrying it still further forward two years later in Berlin. In 1858, John Bell had summarised the close relationship between archaeological research and contemporary art with the following question: 'The first consideration is *Did the Greeks colour their statues?*, the second *If they did, should we?*'[87] Treu addressed this issue himself in his lecture *Sollen wir unsere Statuen bemalen?* The subject had not lost any of its topicality and although his theses, which appeared in book form in 1884,[88] were still somewhat controversial, they quickly gained international recognition. The poet and critic Jules Laforgue translated the work into French; despite the fact that it was not accepted for publication by the *Gazette des Beaux-Arts* it nonetheless attracted considerable attention.[89]

Although Treu was not completely opposed to contemporary marble sculptures inspired by classical Antiquity,[90] he did question the 'colourless, chaste nobility of Greek art' and the 'sugary white of pale abstractions.' According to him, the traditional notion that sculpture was to be 'the embodiment of pure form' had not only hindered the development of the art, it had also offended all 'unprejudiced and natural artistic feeling.' He proclaimed the 'equality of form and colour' and felt the task of polychromy was 'to simplify and ennoble form.' Treu was an advocate of modernity and defended the 'contemporary desire for truth, life and colour.' Unlike the waxworks, the aim of his realism was not deception but rather the depiction of the 'gripping truth of spiritual and physiognomic expression'; he thereby introduced an elevating element into the theory of realism. He wanted the 'virtuosity' of the creating hand to always remain recognisable, so that the 'intellectual appeal of the *artistic* translation of natural forms into a foreign substance' would not be lost.[91] His ideal was the realism of Italian Renaissance portrait busts, a subject on which Wilhelm von Bode had recently published.[92] According to Vasari, these artworks were so natural that they seemed to be alive, and Treu prophesied that modern sculpture would soon come to resemble them[93] – a prediction that came true but only to a slight degree.

The poet Jules Laforgue's position was somewhat different. Between 1881 and 1886 he lived in Germany (mostly in Berlin), working as both a reader to the empress and an art critic. Although reserved, his review of Treu's exhibition in the capital was not 'devastating,' as has sometimes been suggested.[94] Despite the fact that he described it as a 'bazaar, full of commercial and heterogeneous works,' he was open to those polychrome statues dictated not by fashion but by a real desire to expand the domain of sculpture. He took a particular interest in Joseph Kaffsack's bust of a general in uniform, describing it as 'fresh, robust and effective' (present location unknown). He did not particularly admire the work, but he cited it as a successful symbiosis of sculpture and painting. He objected to all 'weaklings' and 'non-believers' who saw polychromy and sculpture as two distinct entities that merely tolerated one another, and who in their works achieved nothing but 'comforting and dubious compromises.' What Eugène Guillaume had found wanting in Ringel d'Illzach, Laforgue discovered in Albert Wolff: in his stearin bust of a woman, tinted with watercolour, the flesh tones were subtly graded and made an integral part of the material through cross hatching, and bits of scratched-away colour enlivened her glance (present location unknown). The overall handling of the surface made the sculptor's work resemble that of a painter. The critic praised the combination of 'poetry and life' which he felt he recognised in Reinhold Begas's tinted plaster model *Nature* (present location unknown). He condemned all examples of 'puerile realism,' searching instead for 'the most rare, the most exquisite reality, treated using the most precious techniques,' such as in the work of his friend Henry Cros.[95] [12-16] He also approved of a marble bust of a young woman – a collaboration between Artur Volkmann and the painter Herrmann Prell – noting her 'unhealthy' but subtle charm (present location unknown).

The unprecedented antipathy towards traditional monochrome sculpture led to a striving for the novel and original. This tendency is particularly recognisable in the female figures of the turn of the century, the so-called *femmes fatales*: Max Klinger's *New Salome* with her bewitching glance [43]; Fernand Khnopff's willful *Vivien* [99]; the lovely *Eve* by Artur Volkmann [42], noted by

Laforgue; or Richard König's dreamy, blue-eyed *Muse*, her white marble head crowned by wrought-iron hair. [20] Colour and coloured materials did not conceal form, as Herder had claimed, but rather allowed for a spiritual and psychological dimension, for a kind of nuance and ambiguity that had been unavailable to the neo-classical sculptor. Employing colour in sculpture became a mark of modernity. Laforgue had correctly perceived that the tenacious but simplifying equation colour = naturalism – one of the fundamental artistic tenets of the 19th century – was no longer valid. Despite his hesitation with regard to certain artists, Laforgue greeted the principle of polychrome sculpture with enthusiasm: 'Whatever may happen, a unique road has been opened and both the public and artists will take it.'[96]

Spirituality versus naturalism in polychrome sculpture

The model of classical Antiquity remained paradigmatic for the examination of polychrome sculpture until long after the middle of the 19th century. Following the dictates of Platonic philosophy, critics associated colour with sensualism or with vulgar materialism. Using their claim to a higher, philosophically grounded ethic, they came to regard the realism achieved through colour with disdain and sought to escape its seductive charm. The border between art and nature became permeable in polychrome sculpture, and for many this illusionism destroyed their ability to judge reflectively and with aesthetic detachment. The somewhat disturbing theme of 'repetition,' of creating a copy or a double of reality, recurred constantly, climaxing in comparisons with morgues and waxworks. In contrast to classical mimesis, which strove to capture the ideal human being, the new *imitatio naturae* – as in Degas's *Little dancer* – oriented itself at least partly on scientifically grounded physiognomic treatises. A sculptor who dared to enter the inferior realms of the human psyche violated not only aesthetic convention but also the morals of bourgeois society. The introduction of 'low' genres into the venerable sphere of monochrome neo-classical sculpture often hampered the objective discernment of artistic quality. What the critics saw instead was 'l'invasion de l'argot dans la langue sculpturale.'[97] Colour was thought to be inseparable from naturalism and evoked comparisons with the novels of Zola, whose art, just as Degas's, was of course more than a mere medical and scientific reproduction of contemporary life.

It was only at the end of the century that the symbolic aspect of colour and coloured materials was fully recognised and discussed. The competition between art and reality was no longer of critical interest. Through colour, sculpture gained an extraordinary independence from the empirical world. Colour not only

69 Edgar Degas, *Little dancer of 14 years*, 1880-81 (cast of c. 1922), bronze and textiles, Paris, Musée d'Orsay

'increased the emotional power of sculpture' but also its 'abstract meaning.' In his *Manifesto tecnico della scultura futurista* (1912), Umberto Boccioni wrote that colour and the variety of multi-coloured materials could lead to 'the discovery of novel *plastic* ideas' in a reality freed from the archaic concept of mimesis.[98]

Philip Ward-Jackson

Sculpture colouring and the industries of art in the 19th century

Industrialisation was a wild card in the hand which economic circumstances dealt the professional sculptor in the mid-19th century. The distinction between the fine and the industrial was heavily stressed in critical discussion of sculpture, and the orderly classification of products in international exhibitions maintained the division. The facts hardly justified so firm a borderline between them. Fine art sculptors were usually dependent on teams of executants, and conversely, many so-called industrial products involved handicraft of a traditional nature. Honoured sculptors, whose performance in monumental art was constricted by training and a stifling respect for academic proprieties, sometimes excelled in decorative commissions. Towards the end of the century, the arbitrariness of these arrangements came to be recognised, bringing an appreciation of the inventiveness and fertility which had graced the humbler spheres.

Between 1892 and 1901, the English sculptor Alfred Gilbert reclaimed for monumental sculpture mixed media and colouristic effects which had previously been associated with the so-called industrial and decorative arts. Before embarking on the huge and elaborate tomb of the Duke of Clarence at Windsor, he had tried out some of the techniques on a smaller, more decorative commission, the *épergne* or table-centrepiece which the British Army were to present to Queen Victoria on the occasion of her Golden Jubilee. The Clarence Tomb itself involved combinations of different metals, incorporated ivory and marble features, and inlays. Parts of its surface were painted or gilded. Immense technical complexity seemed to proclaim the exclusiveness of this art, and Gilbert's royal patrons expected that it would remain in every sense their personal property. They were unpleasantly surprised when they discovered that the sculptor had been reproducing some of its more elaborate figure sculptures for sale elsewhere.[1] [35 36]

The figures of saints for the Clarence Tomb were either cast with sand moulds or by the indirect lost-wax technique and could therefore be produced serially. The handicraft interventions which conferred on them their air of 'princely magnificence' might have ensured that copies would remain the preserve of 'the happy few,' but after the turn of the century the existence of teams of trained craftsmen in Paris or Brussels would permit such products to appear in the catalogues of editors of serial bronzes. Interpretative reproductions of works by Jean-Léon Gérôme, Louis-Ernest Barrias and others, were offered either as negotiable collector's specialities or simply as catalogue items by the firms of Susse and Siot-Decauville. [72]

The suspicions aroused by these combinations earlier in the century are expressed in Louis Auvray's response to the polychrome busts exhibited by Charles Cordier at the Salon of 1863: 'We have hesitated to mention M. Cordier's two busts, because, in our opinion, they belong more to industry than to the fine arts. With the exception of some jewellers and some marquetry specialists who went into ecstasies over these inharmonious mixtures of coloured marbles, everyone has protested against their bad taste [...].'[2] Taste apart, polychromy and mixing of media in sculpture suggested division of labour, loss of artistic integrity, and raised the ultimate spectre of that world of commercialised art in which the authorship of a work was appropriated by the firm exploiting it.

In France, two main press controversies gave publicity to the issue of authorship in collaborative works. The first was provoked in 1855 by Gustave Planche, in an attack, which some considered ill-timed, on the recently deceased goldsmith François-Désiré Froment-Meurice, for having failed sufficiently to credit his artistic collaborators.[3] The second, in the late 1890s, surrounded the self-justificatory protestations of the goldsmith Lucien Falize, concerning the bust of *Gallia*, which he had shown at the Exposition Universelle of 1889.[4] [70] There is some reason to doubt the authenticity of the *Gallia* controversy itself, appearing as it did in decorative arts reviews, but what was implied was

70 Augustin-Jean Moreau-Vauthier, *Gallia*, c.1889, ivory and silver, present location unknown

that things had come full-circle. Whereas Planche had called for the naming of the artists, the sculptor of *Gallia*, Augustin-Jean Moreau-Vauthier, had been permitted by Falize to sign his part of the work, the ivory head. Now that the *Gallia* had been acquired by the Musée du Luxembourg one of the metalworkers who had been involved wished to see his contribution acknowledged also.

Monochromy seemed to ensure to some degree that the artist's original idea had not been tampered with, and departures from it could attract adverse publicity. This was not true of all areas of production. Away from academic centres, in regions like northern Piedmont or Haute Savoie, even in certain parts of the Netherlands, the production of coloured religious imagery escaped the chastening influence of Neo-classicism. With the Gothic Revival, industrialists were able painlessly to move in on a scene in which coloured statuary was a feature of an architectural ensemble, and in which its claim to 'fine art' status was hardly an issue. Such industrially produced *bondieuserie* was much in evidence in the so-called Chapelle du Champ de Mars at the Exposition Universelle of 1867. Looking so much like a church that visitors were surprised to be asked to pay an entrance fee, this ideal church exhibition aimed to tickle the appetites of the clergy with the full array of revived Gothic church furniture. The firms exhibiting sculpture were Froc-Robert, Aubry from Guespunsart (Ardennes), and the iron founders Barbezat, Ducel and Durenne.[5]

France had awoken rather belatedly to the polychrome neo-gothic romance which A.N. Didron described after a visit to Pugin's church of St Giles at Cheadle in Staffordshire. Pugin, he wrote, 'has revived the Middle Ages in their entirety, body and soul [...] all is covered with gilded and painted ornament; the effect is truly magical.'[6] Pugin's detail was bespoke from a chosen group of craftsmen. In catholic countries, with wider requirements, firms which had already been established before the arrival of the vogue for polychrome statuary were at hand to provide for it. There were the French *Sainteries* of Vaucouleurs and Vendeuvre-sur-Barse, their foreign rivals Mayer of Munich and Blanchard of Ghent and a host of others.[7] [71] The credit for the revival of painted ecclesiastical sculpture was given by a reviewer in the magazine *L'Illustration* to the firm of Chovet et Cie., when they exhibited at the 1863 Exposition des arts industriels a selection of coloured wooden and terracotta statues: 'Not content with improving the industry of religious painting, M. Chovet applies the same reform to statuary and to church sculpture.'[8]

Religious sculpture of this sort hardly entered the critical debate on polychromy. Whilst the ecclesiastical metalwork of Poussielgue-Rusand was winning medals at international exhibitions, plaster and terracotta pious images were stealthily populating the provinces at home and missionary outposts around the globe. Viollet-le-Duc, representing the more rational tendency of the Gothic revival, declared these images to be fetishes, and denounced them as encouragements to ignorance in country districts.[9] The novelist and critic, Joris-Karl Huysmans, whose father had won imperial commendation for a neo-gothic missal, found no place for them in his brief survey of the experiments in polychromy leading up to Degas's *Little dancer of 14 years*.[10] [68] They did however form a part of the grotesque backdrop to his evocation of modern urban life, as when they are glimpsed in a shop window in his naturalist novel *Les sœurs Vatard*: 'Grave faced Madonnas suitable for a niche, Christs the size of life, their

71 Specimens of religious terracotta statuary from the workshop of Léon Moynet in Vendeuvre-sur-Barses

tummies lilac tinted, their fingers carmined, crimped blond Jesuses offering a benediction, their arms stretched towards us, welcoming and well-dressed.'[11]

Commercial metalwork, as embodied in the so-called *articles de Paris*, to which promoters of the decorative arts were giving ever more serious attention, and which was a major contributor to France's export figures, was treated by Huysmans with even less respect, even though, in the world of serial bronze production coloration had been a noted feature since the 1830s. Chiselling, patination and mounting were all forms of intervention exploited by editors of bronzes to add lustre to the product, and to compensate for the lack of the autograph touch resulting from an industrial approach to casting. In this case, a sense of the inferiority of sandcast multiples, whose moulds had been taken, not from an original model, but from a dismountable 'master bronze,' made these interventions especially desirable. As improvements were introduced in sand-casting technique, the chiseller, whose contribution was extrinsic and associated with elaborate decorative metalwork and jewellery, might be confined to the less creative task of removing join marks and other defects. Patination on the other hand was intrinsic, to the extent that it worked on the bronze, changing its physical nature as well as its surface appearance. As such it remained an important area of creative choice, in a situation in which speed of turnover prevented the possibility of patination through the operation of natural agencies over time.

The speeding up of the pace of colouristic invention among the *metteurs en bronze*, *bronzeurs*, or *metteurs en couleur sur métaux*, as they were variously known, is described in the relevant volume of the *Encyclopédie Roret*.[12] The authors are hardly generous with practical information, which was jealously guarded, but the requirements of commerce 'qui exigeait sans cesse du nouveau' were held responsible for the kaleidoscopic options suddenly on offer. A certain M. Lafleur is credited with having broken the monopoly of the standard *vert antique* or *vert à l'eau*, in 1828 when he introduced the *bronze florentin* named after him, which involved dipping the piece in a copper solution before applying the oxidising agents. This innovation was followed in 1833 by a *teinte florentin fumé* attributed to a M. Camus. Camus figures in the 1844 *Almanach des fabricans de bronze*, offering his services as 'gilder on metals, produces *artistique* bronzing, and the steamed bronzing called *florentin*, using the new processes of water immersion.' As well as nine different patinas offered by the various specialists in the *Almanach*, there are *bronzes de fantaisie* advertised by amongst others a Mme. Massin.[13] The range is exemplified in the *Encyclopédie Roret* by a M. Masselotte 'ouvrier chez M. Denière,' who combined 'sometimes greenish undertone with high points in yellow, sometimes a black base tone highlighted with varying intensities of red, with powdered bronze and spirit varnishes.'

72 Illustration from the 1905 catalogue of the Susse Frères foundry

Though it may be assumed that some of these more variegated effects were destined for purely ornamental bronzework, candelabra, mounts for clocks and furniture, certain areas of sculpture proper seem to have been privileged with special attention from the patinators. Antoine-Louis Barye was famed for the richness and appropriateness of his colorations. [61] [74] On the other hand he was commended for models which were adequately reproduced by *fonte brute*, sandcasting in which the surfaces required minimal attention from the chiseller.[14] Appreciations of animal sculpture shown in the international exhibitions on a number of occasions allude to the admirable dissimulation of the chiselling 'comme il convient en pareil cas.'[15] The advantage of animal subjects for serial casting was that their naturally rugose surfaces, imitating fur and feathers enabled some equivalent of the artist's touch to survive translation through two successive castings. But, if the chisellers' intervention was to be invisible, variegated patination could be used to enhance the already eventful surfaces. The *Encyclopédie* recommends a 'bronze à fonds noirs' for those wishing to imitate the animals of Pierre-Jules Mêne, and a 'bronze à fond brun' for an effect 'qui imite très bien les animaux de M. Bonheur.'[16]

Inevitably also, the representation of racial types inspired sculptors to vary their patinas to suggest the colour of the subject's skin. Cordier was not the first, even within the 19th century, to do this kind of thing. A critic who appears to have been especially sensitive to such nuances, observed in the pages of the *Journal des Beaux-Arts et de la Littérature*, that Francisque-Joseph Duret's *Chactas*, exhibited at the Salon of 1836 was 'en bronze qui imite la couleur naturelle de la peau du sauvage [...].'[17] This may of course suggest an all-over patination rather than the application of local colours, but a number of statuettes of Indian and African subjects by Charles Cumberworth, which almost certainly date from the 1840s are clearly polychromed.

The examples of multicoloured patination, which are recorded or have survived from the 'romantic period' were from the hands of the modellers most closely associated with industrialised statuary production. Foremost amongst them was Jean-Jacques Feuchère, who, his biographer Jules Janin was unashamed to admit, 'a vulgarisé, tant qu'il l'a pu faire, ses plus charmants modèles.'[18] The decision to colour his bronzes may with certainty be ascribed to Feuchère himself, since on one occasion he is recorded as having subjected an important private commission to this treatment. A reviewer wrote of Feuchère's full-length bronze statue of the Marquis of Stafford that the sculptor had indulged one of his customary manias 'that of aiming at charlatanism of effect by colouring in variegated tints of bronze, which should by rights have only one.'[19] No trace remains in this statue today of the polychrome patination, but in other works of Feuchère, as in those of his contemporaries, Henri de Triqueti, Antonin Moine, Jacques-Auguste Fauginet and Cumberworth, it is on occasion very evident.

A mystique grew up around these *petits maîtres* of Romanticism, whose world was so effectively evoked by Balzac in *Cousine Bette*. Feuchère in particular was credited with an almost occult feeling for materials and processes, deriving from his involvement with the industries of art. According to Philippe Burty, writing later in the century, this hands-on approach distinguished Feuchère's contribution to a much publicised series of experiments in the chryselephantine mode. Various explanations have been offered for the renewed interest in ivory as an artistic material during the July Monarchy.[20] Towards the end of the 1840s the

73   Emile Froment-Meurice, *Venus*, c. 1850, ivory and bronze, present whereabouts unknown

jeweller Froment-Meurice, and his erudite patron, the Duc de Luynes, acting to all appearances independently, set about combining ivory with bronze and gold. For the learned recreation of the chryselephantine *Athena Parthenos* for his château at Dampierre, the Duc de Luynes called upon the services, not only of the sculptor Charles Simart, but also those of the goldsmith Duponchel. [19] Froment-Meurice chose to interpret modern works by Pradier in this form, and to commission an original group, *La toilette de Vénus* designed specifically for such treatment from Feuchère. [73] It was Burty's claim, that Feuchère had understood that the blandness of ivory in such a conjunction, required more support from the metal component in defining the composition than had been allowed for in Pradier's *Leda* [21] and *Bacchante*. In coping with these diverse materials, the Prix de Rome sculptor lost out to the *habitué* of the workshops.[21]

It was Froment-Meurice's groups, rather than the Duc de Luynes's archaeological reconstruction, which established the viability of mixed media for modern sculpture, justifying Louis Auvray's insinuation that the busts of Charles Cordier derived from the world of the applied arts. A further debt of Cordier to this world was his use of enamelled ornamental details, which is

74　Antoine-Louis Barye, *Tatar warrior*, 1855, bronze, partially enamelled and gilt, Paris, Musée d'Orsay

75　*Warrior guard*, Japan, Meiji period, silvered and gilt bronze, Nasser D. Khalili Collection

anticipated in a polychrome elaboration of a model by Barye. A version of this sculptor's *Tatar warrior*, richly enamelled, its face gilded, and proudly displaying the date 1855, is assumed to be a product of the Barbedienne firm, which at that time was making lavish use of enamels in its novelty furnishings. [74] Effective though the work is, this statuette bears all the marks of an editor's intervention, and little relation to what we know of Barye's own colour preferences.

A new ingredient in the polychrome sculpture of Charles Cordier is the use of coloured marbles and onyx from France's recently pacified colony, Algeria. [47–49] The illustrated guide to the 1867 Exposition Universelle emphasised the fact that the onyx quarries in the province of Oran had lain untouched since ancient times, their revival establishing a link between the Roman Empire and the modern French one.[22] The *Compagnie des marbres et d'onyx d'Algérie* showed at the international exhibitions its own *torchères* and clocks, some of which were modelled by Albert-Ernest Carrier-Belleuse. The heads and hands of the torch-bearing figures were cast in bronze, whilst the light from their lamps penetrated their translucent onyx robes. At the end of the century, Leopold II of Belgium would follow this example of the promotion of a colonial product's artistic potential with his celebrated Tervuren Salonnet. [136] Part of the Brussels Exhibition of 1897, this exhibition of sculpture was intended to showcase ivory from the Congo, still at this date virtually a royal domain.[23]

During the Second Empire exploration of polychromy seems to have been delayed rather than encouraged by the development of *galvanoplastie* or electroplating. Use of the Voltaic pile could ensure more even patination, but, as far as surface variations were concerned, it was still a blunt instrument, whose technicalities proved daunting to artists. It did however encourage the move away from dark toned bronzes towards lightness and brightness by increasing the availability of silvered and gilt statuettes. A reaction against the gothic and sombre led also to the search for paler patinations. The inspiration for some of these was the Japanese metalwork which began to appear in Europe in the 1860s. The firms of Christofle and Tiffany vied with each other to produce plausible imitations of the mottled, woodgrain-like *moukoumé* or *moka-meia* of Japan. Japonisme was well entrenched in the statuette industry by 1880, when Barbedienne won praise for a series of small decorative sculptures modelled by Louis-Ernest Barrias, whose *rousseurs*, had they been less exquisitely suitable, might have incurred the criticism that bronze could only descend in the hierarchy of materials by imitating wood.[24] The English sculptor Alfred Gilbert would have encountered these experiments during his Paris period, before being thoroughly schooled in Japanese bronze pickling techniques by the metallurgist William Chandler Roberts-Austen.[25] At the turn of the century, following the symbolist fashion, variegated patinas were revived by bronze editors in altogether blonder tonalities. Siot-Decauville boasted in 1900 of their ability to provide each purchaser with a product whose patination rendered it a unique work of art, whether its substance was bronze or pewter.[26]

On the subject of Siot Decauville's patinas, a commentator, René Mauglas, adopted the exalted and mesmeric tone of the brothers Goncourt: 'there is *le vert Barye*, new or old depending on whether it has chestnut glazes on the higher planes, or paler tones scattering their droplets of light over the extremities; there is the *patine fleurie* in which red flecks sing out like poppies strewn in the rusty pallor of ripened cornfields; there is the *patine giroflée* which gives you an admirable intensity of red on a green ground; there is *vert antique*, there is *patine vieil or*, *patine herbeuse*, *patine d'argent* and more besides [...]. I have seen in the workshop a bronze destined for the museum at Vienne, the *Abel* by Carlès [...] never have such patinas been obtained; there are surfaces on it, in which you can imagine blood circulating beneath the skin; oxydisation has here produced chords whose harmony astonishes.'[27]

The 1900s catalogues of Susse and Siot Decauville represent, not without a touch of vulgarity, the coming of age of sculptural polychromy in the sphere of commercial sculpture. And yet, even at this time, the world of bronze editors was divided. A conspicuous restraint was observed in particular by the honorary doyen of the French bronze casters, Ferdinand Barbedienne, whose de facto pre-eminence seems to have required of him that he remain aloof from certain novelties, even though his firm had indulged in these from time to time in the past.[28] From this point of view, it is perhaps interesting to observe the way in which the models of Barrias were shared out between Barbedienne and Susse. Apart from the series of small ornamental figures with light, Japanese-style patina, Barbedienne adopted those models by Barrias which were suitable for straight monochrome treatment, whilst Susse took on exotic, allegorical and historical subjects, to which inlays, gilding and other embellishments could reasonably be added. [72] In this Susse remained true to its reputation as a retailer of novelties of all kinds. It had dealt in porcelain, customised stationery, cameras, and in 1861 offered to a specific section of its clientele a kit called *décalcomanie* 'which allows the ladies, with the aid of a magic varnish and printed colour transfers, to decorate on the spot, wood, silk, candles, porcelain.'[29]

The virtual confinement of the more ambitious displays of polychromy to the exhibition stand in earlier decades is demonstrated by the struggle into existence of architectural ceramics, in which the deployment of coloured glazes in conjunction with full plasticity might have seemed easy of accomplishment. The interpretation of sculptural ideas in ceramics, not of course for the first time, but certainly on an unprecedented scale, was the keynote of the exhibits at the Crystal Palace in 1851 of the British firm of Minton. [77] What particularly distinguished these exhibits was a sort of schizophrenia about colour. On the one hand, and as if legitimising the annexation of sculpture by pottery, there were the monochrome Parian Ware exhibits, their creamy, light absorbing body imitating marble. These were in many cases reductions of celebrated works of sculpture.[30] In vivid contrast to these respectful reflections of high art endeavour, Mintons showed also conservatory ornaments and other pieces with strong sculptural features in the firm's brightly coloured new Majolica range. Whilst Mintons' artistic director, the Frenchman Léon Arnoux, claimed eminent cultural antecedents for the Parian enterprise, his plans for Majolica would have secured for the firm a more positive and less interpretative role. It would, he hoped, follow the already celebrated Minton encaustic tiles, in becoming a popular adornment for architecture.[31] These hopes were never fully realised.

In the meantime, the sculptural potential of the new clay bodies and high temperature glazes introduced by Arnoux was soon inspiring imitations elsewhere. Spectacular imitations of the works of Bernard Palissy had already appeared in the Expositions des Arts Industriels in Paris in the previous decades, in particular the seminal *Vase de la Renaissance* executed by Aimé Chenavard and Antonin Moine for Sèvres in 1831-32, and the virtuoso imitations of Palissy's more naturalistic mode by Avisseau of Tours, but the example of Mintons gave a further impulse to French firms after 1851.[32] In Italy too, its country of origin, majolica was to enjoy a revival from the mid-sixties, and at the Doccia factory especially, the quality of the modelling was enhanced by the employment of two sculptors Jafet Torelli and Raffaello Pagliaccetti, the former taken on by the firm in 1865.[33] In the case of Italian majolica there was always a suspicion that its pastiches of renaissance originals were aimed at the unwary tourist, in an age when the reputation of the Della Robbias was at its highest, but some of the conservatory ornament produced by the Doccia firm is remarkably similar to work from Mintons, where the main modellers were the Frenchmen, Carrier-Belleuse and Hugues Protât.

76 John Bell, *Dorothea*, c. 1850, Minton porcelain ware, private collection

77 Albert-Ernest Carrier-Belleuse's *Galatea* and other Minton exhibits, illustration of c. 1852

The international exhibitions saw some brave attempts at monumental coloured ceramics. In London in 1862, Minton's showed their 36 foot high St George Fountain, modelled by the British sculptor John Thomas, and with water perfumed by the firm of Eugene Rimmel. In Paris in 1867, Virebent of Toulouse responded with the so-called *Monument Céramique*, a sort of wayside chapel with a Virgin and saints in brightly coloured faience, which inspired comparisons with the work of Luca della Robbia.[34] The application of these principles in real architecture remained limited. After the 1878 Paris Exhibition at which ceramic revetements, including some in low relief, had been used to lend a festive air to iron frame pavilions, the question of architectural ceramics was ironed out, somewhat to the detriment of ceramic sculpture. The enthusiasm expressed for this bright and pollution-resistant form of decoration, was accompanied by reservations about Virebent's more boldly plastic endeavours.[35] It seemed that architectural ceramics could only flaunt their colour if they were flat. A rare example of Della-Robbiaesque ceramic applied to exterior architecture survives at St Bede's College, Alexandra Road, Manchester (1878-84), with its historical relief panels executed by the sculptor John Broad for the London firm of Doulton's. These were carried out in terracotta with vitreous glazes, soon to be supplanted for such purposes in the firm's output by polychrome stoneware. The stoneware did not at first prove popular. Its heyday came during the period between 1923 and 1939, when the sculptor Gilbert Bayes collaborated with Doulton's. Besides the ambitious frieze which once decorated the Thames-side facade of their London offices (now in the Victoria and Albert Museum), Gilbert Bayes modelled polychrome garden sculptures and repeatable motifs for housing estates. [78] However, in the period between 1880 and 1923, Doulton's confined their efforts largely to monochrome ceramic sculpture or low relief tiles and ceramic murals.[36]

78 Gilbert Bayes in his workshop with a Doulton ceramic garden fountain figure

79 Gilbert Bayes, *The Queen of Time*, 1908-31, London, Selfridges

In France, at the turn of the century, the discrepancy between exhibition display and actual practice is confirmed by, on the one hand the large and garishly coloured glazed earthenware frieze representing *Art through the ages* on the western facade of the Grand Palais, and on the other by the preference of Art Nouveau architects for the restrained colouring and mottled glazes of the products of firms like Bigot and Gréber. [80] Bigot in particular was renowned for his sculptural collaborators, who included Pierre Roche, Jean-Antoine Injalbert, René de Saint-Marceaux, Jean Carriès, Alfred-Jean-Baptiste Halou, Jean-Baptiste L'Arrivé and Camille Alaphilippe. His glazes were not the least original aspect of Bigot's product, but in contributions to buildings by the architects Lavirotte, Guimard and Anatole de Baudot, considerations of overall harmony led to the playing down of colouring in individual sculptural features.

That the populace at large should be able to savour splendours once available only to an elite was an axiom to which most 19th century industrialists were inclined to subscribe. This was the message of many of their more fantastic exhibits. If it was not a disguise for a substandard product or a means of adding distinction to an edition of thousands, polychromy existed in the world of industrially produced sculpture as a profession of faith in excess, since it was a luxury added to a work of art which was already in itself a luxury. Chryselephantine sculptures and glazed earthenware fountains were more a forecast of what might be done than samples of actual production, but what they proposed had repercussions, even within the period under consideration, in less commercially constricted areas of creativity. Alfred Gilbert was not alone in reclaiming the endeavours of the industrial arts for his original creations. It was a preoccupation which he shared with some of his fellow practitioners of the New Sculpture in England, and with a number of contemporary Belgian and French Symbolists.

Although the divide between ceramic and serial bronzes was often bridged by artists operating simultaneously in both fields, these activities were generally in practice segregated. However, in the atmosphere of increased craft consciousness generated by the building of Berlin's Kunstgewerbemuseum (1877-81), variegated patination and ceramic made their appearance together in one public monument, on the pretext of setting it off against a dark background of trees. This was the monument to Dr Albrecht von Graefe, by the architect of the Kunstgewerbemuseum, Martin Gropius and the sculptor, Rudolf Siemering. [81] The reliefs flanking the figure of Graefe, made at the March terracotta factory at Charlottenburg, and coloured by the majolica glazer, Bastanier, remain a distinctive feature of this monument. Time, on the other hand, has effaced the lighter, golden patination of face and

80   Facade of the Poterie Gréber, Beauvais

81   Rudolf Siemering, Martin Gropius and Heino Schmieden, *Monument to Albrecht von Graefe*, 1882, granite, bronze and terracotta, Berlin

hands, which reportedly once also drew the portrait statue into the monument's overall colour play.[37] Again, in 1931, Gilbert Bayes, the inheritor and exploiter of so many of the 19th century's cherished technologies, brought bronze and ceramic even closer together in his group, *The Queen of Time*, which supports the clock on the Oxford Street front of Selfridge's department store in London. [79] Conceived by Bayes as an entirely ceramic sculpture, it was eventually carried out in gilt bronze with inset panels in Doulton's stoneware.

Where the efforts of Gilbert Bayes and the New Sculptors often seem trapped in the world of the *haute luxe* product, a greater craft innocence characterises the use of ceramic in the architecture of Antonio Gaudí. The collages of smashed crockery at the Parque Güell seem closer in spirit to some of the promotions of non-artistic products gracing later 19th century international exhibitions. The tradition of cumulative trophies, triumphal arches made up of bicycles, columns of minerals, food sculptures, linked up in the last years of the century with the use of 'mascot' sculptures and paintings by firms like Pears Soap, to produce at least one strikingly original art work. This was the trophy promoting Liebig's Meat Extract, shown at the Antwerp International Exhibition of 1894. Created by two prominent Belgian sculptors, Jef Lambeaux and Jules Lagae, it was a triumphal arch formed by two beef animals, supporting on their heads a colossal jar of the extract, the whole surmounted by a bust of Liebig, and flanked by two vegetal Art Nouveau lamps.[38] [82] With this trophy, the commercial world had produced its own *art incohérent*, a joyous montage, in which combinations of media and the resulting polychromy must have seemed for the moment as welcome as the dietary enrichment it advertised.

82 Jef Lambeaux and Jules Lagae, Meat extract trophy, Universal Exhibition Antwerp, 1894; from *The Illustrated London News* (20 October 1894)

Alison Yarrington

Under the spell of Madame Tussaud

Aspects of 'high' and 'low' in 19th-century polychromed sculpture

The introduction of colour into works of sculpture which were categorised as 'high' art during the 19th century was fraught with difficulty for the sculptor and the viewer. Despite its ancient classical lineage, polychromy seemed to breach the aesthetic *hortus conclusus* of the ideal in sculpture, particularly in the representation of the nude.

As Henry Weekes was to observe in his lecture to the Royal Academy students concerning colour in sculpture: 'The absence of Colour in a statue is, in short, one of the peculiarities that remove it so entirely from common Nature that the most vulgarly constituted mind may contemplate it without its causing any feeling of a sensuous kind. The eye learns to look upon it, not as a real existence, but as a sort of visible representation of some admirable concentrated essence that excites our admiration, or calls forth our imitation; and it must have been a sentiment of this kind that caused the gradual disuse of Colour in olden times.'[1] The Belgian sculptor Paul De Vigne similarly summarised the aims of the sculptor: 'The artist must translate none but great ideas. It is his mission to speak to the soul while pleasing the eye. Art should express none but noble thoughts; the principles of sculpture exclude vulgarity.'[2]

With colour suffusing the form of the sculpted body, the viewer, Pygmalion-like, had to come to terms with the starting point for the sculpture itself, the human body. Although the sculptor introducing colour into her or his work might attempt to 'speak to the soul' of the viewer, this aim might be thwarted by the very tangibility of coloured flesh, eyes and hair, which brought thoughts back to earthly concerns of the flesh. Whilst the public was used to seeing colour in commemorative, popular or practical arts where it performed a specific function of providing an apparently accurate record of physical appearance, historical verisimilitude or anatomical or botanical accuracy, there was a necessary distinction to be made between these forms and those of 'Art.' In the decorative arts, too, colour had a rightful place and its own internal rules which were not seen to challenge the lofty ideals of 'high' art. Indeed, small scale statuettes which used mixed media to create richly jewelled effects were more easily accepted within high art than the larger polychromed ideal gallery works. Jean Dampt's exquisitely worked *Fairy Mélusine and the Knight Raymondin* (1895, private collection) and his equally bejewelled *Domestic bliss* (1900, Paris, Musée des arts décoratifs) provided colour and fantasy through the juxtaposition of ivory, gold, wood and iron without the disturbing realism of fully polychromed statues where wax was first rubbed into the surface of marble, followed by dry colour across the whole surface to suggest fleshiness.[3] Marion Spielmann noted the 'purity' of Dampt's *Fairy Mélusine* when discussing its impact upon Henry Fehr's *St George and the rescued maiden* (present location unknown).[4]

Outside the gallery, colour was used in popular forms of sculpture to provide a heightened sense of realism. In the early part of the 19th century small-scale coloured wax portrait reliefs were a popular means of providing images of loved ones (one collection of these by, amongst others, Mary Slaughter, David Morison and Samuel Percy is in the Victoria and Albert Museum, London). The equally 'low' art of making wax portraits and flowers was an accepted accomplishment for women and lessons in this art were available from private tutors, such as Emma Peachey, 'Artist in Wax Flowers to Her Majesty [Queen Victoria]' who worked from her residence at 35 Rathbone Place, London and her shop at 160-63 Soho Bazaar. In the early part of the century there was also a vogue for small scale coloured wax genre scenes, exemplified by artists such as Johann Christoph Rauschner's *Lady Hamilton as the repentant Magdalene* [83], and Samuel Percy's *Death of Voltaire* (both London, Victoria and Albert Museum). Out in the commercial world tinted wax figures were made to display wigs and dresses. By 1851 the Parisian firm of A.J. Allix won praise for its detailed hair-dressers' wax figures: 'These are modelled with considerable skill, and present a very life-like appearance; the hair, eyelids, and eyelashes being

83 Johann Christoph Rauschner, *Lady Hamilton as the repentant Magdalene*,
c. 1810, wax, London, Victoria and Albert Museum

inserted singly in the wax in such a manner as very faithfully to represent nature [...] their manufacture [...] closely resembles that of doll-making.'[5]

Sculptors attempting to introduce colour into their works, particularly in life-size, full-length figures ran the risk of these being classified as 'vulgar,' the artist committing a cardinal sin by stepping outside the realm of Art into the public arena of the fairground or the waxwork museum. This still held true even in the later years of the century when the barriers between the arts were breaking down and the tourniquet of Neo-classicism was being loosened. As shown by the critical response, tinted works such as Gérôme's *Tanagra* (1890) [112] and *The ball player* (1902) [56] brought Art to the edge, forming a dialectic between the idealised sculptural form of the nude and the overlaying 'skin' of tinted wax. By contrast the introduction of chryselephantine works to create sumptuous colour effects were more easily absorbed into the realm of high art than techniques which 'painted' the surface of the body in a manner which echoed the popular 'low' art of the waxwork.

In effect, the creative freedom to colour idealised sculpture was severely curtailed by a cultural environment in which poly-chromed sculpture was indelibly associated with popular and low arts, where nature was copied rather than interpreted. Thus Huysman's description of Degas's only exhibited statue, the tinted wax *Little dancer of 14 years* [68], shown at the Sixth Impressionist Exhibition of 1881, encapsulates the distinction in a typically emotive way: 'The terrible realism of this statuette makes the public distinctly uneasy, all its ideas about sculpture, about cold, lifeless whiteness, about those memorable formulas copied again and again for centuries are demolished.'[6] Despite its being only two thirds life-size, with its overt realism, the real hair, tinted flesh and muslin and gauze tutu, this iconic work of the new art was only a hair's breadth from the waxworks in the Musée Grévin which were still a popular spectacle in Paris. The Musée Grévin's new 'Galerie de la Revolution' was to open in 1882 and two years later, in London, Madame Tussaud's moved to extended premises in Marylebone Road thereby demonstrating the continuing popularity of this art.[7] However, the essential difference between the waxworks and Degas's statue was the role the work performed in the public context; like a cafe-concert artist singing opera it seemed out of place, lacking refinement, overtly 'vulgar' (a word much used in the critical responses to it) and 'low,' some of the qualities which we now recognise form its power as a work of art. In the Impressionist Exhibition it *became* art and challenged preconceptions which sculptors like Antonio Canova, Harriet Hosmer, James Pradier and John Gibson had previously only hinted at from within the safety of the classical ideal. Had it been placed in the Musée Grévin where complete accuracy of form was required for the sake of historical veracity it would also have been out of place, but, it was additionally so from the perspective of the art gallery that seemed its natural habitat. As Antoinette Le Normand-Romain has noted in the context of Degas's statue, Jean-Désiré Ringel d'Illzach's coloured wax figures, particularly his nude shown at the 1879 Salon, *Le demimonde* and his *Head of St John* at the Salon in 1884 were exciting controversy at this period (both works now lost).[8] Particularly in the case of the latter work, the tradition of wax portraits taken from decapitated heads of the Revolutionary period exhibited in the Musée Grévin and Madame Tussaud's must be considered if an understanding of what constituted vulgarity and 'réalisme horrible' is to be properly gauged. The wider environment of popular culture within which polychromed sculpture evolved is crucial to our understanding of the contradictions and difficulties it raised for the viewing public and sculptors themselves. It is the intention of this essay to explore some of these issues in relation to 'high' and 'low' art of the period and how the well-policed boundaries between them were threatened by the increasing popularity of polychromy in sculpture during the 19th century.

How was the distinction between 'high' and 'low' constructed in the 19th century? At one of the most popular international exhibitions of the era, the 1851 'Great Exhibition of the Works of Industry of All Nations' held in London, sculpture was included as the only representative of the 'Fine Arts' in Section XXX. The jury for this section included the sculptor John Gibson,[9] who was by this date already a protagonist of polychromed sculpture, the architects A.W.N. Pugin and C.R. Cockerell, and Dr Waagen (who wrote one of the official reports). In the original layout of the exhibition and within the official catalogue large and small scale sculptures as well as some waxworks were placed within Section XXX. Two small-scale sculptures in white marble, *Gratitude* and *Fidelity* representing small girls with dogs, prompted one commentator to expound upon the difference between high and low in sculpture: '[...] these children and dogs are specimens of low art, and as such are understood and appreciated by the unlearned million. It is only the critics who look for the high and severe style; and for one who really comprehends the stupendous Godfrey, there are a dozen who linger to admire the Boy with the Broken Drum. Art, like music, needs education ere it can be thoroughly comprehended; – though it is not everyone who has "been to Rome and studied the antique" who is able to distinguish between a good statue and a bad one.'[10] These examples of 'low' art by Giovanni Maria Benzoni, were awarded a prize medal, but as the Jurors noted in their report: 'The motive of these works is attractive, and they are carefully executed in marble, but they are by no means of sufficient importance to be considered adequate representations of the modern school of sculpture of such a city as Rome.'[11]

By comparison waxworks had a more ambiguous role within Art. At the Great Exhibition there were examples on show which (other than dolls, automata and shop models) were placed in the Fine Arts Class. In the United Kingdom section were groups of figures representing different characters, natives of Mexico and the American Indians: '[...] all of these having been modelled in wax by M. Montanari from the living originals, and too much praise cannot be accorded him for the truth and fidelity of his representations.'[12] The figures, arranged in narratives, represented the 'characteristic customs in the several phases of civilized and savage life, with a truthfulness in the varied expressions and anatomical development of the different effigies, which is most remarkable. An Indian, rejoicing in triumph over the despair of a white victim, whom he has bound and is about to scalp, but whose sufferings he is prolonging with savage cruelty, may be especially cited in illustration of this particular excellence.'[13] Other polychromed 'sculptures' of this kind included painted plaster figures from India. These also attracted large numbers of visitors. '[...] modelled in clay or plaster, or else carved in wood, and painted to represent the natural colours of the various objects' they included a group belonging to Mr Mansfield of the East India Company's civil service; 'the double-poled tent of the collector is pitched at a short distance from the village; and he is represented as sitting within it, surrounded by the *Manletdar*, and other revenue officers.'[14] It is clear that these works were used to confirm an established ideology relating to colonial control by their apparent objectivity of representation. Such ethnological figures were popular as part of museum displays and in other 19th-century international exhibitions.

Charles-Henri-Joseph Cordier elevated this genre to the realms of 'high art' when he exhibited ten busts of different native peoples of Algeria at the Salon of 1857.[15] Cordier's government-funded anthropological field work in Algeria during 1856-57 was undertaken to create sculptures for the National History Museum in Paris. [47–49] These were intended, like Napoleon Montanari's figures, to provide precise information concerning the appearance of other races.[16] Although Cordier's busts were full of vivid colour, they were different from the ethnological wax or tinted plaster figures displayed at the Great Exhibition. His were portraits created from the standard materials of sculpture – bronze, coloured marble – presented as individual works of art. These highly decorative works made the transition from 'low' to 'high' art by providing paraphrases of surface colour effects; imitation rather than copying. As portrait busts they were also outside that sacred area of the ideal and not constrained by the problematic role of realism.

At the Great Exhibition the supposed truthfulness and fidelity to nature of the ethnological figures placed in melodramatic tableaux fell outside the category of 'Fine Art' when it came to the award of prizes. Admired by the public that flocked to the exhibition Montanari's figures were duly awarded prize medals but had to be transferred to: 'Class XXIX: Miscellaneous Manufactures and Small Wares, section C: Articles connected with Education (ethnographical models)' to achieve this. Class XXIX also included natural history – taxidermy, botanical specimens in wax – and manufactured amusements, such as toys, umbrellas, soaps, wax candles etc. The criteria for the award of a prize medal here were 'excellence of workmanship, novelty of construction, beauty of design, or goodness of manufacture combined'[17] with no troublesome aesthetic dimension to assess.

The jury of Class XXX: Fine Art adjudicated upon the various works of sculpture in the exhibition following different rules. These necessarily excluded the wax figures of Montanari and others: 'In forming their judgement upon works in the highest branch of art coming within their jurisdiction, the Jury have principally looked for the embodiment of ideas, thought, feeling, and passion; not for the mere imitation of nature, however true in detail, or admirable in execution. They have looked for originality of invention, less or more happily expressed in that style which has for twenty-three centuries been the wonder of every civilized people, and the standard of excellence to which artists of the highest order have endeavoured to attain.'[18] On such grounds they also excluded anatomical models in painted wood and wax, which instead were adjudicated under Class Xc: Surgical Instruments. The Jury for this section desired 'especially to express their admiration of the series of models in wax, which display the anatomy of the torpedo, not only as highly interesting specimens of Florentine art, but as patterns of scientific accuracy and artistic beauty.'[19] These works were made by Professor L. Calamai from Tuscany, and others that were commended were by Dr Louis Auzoux of France and the British makers J. Gordon and G. Simpson.[20]

Collectively the members of the jury for Class XXX, were not over-enthusiastic about the incidence of colour in the works of 'high art' on display at the Great Exhibition, although they did not condemn it as a practice. In the report on the sculpture in the French section, Pradier's slight touch of colour to drapery of his statue of *Phryne* (1845, Musée de Grenoble) caused them concern

84 Napoleon Montanari, A group of Mexican Indians, 1851, illustration

but not sufficient to prevent the work being awarded a Council Medal: 'The idea of ornamenting the hem of the garment with a red "Mæander" border is not happy, for, in contrast with the colourless uniformity of the rest of the marble, such an ornament appears crude and misplaced.'[21] The original statue, exhibited at the Salon of 1845, had pale blue colouring to the edge of the drapery and was further decorated with gold earrings.[22] It is perhaps worth noting that Gibson had introduced a similar element of colour into the drapery of his statue of *Queen Victoria* (1844-47, London, Buckingham Palace). According to his biographer Gibson was aware of the particular distaste for polychromy in the United Kingdom: 'I introduced coloured ornaments upon the mantle, diadem, &c. I was pleased by the effect but it was condemned by all the English who came to Rome; not one had I on my side, but all the artists, Germans and natives, tacitly approved.'[23] The Queen accepted the work with the coloured details, despite extensive adverse criticism of the work in England. However, *The Roman Advertiser* (23 January 1847) observed that the delicate colour used did not produce any 'glaring contrast' that would be detrimental to the statue as a whole.[24]

In contrast to Pradier's modest introduction of colour in *Phryne*, Montanari's highly-coloured wax figures provided almost excessive detail and thereby ensured their 'popular' success. Nothing was left to chance by the waxwork artist and nothing to the imagination. Colour was crucial to this success and there was no room for delicate suggestion or slight tinting to satisfy more aesthetic tastes. These were works to be judged for their apparent realism with no imaginative transference of ideas between the viewer and the object of contemplation. The placing of sever-

85 *The sleeping beauty*, 18th century, wax, London, Madame Tussaud's

al figures in a tableau further added to the idea of the spectator witnessing life as it was really lived, frozen in time. The fact that the figures had been modelled 'from life' heightened the sense of the spectator bearing witness to an actual scene. This was crucial to the success of the enterprise in that it gave the sensation of an imprint of the people from whom the wax casts had been taken. As recently observed by Claudine Mitchell in her analysis of historical events at the Musée Grévin: 'Each tableau stage-manages a realist scenario which positions the visitor as eye-witness to a scene in its moment of occurrence. Its main principle consists in inviting the viewer to focus attention on the specificity of visual quality in an attempt to construct the real on the basis of an equation between the concrete and the true.'25

The development of the waxwork museum in the 19th century was predicated upon this idea, waxworks being presented not as fairground novelties purely for amusement but as a means of educating the public. Madame Tussaud played this card heavily when she travelled with her waxworks in England, Scotland and Ireland before establishing her showrooms in London in 1833. The cover of the guide book to her collection did everything to create the impression that hers was an intellectually serious enterprise. The title *Biographical and descriptive sketches of the distinguished characters which compose the unrivalled exhibition of Madame Tussaud and sons* was followed by a list of deceased and current royal and aristocratic patrons including Louis XVI, Marie Antoinette, the King of Hanover and the Duke of Wellington. Three quotations from Shakespeare's *The winter's tale*, the most well-known, dramatic enactment of a statue coming to life before the amazed onlooker, heightened the sense of artistic quality, whilst the linking lines from the dramatic text which seemed to suggest self-praise and trickery were carefully missed out. Thus Polixenes's cry of 'Masterly done!' is removed leaving the lines: 'The very life seems warm upon her lip,' followed by Leontes's line: 'The fixture of her eyes has motion in't' without the troublesome following line: 'As we are mocked with art.' The lines 'Would you not deem it breath's and that those veins/Did verily bear blood' (V, 3, 65-6) also set the scene for one of the highlights of the exhibit, the figure of *Madame de St Amaranthe* on a couch, 'the most lovely woman in France'26 lying down with an arm raised across her face appeared to breathe as her chest rose and fell in sleep mechanically operated by a clockwork mechanism.27 Madame Tussaud took care to place her own self-

86 Madame Tussaud, *Self-portrait*, 19th century, wax and textiles, London, Madame Tussaud's

portrait against this 'sleeping beauty' in the exhibit, heightening the contrast between her own plain features and the prettiness of the young woman who had met her death at the guillotine rather than dishonour her husband. [86] Placed alongside this duo was a third figure, the raddled coquette, *Madame Sappé*, her ageing face twisted in a ghastly smile. This figure, 'taken from life' as the guide book proclaimed, was an ironic reference to the bewitching nature of the waxworks and the Pygmalion myth: 'We have read of a young man having become enamoured of a statue; we caution young gentlemen to beware the same does not happen to them, while gazing on the charms of the interesting Madame Sappé.'[28] Madame Tussaud's self-portrait, bonneted and heavily bespectacled – the third of these three graces – provided an image of probity and hard work in which physical beauty was of no consequence. Such an unadorned and unflattering self-portrait was a means of strengthening the impression that the waxworks were empirical evidence of actual physiognomy and did not allow for any intervening, fictional element which would detract from their role as objects of historical value.

Madame Tussaud's aim to provide her visitors with absolute knowledge of the physical appearance of historical personages was built upon this myth. Her activities during the French Revolution when she was called upon to take casts from the freshly guillotined heads of victims of the terror were well known. By the 1840s her early history had been further disseminated by *Madame Tussaud's memoirs and reminiscences of France*, first published in 1838.[29] Part of the attraction of the waxworks was undoubtedly the grisly nature of such exhibits, which in order to keep the public attention were constantly updated by the addition of further, topical figures made from death or life masks taken immediately after execution or during imprisonment. Particularly popular were her waxworks of the criminals Burke and Hare who had been tried for supplying freshly murdered corpses to the Edinburgh medical school: 'the Model of Burke, taken within three hours after his execution [27 January 1828], and that of Hare from Life, in the prison of Edinburgh.'[30] In 1844 these were grouped together with amongst others, the famous waxwork of Marat 'Taken immediately after his assassination, by order of the National Assembly' to form the newly designated 'Chamber of Horrors.' [87]

Despite this supposed veracity it is noticeable that Madame Tussaud's collection contained several works which were not taken from life, but relied upon Art for their source material. For example, the figure of Lord Byron was taken, according to the guidebook, 'from a Bust for which he gave sittings in Italy,'[31] George Washington 'taken from a Bust, executed from Life,'[32] William Pitt and Charles James Fox both from busts 'taken a short time before [their] death[s].'[33] Early figures of the kings and queens of England had to be constructed from portraits, and although the head of George IV was taken 'from life' the pose of the figure was 'copied from a picture by Sir Thomas Lawrence.'[34]

It is therefore not surprising that when life-size or nearly life-size fully polychromed statues were presented to the public in public exhibitions there was unease over their status as 'high' or 'low' art. Even the small touches of colour and gilt ornament found in some of Canova's ideal figures such as *Hebe* [10] brought the works too close to earth for some viewers and Gibson's later attempts at full-blown polychromy applied to a life-size statue of a nude woman were particularly problematic for the Victorian public. Based upon his understanding of Greek sculptural practice the introduction of colour into sculpture was one that he recognised might be difficult for the public to accept, despite the high ideals that motivated its introduction: 'It was as though through Polychromy the ancients gave expression to the brighter and more ethereal impulses of the mind. Polychromy was the link connecting the forms of matter with the airy fancies in which genius was rife.'[35] Other polychromed statues of Venus had been on display prior to Gibson's own *Tinted Venus* [7], but

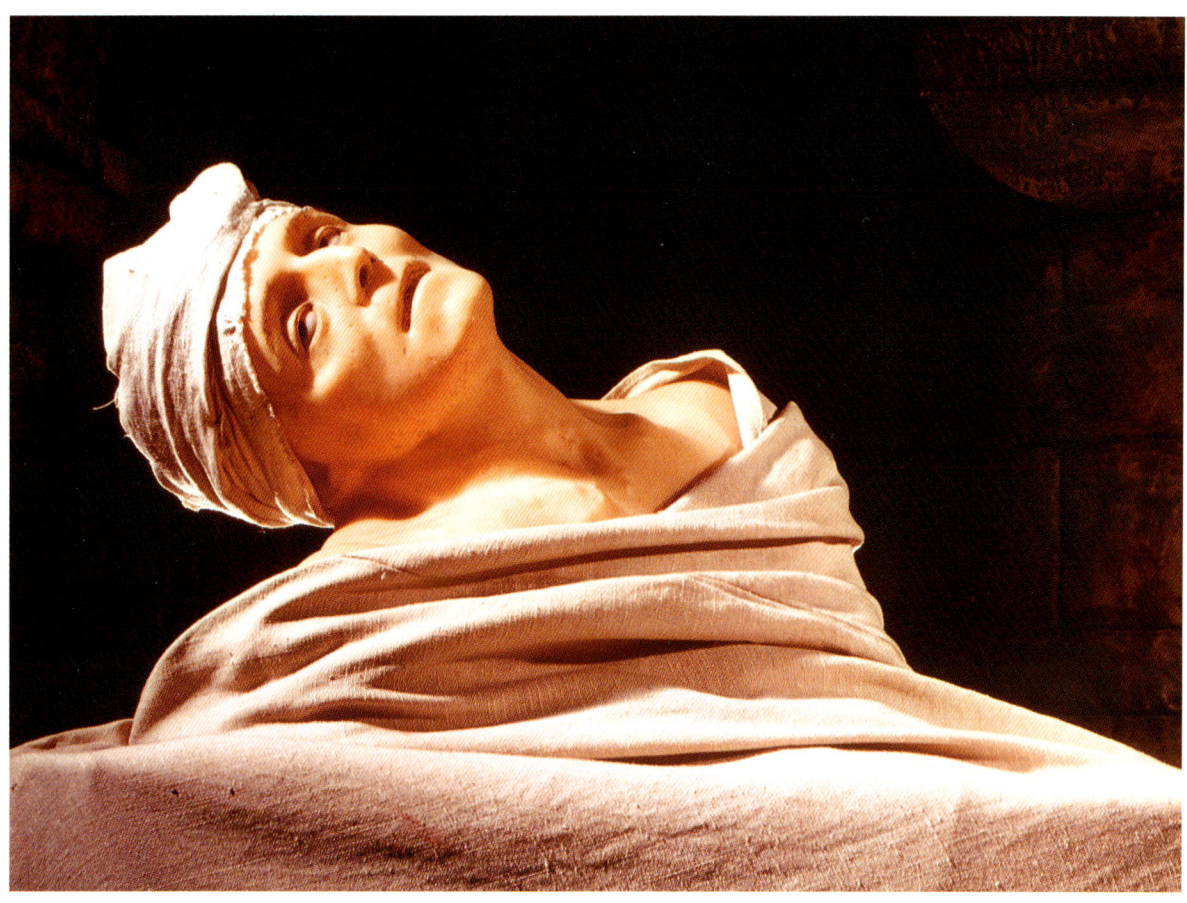

87   The death of Marat, 18th century, wax, London, Madame Tussaud's

these were firmly within the realm of the popular and educational entertainments and had very little to do with 'airy fancies in which genius was rife.' In 1826 in a London showroom an anatomical wax figure with an exterior form representing the *Medici Venus* was opened up to display: '[...] on dissection the various functions of the Human Body, and displays to perfection the order and beauty that prevails throughout the works of the CREATOR [...].'[36] In 1844 a *'Parisian' Venus*, not apparently modelled on a statue, was on display presented as an educational exhibition likely to be of benefit to 'young medical students.' In 1853 at Reimer's Anatomical and Ethnological Museum, a display of several hundred wax anatomical figures 'for gentlemen only' included a 'Florentine Venus, which is dissectable in all its parts [and a] Greek Venus, Displaying the Muscular System.'[37]

Whilst wax Venuses were dismantled and their body parts offered up for popular entertainment, living bodies parodied statues in *tableaux vivants* or *poses plastiques*. This popular entertainment was widespread in Europe, often basing the composition of the living figures upon the 'high' art of painting and sculpture in order to give the entertainment credibility. 'Living sculpture' had been long been a form of private and public entertainment, Lady Hamilton's Attitudes being one early example of private theatre with which the aristocracy amused themselves.[38] But these were (despite the mixed response they received) a far cry from 'an evening with Canova and Flaxman' presented to the London public by Madame Wharton in 1847 where live models posed as famous statues by the two sculptors.[39] This kind of live entertainment was still popular in the 1890s, although the focus of controversy. 'Living Pictures' presented at the Palace Theatre of Varieties was thought by Arthur Symons 'to be directly opposed to sculpture because the women, held fast by corsets and plasters, took on that very rigidity that good sculpture struggled to transcend. They were at best an aesthetic curiosity, rather like a juggling act.'[40]

Funeral effigies, death masks or votive sculptures were other examples of polychromed three-dimensional works which had, necessarily, to provide an accurate record of the deceased or saved person. The long tradition of this practice of providing life-size wax portraits flourished in Catholic Europe, particularly in southern Germany, Austria and northern Italy. The continuing popularity of this form of commemorative votive work is evident in the many wax votives of children which survive in Franconia.

88   Anatomical model of a mans head, 18th century, wax, Vienna, Josephinum

Here life-size wax coloured statues of children dressed in real clothes served a religious purpose of thanksgiving for recovery from illness and in some instances themselves becoming the object of pilgrimage associated with Mariology.[41] In contrast, in Protestant England the wax effigies of the kings and queens of England had, by the mid-19th century been removed from public view in Westminster Abbey.[42] They had lost their value as *memento mori* and were considered no better than fairground dummies. In Allan Cunningham's biographical account of the sculptor Joseph Nollekens published in 1830 the low status of such polychromed works is clear from Nollekens's reported reaction: '[...] well, my wife wants also to know what you have done with the wooden figures in wax masks, all in tattered silk, which the Westminster boys called the ragged regiment – she says they were borne before the corpse formerly [...]. I wonder you keep such stuff. I don't mind going to Mrs. Salmon's wax-works, where Mother Shipton kicks you as you go out. You should not have such rubbish in the Abbey – and then take money for this foolish thing and the other foolish thing [...].'[43]

Against this wider popular culture Gibson's *Tinted Venus* executed in his Roman studio and shown at the International Exhibition of 1862, can be seen to have been made in the spirit of Pygmalion with the noblest of intentions: 'I forgot at moments that I was gazing at my own production. There sat I before her long and often. How can I ever part with her!'[44] But in colouring his statue Gibson was seen by many to allow vulgarity to clothe the pristine white marble form, and in so doing defiled the purity of the ideal. The critical response to the *Tinted Venus* classed the statue, because of its colouring and heaviness of limbs, as an earthly, modern woman, rather than as a heavenly form which had sprung from the imagination of the sculptor: 'Her heavy English limbs, stained, as was currently reported, – whether in jest or not, we cannot say, – with tobacco juice, to suggest the rosy-tinted Aphrodite; her hair, a pale straw-color; the pupils of her eyes, a light blue; golden earrings in her ears, and a golden collar about her neck; with a face of a common-place, house keeping type, and an attitude devoid of character or intention – it was, to us, a work of unmitigated vulgarity.'[45]

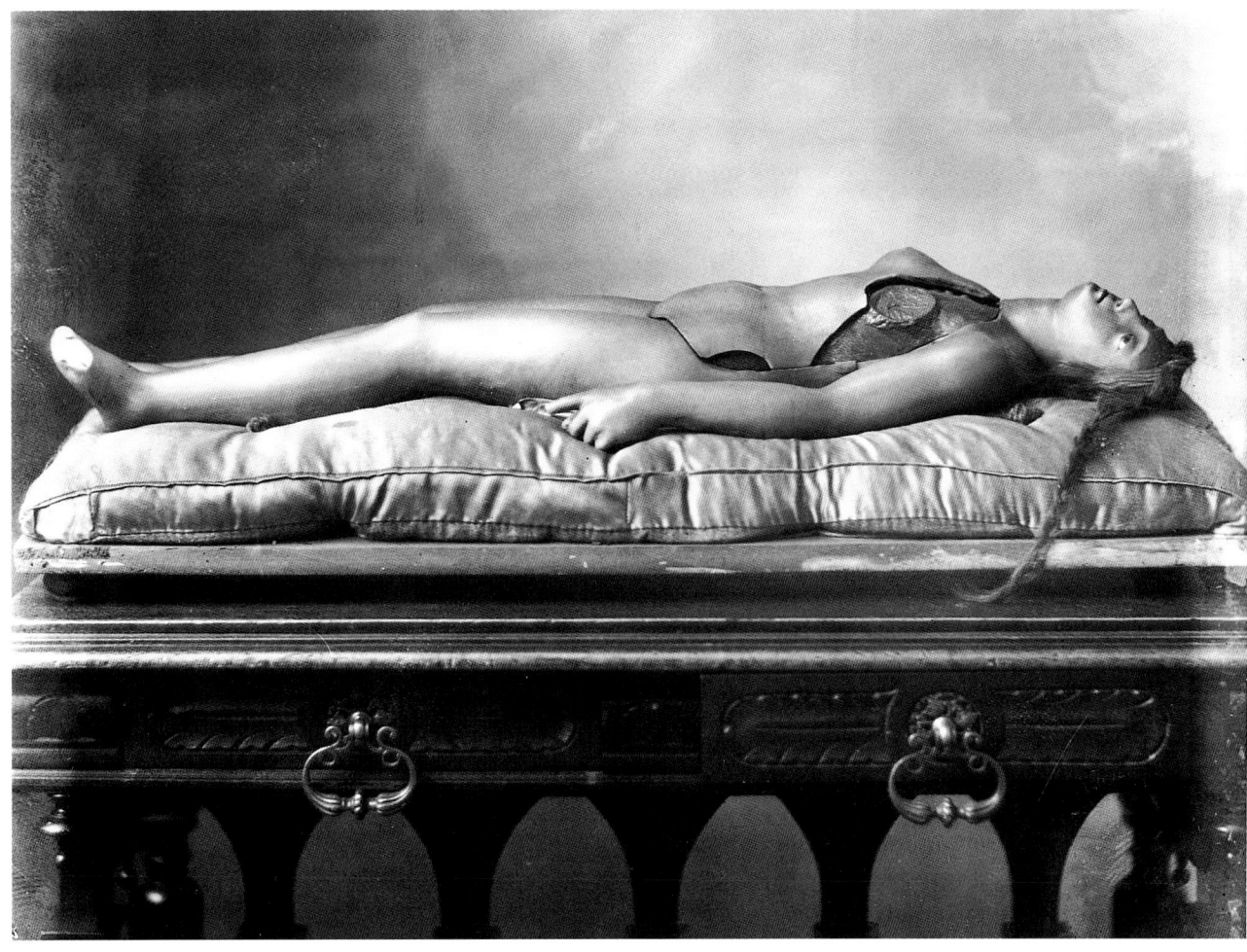

89 Female anatomical model with removable front torso, 18th century, wax, London, Wellcome Library, on loan to Science Museum

It was easier for the public to accept a less complete adherence to polychromy in complete figures. Harriet Hosmer, Gibson's pupil exhibited her own statue of the captive *Zenobia* (present location unknown) alongside the *Tinted Venus*. As one American visitor to Hosmer's studio noted of: 'Zenobia's rosy tint' [...] 'much as I dislike colored statues, I cannot object to the delicate tinting of this,' seeing it as 'catching the better part of Gibson's idea of tinting the marble.'[46]

But even by the end of the century the practice of colouring a wax skin over a full size statue had failed to meet with approval and the need to separate nature from art became more crucial as sculptors produced works with greater surface naturalism. As Marion Spielmann noted in the opening pages of *British sculpture and sculptors of to-day* (1901): 'Nature is but the model which has to be idealised, or the result is commonplace – a vulgar copy, uninspired in its imitation.'[47] Taking Ruskin's statement that a statue 'is not like the form of a man; it is a man' the practice of colouring statues 'like waxworks became offensive.' It is interesting to note that as an example of this offensive practice Spielmann cites a 'well known painter in Paris' who possessed a statue of Venus in wax 'variously coloured to imitate nature,' which although 'exquisitely modelled' was 'supremely ridiculous' to look upon.[48]

Whilst Gibson's and later Gérôme's use of colour for ideal subjects in which the nude played a central role brought the body too close to nature with the use of tinted wax surfaces, evoking a strong critical response, other sculptors sought to preserve the ideals of high art by a more subtle use of mixed media. The purity of high art could best be maintained within polychromed sculpture if the body was made from a single, uncoloured, sculptural medium such as marble or ivory, the latter being the material closest to flesh because of its animal origin. This could then be incorporated with other, richly contrasting secondary elements in gilt bronze and coloured stones and marbles to achieve polychromy. The sensuality of the figure could therefore be conveyed by the subtle manipulation of surface in a traditional way without vulgarity. Spielmann stated that the mingling of ivory and gold in chryselephantine works produced results which were sufficiently removed from reality, though these could still be questionable.[49] This was certainly the case with Désiré-Maurice Ferrary's life-size *Salammbô* (1899). [91] Here the figure of Salammbô is represented at an erotically charged moment, when she submits (as she has been instructed to do without resistance) to the embrace of a black python of the Temple of Eschmoun. In the sculpture the pillar around which the python normally wraps itself is surmounted (in a departure from Flaubert's original text) by a series of phallic horses' heads above which is seated the ruby-eyed figure of the goddess, Tanit, placed against a crescent moon. Salammbô is held by golden chains, an echo of Albert-Ernest Carrier-Belleuse's controversial marble statue of *Angelica* held by gilt bronze chains, exhibited at the Paris Salon in 1866.[50] As though witnessing the private ritual, which in the novel 'Salammbô did not want to be seen, even by the walls'[51] the viewer is aware of the bronze serpent which begins to twine itself around the woman's form. Ferrary's *Leda and the swan* [59] exhibited with *Salammbô* at the Exposition Universelle of 1900[52] also utilises the more richly-coloured material to represent the violating presence of animal nature against the pale marble or ivory form. In many ways these fin-de-siècle sculptures with their vivid use of colour contrasts correspond to Weekes's ambivalent feelings concerning what he described as the 'florid style' in his lecture on 'Style' to Royal Academy students. This he understood to be particularly appropriate for some settings: '[...] for instance, in the decoration of the theatre, the ball-room, and other places of amusement.'[53] In this transient and more popular context that sculptors may allow themselves to be lead away into a 'realm of Ideality [...] It is here, if anywhere, that colour may be introduced into your statues as well as into the ornaments about them. The danger is of their becoming sensuous; but the refinement, whether of design or execution, which you will introduce will keep that down as [Shakespeare] has done in [*The tempest*].'[54] Thus the taste for polychromed sculptures which evoked mysterious and magical effects in the last years of the century allowed polychromy to develop away from the vulgar, popular arts with their emphasis upon the 'real.'

Emmanuelle Héran

Art for the sake of the soul

Polychrome sculpture and literary Symbolism

As far as we know, no one has ever offered a specific definition of symbolist sculpture. Certainly, we have the resonant pronouncements of writers and critics such as Stephane Mallarmé, Jean Moréas and Albert Aurier, but they were all inspired by literature and painting, and none are really appropriate to sculpture. As the most physical of arts which, more than any other, forces the artist to confront matter in its hardest form, how indeed could sculpture be expected to lend itself to the expression of mystery, to the suggestion of soul? If the aim of Symbolism is 'to clothe the idea in sensuous form,' then the task of the symbolist sculptor was a difficult one indeed.

For the sake of concision, I shall limit this discussion to two main themes: cosmetics and jewellery. Not surprisingly, perhaps, both are inspired by Charles Baudelaire, who on numerous occasions stated his taste for artifice and his hatred of naturalness. In *Le peintre de la vie moderne*, notably, he delivered a vibrant *Eloge du maquillage*, and the women of *Les fleurs du mal* are painted and bejewelled.

To understand why these texts were provocative, one must remember that in Baudelaire's time whiteness exerted a truly tyrannical dominance. Throughout the 19th century, in the discourses both of fashion and medicine, white was the only colour. Health and beauty were associated not, as today, with a tan, but with extreme pallor. Thus it was imperative that George Sand's wild heroine, Indiana, should whiten her coppery skin. And there was no shortage of cosmetic solutions to help her: women were advised to 'wash your face with chicken's blood' or 'the urine of breast-fed nurselings.'[1] Balzac's César Birotteau invented 'Carminative water' and 'Double paste for Sultanesses.'[2] Women followed 'the dire fashion of coating their faces, breast and arms with the white of lead, bismuth or baryta [...] the absorption [of which] can lead to grave health problems.'[3] The aim was to eliminate the slightest blotch, beauty spot, freckle or ruddiness, even when this meant using violent acids, 'the external application of excrement of dogs, donkeys, chickens, crocodiles, foxes or pigeons.'[4] Less harmfully, rice powder and starch reigned supreme: 'what our age vulgarly calls cosmetics, which envisages only the use of rice powder, what is so stupidly anathematised by our philosophers of candour, has the aim and result of removing from the complexion all the stains that nature has outrageously scattered there, and of creating an abstract unity in the grain and colour of the skin, which unity, like that produced by the singlet, immediately brings the human being closer to the statue, which is to say, to a divine and superior being.'[5]

It had become a commonplace to compare women to sculptures: feminine beauty was measured by the yardstick of statuary. The goal was to be as fair as a statue, i.e., above all else, white. Théophile Gautier was the great apostle of this ideal, which he praises with remarkable consistency throughout his writings, from his critical and aesthetic texts to his poems. He dispenses absolutely identical advice both to a sculptor and to a woman, urging the former to:

> Keep to Carrara rare,
> Struggle with Paros cold,
> That hold
> The subtle line and fair.[6]

To the latter he recommended that she adopt 'a unity of tone which is to be preferred to the insistent white, yellow and pink offered by even the purest complexions. It might be a vague shudder of modesty that prompts women to lay on their necks, their shoulders, their breasts and their arms that light veil of white dust which attenuates nudity by removing from it the warm and provocative colours of life. Thus the figure draws closer to statuary, becoming more spiritual, purified.'[7] Gautier even wrote a poem entitled *Symphonie en blanc majeur* about whiteness as the *sine qua non* of beauty.[8]

These texts reveal all the basic connotations of whiteness: philosophically, it represents the spiritual as opposed to the corporeal, the soul over the body; morally, whiteness is to colour as the immaculate is to the soiled. Whiteness is conducive to abstraction, makes woman like a white statue, a divine and superior being. And on the side of the statue, of marble, of whiteness, the absence of colour which emphasises form, we find the mind, the idea. Hegel's famous assertion that 'only the spiritual is true' dominates the century.[9] If woman is to approach the ideal, then she must imitate statuary. The mimetic process is reversed: art no longer seeks to imitate life, it is life that must imitate art. Baudelaire stigmatises this aesthetic:

> I leave to Gavarni, anemia's laureate,
> his twittering flock of insubstantial girls
> in all those sallow blossoms who could find
> one rose to reconcile my red ideal?[10]

But he is no advocate of naturalness. On the contrary, he wants to heighten life, to emphasise its most shocking colours, its most sensual and even its most morbid realities. Better real death than false sickliness. One recalls his well known (and, at his trial, much decried) passion for carrion, a theme that became incorporated into the symbolist aesthetic.

We thus have a dichotomy with, on one side, flesh, coloured by blood, charged with life but liable to decay and become carrion, and, on the other, immaculate, bloodless marble that is lifeless but, by the same token, immortal. The statue metaphor and the carrion image are often combined in a spectacular contrast. Thus, when Zola's 'marble-fleshed' Nana dies of syphilis, her body becomes 'a shovelful of putrid flesh [...] the greyish colour of mud.' On the last page, we read the words we were waiting for: 'Venus was decomposing.'[11] In *L'éternelle poupée*, Jules Bois convokes the image not of a statue but of a doll containing carrion: 'a scrubbed, varnished, painted doll' beneath whose 'crust a little ordure is fermenting.'[12]

It is important to emphasise the aesthetic break introduced by Baudelaire in order to establish the context in which the Symbolists would revolutionise and enrich the imaginary status of the body. Their references were moral as well as aesthetic. Symbolist writings are full of morbid myths revolving around the transition from flesh to marble, wax, metal or ivory, as if the fundamental nature of the human body were morally unsatisfactory. The body is despised because it is mortal, subject to decay. The idea of the superiority of marble over flesh is clearly expressed in Henri de Régnier's short story, *La femme de marbre*: 'The vain flesh that she animated is rotting in the earth. She now inhabits the eternal form that you had prepared for her in incorruptible marble.'[13] By insisting on coloured representations of the body, Baudelaire and his symbolist heirs overturned this hierarchy and affronted prevailing moral standards.

One should realise that the moral condemnation of polychromy is implicit in many of the writings of sculptors and art critics from the 1830s onwards. Again and again, the moral perfection of white marble is contrasted with the flesh and its natural colour, but also with the practice of painting, to the addition of ornament and use of cosmetics. The definitive statement on the subject comes from the sculptor David d'Angers: 'As a woman gets on in life, she increases the finery of her apparel. She believes that finery will palliate the fading of her beauty. How touching and beautiful is a young woman adorned with the graces bestowed on her by nature. She has no need of the ornament of art. And might not the same be said of modern art, which is obliged to colour its statues? Does this not reveal an absence of feeling for beauty?'[14] Or again: 'Those who put form before colour are quite right. Is it not form that initiates one into the most secret states of a young girl's soul? Colour paints creaturely health: it is the egotism of nature, it is the material expression of life.'[15] The intensely hostile reaction to certain polychrome sculptures is equally eloquent. Shocked by Auguste Clésinger's *Sappho*, Paul Mantz wrote: 'these jewels, these lies, do not enrich the form, they hide and sometimes disfigure it.'[16] What emerges here is an aesthetic and moral opposition between form, guaranteed by whiteness, which expresses the soul, and an externally imposed colour which muddies its clarity.

With the Symbolists, however, colour is brought over onto the side of the ideal, in continuity with the ideas of Baudelaire. For them, it was colour that represented the soul. For this idea, we must look not to Paul Verlaine, whose deceptive encomium to whiteness is drawn directly from the aesthetic of Gautier – 'With the chisel of thought we sculpt/Virginal beauty, immaculate Paros'[17] – but to more obscure writers, many of whom are no longer read, or are just being rediscovered.

Certainly, we are familiar with the writings of the first critics to express their interest in the idea that the colours of the real body could be represented in the form of painted statues. Paul Mantz, for example, notes that in 'the reign of Louis XV [...] this declining art was rarely employed,' and recalls 'certain coloured figures which, precisely because they appeared too true and almost alive, gave me one of the great frights of my childhood.'[18] Upon seeing Degas's *Little dancer of 14 years*, Joris-Karl Huysmans declared that 'the terrible reality of this statuette makes one distinctly uneasy; all one's ideas about sculpture; about these inanimate whitenesses, about these memorable clichés copied down the centuries, all are overturned.'[19] Guy de Maupassant apostrophised the 'Eternal and insipid model of beauty, perfect Venus, known as the Venus of Milo,' and asked 'who will make bold to shatter those famous loins that for so many years have inspired all the scrapers of pallid marble...? You were sublime, no doubt, but you are not the woman of today, just as rigid marble is no longer the material desired by our eyes that hunger for colour, for movement, for life. Let us shatter our antique marbles, moulds and admirations. Seek, imagine, find. Dig deep into wood, knead clay, model wax!... And as colour combines with form, so we may soon be seeing painted statues.'[20]

However, what these naturalist writers and critics are calling for is more reality. Less commonly quoted are those texts which associate sculpture not with reality but with artifice, like this declaration by the Parnassian poet, historian and moralist, Louis Ménard:

> Real women I cannot love:
> The ideal is a gulf between us [...]
> Each should have a sculpted virgin,
> Like Pygmalion[21]

The Symbolists were even more keen on these 'sculpted virgins,' and created many painted statues, dolls, wax figures and painted women. In keeping with the customary distinction between natural polychromy (the combination of naturally coloured materials, mainly stones and marbles) and artificial polychromy (the application of paint), I shall begin by looking at the texts and sculptures relating to the first category, then go on to those that come within the second.

Encrustation

The encrustation of precious stones is a recurrent feature of symbolist sculpture, especially for the representation of the eyes. Working as a 'psychologist of gems,'[22] Philippe Wolfers used opal to figure the eyes of the ivory Medusa head on a necklace: given Medusa's petrifying gaze, stones are a particularly appropriate way of representing her hypnotic glance.[23] However, the best example of this procedure is the sculpture of Max Klinger. His *Cassandra* in the Musée d'Orsay is particularly striking for what, as far as we know, is its unique combination of black bronze, for the darkness of her prophecies, and contrasting red amber for the eyes, suggesting the horror of her vision of the fall and fire of Troy. [19] In the *New Salome*, the amber eyes contrast with the marble of the body and represent the thirst for blood which Salome slaked with the decapitation of John the Baptist. [43] In this piece Klinger goes beyond the strict illustration of Théodore de Banville's founding text, *Hérodiade*, in which the poet suggests Salome's sanguinary nature by having her wear red and purple stones:

> On her ruby fingers, sapphire and amethyst
> Glitter seductively: on a golden plate
> She carries the bloody head of John the Baptist.[24]

He thus creates a literal transcription of Baudelaire's description: 'Precious metals form her polished eyes.'[25]

However surprising, this idea of encrustation was used frequently by symbolist writers. The most often-quoted example is of course Des Esseintes's tortoise, which eventually suffocates under the weight of the gems that its owner has had set in its shell.[26] In his novel *Monsieur de Phocas*, Jean Lorrain creates a character called Ethal who collects gemstones. He is fascinated by the marble *Antinous* in the Louvre, but deplores its empty gaze: 'If this bust were mine,' he declares, 'I would have its eyes inlaid with emeralds.'[27] This theme of emerald eyes runs through the whole novel. In one of his *Moralités légendaires*, Jules Laforgue imagines the punishment of Salome: she falls from her terrace and is dashed on the rocks below, where her diamonds pierce her flesh.[28] More curious is Jean Lorrain's marked penchant for inlaying stones in the actual flesh of his heroines: one loses an eye and has an emerald set in the empty socket, which kills her;[29] another, an old woman, commemorates the 15 times she has been raped by having the same number of rubies set in her décolleté: '15 sparkling gems on shoulders transpierced by 15 wounds.'[30] In *Le jardin des supplices*, Octave Mirbeau evokes a leper woman whose necklace of rare pearls is gradually absorbed and destroyed by her skin.[31] It is clear that this inlaying of jewels can have a moral meaning: their implantation in the flesh is very similar to torture and can sometimes be mortal.

On most occasions, however, the ornament in question is simply that of a courtesan. No sadistic or masochistic encrustation is involved. All women (and, for some, all men[32]) become beautiful when they wear jewellery and stones. Symbolist taste is in thrall to 'that scintillating world of metal and stone.'[33] This aspect of the movement has been extensively studied, for there is no shortage of literary descriptions of bejewelled women to be compared to similar sculptures using artificial colour and the combination of precious materials.[34] I shall therefore limit myself to what seem to me the two most extreme examples. The first is the series of *Princesses* by Théodore de Banville, including the *Hérodiade* mentioned earlier and also his *La Reine de Saba*:

> Bejewelled Queen Nicosis, bedecked
> With a calm and marvellous concert
> Of stuffs, where a flashing wave of stars is lost
> In lakes of light and flowering flames.

90 Théodore-Louis-Auguste Rivière, *Salammbô at the house of Mathô*, 1895, bronze, ivory and jewels, Paris, Musée d'Orsay

91 Désiré-Maurice Ferrary, *Salammbô*, 1899, marble and bronze, National Museums and Galleries on Merseyside, Port Sunlight, Lady Lever Art Gallery

Her shimmering gilded gown
Is of rare cloth veering on purple
Where dazzling gold, glowing red and green,
Is put a poor foil to rich embroideries.

She has heavy ear pendants, copies
Of the sky's fiery suns, and on her feet
A thousand escarbuncles make the livid day pale.

Proud in the bright red glow of her apparel,
On the knees of King Solomon
She pours rubies from a sapphire vase.[35]

The sculptural equivalent of this at the end of the century would be the work of Georges-Henri Lemaire, who specialised in precious representations such as *Silence* (also known as *Immortality*, Paris, Musée du Petit Palais) made up of lapis lazuli, jasper, agate, opal and gilded copper, or *Fate* (1908, gem quartz, pink quartz, marbled agate, arborised agate, labradorite and yellow silica). Generally speaking, sculptures representing a *femme fatale* would tend to be polychrome, laden with jewels and saturated with precious materials. This approach soon became a convention, as is indicated by the abundance of polychrome Salammbôs. In 1892, Théophile-Eugène-Victor Barrau sculpted *Mathô and Salammbô* in polychrome marble (Saint-Maur-des-Fossés, Square de la Pie). Three years later, Théodore Rivière produced a small group in bronze and ivory entitled *Salammbô chez Mathô: Je t'aime! Je t'aime!* which he decorated with jewels. [90] In 1899, Désiré-Maurice Ferrary presented a languorous *Salammbô* in painted marble and bronze.[36] [91]

Paint

I have already mentioned the opinion that paint concealed the soul. However, from the 1860s onwards, in the tradition of Baudelaire's *Eloge du maquillage*, make-up was assigned the task of *revealing* a woman's soul. So much so that, writing in 1905, Heinrich Mann could maintain that 'living in contact with fabrics and paints is almost like touching and breathing the soul of woman [...] powder and stuff are little less than the soul itself.'[37] Already, in 1894, Max Beerbohm, one of the theorists of the Pre-Raphaelite movement, had rehabilitated cosmetics in an influential essay in which he went so far as to assert the precedence of cosmetics and polychromy over all the other arts: 'The painting of the face is the first kind of painting men can have known.'[38] Not only did symbolist writers portray painted women (and men) but figures such as Jules Barbey d'Aurevilly and Jean Lorrain themselves practised the art of *maquillage*.

There is surely no need here to recall that symbolist literature abounds in descriptions of painted women.[39] It would be more interesting to look at the many unsettling cases where the application of paint is associated with polychrome sculpture. In most cases, these fictions relate how either the original or the cast of an ancient work is transformed into a completely different object by the application of colour. Thus, when Jean Lorrain describes his own taste for painted sculpture in his short story *Réclamation posthume*, he sets about changing 'a simple cast from the Louvre [...] of Donatello's famous *Femme inconnue*' by decapitating and then colouring it with the 'sea-green of blind eyes, the faded pink of the lips, the flecks of gold in the hair.' He even dedicates some poems to it. I shall spare the reader and limit myself to two lines: 'Hanging by the bed, the head with painted lips.../He gave that roseate mouth a languorous kiss.'[40]

There is an obvious parallel between what Lorrain is doing here and the practices of sculptors such as Franz von Stuck and Fernand Khnopff. In his villa in Munich, Stuck raised up an altar comprising various paintings and sculptures of his own making but also antiques from his personal collection, which he had no qualms about enhancing with colour. [97] Looking beyond the erudition involved here (Stuck, the great lover of classical culture restoring his antiques to their original polychromy), it is important to note the sacred dimension of this procedure: to colour a statue is a way of loving it, of worshipping it, of making it sacred. We, of course, would see this as sacrilege.[41]

Khnopff also came under the charm of an antique bust. In the British Museum, his admiration for a small bronze head of Hypnos attributed to Scopas prompted him to make a copy (unless, of course, it was a commercial cast) which crops up in all kinds of forms and places in his subsequent work.[42] It would seem that he made a plaster or marble transcription of the piece which stood on a kind of altar bearing the motto ON NE A QUE SOI. Unfortunately, Khnopff's house was destroyed in 1921. This piece makes its first appearance in an oil painting on canvas, *I lock my door upon myself* (1891, Munich, Bayerische Staatsgemäldesammlungen, Neue Pinakothek), where it stands on a shelf at the centre of the composition. Khnopff has clipped one of its wings, on the left, but has added a poppy and echoed the wing on the right with a wing in real feathers in a strange gradation of blues. Khnopff returned to this theme in 1894 (or thereabouts) with a smaller, vertical panel entitled *Blue wing* in which the poppy has disappeared and the bust now stands in the foreground as a still life.[43] [92] In a work from 1901, *White, black and gold* (Brussels, Musées royaux des Beaux-Arts de Belgique), the bust is set in an identical composition but the brow is now decorated with wavy locks of hair parted in the middle and the face is more masculine, similar to that of a classical ephebe.[44] Lastly, a

92 Fernand Khnopff, *Blue wing*, 1894, private collection

pastel from 1909 (private collection) shows the bust on a sandy beach with a crow perching on it and, in the distance, a cliff and the sea against a very hazy sky. The head seems to be floating on a mirror of smooth water.[45]

A similar process of transformation and repetition can be observed in the history of the polychrome mask of a woman's face that Khnopff made and displayed in his house. The first version, in ivory, bronze and enamel, was exhibited at the Exposition Congolaise in Brussels-Tervuren in 1897. Several others are mentioned but we cannot be sure of the materials, in spite of the photographs taken by Arsène Alexandre at Khnopff's behest. It would appear that for Khnopff polychrome plaster was an object of real veneration. Photographs of his home show the work affixed at the top of a thin Corinthian column, sometimes surmounted by a single flower, a bouquet, palms or a vase, like offerings to a goddess in an ancient temple. The same cult is apparent in the two pastels entitled *Secret* (1902, Bruges, Groeningemuseum, and c. 1902, Ghent, private collection) in which we see a young woman (Marguerite Khnopff, the artist's beloved sister) in the robe of a vestal virgin, respectfully touching the mask. [137] It is clear here that polychromy does not strengthen the mimetic quality of the work or bring it closer to reality, but, on the contrary, establishes a distance, endowing it with 'a little more soul,' a mysterious and undefinable interiority. The hypnotic aspect of the mask, its perfect frontality, its preciousness, make it the object of an idolatrous veneration. From now on, the role of colour is to represent the soul.

Reproduction

What is most striking here, as in the short story by Jean Lorrain, is that the work that inspires love is anything but an original. It is a copy, a cast, one that has been transformed by the application of modern colour: in other words, it is an adulterated object which no longer deserves to be called a 'work of art.' This adoration of a copy, as opposed to an original work, is a theme that occurs in a large number of symbolist texts. This is to be contrasted with the status of white marble as the noble material *par excellence* at the beginning of the 19th century, when the idea of revering plaster would have been considered a perversion.

The most famous case (in the pathological sense of the word) is that of Norbert Hanold, the young hero of Wilhelm Jensen's *Gradiva*.[46] This short story enjoyed considerable success when it was published in 1903 and, as a result of the brilliant interpretation written by Freud in 1907, is the only one of Jensen's works still read today. The hero is a young German archaeologist with a passion for ancient Greek and Roman art and literature who falls in love with a young girl represented on an ancient relief. Since she walks with an airy step, he calls her 'Gradiva,' which means 'the girl who steps along.' The hero's love for sculpture leads him to overlook real women and to love only marble or bronze statues: 'Hitherto, the female sex had been to him no more than the concept of something made of marble or bronze, and he had never paid the slightest attention to its contemporary representatives. [...] He considered marble and bronze not as lifeless matter, but as the only thing that was truly alive.'[47] When he dreams, he dreams of antique sculptures: 'he dreamt that he was in Pompeii the day Vesuvius erupted [...] and, in the middle of the confusion, he saw the Apollo Belvedere carry away the Venus from the Capitol, then put her down in a dark corner, out of harm's way.' However, the hero is in love not with an original but with a reproduction – the plaster cast he has installed in his study. Moreover, not only does the fascinating exchange of letters between

Freud and Jensen tells us that the writer himself possessed a cast of this relief, but photographs indicate that Freud too had hung a cast of the *Gradiva* on his own wall. Hanold dreams of meeting Gradiva, and his desire leads him to Pompeii, where he encounters a young girl whom he takes for the ghost of a Roman who was buried and killed in the eruption of Vesuvius in 79 B.C. It is some time before he realises that this young woman is actually alive, that she is one of his contemporaries, is in fact his neighbour and childhood playmate. *Gradiva* is thus the story of a statue which, through a particular state of awareness, by a mental operation on the part of the beholder, becomes a real woman. The marble becomes flesh, but only because it was flesh to begin with, and above all because it has been plaster. The process described here is a reversal of sculptural creation.[48]

In this situation, it is as if the reproduction were the necessary transition between reality and art. The first step is to appropriate the work by possessing its reproduction. The next stage is to transform it by the application of polychromy. It is an intriguing paradox: the artist coats the work of art with paint in the belief that this is an act of respect. What, then, is the difference between veneration and degradation? This is the theme of the Jean Lorrain novel, for the aesthetic propriety of the Donatello cast is violently contested, first by a visitor who denigrates it because he believes that Lorrain has degraded it, and then by the body of the statue itself which comes to haunt the apartment and demand its lost head.

This veneration of non-noble materials and advocacy of polychromy, together with the use of multicoloured combinations of diverse materials, are salient characteristics of the symbolist aesthetic. Its practitioners delighted in provocative reversals of the prevailing dogma, proclaiming, as did the young Laforgue in a text that would have made a fine manifesto of symbolist sculpture, that: 'above a bust in marble or bronze, I place, for example, this bust in wax, with blue or black eyes, red or bloodless lips, hair and ornament, etc.'[49]

Wax

For wax was indeed the Symbolists' favourite material. It fascinated them as a kind of intermediary between human skin and marble. Its colour, its capacity to hold pigment (either on its surface or by dying) made it ideally mimetic. Although it hardened, this was not irreversible. It could recover all the malleability and suppleness of skin. And the fact that it melts added to its charm as a paradigm of possible decomposition. We are a long way here from changeless marble. Not only is wax not a noble material, it is also and above all a material that is liable to deteriorate, able to materialise the ambiguous relationship between real and artificial flesh, to accomplish the metamorphosis from one to the other. It is abundantly present in both symbolist sculpture and literature.

Rachilde, the sulphurous woman writer of the fin de siècle, used these properties in her notorious novel *Monsieur Vénus*.[50] Its heroine, the beautiful Raoule de Vénérande, has a dual, androgynous sexuality, and is in love with a young man of weak character named Jacques Silvert. In the end she kills him, removing from the corpse the nails and teeth she needs to make a surrogate, 'a wax mannequin covered with a transparent rubber epidermis.' Silvert is immediately compared to a sculpture. Rachilde calls him 'the Antinous of Montparnasse' because of his beauty and lower class origin. And so the process of degradation begins. Not surprisingly, before it is transformed into a waxwork, the lover's body is described in terms of sculpture: 'Worthy of Venus Callipyge, the small of the back where the line of the spine disappeared in a voluptuous plane then rose, firm and plump in two adorable mounds, had the amber transparency of Paros marble.' To this can be added the metallic connotation of the character's name, a French phonetic adaptation of the English 'silver.'[51]

While we know little about the relation between another writer, the poet Maurice Rollinat, and the wax moulder Jean-Désiré Ringel d'Illzach, this may have had something to do with their shared love of wax figures. Certainly, Ringel d'Illzach made a polychrome wax mask of Rollinat (Strasbourg, Musée d'art moderne et contemporain), whose poem *La dame en cire* evokes a voyeur's fascination with wax models:

> Watching the mannequin turn around
> I was admiring her waist, her breast,
> Her golden hair and mischievous face,
> When I saw her nostrils quiver
> As did her thin viperine neck.
> 'So she is alive!' I said, aghast:
> And since then, haunted at each moment
> By a love that nothing can slay
> I am afraid and curious
> To see the wax lady enter my home.[52]

Jean Lorrain was also fascinated by waxes and wrote a text about one of Ringel d'Illzach's coloured pieces, *Young Medici prince*. [93] Many of the writer's characters also own wax figures. The best known is the English painter Lord Ethal, the hero of *Monsieur de Phocas*, a collector of wax dolls and busts whose penchant for emerald eyes we have already observed. In Leiden, Ethal buys 'a doll' which is in reality 'a wax model representing a young girl of about 13 years old, life-size [with] heavy clothes thickly inlaid with embroideries, silk arabesques and flourishes

of pearls.' Lorrain indulgently emphasises the morbidity of the theme, pointing out that the doll has 'that appearance of an embalmed body common to all wax figures. Ethal's eyes glittered intently as he looked fondly and caressingly over the livid transparencies and dulled pinks of that factitious flesh.' The second piece in his collection corresponds to the work by Ringel: 'the head of an adolescent with a prominent nose, the chin cleft by pressure from the thumb, with a striking expression of energy in the bulging forehead and the protuberant arches of the eyebrows above deep-set eyes: the distressing and suffering face of a tragic child, a mute and obstinate head, handsome in the silence of its fine, full lips. The greenish pallor of this thin, foolish, yet stubborn face further accentuated the bitterness of the mouth. Above, in a coat of arms, three tear-shaped pearls: the three pills of the Medici.'[53]

The waxes of Henry Cros also held a considerable fascination for many novelists and poets, including Alexandre Dumas *fils*, who commissioned a number of busts from him, François Coppée, of whom Cros made a wax portrait, and José-Maria de Heredia, who was the owner of *La Belle Viole* (location unknown) and *Isabeau de Bavière* (1875, Paris, Musée d'Orsay). Cros's brother, incidentally, was the poet and inventor Charles. But the only person to have actually written on Cros's art is Jules Laforgue, who owned a number of his waxes and lent two of them to the exhibition of polychrome sculpture held in Berlin in 1885. In 1884 he published an enthusiastic review of Cros's book on wax.[54] Praising the final chapter, entitled 'Notre pratique personnelle,' he urged 'artists to take a look and have a try [...] one senses that there are great possibilities [...] at this decisive moment when circumstances make it urgent to rejuvenate, to reinvent our decorative arts.' He recommended that they follow in the footsteps of this 'delicate wax-maker who has the sincerity of a primitive.'[55] Huysmans also made a bold statement of his predilection for wax sculptures, but then went even further when, considering the mannequins in the windows of couturiers' shops, which have absolutely no artistic pretensions, he exclaims: 'How superior to the dreary statues of Venus are these lively dressmaker's dummies.'[56]

Metamorphosis

In his *Journal*, Edmond de Goncourt describes a visit to Henry Cros: 'He is an extremely thin, dark and bearded young fellow with an unsettling fixity in his deep-set eyes. And, after a while,

93 Jean-Désiré Ringel d'Illzach, *Young Medici prince*, c. 1890, wax, Strasbourg, Musée d'art moderne et contemporain

that glowing lamp, those little bits of wax that looked like small bits of flesh in their cigar boxes [...] filled me with a kind of dread of the magical life cooked up in that cave by that pallid boy.'[57] Goncourt makes clear the ambiguity of the wax as flesh and the artist as alchemist.

This uncertain boundary between flesh and the material of sculpture, the permanent possibility of the transition from one to the other, is a constant of the symbolist imagination. Countless novels, short stories and poems describe this creative transition whereby a statue metamorphoses into a real woman or vice versa, producing indefinable creatures who are neither women nor statues, or are both at the same time, and who drive those who approach them mad with love. It is clear that the fictions based on this ambiguity draw on ancient sources. One need only mention the much-studied Pygmalion myth and its variants. In the second half of the 19th century, its most famous representations are the sculptures of Jean-Léon Gérôme and the paintings of Edward Burne-Jones.[58] [47 55 56]

As for the novel, the most disturbing work on this theme is undoubtedly Auguste de Villiers de l'Isle Adam's *L'Eve future*, begun in 1877 and published in its complete and definitive form in 1886. Its hero, Lord Ewald, loves the body of his mistress, the singer Alicia Clary, but finds her soul stupid. The text is laden with sculptural comparisons. Confiding in the scientist Edison, Ewald tells him that Alicia's 'body offers an ensemble of lines that would surprise even the greatest sculptors [...] In truth, it is the splendour of the Venus Victrix made human [...] her feet have the same elegance as the Greek marbles.' And when he shows Edison a photograph of Alicia, his friend exclaims: 'Remarkable!... it is indeed the famous VENUS by the unknown sculptor! [...] it is more than remarkable, it is truly astounding!' The trouble is that Alicia talks a great deal and utters only inanities. 'When Alicia stopped speaking, her face [...], her marble, which had remained divine [the expression 'divine marble' occurs frequently here] contradicted the fading language [...] the incompatibility of the physical and the intellectual made itself felt constantly and in paradoxical proportions [...] On the outside – and from the forehead to the toes – a kind of Venus Anadyomene: within, a personality that was utterly FOREIGN to this body.'

For Lord Ewald, a beautiful woman should be neither stupid nor even intelligent: 'If she were completely without thought, I could understand her. The marble Venus has no need of thought. The goddess is veiled by her mineral silence. The Word that issues forth from her appearance is this: "I am only Beauty itself. I think only through the mind of the beholder."' And Ewald concludes his confession with the exclamation: 'Ah! Who will remove the soul from this body.' His desire is to create woman without a soul, a woman who is purely material. Her name will be Hadaly, which is Persian for 'ideal.' And if Ewald is constantly comparing Alicia to the *Venus de Milo*, which wrenches sobs of ecstasy from him each time he sees it in the Louvre, Hadaly will be no marble statue but a veritable chryselephantine composition of gold, silver, steel, ivory and crystal. At the same time, the 'epidermis' created for her by Edison will be made of a special material that is supple, warm and alive like human skin. In order to prove this, the scientist presents Hadaly to Lord Ewald without forewarning. Not even Ewald's sense of touch can detect that Hadaly has replaced the real Alicia, whom he believes is still standing there before him.

At the beginning of the novel, when Ewald visits the scientist, he touches an object that is lying on the table: 'a human arm placed on a cushion of purplish silk [...] It was the left arm and hand of a young woman. [...] The tint of the flesh had remained so lifelike, the skin was so pure and silky that its appearance was both cruel and fantastical.'[59] It is this 'bloom' that Edison will use to complete Hadaly. As he explains, 'This flesh, which lends itself to the penetration of caloric warmth [...] offers to the touch the marvellous impression, the vigorous, smooth elasticity of Life. [...] Showing through just as it should, its brightness softened by the epidermis, its hue is that of snow tinted with the smoke of amber and pale roses, with a vague shine that comes from a small dose of powdered asbestos. A photochromic effect then saturates it with its definitive tone.'[60] A similar revelation occurs when Norbert Hanold's hand touches that of Gradiva and senses something living: 'rather than thin air, his hand came up against – not something hard and cold, but a real, warm, living hand.' In Villiers's novel, we witness the creation of a veritable polychrome sculpture which is supposed to resemble an antique marble, but which ends up becoming the simulacrum of a real woman.

One of Villiers's biographers, his cousin Robert du Pontavice de Heussey, claimed that the writer based his tale on the true story of a young English aristocrat who, not long after he met him, killed himself beside a wax effigy of his fiancée. The figure had been modelled by a great sculptor after a woman of outstanding beauty. One notes the interesting transition from wax figure to chryselephantine.[61]

Was the work of Ringel d'Illzach influenced by Villiers's novel? We are aware from contemporary photographs of the allegories created by the former in 1901-02: *War*, *Victory* and *Defeat*. These are extraordinarily sophisticated polychrome busts with wax faces and wooden frames supporting a composite metal armour of bronze, copper, tin, zinc, brass, iron and lead, and decorated with rock crystal and agglomerated enamels. This irresistibly brings to mind the work of Edison, the mad scientist in his mysterious den.

The comparison of the colourist and sculptor to an alchemist also occurs frequently in the writings of critics and artists. Defending his experiments with ceramics, Gauguin argued that 'God made man with a bit of mud. With a bit of mud, one can make metal, precious stones, with a bit of mud and a bit of genius! Surely, then, this a most worthwhile material?'[62] Praising the remarkable and colourful innovations of Emile Gallé, one critic wrote that 'An artist such as Gallé makes one think of an extractor of quintessences who had tried to materialise the impalpable and to vitrify dreams.'[63] And another, that 'The alchemy of this "forger and lapidary" metamorphoses vitreous substance into precious stones.'[64] What the Symbolists did to the aesthetic of sculpture was indeed to transform it in the alchemical sense of the word. Their use of paint, ornament and colour to represent the soul ultimately overturned the traditional, moral conception of the human body. Perhaps the most apposite definition of the aesthetic of symbolist sculpture can be found in Alphonse de Germain's description of the work of Henry Cros, in which: 'Colour heightens the mystery and spiritualises matter. [...] For the aesthete, the transmutation achieved by the alchemist in his crucibles is but the cement of his ideal, a precious means of representing his dreams; he etherealises the tangible and makes tangible the immaterial.'[65]

June Hargrove

Painter-sculptors and polychromy in the evolution of modernism

No century prior to the 19th saw such an abundance of artists who oscillated between painting and sculpture.[1] While great exceptions jump to mind – Michelangelo, Bernini – only in the 19th century did such cross-overs become routine practice.[2] This fostered a dynamic exchange between the arts, stimulating innovative hybrids that were to modify irrevocably the definition of art. Fundamental to this was the reintroduction of colour and of mixed media into the fine art of sculpture.

Although numerous artists embraced the trend to enhance sculpture, through multiplicity of hue or substance, among the most intrepid practitioners of polychromy were the painters who delved into sculpture. Receptive to colour, they boasted little formal training in sculpture to compromise an open mind. If anything, they shared a vision of polychromy as a vehicle of change. Their attitudes toward the use of colour and of mixing materials manifest an autonomy at once eccentric and pragmatic that anticipates modernism.[3]

More willing to jettison their era's preconceptions, the painter-sculptors provided the springboard for the 20th century. A hint of their audacity can be gleaned from remembering the recent case of David Smith, whose painting was ruthlessly eradicated from his sculpture after his death.[4] And a measure of their triumph can be seen in the work of an artist like Robert Rauschenberg, whose collaborations with John Cage dissolve the barriers between painting and sculpture, music and the visual arts, poetry and dance, striving for a total synthesis.[5]

Focusing on the painter-sculptors, this short essay privileges the use of polychromy as an attack on the status quo. The transnational dialogue that precipitated the widespread popularity of coloured sculpture in the 1890s occurred a decade earlier among artists of the avant-garde. They benefitted from ties between them at the generative stages of their ideas. Seeking to escape from the limitations of creativity foisted onto them by an oppressive establishment, these artists were attuned to an art uninhibited by convention. Their quest for expressive freedom tapped into the revival of polychrome sculpture, revealing a fresh potential for colour, which they manipulated in their experiments with unorthodox materials, including those relegated to the minor arts.

They were pioneers of the larger trend to prospect the interconnectedness of the arts that gained momentum through the Symbolists, who assimilated emerging principles of synaesthesia into their program. The Symbolist's speculation on equivalency within the arts strengthened the belief in the unity of the arts, inherited from the Romantics. Consequently colour acquired an urgency that transcended the decorous premise for a harmonious ensemble to become an integral component of an environment where the aesthetic fusion of the formal elements conveyed the spiritual complexity of the total work of art.

Resistance to polychromy in statuary lingered after mid-century despite mounting evidence to the contrary. For sculptors, the process from inception to completion was labour intensive, and traditional materials necessitated an arduous training if the piece was to survive the numerous stages of realisation. So deeply engrained was the hierarchy of marble and bronze that very few professional sculptors were willing to risk applying colour to their serious, large-scale works bound for exhibition. As Jean-Léon Gérôme later recalled, 'anyone who would have ventured to suggest that many [ancient sculptures], if not all, were tinted and sometimes really coated with paint would have been considered mad – a man of pitiful taste.'[6] The monochromatic ideal dominated the Salons, an exclusionist agenda that stiffled any attempt to deviate from the norm. Even a nonconformist as inventive as Rodin rarely pushed polychromy beyond various patinas. Small wonder then that transgressions against the entrenched aesthetic came from outside the mainstream of the metier.

Although the Romantics had advocated innovation at any price, their attitudes, more than any body of work, were central to the breakdown of traditional hierarchies that tacitly encouraged arbitrary combinations of materials and techniques. They encouraged a taste for the historical and the exotic, closely aligned with the decorative arts.

The Romantic propensity for intertwined media laid the foundation for the sundry theories about the unity of the arts that were to proliferate in the second half of the century. The ideas of Richard Wagner about the artwork of the future, what came to be called the *gesamtkunstwerk*, served as the global touchstone for an avant-garde obsessed with the total work of art. Implicit in this yearning is the contextual foundation for the promotion of polychrome sculpture.

The influence of the English Arts and Crafts Movement on fashionable decors accelerated the taste for polychrome sculpture. William Morris extended the aesthetics of John Ruskin and the Pre-Raphaelite Brotherhood into a theory of design that encompassed the notion of a harmonious environment, wherein the arts conspired to achieve a unified spiritual and aesthetic effect.

The revival of the styles of the Middle Ages and the Renaissance went beyond the obvious elements of historicism – subject and detail – to lend itself to a heightened awareness of technique. The renewed admiration for polychromy was reinforced by the predilection for richly coloured interiors. The imitation of historical objects in mixed media encouraged new combinations with metal, ivory, stones, and the like. The insistence on the handmade, reacting against the products of the Industrial Revolution, promoted a freely handled surface that authenticated the object's originality. This validation of the traces of the artist's presence filtered into the thinking of the avant-garde. Morris's fervent disapproval of the mechanical was matched by a preference for materials not subjugated to the prejudices of academic art, hence the amplification of the status of the decorative arts.[7] The dictums pronounced by Morris resonated across the Continent, meshing with parallel concepts advanced by Viollet-le-Duc and Wagner.[8]

The artist who did the most to translate Morris's ideas into visual terms was Edward Burne-Jones. Primarily a painter, a disciple of the Pre-Raphaelite circle, Burne-Jones was much admired for his retrospective, soulful scenes from legends enacted by languid androgens. He collaborated extensively with Morris and Company on decorative ensembles, providing designs resembling his paintings. Partial to the technique of *gessoduro*, his polychrome reliefs established a precedent that was quickly copied by younger sculptors.[9] In the *Feeding of the dragon in the Garden of the Hesperides* (London, Victoria and Albert Museum), the silver and gold background in combination with the naturalistic coloration of the figures and the details accentuates the other worldly atmosphere that gave his art its widespread appeal.

Burne-Jones maintained an exhibition record of truly international scope, promoting the aesthetic of the Arts and Crafts across the Continent. Not only was his painting a source for both the subjects and the style of the next generation, he offered a pivotal example of a painter who actively participated in the creation of sculpture.

Meanwhile in France, a similar flirtation with the past animated a vogue for coloured waxes. Touted in lectures, articles, and exhibitions, historical pieces were prized by museums and collectors alike. Trained as a painter, Henry Cros saw the pictorial possibilities of the medium, which he saturated in warm hues.[10] He chose subjects, like the *Tournament prize* [94], that emulate his technical prototypes, rendering chivalresque themes in a medievalising style. Cros's nostalgic vignettes have more in common with the Pre-Raphaelites, whose insistence on the handmade encouraged his sketchy handling of the wax overall.[11] In any event this soft-focus effect belies the influence of the photographic experiments of his brother.[12]

Although Henry Cros has been marginalised as decorative, he was a conspicuous presence, with his brother, the poet Charles Cros, in the avant-garde circles of his day. At the Nouvelle Athènes, a hotbed for nascent symbolist theories, the pair were often in the company of Manet, Duranty, and Degas, among others,

94 Henry Cros, *Tournament prize*, 1873, wax, Paris, Musée d'Orsay

including symbolist poets.[13] Besides their artistic pursuits, both were inventors, Henry rediscovering the lost techniques of encaustic and of *pâte de verre*, while Charles pioneered in the areas of colour photography and the phonograph.[14] Their mutual concern with colour was part of a larger philosophy of the interrelatedness of the arts. No doubt encouraged by their friend Charles Henry, they actively espoused the notions of synaesthesia fundamental to the aesthetics of Symbolism. Not only did they believe in the reciprocity among all of the arts – notably music, poetry, and the visual arts – but also with the sciences. To promote these ideas in 1874 Charles edited a new journal, the *Revue du Monde Nouveau. Littéraire, Artistique, Scientifique*.

In 1884, after 15 years, Henry Cros published the results of his historical and technical research on wax, *L'encaustique et les autres procédés de peinture chez les anciens*, in collaboration with Charles Henry. The latter, a physiologist and mathematician, was acknowledged by the Symbolists for his theories about a scientific foundation for aesthetics, one that explained how artistic components trigger emotional responses.[15]

Seeking to find a more durable medium, Cros revived in 1883 a forgotten ancient method of casting coloured-glass paste, the so-called *pâte de verre* technique. [12–16] For him, the historical sources were inseparable from the conceptualisation of his work. Inevitably the change in materials entailed a corresponding shift in subjects, away from medieval pageants to classicising allegories in the spirit of the Parnassian poets, such as the *Incantation*.[16] [12] These pastel reliefs are sheathed in a muted veil that imbues them with a dreamlike atmosphere. Exhibited at the Salons with his more traditional paintings and sculptures, which he never abandoned, his wax and his glass objects render meaningless the distinctions drawn between the fine and decorative arts.

Undeniably wax figures had long been modelled by painters as a compositional device. The example of Ernest Meissonier proves how polished and precise such tools could be. His polychrome equestrian *Voyager*, complete with its detailed bridle and its cloth cape billowing in the tempest, asserts the perfectionism for which Meissonier was famous. [95] Although the *Voyager* corresponds to sketches from as early as 1878, his sculptures remained studio props, unknown to the public until the retrospective exhibitions after his death in 1891. Despite their attraction for Degas, who admired these waxes for their studied craftsmanship, they did not contribute to the use of wax as a definitive medium.[17]

A more persuasive candidate as a stimulus for Degas to explore the expressive range of wax was Henry Cros, whom he knew personally. Cros must have introduced Degas to the technique of encaustic, which prompted the latter to add wax intermittently to his pastels.[18] Precisely when and why Degas began to

95   Ernest Meissonier, *The voyager*, 1878, wax, textile, metal and leather, Paris, Musée d'Orsay

model in wax remains the subject of a debate in which the *Little dancer of 14 years*, exhibited in 1881, offers the only fixed point. [68] The related drawings suggest that Degas conceived his statue sometime around 1878.

The *Little dancer*, quite innocuous to modern eyes, was seditious, if not downright prurient, from the perspective of her contemporaries. She smacked of a pseudoscience borrowed from anthropological specimens, such as those seen at the 1878 Exposition Universelle, a case study drawn from the France of the Third Republic. Her vocation as a ballerina trapped her in a web of circumstances that made inevitable the fruition of the degeneration stamped on her face. To a society convinced of Darwinian social evolution, she had the unmistakeable aura of incipient adolescent vice, a fact that Degas emphasised by juxtaposing her at the Salon des Indépendants to his pastel *Physionomies de criminels*.[19]

The modernity of the *Little dancer* stemmed as much from the deliberately mundane materials as from the subject matter, prosaic to the point of the perverse in more ways than one. Mocking the prestige of marble, the wax figure dons the signifiers of her trade – the tutu and ballet slippers. The use of real hair and clothes vests the resolutely unidealised little dancer in truth, without fussing over illusionistic handling.[20] The realism is not of surface but of effect – impressionist in the way his paintings are. That is to say concerned with modernity in ways that inextricably weld the subject to the materials. Standing on a wooden plinthe, alluding to the stage, the dancer is observed in her natural habitat, denying the distance between art and life.

Degas was not exactly indifferent to technique, rather he was impatient with prescribed methods, even at the expense of his creations. Fascinated with technical novelties, he was always fiddling with the process of making art.[21] The loose surfaces characteristic of his style in two and in three dimensions may reflect this restlessness. His curiosity spilled from one medium to the next, so that the conceptual basis of his creative productions goes beyond the question of common subjects. They share the same motivation, to find a means of expression that served as a cutting-edge for the topical slice of modern life.

The step taken by Degas was so extreme in its renunciation of the condoned criteria for serious sculpture that it could only have been taken by someone outside the metier properly speaking. However indebted he was to the Mediterranean custom of dressing the polychrome effigy in real fabric and jewels, his use of wax and real accessories was intended from the onset to tweak the pretensions of the ordained authorities. Whatever opinion of himself as a sculptor that Degas may have harboured, he was not hampered by the professional biases of the *statuaire*.

Although Degas's insurrection was to leave a legacy in the 20th century to such artists as Duane Hanson, only a few of his peers rose to the challenge.[22] His influence on Medardo Rosso was initially indirect. The Italian artist found the immediate impetus for his art in the Milanese movement of the Scapigliatura, whose name means dishevelment or bohemian. This circle of rebellious painters, writers, and composers imitated the French example of breaking with the past through a similar insistence on the ephemeral appearances of everyday life. Among the earliest in Italy to revere Wagner, they based their goal of creating a synaesthetic experience in art – i.e., pictorial sculpture, musical painting – on his concept of the *gesamtkunstwerk*.[23]

This fusion of the arts is at the core of Rosso's aesthetic, wherein 'les limites qui séparent la peinture de la sculpture n'existent pas.'[24] Although he abandoned painting early on, that experience led him to react against the isolated mass in space. The Scapigliatura paintings of Daniele Ranzoni and Tranquillo Cremona gave Rosso the insight 'for blurring the outline, attenuating the edges of intersecting planes and creating a vibrant light and atmosphere [...].'[25]

The French were no doubt critical to awakening in Rosso the potential of wax as he pushed beyond the studio practice of altering a plaster cast with wax. The achievements of Degas and Cros were well known in Italy.[26] And Rosso openly acknowledged his debt to Baudelaire's assertion 'that painting was superior to sculpture because painting has but one possible point of view.'[27] Hence his obsession to establish a fixed link between the viewer and the sculpture in order to dissolve the boundaries between them through the dynamic interaction of light and form.

The turning point seems to have been around 1883, when Rosso exhibited works like the *Flesh of others*, where the prosti-

96 Max Klinger, *The judgment of Paris*, 1883, Vienna, Kunsthistorisches Museum

tute seems to putrefy, devoured by vice, at the very moment she is glimpsed. [76] The suggestion of a mass disappearing into the atmosphere reinforces the impression of a fleeting moment. The choice of a prostitute as a subject suggests a familiarity with French art, if not Degas.

Degas's sketchy surfaces anticipate the way that bits of wax in Rosso's compositions catch the light. Such free handling bears a superficial rapport with impressionist paintings that is deceptive.[28] The dissolution of form in Impressionism results from the pursuit of colour and light, whereas Rosso's goal is to disperse the form in space through manipulating light and colour. He sought to liberate sculpture by counteracting the customary insistence on mass. In his modelling, Rosso aimed to surpass 'les plus vigoureux effets des plus audacieux coloristes.'[29] His fascination with the coloration of his wax models, which had no imitative basis, paralleled his interest in the infinite variety of patinas possible with bronze.[30] After several lengthy visits, Rosso settled in Paris in 1889 to be near kindred spirits, who rejected dogmatic categories.[31]

The propensity to focus on Paris as the hub of the art world, however justified its pre-eminence, obscures the multiple points of contact around the periphery. Not to mention the reverberations back to Paris. The cosmopolitan Max Klinger formulated the essence of his aesthetic credo in the 1880s, while living intermittently in the French capital. Whereas the sojourns indubitably helped shape his thinking, his role in formulating a progressive philosophy of polychromy as integral to the synthesis of the arts has been given little consideration outside of Germany.

A painter well-known for his graphic art, Klinger was attracted to polychromy as a means of liberating German sculpture from the artists and critics who held sway over the established order.[32] During his 1883 trip to France, he implemented the *Judgment of Paris* [96], wherein the painting incorporated trompe l'oeil architecture and sculpture with the actual structure of a sculpted frame. At the same time he carried out the decor of the vestibule of the Villa Albers in Berlin. With these two projects, he refined his thoughts about the relationship among the arts, which he christened 'Raumkunst.'[33] In spite of the plastic dimension of his goal, Klinger articulated his theories under the title of *Malerei und Zeichnung*, first published in 1885 in Leipzig.[34]

Derived from the union of the arts exalted by Wagner and the *gesamtkunstwerk*, Klinger went beyond the fashion for a harmoniously coordinated environment. Without specifying exactly how this goal was to be achieved, his *raumkunst* was aimed at the soul, plumbing the depths of human existence.[35] In the symbolist vein, Klinger dismissed the mimetic function of colour, giving priority to its emotional and aesthetic resonance.[36] That said, his painting was always more realistic in colour than his sculpture.

He embedded colour in a three-dimensional continuum that no sculptor had yet dared suggest.

From Paris in 1883 and 1885-1887, Klinger maintained a lively correspondence with his friends in Berlin, including Jules Laforgue.[37] Although Klinger claimed to be leading a solitary life, it is inconceivable that he did not arrive with letters of introduction to Laforgue's friends, such as Henry Cros.[38] One of Klinger's closest friends was the Danish author and critic Georg Brandes, the brother-in-law of Gauguin, which makes some encounter seem probable.[39]

With his own theories of *raumkunst* in progress, Klinger would have been drawn to those individuals who were exploring similar concepts. Even in the unlikely event that he were ignorant of Charles Henry's *audition colorée*, he was surrounded by a milieu in which such ideas were the subject of animated polemics. The young German hardly needed to go to Paris to reinforce his attraction to the ideas of Wagner – who was also born in Leipzig – but he arrived at a critical moment when the French were falling under the composer's thrall. (The *Revue Wagnérienne* was founded in 1886.) Their sophisticated application of these ideas to theories about equivalencies within the arts must have magnified his esteem for his compatriot.

Embryonic symbolist theories equating colours with musical tones are at the heart of Klinger's account of the inspiration for his *Beethoven Monument*. [62] He claims to have envisioned this homage to musical genius while he was himself at the piano.[40] If one follows the transmedia dialogue, this theme recurs in his prints, as in the *Brahmsphantasie Opus XII*, where music, inspiration, and the artist meet in an irrational atmosphere that was a hallmark of Klinger's symbolism. The bizarre imagery of his graphic art betrays the subliminal malaise underlying his entire oeuvre.

By the summer of 1886, Klinger had finished the model for the *Beethoven Monument* in plaster which he painted, visualising the definitive version in more lavish substances. He had also sketched the *New Salome* before leaving France, but his visibility as a sculptor prior to finishing it in marble in Rome in 1893 is uncertain.[41] [43] What is indisputable is his early role both practising and preaching a gospel of polychromy. Had any of Klinger's polychrome endeavours been finalised sooner after its conception, he would have pre-empted Gérôme in introducing monumental polychrome sculpture, free of the decorative or the exotic, at the Salon.[42]

When the *Beethoven Monument* was finally realised for the 1902 exhibition of the Vienna Secession it fulfilled his ideal of *raumkunst*.[43] Of course by this time, the synthesis of the arts was a widely-held creed, whatever the terminology bestowed upon it by a particular group. The inauguration in the Secession Hall

97 The 'Orpheus wall' in the music room of the Villa Stuck, Munich

rotunda, decorated with a frieze by Gustav Klimt, was celebrated with the fourth movement of the Ninth Symphony, itself a testament to the symbiosis of music and poetry.[44] [63]

Realism was the last thing he sought. The multicoloured marble and bronze statue is neither a reconstruction of antique polychromy nor an attempt to render a lifelike resemblance of the great composer; on the contrary, it is the deification of genius.[45] The multiplicity of materials, united in the form of a cult statue, is synomymous with the protean gifts of Beethoven. The materials were intended to augment the meaning of the image, but their insistent presence vies with the illusion in disturbing ways. Subsequently confused with a retardataire Neo-classicism, the *Beethoven Monument* aimed for a radical synaesthesia that transcended convention – not because polychromy was any longer perceived as inimical to the Antique but because Klinger conceived it in symbolist terms that were anti-academic.

Despite the honoured position Klinger enjoyed at the Vienna Secession, he had few imitators, in part because his balance of Classicism and Symbolism was too precarious to sustain. However, his doctrine of *raumkunst* supplied a rationale for ensuing environments, such as those realised by Stuck, Khnopff, and Gauguin, meaningful to the individual through their artistic and spiritual coherence.

Franz von Stuck, another painter-sculptor, designed a secessionist villa for himself in neo-antique taste in Munich at the end of the century.[46] Stuck knew Klinger personally, perhaps through their mutual friend, Arnold Böcklin. The polychrome interiors of the villa aspire to the philosophical import that Klinger loaded into the space of the total work of art. There is a quasi-religious atmosphere from the painting, sculpture, and architecture, bound together through colour, that climaxes with the artistic altars that the owner dedicated to himself. The sculpted polychrome elements are the by-product of the painter's desire to meld the arts into an ensemble that functions as his temple of creation. [97]

Fernand Khnopff pursued the morose elegance of his idol, Burne-Jones, with an edge that cut deeper into the theoretical core of Symbolism vaunted by the Continental artists. He learned the technique of *gessoduro* in 1891, probably from George Frampton on one of many trips to England.[47] The British *Mysteriarch* (Liverpool, Walker Art Gallery) served as the prototype for his *Sibyl*, personifying a mute but knowing oracle by the idealised bust of a woman placed against a circular backdrop. [98] His goal in colouring the plaster was not to render forms more lifelike but to exploit the ambiguity between sculpture and painting as a metaphor for art and reality.[48] The sculpted imagery reappears in his paintings, such as *Incense* (Tokyo, Art Point), that often redound with synaesthetic evocations of sound or smell.[49] His

98 Fernand Khnopff, *Sibyl*, 1894, tinted photograph, Brussels, Bibliothèque royale Albert Ier, Cabinet des Estampes

99 Fernand Khnopff, *Vivien*, 1896, plaster, painted, Vienna, Österreichische Galerie Belvedere

palette is consistent, with figures of unhealthy pallor, exacerbated by wan complements of silvery blue and orange.

The Belgian artist became friends with Stuck in 1894, when he exhibited with the Munich Secession.[50] The assumption that he was familiar with Klinger's work, perhaps through Stuck, seems plausible, if for no other reason than the striking resemblance of the *Vivien* to the *Cassandra*.[51] [99 114] By extension, Klinger's *raumkunst*, via Stuck's design, may have been the catalyst for the house that Khnopff built four years later in 1901. The Munich studio featured an homage to Athena that was a precedent for the one in Brussels in tribute to Hypnos.[52] Dear to Khnopff, the bust of Hypnos metamorphosises through his oeuvre, inspiring countless variations in sculpture and painting, as in the *Blue wing*, eventually achieving the status of a household icon. [92] The unremitting recurrence of motifs – in paintings, sculptures, and photographs – culminates in this abode where the artist hovers between art and reality. Khnopff substitutes the neurasthenic sensitivities of an aristocrat for those of a self-professed savage, but his creative preoccupations betray an ego no less narcissistic than that of Gauguin.

The artist's oeuvre as the ultimate total work of art was the achievement of that most truculent of innovators, Paul Gauguin. He charted his own idiosyncratic course on a path that intersected with these same circles. In the summer of 1879 he began to frequent the Nouvelle Athènes, where he must have encountered the brothers Cros and their friends among the Impressionists and symbolist poets who gathered there. He gravitated to Degas, whose *Little dancer* sparked the bust of his son *Clovis*, rendered in painted wax and wood (private collection).[53]

Even as Gauguin borrowed specific motifs of ballerinas from Degas's paintings for his enigmatic *Wooden box* (private collection), he was moving in the direction of Symbolism. The inscrutable figures and faces accompanying the straightforward images of the dancers anticipates his subsequent irrational mélanges.[54] The way the box is made – carved and assembled, with its colour – red stain plus the diverse matter of the parts, is proof of a style germinating from the outset of the artist's career.

Around this same time, Gauguin summarised his thoughts in *Notes synthétiques*, comparing painting to other arts, music, and literature in its capacity to evoke sensations.[55] His avowed opinions about the relationship between art and music were fortified by exposure to the theories of Wagner, whose words the Frenchman embraced and made his own.[56]

Gauguin had made painted furniture in a rustic style, where faux-naive craftsmanship, like that of the rough-hewn box, is not without a debt to the thinking of Ruskin.[57] The reaction to mass production occurred slightly later in France, as had the Industrial Revolution, but the ardour for the conspicuously handmade, championed by Viollet-le-Duc, shared the principles of the English Arts and Crafts Movement. The tendency to unify the arts strengthened the status of the decorative arts by integrating them into a comprehensive philosophical context. It concurrently expanded the options for communicating through unexpected combinations of materials, colour and form.

Quite apart from its affinity with European crafts, the box heralds Gauguin's drift towards non-western sources. The reclining figure in the interior resembles coffers from the Congo.[58] Its *netsuke* appliqués reveal the nonchalance with which the artist began to incorporate the found object into his own creations. Taking a cue from Degas, who still planned his piece before adding accessories, Gauguin displayed a voracious aptitude for turning virtually anything into art – even the odd wine cask.[59] Whatever the practical considerations, dictated by financial constraints, he made a virtue of necessity. If his creative Midas-touch brought him no gold, this artistic laying-of-hands, consecrating the prosaic, struck pay dirt for future generations.

Moreover the irregular route by which he became an artist, by-passing the prescribed avenues of training, left him unscathed by structured definitions of what the arts were. His open-minded approach allowed him to take risks with the creative process that encouraged the inventive and welcomed the accidental. Gauguin did not set out to obliterate the sacrosanct divisions between the arts; for him they never really existed.

The new dynamism in the decorative arts further stimulated Gauguin's receptivity to diverse materials. His plunge into ceramics was decidedly unorthodox despite his fantasies of easy money.[60] In 1886 he started to collaborate with Ernest Chaplet, who revolutionised the production of stoneware. The nature of glazes influenced the artist's handling of colour, noticeably in the abstract areas in his later paintings.[61] Works such as the *Jar with self-portrait* then reappear in paintings and in sculpture.[62] The appearance of his ceramics in his paintings exemplifies his intuitive allegiance to the interconnectedness of the arts.[63]

Gauguin disdained the rational, searching to communicate on an emotional plane without an intellectual filter. This is not to say that the content is forthright. The polychrome relief *Be in love you will be happy* illustrates the conflation of idealism and cynicism that makes the myth inseparable from the man (Boston, Museum of Fine Arts). The likeness from the jar, sucking his thumb, is present with his alter-ego the fox, among a complex plethora of emblems.[64] His autobiographical iconography is only comprehensible, such as it is, by referencing previous works, in combination with his prolific literary and epistolary allusions that help to clarify some of the esoteric symbols, derived from visual and textual sources that lay outside the European tradition. The appeal of non-western art was enhanced by his longstanding infatuation with wood as an escape from mandated protocol. The

100 Paul Gauguin, *Be mysterious*, 1890, wood, painted, Paris, Musée d'Orsay

palpable traces of his assault on the panel contribute to the image of brutality, at odds with the exhortation to love. Contrary to what the primitive effect suggests, the composition was carefully worked out in a model. He used the natural colour of the wood for the figures, staining other parts, never as colourful as his painting. Not a tactile extension of his painting, his sculpture is less pictorial. The rapport is infinitely more subtle.[65]

The rusticity of wood made it popular among many of the painters associated with the colony at Pont Aven. Georges Lacombe followed the symbolist creed of expressive colour in his painted relief of *Isis* (Paris, Musée d'Orsay). The painter-sculptor achieved disconcerting effects by subverting the tendency of polychromy to make a scene more lifelike to intensify the irrational; hence blood rather than milk flows from Isis's breasts.[66] Like his mentor Gauguin, he capitalised on primitivistic carving to reiterate the primordial nature of his theme, though he used more intense colours.

Against the foil of the free-wheeling adaptations of materials and techniques urged by the Symbolists, Salon sculpture, straight-jacketed in a monochromatic ideal, looked increasingly hackneyed. At the pinnacle of France's official hierarchy, Gérôme felt an almost messianic duty to protect the academic legacy from the modernist onslaught.[67] To keep classicism viable, rather belatedly he opted for change within the limits of the archaeologically justifiable. His witty painting entitled *Sculpturae vitam insufflat pictura* (*Painting breathes life into sculpture*) serves as a mini-manifesto of his intentions, playing a self-referential game in which each art form validates the other's authenticity.[68] [45]

For his first polychrome endeavour, exhibited in 1890, Gérôme referenced the painted figurines discovered in 1873 at Tanagra, but his marble abandons the naturalism of its terracotta namesakes in favour of an idealised personification that refrained from jarring his audience too abruptly.[69] [112] It may not be coincidence that Gérôme chose the very antique source that had en-

101 Paul Gauguin, panel from the Maison du Jouir, 1901, Paris, Musée d'Orsay

couraged his friend Degas to break with propriety.[70] Struggling to reconcile his esteem for ancient art with the lure of modern life, Degas found the Tanagra figurines particularly gratifying because they vindicated his attraction to naturalism with an impeccable pedigree.[71] Although Gérôme never revealed a source for his revived technique, the ancient process of applying tinted wax to marble was described by Cros in his book on encaustics.[72]

Likewise, the opulent *Corinth* embodies more than a place (private collection). Gérôme's marble exudes rarified luxury, 'Non licet omnibus adire Corinthum' (Not everyone can go to Corinth). In comparison, the *Idol with a shell* (Paris, Musée d'Orsay), would truly appear to be from another world, but, in fact, Gauguin transposed an institutional tenet, that is the imitation of models from the past, onto sources from alien cultures. Both statues are seated nude icons enhanced with encrustations that emphasise their dangerous exoticism. Whereas the orientalism of Gérôme translates the exotic into the soigné language of academic sculpture, Gauguin assimilated the immediacy of the primitive into his own sophisticated sensibilities. Gauguin applied shell and bone to wood to achieve the antithesis of the beaux-arts style. Unlike any object found in the Marquesas (where he was not yet living), this diminutive fetish nonetheless owes many of its particulars to an array of Marquesan customs – not the least of which was cannibalism. The intrinsic shock of the sharp ossiferous teeth animates the *Idol*'s essence as one of Gauguin's 'ultra-sauvage sculptures.'[73] Uniting Buddha with Ta'aroa, from the *Ancien culte Mahorie*, the *Idol* attests to the syncretic beliefs that Gauguin brought with him from Europe.[74]

The portability of Gauguin's eclecticism transcended geography, even when locale was indispensable for actual fabrication. Taking advantage of proximity to a kiln during his return to Paris in 1893-1895, Gauguin modelled the *Oviri*. [95] The coarse texture of the unglazed body undermines any vestige of polite refinement in his nude, and the splattered red glaze (appropri-ately called *sang de boeuf*) conveys violence more graphically than the notion of the blood it represents.[75] Less a description than an incarnation of the savage, the *Oviri* repudiates the aesthetic cherished in the western tradition since the Renaissance. Gauguin's scheme to support himself by the sale of such ceramic sculptures seems ludicrous in the context of a society where the terracotta nymphs of Clodion were the epitome of good taste.[76]

Gauguin's strategy of repeating a figurative motif across media results in a creative dialogue among his works over time. Whereas such repetitions remain coyly self-congratulatory in the art of Gérôme, they accrue autobiographical significance with Gauguin. Building on accumulated allusions to the motif, the *Oviri* has been convincingly interpreted as a self-portrait of the artist as a creative/destructive force, a summation of his ideas of 'artistic creation and personal rebirth.'[77]

Polychrome sculpture is the ubiquitous ingredient around which Gauguin's thematic transmutations revolve. The interchangeability of materials is indispensable to his overarching construct because it is the permutations of his themes that constitute the metanarrative of himself as god-like creator and Christ-like martyr.[78] The syncretic strain of theosophy that pervades Symbolism finds its analogue in the fin-de-siècle attitude toward the universal harmony of the arts. In his oeuvre, this synthesis is the axiom indispensable to the transmedia correspondences central to his metanarrative. The emotional thrust of colour makes it a powerful aesthetic mortar for his rapacious appropriation of heretical materials.

Since Gauguin's paradise existed only in his fantasy, his art probed deeper into the interior landscape of his psyche as he retreated further from civilisation, eventually moving in 1901 to the Marquesas. His final total work of art, the decor of his house at Atuona, recapitulates his life as a man and as an artist.[79] The most striking remnants of this decor are the five sculpted panels that framed the entrance to the second floor, accessible by an

Painter-sculptors and polychromy

102 Paul Gauguin, *Idol with a pearl*, 1892, wood, painted, Paris, Musée d'Orsay

103 Ernst Ludwig Kirchner, *Woman dancing*, 1908-12, wood, painted, Amsterdam, Stedelijk Museum

exterior ladder. In these polychrome reliefs, Gauguin wove recurring themes and motifs into an intensely personal re-evaluation of his existence. [101]

The words 'Maison du jouir,' carved on the lintel, play on the French equivalent for House of Pleasure, pleasure of a special kind.[80] Characteristically, Gauguin grafted this allusion onto an indigenous visual form, the elaborate reliefs on the facades of the 'bachelors' house,' where young people congregated for social and sexual encounters.[81] The reference suited the nightly cavorting with the locals that gave the colonial authorities fodder for their censure of Gauguin.

The repetition on two panels of favourite aphorisms from the 1880s, 'Be in love you will be happy' and 'Be mysterious,' announces the continuing irony of Gauguin's frustrations and aspirations.[82] The imagery also resounds over the years, wherein depictions of Eve-like nudes and fruits alluding to innocence and abandon, intertwine with motifs of lust and life, creativity and suffering, that recur in a concurrent series of woodcuts. For example, most of the emblematic elements from the 1889 panel *Be in love...* turn up in the series and/or panels. The puzzling references to Brittany scenes in the prints are surely clues that these works share a subtext as a life cycle. Impressions of these woodcuts were tacked to the walls inside the second floor rooms, along with pornographic photographs and reproductions of paintings.[83] Beyond the bed ornately carved by Gauguin was the studio, the inner sanctum where paintings and works in progress were scattered among his paltry worldly possessions.

Outside at the foot of the ladder stood two satirical temple guardians, the caricatures of *Père Paillard* (Father Lechery), the prelate who was Gauguin's *bête-noire*, and the priest's alleged mistress, *Thérèse*.[84] If the underlying connotations of the ensemble revolve around the Temptation and the artist's failed Garden of Eden, these statues become the paradoxical Adam and Eve at the Gates, à la Rodin.[85] Gauguin orchestrates his Wagnerian leitmotifs into a total work of art. The *Maison du jouir* is *raumkunst* in another time zone, a culture warp.

The retrospective of 1903, organised by the dealer Ambroise Vollard, exposed artists of the next generation to Gauguin's brilliant accomplishments. Pablo Picasso seized upon their raw energy and inventive disregard for pat solutions to mould his own rebellious track. Given that the multiplicity of Picasso's sources is as breath-taking as the explosion of ideas that he tossed into the avant-garde mix, the contributions of Degas and Gauguin are nonetheless essential to his development.

The *Absinthe glass* could be seen as Picasso's homage to Degas, who popularised the subject with his famous painting of 1876, because the Frenchman was the progenitor of the real thing as the startling crux of the meaning of the created object (New York, The Museum of Modern Art). Gauguin amplified the merger of the real or the found with the unrefined. He exercised an autonomy in his use of materials that ushers in Picasso's omnivorous composites. With his cubist constructions, such as any one of his assembled guitars, the Spaniard calls into question the very nature of separate designations for painting and sculpture. His blend of art and life is synonymous with modernism. [104]

Polychromy began as an extension of tradition, grounded in archaeology, to become a reaction to the norm as colour was progressively energised as an agent of reform. The painter-sculptors discussed in this essay moved away from prevailing academic canons, endowing colour with purpose beyond its mimetic capacity or sensuous appeal. If Gérôme sought to coopt polychromy to reinvigorate the waning academic tradition, the others were engrossed in rethinking the materials of sculpture on a fundamental level. Because they came from outside the discipline, they felt free to conceptualise their ideas in three-dimensions without regard for the procedures long venerated in the sculpture studio.

This rupture cleared the way for a greater unity among all of the arts. Those who sought such an amalgamation were themselves affiliated on an international circuit, and the very fact that they were painter-sculptors defined the matrix of their mutual interests. Their history is indissoluably linked to the collapse of artificial boundaries between painting and sculpture, the fine and the decorative arts, and ultimately between art and life. Not the only conduit to modernity, their contributions were nonetheless essential to the cross-fertilisation among the arts that was to liberate artists in the 20th century from the tyranny of categories.

104 Pablo Picasso, *Violin*, 1915, Paris, Musée Picasso

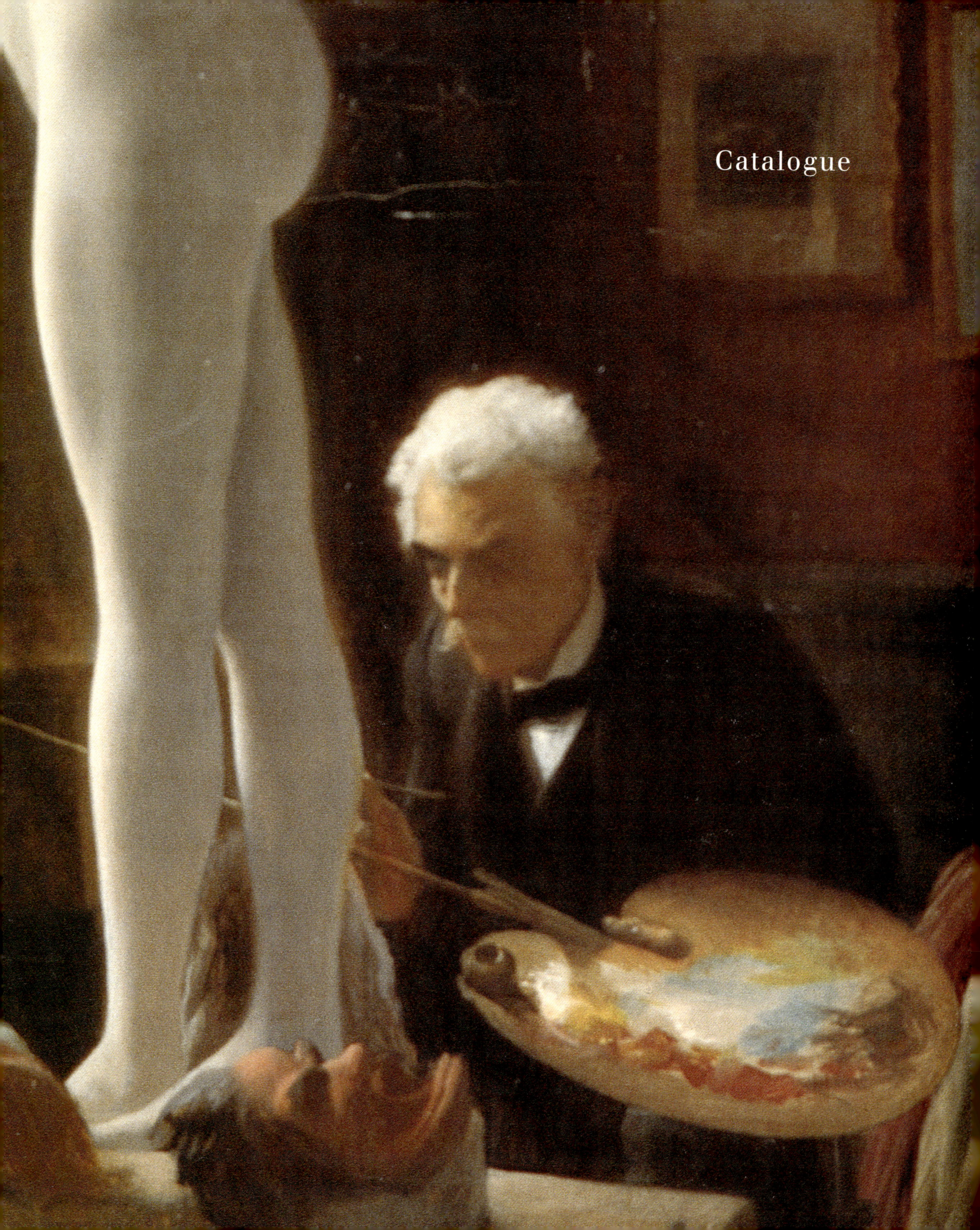

Catalogue

The classical heritage

1 Medusa early 19th century
Alabaster, 42.5 x 20.5 cm
Martin von Wagner-Museum der Universität Würzburg

Colour and volume can come together in an endless variety of ways. Even before the addition of pigment or the combination of materials, it is the incidence and reflection of light that is the most important source of colour.

Since the Renaissance it had been a pastime of the educated to visit sculpture galleries by torchlight. The flickering light created a mysterious atmosphere and the statues appeared to move. In the case of this *Medusa*, the sculptor has made certain his work would always be seen in the proper light: the alabaster bust is hollowed out and at the back there is a gap designed to hold a candle. The transparency of the alabaster is used to great advantage and the *Medusa*, come to life, captures and immobilises the viewer. Goethe was fascinated by this effect: 'I own quite a good cast, but there is nothing left of the magic of the marble. The noble, partially transparent yellow, the stone imitating the colour of flesh has disappeared. The plaster looks chalky and dead by comparison' (*Italienische Reise*, 25 December 1786).

The *Medusa* was once considered as a work of Antiquity. Scholars today, however, mostly agree that it is a 19th-century copy after the famous *Medusa Rondanini* of the 2nd century A.D. (Munich, Glyptothek).

105 The *Medusa* without illumination

106 The *Medusa* from the back

118　　　　　　　The colour of sculpture

2 The 'Psyche of Capua'

cast of c.1893
After a Roman copy of a Greek original
(c.100 B.C.)
Plaster, painted, 85 cm
Staatliche Kunstsammlungen Dresden,
Skulpturensammlung

This plaster cast after the original work found in 1726 in Capua (Naples, Museo Nazionale Archeologico) belongs to the ample collection of the Albertinum in Dresden. In 1882, the archaeologist Georg Treu became director of the museum. He was a great champion of colour in antique sculpture, and also encouraged its use in the present. By this period there was no longer any doubt that the Greeks had painted their sculptures, and under his direction conservators and artists painted casts of faded ancient works in order to recreate their original appearance and effect.

The so-called 'Psyche' was painted by Ernst Sattler. The coloration is very restrained, limited to the hair and garment. The body is made to seem even whiter by this contrast.

The classical heritage

3 The 'Antinous Albani' cast of 1893
After the Roman original (2nd century A.D.)
Plaster, painted, 56 x 50 cm
Staatliche Kunstsammlungen Dresden, Skulpturensammlung

Ernst Sattler painted this copy after the famous relief in the Villa Albani in Rome with considerably more daring than the 'Psyche' [2]. The face is subtly tinted, and the lips, eyes and eyebrows are clearly accentuated. The abstract marble countenance is thus transformed into the portrait of an historical personality with a true physical presence. For many, even at the end of the century, this was still something of a shock, a violation of the rules. Experiments such as this fuelled the debate on realism in Antiquity. Comparisons with wax figures were often used to discredit the advocates of polychromy, whether in ancient or modern art. The *Antinous* relief proves, however, that colour can actually aid in distinguishing and emphasising the arrangement of plastic forms.

4 Mask of a satyr cast of 1883
After an original marble from Pompeii (late 1st century B.C.)
Plaster, painted, 28 cm
Staatliche Kunstsammlungen Dresden, Skulpturensammlung

5 Mask of a satyr cast of 1893
After an original marble from Pompeii (late 1st century B.C.)
Plaster, painted, 28 cm
Staatliche Kunstsammlungen Dresden, Skulpturensammlung

These casts, painted ten years apart by Paul Kiessling [4] and Ernst Sattler [5], are excellent for comparing two approaches to reconstruction. Both efforts are based on the traces of colour found on the original, bought for Dresden in 1841. Their great differences demonstrate the extent to which reconstruction is actually interpretation. Georg Treu was unhappy with the earlier one, feeling it did not adequately distinguish the satyr's facial features. Sattler's essay is much more cautious. Treu had sought to determine the colours of the original himself. The 'truth,' however, probably lay somewhere between the two examples.

120 The colour of sculpture

107   Benvenuto Cellini, *Saltcellar*, 1539-43, gold and enamel, Vienna, Kunsthistorisches Museum

6 James Pradier 1790-1852
The birth of Cupid c.1840
Bronze, 14 x 21.5 x 9 cm
Amsterdam, Van Gogh Museum

In the 1840s, the Swiss sculptor James Pradier sought to combine colour and sculpture in numerous ways, sometimes by joining ivory and bronze, sometimes by delicately painting his marble statues. In the area of small-scale bronzes, his most convincing effort is this variation on the *Birth of Cupid*. Having no antique precedents, Pradier's interpretation of the theme is highly original. Cupid is a winged putto and, like his mother, represented half asleep. The open shell is not only a kind of cave or womb but also a reference to the mythical birth of the goddess herself. A comparison with Benvenuto Cellini's famous saltcellar is certainly not farfetched, as Pradier represents the goddess in a glittering gold that stands out from the bronze. The non-gilded parts are also given different coloured patinations: the shell is dark brown, while the waves are green.

108   James Pradier, *The birth of Cupid* from the back

The classical heritage

109 John Gibson's *Tinted Venus* in Owen Jones's pavilion at the Crystal Palace at Sydenham, stereo photograph, c. 1862, Amsterdam, Rijksmuseum

7 John Gibson 1790–1866

Tinted Venus c.1851–56

Marble, painted, 175 cm, signed in Greek on the turtle: ΓΙΒΣΩΝ ΕΠΟΙΕΙ ΕΝ ΡΩΜΗΙ ('Gibson made this in Rome'); inscribed on the apple: Η ΚΑΛΗ ΛΑΒΕΤΩ ('The beautiful one must take this')
The Board of Trustees of the National Galleries and Museums on Merseyside, Liverpool, Walker Art Gallery

This statue of Venus, by England's greatest Neo-classicist, is probably the most important polychrome sculpture of the 19th century. With the aim of becoming a disciple of the Greeks in practice as well as spirit, John Gibson toyed with the idea of colouring his statues as early as the 1820s. In 1849, he was commissioned by Joseph Neeld to make a statue of Venus. Even before it was finished, Mr and Mrs Robert Preston of Liverpool had already ordered a replica. It is that version which now belongs to the Walker Art Gallery. Gibson worked on the piece from 1851 to 1856. When it was shown in 1862 at the International Exhibition in London – in a pavilion designed for it by Owen Jones – it became famous instantly. The reactions of both the critics and the public were mixed: although most viewers had no problem accepting a naked goddess in *white*, a *coloured* Venus appeared unchaste. In all other respects, however, the statue represents the classical ideal and is indebted to both Antiquity and the Italien sculptor Antonio Canova. Gibson was 60 at the time of its creation, so that it is not only a 'late' work in terms of style but also within the sculptor's oeuvre. Despite the revolutionary nature of the *Venus*, Gibson cannot be placed among the more radical advocates of polychromy. Only the hair and lips, the pomegranate and the turtle are strongly accentuated; the tinting of the skin, on the other hand – probably achieved using a thin layer of wax – is barely noticeable. The appearance of the figure today is based on a restoration of the 1960s that was recently carefully re-examined. Early photographs lead to the conclusion that the surface now conforms to that of the original. One should be especially cautious, however, with regards to the skin, whose coloration cannot be determined with any certainty. Other sources, documented by the Walker Art Gallery, speak of an overall ivory tinting, blue eyes and gold earrings.

Another version of the *Tinted Venus*, with traces of colour, 76.5 cm high, was auctioned on 22 November 1983 at Sotheby's in London and is now in a private collection.

8 Prosper d'Epinay 1836–1914

Medusa c.1865–70

Terracotta, 42 x 32.2 x 20 cm, signed on the back: d'Epinay

Amsterdam, Van Gogh Museum

This head was probably created by Epinay at the beginning of his stay in Rome. Chronologically speaking, it is thus related to the work known as the *La ceinture dorée* [9]. Stylistically, however, the bust is so different from this popular Salon piece that one does not immediately believe they are by the same hand. The head is of course a *bozzetto* in clay, and therefore subject to completely different laws than a polished marble. Beyond this, Epinay proved himself a skilled eclectic, employing in the one case a classicising, in the other a more baroque vocabulary. The sculptor certainly became acquainted with the method of distinguishing face and hair by studying the work of Bernini, and it is possible he even saw the master's own *Medusa* (Rome, Palazzo dei Conservatori). Epinay additionally emphasised the painterly quality of the bust by giving the hair a blueish tone. It appears almost as if he had kneaded the colour into the clay while modelling the wild curls, which do not yet have the appearance of snakes.

It is thought that the *Medusa* is a portrait of a certain Assunta, the wife of Dambrosio della Ruella, a bandit whom the French had sentenced to death in Rome in 1866. The exact circumstances are unknown, and whether there were aspects of the woman's character that might have led to her representation as Medusa is pure speculation. Among the many 19th-century variations of this mythological creature, Epinay's head takes a middle position between Neo-classicism and the Neo-baroque.

The classical heritage 125

9 Prosper d'Epinay
The golden belt c.1874
Marble, gilt bronze, 45 × 14 cm, signed: P. d'Epinay
Roma; inscribed: CEINTURE DOREE
Paris, Galerie Elstir

The success of *La ceinture dorée* at the 1874 Salon and at the 1878 Exposition Universelle in Paris brought renown to its creator: 'The best figure of a nude woman, certainly the most agreeable and in our opinion the most elegant, is Mr d'Epinay's *La ceinture dorée*, a curvaceous and supple young woman in the flesh, her body lovingly carved in the whitest, purest marble, with a few gold highlights in her hair and on the belt she is fastening. This is perhaps not the severest form of art, but it charms at once and reminds one of Canova.' So wrote the influential critic Louis Gonse in the *Gazette des Beaux-Arts*.

Epinay's art had two masters: women and antiquity. *La ceinture dorée* expresses his conception of modern woman. The idea was suggested by Madame de Cassin, who probably commissioned the work in 1871. This very classical purity, worthy of Canova, is fashionably sweetened by a fairly conventional and decorative polychromy. While the gold highlights recall several works by James Pradier, Epinay's bases are always done with a very sure decorative sense redolent of the rich ornamentation and colours of his stone vases. Two large versions of *La ceinture dorée* in private collections have remarkably rich pedestals: high classical white marble with fluting and garlands on one, dark red veined marble with gilded bronze decoration on the other. This statuette, lot no. 8 in the Epinay auction held at the Hôtel Drouot, Paris, on 14 April 1902, still has its original base in rare marble. Other versions of this size were issued in bronze by Ferdinand Barbedienne with a brown patina and gilding on the hair, belt and drapery, and in biscuit by the porcelain manufacture at Sèvres.

110 Denis-Antoine Chaudet, *Peace*, 1805, silver and bronze, partially gilt, Paris, Musée du Louvre

111 Jacopo Alari-Bonacolsi, called Antico, *Goddess of the Via Traiana*, c. 1500, bronze, Staatliche Museen zu Berlin, Preußischer Kulturbesitz, Skulpturengalerie

10 Auguste Clésinger 1814–1883

Helen 1860

Bronze, 78 × 41 cm (with socle), signed: J. CLESINGER.ROME.1860; foundry mark: F. BARBEDIENNE
Paris, Collection Lucile Audouy

Auguste Clésinger was in Italy when he represented 'the beauteous Helen in the form of a large, robust and calm woman, somewhat lacking in charm, grace and smiling voluptuousness' (A. Estignard). Now lost, this full-length marble statue of the heroine of the *Iliad* was preceded by a marble bust with shoulders (also lost), which he presented at the Salon in 1861. In 1868, Clésinger was again inspired by the saga to produce two new marble busts, this time without the shoulders: another *Helen*, and a *Paris* (private collections).

Ferdinand Barbedienne, the first founder to sign commercial contracts with sculptors, bought the advance rights to reproduce Clésinger's entire oeuvre, whatever the format or technique used. He produced six copies of the full-length *Helen* and of the accompanying bust. The one here is the biggest of all, having the same dimensions as the original marble made in Rome in 1860. Barbedienne's catalogue also proposes the same bust without the shoulders. The founder presented these models at prestigious events such as the International Exhibition in London, in 1862, where he showed bronzes of this *Helen* and a bust of *Paris* with the shoulders (now lost).

Clésinger was certainly not opposed to colour in sculpture. He experimented with it on his *Cleopatra*, a white marble statue richly decorated with real coloured enamel jewellery (Fontainebleau, private collection). Reactions to this work at the 1869 Salon were more astonished than enthusiastic. As can be seen from the hair, drapery and jewels of *Helen*, Barbedienne enriched his bronzes with various patinas and gilding. This endowed the castings with a crafted rather than industrial character. Indeed Barbedienne's contract with the sculptor foresaw the possibility of adapting or even changing the model to suit the taste of the day. This part of the creative process belonged to the manufacturer. It is clear that these bronzes edited by Barbedienne and other foundries helped to popularise a somewhat facile, spectacular and decorative use of polychromy.

112 Jean-Léon Gérôme, *Tanagra*, 1890, marble, Paris, Musée d'Orsay

11 Jean-Léon Gérôme 1824–1904
Head of Tanagra c.1890
Marble, painted, 57 × 34 cm, signed: J.L. GEROME
Paris, Collection Lucile Audouy

This little known bust is a partial copy of Gérôme's famous *Tanagra*, one of the great successes of the 1890 Salon. [112] Its life-size model is the personification of the town of Boeotia. Sitting straight as a column, it holds in its hands the *Hoop dancer*, an imitation of the Tanagra figurines. At its feet lie other statuettes which, as the pick axe suggests, have been freshly excavated. The sensational discovery of these innumerable little moulded and painted terracottas produced in the studios of Boeotian coroplasts, often representing young girls, revived the debate about ancient polychrome sculpture.

As both painter and sculptor, Gérôme was fascinated by archaeology and a keen advocate of historical realism. He chose this subject to justify the use of colour on the marble. 'I have always been dismayed by the coldness of statues when the finished works are left in their natural state [...],' he wrote, remembering the painted marble metopes from the temple at Selinunte which he had seen in the museum in Palermo. No doubt, Gérôme had also read Henry Cros's and Charles Henry's treatise *L'encaustique et les autres procédés de peinture chez les anciens* (1884), which included a chapter on statuary. Gérôme ordered a special Apennine marble known for its capacity to absorb pigment, which he applied in moderate quantities using a wax solution. And indeed, while the model has whitened with age, this bust has kept its colour admirably.

Gérôme did not imitate antiquity, but used it as a source of inspiration. His concern for historicism and archaeological recreation led him to dress his own period in the antique style, whereas prevailing academicism forced modernity into the mould of an impersonal Graeco-Roman canon. Thus, the body and face of this *Tanagra* are more those of a modern *Parisienne* than a classical Greek beauty. It has, in fact, been said that the work is a portrait of Madame Siot, Gérôme's mistress at the time.

12 Henry Cros 1840–1907

Incantation 2 1891

Glass paste, 35 x 26.5 cm, signature carved in the upper left corner:
H. CROS
Paris, courtesy of Brame & Lorenceau

The first copy of *Incantation* was shown at the 1892 Salon and acquired by the French state for the Musée du Luxembourg. The terracotta model is dated 1 June 1891. The museum catalogue describes the work as follows: 'Seen in profile, a young woman, the lower part of her body clothed in a yellow robe, squats to the right of a clay urn out from which a snake emerges. She is playing a double flute. To her right a young naked woman stands facing us, her two hands holding the ends of a fine pink scarf; at her feet lies a black ram; behind them, in the middle, a young woman in a white dress knotted below her breasts holds two torches, while to the left the head of an old woman appears through the opening of a green curtain.' Drawing on the technical and thematic melting pot of the ancient Mediterranean, Cros combines mythology and invention in a spirit of moderate Classicism like that of the Parnassian poets and the paintings of Puvis de Chavannes, to whom he was compared. In addition to his masks and medallions, Cros made large reliefs in his atelier in Sèvres. His polychromy was considered seductive because it was French and not Germanic. Bourdelle wrote that in Cros's work 'Egypt calculates, Syria decorates, Greece sculpts and quivers and all France smiles.'

13 Henry Cros Woman with a bird (yellow) 1890
Glass paste, 14.5 x 11 cm, signed on the back: H.C. 90
Paris, courtesy of Brame & Lorenceau

14 Henry Cros Woman with a bird (blue) 1890
Glass paste, 14 x 10.5 cm
Paris, courtesy of Brame & Lorenceau

15 Henry Cros Nude c.1895–1900
Glass paste, 19 x 45.5 cm, signed at upper left: H. CROS
Paris, courtesy of Brame & Lorenceau

16 Henry Cros Venus drawn by hippocampi 1897
Glass paste, 12.5 x 23.5 cm, signed on the back: H. CROS
Paris, courtesy of Brame & Lorenceau

A man with a solid knowledge of scientific matters and extraordinary erudition in Greek and Latin, Cros learnt to sculpt in the studios of François Jouffroy and Antoine Etex. His eclectic and imaginative mind was constantly on the lookout for new ways of combining these two arts, while his classical background inclined him to the study of ancient techniques. In 1887 Cros exhibited a painted marble bust of a young woman at the Salon and fashioned a number of glazed ceramics. But since the colour remained external to the sculpture, Cros decided to tint the material itself in order to make the two indissociable. Though a success, his revival of polychrome wax technique produced works that were too fragile and Cros began exploring the secret of ancient sintered glass, used among others by the Egyptians. His first attempt, a medallion portrait of his niece which he fired in a simple stove, dates from 1884. In 1891 the French state gave him a studio at the Sèvres porcelain manufacture as well as a research and publishing allowance. Cros continued his discreet investigations into *pâte de verre* up to his death in 1907.

Cros proceeded by placing coloured crystal powders in the mould of the sculpture, which had already been modelled, then putting them in the oven. He produced mainly reliefs, that eminently pictorial form of sculpture which combines the tactile and visual dimensions of both painting and sculpture. The two versions of his *Woman with a bird* are images of innocence or evocations of the ancient theme, Lesbia's sparrow. Like coloured cameos, they illustrate the results of his research: in the yellow version, the glass paste melts like sugar, absorbing the colours in a crystalline glow. In the blue version, the matt, saturated paste accentuates outline in the manner of biscuit porcelain. Like pastel, his colour suggests without describing.

113 Arnold Böcklin and Peter Bruckmann, *Mother and child*, 1888, plaster, Staatliche Kunstsammlungen Dresden, Skulpturengalerie

17 Arnold Böcklin 1827–1901
Shield with the head of Medusa 1887

Plaster, diametre 60.5 cm
Heirs of Dr. Roland Fleiner, on loan to Kunsthaus Zürich

Böcklin never disguised his deep contempt for those theoreticians who for centuries had condemned Greek sculpture to colourlessness. He claimed to have always been certain that the sculptors of Antiquity had employed colour, even before this was proven in the writings of Gottfried Semper and Georg Treu. Together with his pupil and son-in-law, the sculptor Peter Bruckmann, he created a number of polychrome sculptures, the two occasionally changing roles: sometimes Böcklin himself did the modelling, sometimes he was merely responsible for the painting.

The artist often turned his hand to the Medusa myth. She appears in a series of paintings, and twice he sought to give her plastic form. The first version of this relief, executed in 1885, no longer exists, having been broken during its return from the polychrome sculpture exhibition in the Nationalgalerie in Berlin. There are, however, several casts of this second version.

Böcklin's *Medusa* is more expressive and intense than other such figures created by the painters and sculptors of the turn of the century. The masklike rigidity of her almost archaic face is further emphasised by her wild hair and the snakes. This *Medusa*, modelled by Bruckmann, also demonstrates Böcklin's love of dark, saturated colours.

The illustration shows another, almost identical version belonging to the Kunsthaus Zürich.

114 Max Klinger, *Cassandra*, 1895, marbles, Leipzig, Museum der bildenden Künste

18 **Max Klinger** 1857–1920

Bust of Cassandra c.1895

Marble, amber, painted, 62 x 31 x 27 cm, signed at the right: MK; marked on the socle: AKTIEN/GESELLSCHAFT/GLADENBECK/BERLIN/&/FRIEDRICHSHAGEN
Hamburger Kunsthalle

19 **Max Klinger**

Bust of Cassandra c.1903

Bronze, amber, 58 x 31 x 36.5 cm (with socle), signed: M. Klinger fct
Paris, Musée d'Orsay

Klinger worked simultaneously and over several years on his large sculptures *New Salome* and *Cassandra* (both Leipzig, Museum der bildenden Künste). Inspired by Georg Treu, director of Dresden's Antikensammlung and advocate of sculptural polychromy, the artist not only combined different materials but also painted his figures. While in Paris in 1886, he began work on a *Head of a Roman woman*, finished and painted in Rome in 1891, which was probably the starting point for the variations of *Cassandra*. More than her counterpart *Salome*, *Cassandra* is indebted to Greek sculpture. The modest coloration of the marble version makes her comparable to the Dresden plaster reconstructions, with which Klinger was certainly acquainted. [2–5]

The Gladenbeck company in Berlin produced marble and alabaster versions and, since 1903, authorised bronze casts of the bust. The Hamburger Kunsthalle's marble and the Musée d'Orsay's bronze are both special variations, and the former was probably executed by Klinger himself. In both cases the eyes are amber. By placing so much emphasis on the Trojan seeress's eyes the artist spanned a bridge between Neo-classicism and Symbolism.

The classical heritage 137

20 Richard König 1863–after 1920
Bust of a muse 1901
Wrought iron, marble, painted, 46.7 cm, signed: R.KÖNIG
Staatliche Kunstsammlungen Dresden, Skulpturensammlung

Within the broad spectrum of possible combinations of material in sculpture, the association of iron and marble is certainly one of the most original. The value of this bust does not, however, lie purely in its experimental character: the sculptor in fact here proves himself to be a talent unjustly forgotten. The head, turned to the left, is highly expressive, and the marble is modelled with assurance and feeling. König ends the sculpture abruptly at the shoulders, giving it a sense of immediacy. The wrought iron used for the broad curls of the hair appears perfectly natural. The classicising muse, her eyes and lips additionally painted, has an almost archaic appearance. The sculptor employed the company Kühnscherf & Söhne in Dresden for the wrought iron. The work appeared in Georg Treu's exhibition of polychrome sculpture in the Nationalgalerie Berlin in 1884.

21 Franz von Stuck 1863–1928
Fighting fauns 1903–04
Plaster, painted, 78.7 x 116.8 cm, signed below: FRANZ/STVCK
Amsterdam, Van Gogh Museum

For his private villa, Franz von Stuck united stylistic elements from his native Bavaria with those of ancient Rome in order to create an extraordinarily colourful *gesamtkunstwerk*. In his works, the artist relied on the Antique to varying degrees. The fighting fauns, which also appear frequently in his pictures, are probably derived from vase painting, without, however, immediately revealing their origins. Stuck was thus able to create a pseudo-Pompeiian ambience very much in accordance with his own tastes.

The figures themselves are not actually painted. The decorative effect is achieved through the red background, which helps to accentuate the figures. This was Stuck's comment on the age-old debate among museums of ancient art about the 'correct' background for white marbles. The dark red employed here is more or less the same colour used by the British Museum for its classical art collection. It is no accident that an artist of the turn of the century, publicly celebrated as a genius, not only surrounded his paintings with frames of his own design, but also took the eventual museological presentation of his creations into account.

The classical heritage

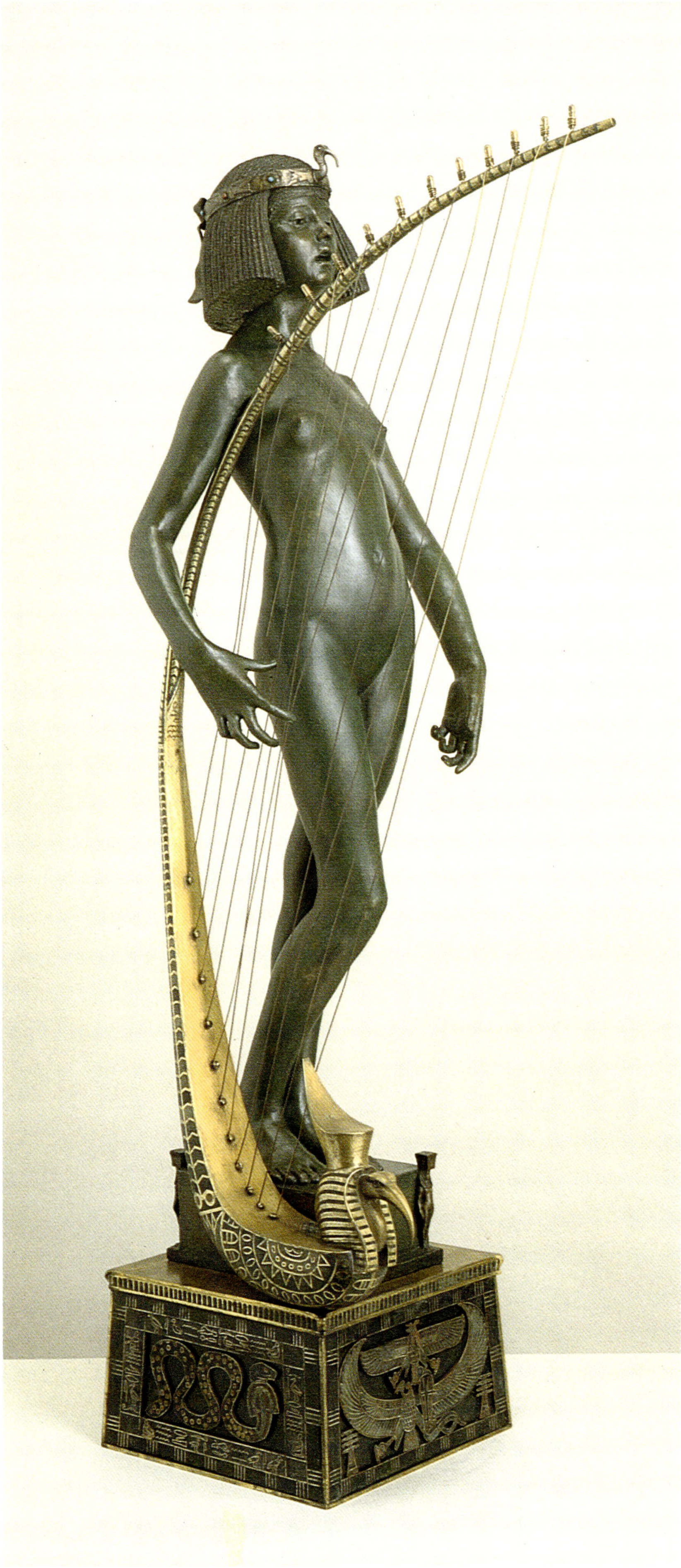

22 Edward Onslow Ford 1852–1901
The singer c.1889

Bronze, coloured resin paste, semi-precious stones, 90.2 × 21.6 × 43.2 cm
London, Tate Gallery

Initially trained as a painter, Edward Onslow Ford became, with Alfred Gilbert, one of the two or three most important and successful creators of the English New Sculpture movement. The two artists held neighbouring studios in the mid-1880s, and Ford collaborated with Gilbert in experiments with reviving lost-wax bronze casting. This technique allowed greater specificity and liveliness in surface handling, a quality that came to be called *couleur* (deriving from contemporary French criticism, and referring to a sculptor's ability to give a lifelike quality to his work *without* the use of actual colour, mainly through surface qualities). Ford won praise for the *couleur* in his work, and *The singer*, which depicts a nude Egyptian girl playing a harp and singing, was acclaimed for its truthfulness to its model.

In *The singer*, Ford introduced the use of actual colour (in the polychrome sense) by the insertion of real turquoise and garnets in the girl's circlet, and with coloured resins laid in the harp and the base in imitation of enamel. Gilbert had earlier begun using colouristically diverse materials, in his memorial to Henry Fawcett (1885-87, London, Westminster Abbey), which, probably significantly, was also set with turquoise and garnets. In *The singer*, the use of turquoise is likely related to its subject matter, since that stone is often associated with Egyptian art.

115 Edward Onslow Ford, *The singer* (detail during restoration)

23 George-Henri Lemaire 1853–1914
An Egyptian woman c.1890
Blue and red marbles, coloured stones, metal, lapis lazuli,
47 × 11 × 10 cm, signed on the base at the left: Georges Lemaire
Beauvais, Musée départemental de l'Oise

Reflecting the contemporary fascination with all things Egyptian, the hieratic form, clothing and decorative motifs of this precious *Egyptian woman* look back to ancient art, but the figure has more to do with the stereotypical representations that began to circulate in the 18th century: thus its head-dress, or *nemes*, should only be worn by a pharaoh, while its rounded forms reflect western canons of beauty. Even the theme, that of the offering, would appear to have more to do with the myth of Pandora.

The iconography of this statuette is less important than the choice of precious materials and the formal difficulty of the work. It may be that its lapis lazuli blue was inspired by the large neo-classical statues of *Antinous* in bluish-grey marble from the Hôtel de Beauharnais in Paris or by the countless little funerary servants, or *shawabtis*, in blue frit, placed in Egyptian tombs. The red marble of the *nemes* and turquoise of the chest display Lemaire's skill at polychromy. As a sculptor and engraver in stone, he specialised in glyptics and was renowned for the finesse of his medallion portraits and antique style cameos. Like the symbolist *Silence* (or *Immortality*, Paris, Musée du Petit Palais) in lapis lazuli, agate, jasper, opal and copper, Lemaire's statuettes appear to have been fashioned in a jeweller's workshop. Indeed, Lemaire himself created jewellery in collaboration with J.L. Bonny.

Like the Orient in general, Egypt was a stock pretext for sculptural polychromy. During the First Empire, the sphinxes, Antinous, Nubians and other decorative bronzes of the 'retour d'Egypte' style all had gold *nemes*, loin cloths and jewellery contrasting with their black patina. Edition bronzes continued this polychromy all through the century.

The Gothic and Renaissance Revivals

24 Félicie de Fauveau 1802–1868

St Louis c.1840

Marble, painted and gilt, 59 x 26.5 x 20.5 cm, inscribed on the baldachin: LE.S^{ct}.ROY.LOYS

Château d'Ussé

Nostalgia for the Middle Ages informed not only Félicie de Fauveau's art, but also her politics. Following the July Revolution, she was forced to pay for her armed advocacy of the Legitimists with prison and exile. However, she remained true to her convictions, as the sculptures and decorative objects created for her aristocratic patrons and friends demonstrate.

This statuette of Louis IX, also known as St Louis, was made for the Comtesse de la Rochejacquelein, a comrade-in-arms who had shared Fauveau's cell in Paris and joined the sculptress in her exile in Florence. Following the medieval tradition, the artist gave her figure the countenance of the currently reigning monarch, or rather, of the man to whom in her opinion the French throne truly belonged: Henri Charles d'Artois-Bourbon, duc de Bordeaux (1820-1883). The H on the base stands for 'Henri V,' who would have succeeded Charles X upon the latter's death in 1836. St Louis, seated in a niche, is represented crowned and apparently about to bless the people. The sword stands for his position as the country's highest judge and his role as a crusader. His reign was a period of stability in which power was centralised, and he is known to have campaigned against corruption. The life of this popular king therefore offered many points of reference for Fauveau's contemporaries.

The manner in which the artist coloured the statue and throne reflects the influence of the polychrome debate among the Neo-classicists: it is limited to the gold background, the starry sky, and the figure's accessories: the crown, the handle of the sword and the fleur-de-lys pattern on his mantle. Fauveau never went as far as the neo-gothic sculptors of the following generation, who completely painted their statues. A comparable *Font of St Louis*, c. 1834, can be found in Florence, Galleria d'Arte Moderna, Palazzo Pitti.

25 Anonymous The Four Evangelists c.1895–1900
Terracotta, painted, all c. 65-70 x 20 x 18 cm (two exhibited)
Stedelijk Museum Roermond, on loan from the
St Christoffelparochie, Roermond

26 Anonymous St Gregory c.1895–1900
Plaster, painted, 145 x 50 x 30 cm
Stedelijk Museum Roermond, on loan from the
Rijksdienst Beeldende Kunst, The Hague

All of the Evangelists were given the faces of artists from the workshop of the architect Pierre Cuypers. Cuypers was one of the leading historicist builders in The Netherlands, comparable to Viollet-le-Duc in France, Pugin in England or Bodo Ebhardt in Germany. These architects furnished all of Europe with new buildings in old styles, differing from region to region but all with the same intention. Organised in large workshops, generally under the supervision of an architect, their labour divided, the individual artists who participated in these projects mostly remained anonymous. The Evangelists bear the features of Cuypers (*St Matthew*), the sculptor Henri Leeuw (*St Mark*), the painter H. Linssen (*St Luke*) and the chaplain Boermans (*St John*), who comissioned the works for an altar in the Munsterkerk in Roermond.

The colouring of the figures is almost classical, dominated by white and gold. In contrast to academic sculpture, however, the faces and hands are painted in flesh tones, a kind of realism which, by the later 19th century, had once again become perfectly acceptable for church decoration. The enormous productivity of such workshops was most often achieved at the expense of sculptural quality. This was not a problem *in situ*, the figures having been designed to be seen from a distance.

The statue of *Gregory I* from Cuypers's workshop is a triumph of Historicism under church patronage. Gregory the Great is represented in papal regalia, holding a book – thus as one of the Church Fathers. It may very well be that the figure was once part of a cycle. By the end of the 19th century, the storehouse of knowledge about the past had grown so enormously that it had become difficult to distinguish between old and new, restoration and reconstruction, the real and the forged. While the overall form and fall of the garments is borrowed from the late Gothic, the strong colours are reminiscent of the Baroque. Perhaps this unknown sculptor was fooled by 17th-century restorations of medieval works.

146   The colour of sculpture

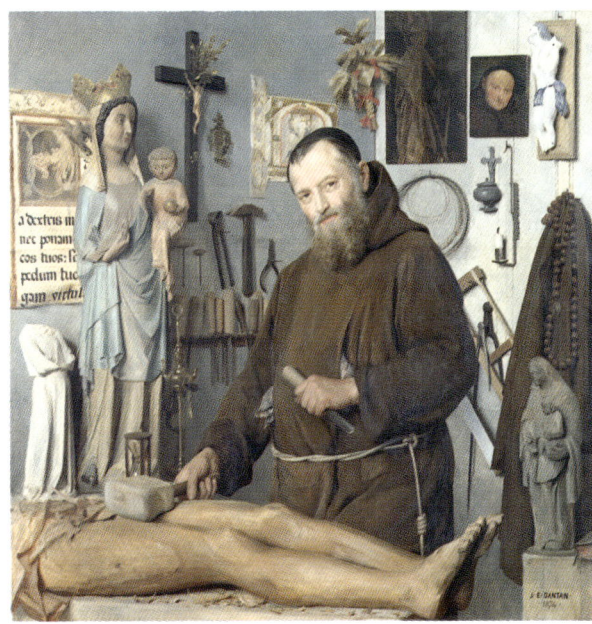

116   Edouard Dantan, *Monk sculpting a Christ*, 1874, Nantes, Musée des Beaux-Arts

117   Alphonse Mucha, *Young woman painting a Madonna*, date and present location unknown

27 Félix Bauer 1854–1933

A lesson in illumination 1892

Oil on canvas, 138.5 × 98.5 cm, signed on the bottom left: F. Bauer
Beauvais, Musée départemental de l'Oise

Painting seems to have been considered more suitable for depicting medievalising genre scenes than sculpture. Highly original, and particularly interesting in this context, is the scene shown here, in which a monk teaches his apprentice how to colour a statue, in this case of St Martin. The teacher's gesture is self-explanatory. Although it cannot be proven, it is possible that the pupil is meant to represent a famous artist as a young man. Anecdotes about the discovery of artists who exhibited great talent in their youth – for example, Giotto or Leonardo – were very popular, and were often the subject of paintings. Here we find ourselves in the 15th century, the style of the figures and their clothing points to the transitional period between the Gothic and the Renaissance. The painter, a native of Lyons, was obviously pleased with his subject, and he clearly indicated the strong colours he believed late medieval artists had employed. The partially finished equestrian statue and the sculptures at the back of the studio indicate that in his opinion a figure was only complete once it was coloured. Whether consciously or not, Félix Bauer thus made a contribution to the ongoing debate about the hierarchy of the arts.

The Gothic and Renaissance Revivals 147

118 Château de Pierrefonds, Chimera by Fremiet

28 **Emmanuel Fremiet** 1824–1910
Chimera c.1878
Stoneware, glazed, 60 × 76 × 31 cm, signed:
Fremiet; marked at the right: Emile Muller
Paris, Galerie Elstir

29 **Emmanuel Fremiet**
Chimera c.1878
Stoneware, glazed, 60 × 75 × 31 cm, signed:
Fremiet; marked at the right: E. Muller
Paris, Galerie Elstir

These two fantastical creatures are reductions of sculptures installed on the staircase at Pierrefonds, a ruin that was transformed into a medieval dream-castle by Viollet-le-Duc for Napoleon III. The versions are different from the usual reductions and editions that Fremiet and other sculptors allowed to be made after their works. Here, he collaborated with the ceramic manufacturer Emile Muller, experimenting with the glazing and creating a various and bizarre mixture of colours. Like Jean Carriès, Muller and Fremiet were inspired by Asian, particularly Japanese, ceramics. These could be seen in Europe beginning in the mid 1860s, but it was the Exposition Universelle of 1878 that represented the breakthrough and *Japonisme* soon captured the imaginations of such very different artists as Vincent van Gogh and Fremiet.

The techniques employed by ceramicists such as Emile Muller and Alexandre Bigot are difficult to reconstruct in detail. A red made with copper, called *sang de bœuf* and adapted from the Chinese, was particularly popular. As can be seen here, oxidation turned it turquoise. An uninhibited creative fantasy was needed for this combination of eastern technique and loosely interpreted Gothic form.

The Gothic and Renaissance Revivals 149

30 Albert-Ernest Carrier-Belleuse 1824–1887
The reader c.1880

Bronze, ivory, 62 cm, signed on the base: A. Carrier-Belleuse; marked on a separate plate: LISEUSE/Par Carrier Belleuse/Grand Prix du Salon
Leeds Museums and Galleries (Lotherton Hall)

Carrier-Belleuse began his career as a chiseller. He received his training in the decorative arts at the Petite Ecole, Paris, before entering the employ of the Minton China Works in Staffordshire. He became the director of art at the Sèvres porcelain manufacture in 1875, where he led the revival of interest in biscuit ware. This 'sculpting machine,' as Edouard Lockroy called him, used all the productive resources available to him in his vast studio.

Medieval subjects are rare in Carrier-Belleuse's oeuvre, but this damsel, dreamily leafing through her book, was one of the most popular statuettes of the 19th century. She was reproduced in numerous variations and sizes. The combination of bronze and ivory indicates that this was one of the more luxurious versions. The idea probably stems from the artist's exile in Brussels after 1870. Her dress – with *poulaines*, coif and tight corsage – was inspired not only by 16th-century fashion but also by the *cul de Paris*.

This genteel portrait of feminine innocence was assured popularity and the use of ivory for the face and hands made her seem all the more fragile and delicate. The artist generally enjoyed using colour in sculpture and did so in a variety of ways: he combined bronze with coloured marbles, added coloured enamels to his ceramics, and even enhanced his bronzes and plasters with paint. This penchant for polychromy was criticised by Charles Blanc, then Directeur des Beaux-Arts, who addressed him as follows: 'Frightful heresiarch! You shall perish on the scaffold where the colourist sculptors shall be burnt, and quite rightly too.'

31 Emmanuel Fremiet

Credo 1885

Plaster, painted, cloth, 40.5 x 32.3 x 10.3 cm, signed on the socle at the left: E.FREMIET; on the base: FREMIET; inscribed on the banner: CREDO
Paris, Musée d'Orsay

The knight is shown holding a banner between his outstretched arms; the inscription is both his and the sculptor's profession of faith. According to family tradition, it is a self-portrait, and this is confirmed by Henri Gréber's – polychrome – likeness. [53] Although of deeply personal significance, the sculpture was not only known in Fremiet's intimate circle. On the contrary, the sculptor-entrepreneur allowed the figure, like most of his creations, to be reproduced. In fact, *Credo* was probably one of his greatest successes, selling over 100 bronze casts in the first three months. In the year of the Boulanger crisis, this steadfast Catholic crusader was certainly a useful symbol for a France preparing to take revenge. The lone figure of the knight is in many ways comparable to the numerous paintings and sculptures depicting the brave soldiers of the Franco-Prussian War.

No matter how subtly patinated, however, the casts cannot compete with the colourfulness of this model. Still more exceptional is the use of textiles. Meissonier's *Voyager* [95], a studio model employed in paintings and, of course, Degas's *Little dancer of 14 years* [68] were precedents, although there is no direct connection between these two works and the present example.

32 Jean-Baptiste Hugues 1849–1917

Ravenna c.1885

Marble, bronze, blue stone, painted, 45 cm, signed on the left shoulder: Jean-Hugues

Musée d'Arras

Hugues's eclectic production included a good number of polychrome statues. The tradition of using feminine allegories to represent towns goes back to the tyches of ancient Greece and was a part of the academic vocabulary of this laureate of the 1875 Prix de Rome. Representations of the eastward-looking cities of Europe offered a historic justification for the use of decorative colour, their oriental splendour calling for an exotic polychromy to be added to the classic form. Hugues imagined Ravenna and its pendant, Venice, shown at the 1900 Exposition Universelle (Le Mans, Musée Tessé), as marmoreal young women bedecked with heavy bronze ornaments.

Sometimes known by the erroneous name of *Byzantium*, this bust of Ravenna evokes the rich Byzantine architecture of the Emilian city. The delicacy of the features is highlighted by the brown paint of the eyebrows and the mass of hair; the pupils are inlaid with blue stone. The graceful face contrasts with the opulence of the bronze jewellery made up of cameos, gemstones, pendeloques and fibulas that hold back the chlamys, and above all with the massive crown worn by this frail yet wilful young head.

In 1884, Sarah Bernhardt glorified the memory of the 6th-century Byzantine empress Theodora in the play of the same name by Victorien Sardou. French and other European audiences were dazzled by the sumptuousness of the costumes and staging, for which the actress had carried out historical research in Ravenna and elsewhere. The influence of Byzantine art on Art Nouveau and Symbolism is evident in the paintings of the Viennese Gustav Klimt and the Russian Mikhail Vrubel. In keeping with this contemporary fascination, Hugues evokes the mosaic portrait of Theodora in the church of San Vitale, Ravenna.

The Gothic and Renaissance Revivals 153

33 Théodore-Louis-Auguste Rivière 1857–1912

Charles VI and Odette de Champdivers 1897

Bronze, marble, ivory, 41.5 cm, signed on the base: THEODORE-RIVIERE
Paris, Musée des arts décoratifs

Rivière specialised in genre scenes and statues created using different materials. This representation of the passionate meeting of Charles VI ('le Bien-Aimé'), king of France from 1368 to 1422, and his mistress probably had no higher aim than to depict the universally human side of royal dynasties for a bourgeois public. After Isabella of Bavaria had abandoned Charles due to his increasingly violent tendencies, the king found comfort with Odette de Champdivers. That she was in fact the daughter of a horse dealer is a rumour that was already disproved in the 19th century.

The sculptor has combined the different substances with great technical skill. In groups such as these, history and *genre historique* – motifs generally reserved to painting or monumental sculpture – were reduced to domestic format.

34 Jean-Baptiste-Gustave Deloye
1848–1899

The captain's share 1898
Bronze, partially gilt, marble, 49 cm,
signed on the socle: G DELOYE
Paris, Musée des arts décoratifs

Deloye was a multitalented sculptor who gained a modest fame with portraits of his contemporaries and historical personalities of the 18th century. During his long stay in Vienna he frequently convinced members of the Austrian nobility to participate in a series of elaborate *tableaux vivants*, given the telling title *Le rêve du collectionneur*. Accompanied by music, the Auerspergs, Metternichs and Kinskys recreated not only famous paintings by artists from Caravaggio to Rembrandt but also a 'divinité indienne,' a 'négrillon vénitien' and a bust by Luca della Robbia. A love of *genre historique* was also the inspiration for this small group, *La part du Capitaine*, a male fantasy set in the Middle Ages. The materials employed – bronze for the armoured knight and marble for his nude prize – are differentiated in a highly decorative manner. In the same year, Deloye and Jean-Léon Gérôme founded the Société de l'art précieux.

35 **Alfred Gilbert** 1854–1934
St Elizabeth of Hungary 1899
Bronze, ivory, tin inlaid with mother-of-pearl and semi-precious stones, 53.3 cm
A parish church in Scotland

36 **Alfred Gilbert**
The Virgin 1899
Bronze, painted, 49.5 cm
A parish church in Scotland

Gilbert, the most famous British sculptor of his period, conceived these two figures for his most important commission, the tomb of the Duke of Clarence at Windsor Castle. Gilbert's early works, such as his *Icarus* of 1884, had been widely praised for their lively naturalism, especially in their surface qualities. Gilbert himself wrote on this concept, then termed *couleur*. In the Fawcett Memorial (1885-87) the sculptor first explored the use of colour or polychromy, especially through the use of diverse materials, a tendency he took furthest in the Clarence Tomb, begun in 1892. The tomb comprises a sarcophagus upon which rests the Duke's effigy in dark bronze with contrasting white marble hands and face. A silvery aluminum angel holds a crown over the Duke. Surrounding these elements is an elaborate bronze grillwork, highlighted with gilt and incorporating twelve statuettes, including versions of *The Virgin* and the *St Elizabeth*.

St Elizabeth of Hungary, a Christian queen and ancestor of the Duke, was carrying food in her cloak one day to feed the poor when her pagan husband demanded to see what she concealed. A miracle occurred when she responded that it was only roses, the food becoming flowers as she revealed her garment's contents. Inset gems in her headdress and on her staff connote her worldly wealth, while her carved ivory face is a pale, ethereal signifier of her inner spirituality. A similar contrast of elaborate clothing and a peaceful face is found in *The Virgin*, whose calm painted visage is set against a gold-flecked white robe, the whole encircled by red roses whose colour recalls Christ's blood and whose thorns recall his crown.

Initially, all twelve statuettes on the tomb were to have been as elaborately colouristic as these, in keeping with the polychrome effect of the monument as a whole. Most of them, including the versions of *St Elizabeth* and *The Virgin*, are less complicated, however, their polychromy due mainly to paint applied to bronze. For financial reasons, Gilbert sold the present statuettes (which had been made for the tomb) as independent works.

37 **William Ernest Reynolds-Stephens** 1862–1943
Sir Lancelot and the nestling 1899
Bronze, ivory, mother-of-pearl, enamel, 86 cm, signed: W. Reynolds-Stephens 1899; initialled on the base: W.R.S. 1899; inscribed on the base: SIR/LANCELOT/AND THE NESTLING
Private collection

38 **William Ernest Reynolds-Stephens**
Guinevere and the nestling 1900
Bronze, ivory, mother-of-pearl, enamel, 86 cm, signed: 1900 W. Reynolds-Stephens; initialled on the base: W.R.S. 1899; inscribed on the base: GUINEVERE AND/THE NESTLING
Private collection

Reynolds-Stephens exhibited both paintings and sculpture at the Royal Academy, switching from mainly painting to mainly sculpture by the mid-1890s. Influenced by Gilbert and Frampton, he was also dedicated to the polytechnical ideals of the Arts and Crafts movement, even more so than the younger Gilbert Bayes. This accounts for Reynolds-Stephens's interest in gold and silversmith work (he exhibited a silver bonbonnière at the Royal Academy in 1897). Later in his career, he would be among the first artists to explore the recently-invented electro-deposition process as a means for making metal sculpture.

The companion sculptures were among Reynolds-Stephens's first endeavours in polychromy. The two statuettes share identical bases (that for *Guinevere* probably recast from the other, since it is dated 1899 while the figure is dated 1900), and reflect the artist's interest in medieval legend, especially the tales of King Arthur. In a manner markedly similar to Gilbert's procedure for his *St George* for the Clarence Tomb, Reynolds-Stephens cast many small parts for the armor of his *Lancelot*, which were then combined for the final work. The jerkin worn by the knight was covered with oxidised silver, with patterns cut into it to show the colour of the bronze beneath.

Both statuettes also include enamel and mother-of-pearl, the latter used to fine effect in *Guinevere*'s belt and hair pieces. The ivory employed by the artist, particularly effective in the nestling held by Lancelot and in the half-figure on the handle of his sword, was perhaps inspired by Gilbert's use of it for the faces of some of the statuettes related to the Clarence Tomb. In *Lancelot and the nestling*, the material lends a certain realistic vulnerability to the naked infant, in contrast to the sense of spiritual removal in Gilbert's *St Elizabeth*. [35]

The Gothic and Renaissance Revivals

119 Gilbert Bayes, model of *St George*, tinted photograph, The Gilbert Bayes Family Archive

39 Gilbert Bayes 1872–1953

St George c.1900

Bronze, enamel, mother-of-pearl, 76 cm (with base),
signed: GILBERT BAYES
London, The Fine Art Society PLC

Gilbert Bayes, though considerably younger than many of the 'New Sculptors,' was influenced and led by them, particularly George Frampton, who sponsored him for his training at the Royal Academy; Bayes may have also been influenced by his father and brother, the painters A.W. and Walter Bayes.

Bayes was particularly attuned to the ideals of the Arts and Crafts movement, especially its emphasis on the artisan who is capable in many media and who can, therefore, combine them in single sculptures. In his *St George*, Bayes has enhanced the bronze with subtle touches of mother-of-pearl and enamelled areas, such as the rich red of the figure's cloak. Many of the sculptor's subsequent works also take this combinatory approach, and it is certainly significant that he was later employed by the famous Doulton Pottery, modelling forms that were glazed and fired as multicoloured stoneware reliefs and figurines.

Like other 'New Sculptors,' Bayes often explored medieval chivalric subjects. It is worth noting that both Frampton and Gilbert tried their hand at the St George theme. Bayes's figure, however, here subtly recalls the stance of Donatello's more famous *St George* in Florence, the early Italian Renaissance being an ever-present influence in this period.

40 Henry Cros
Bust of a girl c.1880-90
Glass paste, 14 × 10 cm
Paris, Musée des arts décoratifs

If his works in *pâte de verre* draw on bucolic Latin themes, Cros's early attempts in polychrome wax suggest a romantic vision of medieval northern Europe in their historical realism, their composition, their aesthetic values (close to those of primitive painting) and their evocation of the days of chivalry. But this apparent dichotomy between the Middle Ages and Antiquity is united by a shared nostalgia for a lost paradise. Quite simply, Cros adapted his polychrome subjects to their medium. Where the precision and malleability of wax lends itself to the historical creation of the age of the troubadours, using mass-tinting and the inlaying of stones and pearls, moulded *pâte de verre* dilutes colours and softens outlines, its suggestive imprecision harmonising perfectly with the fin-de-siècle longing for a Virgilian golden age.

While Cros's wax figures usually represent scenes from the medieval world, he generally chose motifs from Antiquity for his reliefs in glass paste. Occasionally, however, he would also make excursions into the stylistic realm of the Renaissance, as in this frontal view of a girl. In contrast to most of his other reliefs [12–16], this one is clearly raised. It is possible that Cros intended the work, which he additionally had framed as if it were a canvas, to illustrate a compromise between painting and sculpture. The stylistic reference to the Renaissance was a means of legitimising this aim, as he could claim a precedent in the supposedly daring balancing acts of his Quattrocento colleagues. The contemporary critic Alphonse Germain sought, however, to differentiate: 'Sansovino, Vecchietta, Mino da Fiesole, Donatello, Germain Pilon, *coloraient*, lui, *nuance*.'

120 Henry Cros, *Bust of a gipsy from the Pyrenees*, 1881, terracotta, Sèvres, Musée national de la Céramique

The Gothic and Renaissance Revivals

41 Adolf von Hildebrand 1847–1921
Elisabeth von Herzogenberg as St Cecilia 1893–97
Terracotta, tinted, 79 x 44 cm
Marburger Universitätsmuseum für Kunst und Kulturgeschichte

It is somewhat surprising to discover that the promoter of classical sculpture and author of the influential treatise *Vom Problem der Form in der bildenden Kunst* (1893) made excursions into the 'borderline' area of polychromy. Like so many of his contemporaries, however, even Hildebrand could not resist the temptation. Although not numerous, these unjustly neglected works have an important place in his oeuvre. Most are likenesses of family or friends and are clearly inspired by Florentine portraits of the Renaissance. The rehabilitation of coloured sculptures by artists such as Donatello and Laurana in the wake of contemporary discussions about polychromy was probably another motivating factor.

In 1885-86 Hildebrand had created a colourful portrait relief of his friend the composer and pianist Elisabeth von Herzogenberg, a student of Johannes Brahms. Upon her death in 1892, the sculptor also made her memorial, this time in majolica (San Remo, Cimitero Vecchio). She is represented in the role of St Cecilia, the patron saint of music. The version illustrated here, made for the widower, is partially gilt, giving it an unreal, almost supernatural appearance.

121 Adolf von Hildebrand, *Elisabeth von Herzogenberg*, 1885-86, terracotta, painted, Vienna, Österreichische Galerie Belvedere

42 Artur Volkmann 1851–1941

Eve c.1890–93

Marble, painted, 76 cm, signed with monogram: ·AV·

Staatliche Kunstsammlungen Dresden, Skulpturensammlung

As a member of the circle around Hans von Marées and Adolf von Hildebrand, the so-called 'Deutsch-Römer,' Volkmann was one of the most important exponents of German *Neuklassizismus* at the turn of the century. Max Klinger first experimented with colour in sculpture using his plaster busts. Volkmann polychromed his own life-size statues, applying the colour with a restraint that stresses rather than hides the plastic form.

The relief of *Eve*, however, was painted by Hermann Prell, who, although he often collaborated with Volkmann, is actually better known for his monumental historical wall paintings. Both the niche and the realistic apple tree, from which a self-assured Eve is about to pluck the fruit of knowledge, recall works of the Renaissance. The figure is completely white (except for her blond hair) and stands out effectively against the blue background.

Volkmann, like his more famous colleague Hildebrand, later rejected this kind of painterly sculptural polychromy. In his treatise *Vom Sehen und Gestalten* (1912), dedicated to Marées, he saw no justification for the use of colour as an end in itself, claiming that 'colour is only permissable when it is subordinate to form.'

43 **Robert Anning Bell** 1863-1933
Mermaid 1900
Plaster, coloured and gilt, 37 x 32 cm, signed at upper left:
R.A. Bell 1900
Private collection

44 **Robert Anning Bell**
Mother and children 1906
Plaster, coloured and gilt, 37 x 28 cm, signed at upper left:
R. An. Bell/'06/no. 2
Private collection

Bell was primarily a painter, his sculptural work consisting of very low reliefs. Small in size and made of plaster coloured with pigmented wax, they were meant to be cheap to manufacture yet capable of taking the artist's original touch. In different versions of the same relief, Bell was known to alter the colour scheme. Bell collaborated with George Frampton on several multimedia projects, and the two shared a house and studio in the late-1880s. Frampton's 1893 article 'On colouring sculpture' described the methods used in colouring plaster reliefs like these, which Frampton sometimes made in imitation of Bell. Frampton advocated the lowest possible degree of relief, suggesting no more than half an inch at the highest point. Matthew Webb, in the second part of the same article, called such coloured low reliefs a 'meeting-point between sculptor and painter.' Stylistically, Bell's reliefs relate both to his own painting and to the early Renaissance. The *rilievo schiacciato* ('squashed relief') invented by Donatello is here revisited. Bell's *Mermaid* evokes the paintings of Sandro Botticelli, especially in the elegance of the figure and her long wafting hair. The colouring is conceived as broad areas of hue, sometimes enlivened by being thinly applied over gold. Eschewing white pigment, he allowed the plaster itself to serve that function, in a manner analogous to the practice of the watercolourist. The whole composition typically was given a gilt border, which highlighted the gilding of the details and unified the composition.

True to his Arts and Crafts versatility, Bell for a time modelled reliefs for the Della Robbia art pottery (in operation 1893-1906), which were coloured and glazed in imitation of the works of the Italian Renaissance Della Robbia family. Interior decoration was his main concern. The *Mermaid*, e.g., is one of a series of panels made for the banker M. Malet for his country home in Varengeville near Dieppe. His version is fixed above a door and the series is still in place in the house.

122 Donatello, *Madonna and child*, c. 1440, terracotta, Paris, Musée du Louvre

The Gothic and Renaissance Revivals

The art of the Salon

123 Charles Francis Fuller, *Monument to Rajaram Chuttraputti, Maharajah of Kholapur*, 1874, Florence, Cascine

45 Carlo Marochetti 1805–1867
Princess Gauramma of Coorg c.1856
Plaster, painted, 60 x 40 cm
Paris, Association des amis de Carlo Marochetti

46 Carlo Marochetti
Dalip Singh c.1856
Marble, painted, 85 x 60 cm
Paris, Association des amis de Carlo Marochetti

The subjects of both these busts were 'human trophies' of British supremacy in India. Dalip Singh (1838-1893), Maharajah of the Punjab and secular leader of the Sikhs, was persuaded to abdicate in 1849. He was converted to Christianity and settled in England in 1854, becoming for a time a protégé of the royal family. Growing resentment with his treatment by the British authorities caused him to revert to Sikhism, and he ended his days in France. Princess Gauramma was the favourite daughter of the deposed Rajah of Coorg, in the State of Mysore in southern India. In 1852, the ex-Rajah brought Gauramma, aged ten, to England, in order that she should receive a western education. Queen Victoria stood sponsor at her baptism and took a special interest in her. An unhappy marriage to a British officer ended in Gauramma's early death in 1864, after which her husband and child both mysteriously disappeared.

These are versions of busts commissioned from Marochetti by Queen Victoria in about 1856. They are from the sculptor's own collection. The versions in the royal collection are both in marble, but only that of Princess Gauramma retains its original colouring, Marochetti having been requested by Queen Victoria to 'clean off' her Dalip Singh. The colouring of all of the busts appears to have been the work of William Millais, brother of the Pre-Raphaelite painter. Regrettably, these busts are the only surviving coloured sculptures by Marochetti. No doubt Marochetti was influenced in his decision to colour his marbles by the contemporary debate on polychromy in the ancient world. He was acquainted with John Gibson (who also sculpted a bust of Dalip Singh), and would have seen the reproductions of the Parthenon sculptures coloured by his compatriot Raffaelle Monti for The Greek Court of the Sydenham Crystal Palace.

The art of the Salon 169

124 *The dying Seneca* or *The fisherman*, Roman copy of a Hellenistic original with later additions, Paris, Musée du Louvre

125 Pietro Calvi, *Othello*, 1879, marble and bronze, private collection

47 Charles-Henri-Joseph Cordier 1827–1905
Sudanese in Algerian dress 1856–57

Marble, onyx, bronze, 76 × 66 × 36 cm, signed on the right:
C. CORDIER
Compiègne, Musée national du Château

In 1850 Cordier was commissioned to produce a series of busts for the new ethnographic gallery planned at the Muséum d'Histoire naturelle in Paris. On his return from a mission to study racial types in Algeria, Cordier exhibited 13 busts at the 1857 Salon, including this 'Ethiopian type of the Sudanese race.' Copies of the *Nègre en costume algérien* (also known as *Nègre du Soudan*) were acquired by Napoleon III in 1857 (Paris, Musée d'Orsay) and 1860 (exhibited here). The works represent a unique attempt to combine science and art in the form of ethnographic sculpture. As he explained himself in the *Bulletin de la Société d'Anthropologie de Paris* (6 February 1862), Cordier set out to produce 'a general type combining all the beauties specific to the race under study.' In his effort to show the ubiquity of beauty by revealing the canon, the ideal beauty, of each race, he overturned the canon of classic, marmoreal beauty and developed a new aesthetic.

In defining this aesthetic, Cordier also claimed to be renewing the art of polychrome sculpture. As the poet and critic Théophile Gautier observed, 'Mr Cordier is a colourist and has developed a rich palette of marble, materials and stones [...]. He has dared to be original in an art that has little tolerance of originality' (*Le Moniteur*, 13 January 1865). Cordier's experiments with colour were the result of several factors: the examples of polychrome sculpture in the Louvre (e.g. the so-called *Dying Seneca* [124] and at Versailles (the *Moro Borghese* by his Baroque namesake, Nicolas Cordier); the romantic vision of a colourful Orient, heightened by French colonial conquest; his interest in the alliance of art and technologies both new (galvanoplasty, used here for the silver-plating) and traditional (enamelling); and finally, his passion for stones, such as this onyx marble with multicoloured veins that he brought back from Algeria.

The art of the Salon

48 Charles-Henri-Joseph Cordier
Arab sheik c.1862
Onyx, partially gilt, bronze, 94.2 x 58.5 x 41 cm, signed: CORDIER
Amsterdam, Van Gogh Museum

49 Charles-Henri-Joseph Cordier
Jewess from Algiers c.1862
Onyx, partially gilt, bronze, silvered bronze, enamel, semi-precious stones, 92.8 x 63 x 31.2 cm
Amsterdam, Van Gogh Museum

Cordier's 'types' were particularly popular in the wealthy circles of the Second Empire. The demand for replicas in various formats and more or less luxurious editions was gladly met by the sculptor. One of his most successful busts was the *Juive d'Alger*. As in a number of other instances, this work was originally exhibited as a pair, in this case with the *Cheik arabe*. At the Salon of 1863 Cordier exhibited a portrait of his patron the Empress Eugénie which was sharply criticised (present location unknown). Particularly the union of metal and enamel, a technical innovation for which this sculptor could justly claim the copyright, was seen as irrational, a combination of materials that had no relation to one another. The critic for the *Gazette des Beaux-Arts*, Paul Mantz, claimed Cordier had sunk even lower than the waxworks. Such attacks were not surprising: the debate about polychromy in contemporary sculpture had begun just one year earlier with the exhibition of John Gibson's *Tinted Venus* in London. [7]

The different materials are employed in a highly decorative manner in the *Jewess*. Even the bronze of the skin and the hair are differentiated. The inlaid eyes add to the overall lifelike effect. The supposedly original version of the *Jewess* is in Troyes, Musée des Beaux-Arts. Reductions can frequently be found in the art market. Another pair, just like this one, but without gilt applications on the drapery, is in a private collection in Switzerland.

50 Louis-Ernest Barrias 1841–1905
Girl from Bou-Saada 1890
Marble, gilt bronze, 70 cm, signed: E. Barrias
Paris, Musée des arts décoratifs

This statue was designed as a funerary monument for Barrias's student and friend, the orientalist painter Achille Guillaumet, who died in 1887. Bou-Saada was a French guard post in the Sahara and a popular site with many Orientalists. The girl, who was also the model for a painting by Guillaumet, *La cardeuse de laine*, exhibited in the Salon of 1885 [126], now sits on her bronze carpet in the Montmartre cemetery, strewing flowers over a portrait-medallion of the painter. Even without this anecdotal connection, the little girl was a great success at the Salon, which resulted in the production of a large number of variations by the company Susse Frères. Her sentimental expression, the essence of the figure, was also captured in a series of busts. A common strategy was to introduce various 'models' in differing price categories onto the market. The life-size marble and bronze combination shown here was, of course, one of the more elaborate.

126 Achille Guillaumet, *Wool carder in Bou-Saada*, 1885, Rouen, Musée des Beaux-Arts

51 Emmanuel Fremiet
Orang-utan and the savage from Borneo 1895
Plaster, painted, 58.5 × 55 × 21 cm, signed at bottom right: FREMIET; inscribed on the front: ORANG-OUTAN
Dijon, Musée des Beaux-Arts

52 Emmanuel Fremiet
Orang-utan and the savage from Borneo c.1895
Stoneware, enamelled, 58.5 × 55 × 21 cm, signed at bottom right: FREMIET – Grès – Emile MULLER
Paris, Galerie Elstir

The small plaster model and stoneware cast of Fremiet's *Orang-utan and the savage* illustrate two variations on the possibilities of polychromy. The work was originally planned in bronze and was to stand outside the new natural history museum in Paris. In the end, however, the architect Ferdinand Dutert suggested that Fremiet choose marble instead, a less emphatic material which would give the composition a greater suggestiveness and simplicity.

Fremiet had a highly precise sense of observation and, having worked as a draughtsman with naturalists and doctors, he argued for an extreme historical and ethnographic realism. As he saw it, a work of art served to document and not to suggest, and he strove for a rigorous, nonselective verism. The transcription into marble gave him the idea of using artificial polychromy (which he tested on this plaster version) in order to heighten the illusionism he had already created by means of the contrasting lighting on the smooth finish of the man's body and the thick, rough texture of the animal's fur. In 1898, the coloured marble was finally set in the vestibule of the museum. Defenders of ideal beauty warned that such verist polychromy, devoid as it was of sublime feeling, ran the risk of producing no more than garish false corpses, a wax museum devoid of meaning and nobility.

Like many other sculptors, Fremiet sold the reproduction rights to a number of his sculptures to Emile Muller, who founded a huge factory specialising in artistic and architectural decorative stoneware in Ivry in 1854. This material was immensely popular at the end of the century: its plasticity guaranteed accurate casting; when vitrified it was impermeable, and it could withstand extremely high firing temperatures, thus allowing for solid colouring, notably the copper oxide *flambé* effects inspired by Far Eastern stoneware. Muller's commercial priorities led him to transcribe the *Orang-utan* into a smooth, bluish material that seems utterly incongruous with such a subject.

53 Henri Gréber 1854–1941
Emmanuel Fremiet 1908
Marbles, bronze, 48 × 18 × 13 cm, signed on the socle at the right: H. Greber Paris, 1908; inscribed on the front of the socle: Au maître Frémiet
Beauvais, Musée départemental de l'Oise

In addition to his more classical bust of this subject and the public monument in the Jardin des Plantes, Paris, Gréber's small full-length portrait of his teacher is one of the lively representations of his contemporaries in the form of indoor statuettes for which he became famous at the turn of the century. To make this sculpture, Gréber worked from four photographs of Fremiet in a familiar standing position, carefully and faithfully combining the different views and thus sparing the subject the tedium of long sittings. More so than in the first versions, the use of colour – grey marble for the clothing, white for the skin – contributes here to the illusionistic effect.

As the son of an *ornemaniste*, Gréber gave his statuettes the look of small and refined decorative objects, using rare stones in colours that are unusual for sculpture. This decorative polychromy contrasts with the white biscuit used for miniature full-length portraits in the previous century and with the bronze or, occasionally, ivory or silver of the Romantic era. It was very popular for small whimsical pieces at the end of the century, but Gréber's originality was to adapt it to portraits.

127 Fernand Cormon, *The sculptor at work (Jean-Léon Gérôme painting the Bellona)*, 1891, Vesoul, Musée municipal Georges Garret

128 Head of the Medusa by René Lalique, detail of Gérôme's *Bust of Bellona*

54 Jean-Léon Gérôme
Bust of Bellona 1892

Bronze, terracotta, glass, porcelain, 87 × 47 × 30 cm, signed on the base at the left: J.L. GEROME; inscribed at the front: BELLONE
Vesoul, Musée municipal Georges Garret

At the 1892 Salon Jean-Léon Gérôme, the renowned official painter and sculptor, caused a sensation with his life-size statue of *Bellona*, a fearsome allegory of war (Toronto, private collection). Gérôme's aims in making this statue at his own considerable expense were threefold. First of all, and notwithstanding his denials, he was competing with the *Athena Parthenos* made by Charles Simart in 1855. [19] Both works were an attempt to recreate a historic phase of ancient chryselephantine statuary, and in particular the lost and little-known work of Phidias. But if Simart's *Athena* is in strict compliance with the canon, the only antique thing about *Bellona* is its subject. This brings us to Gérôme's second objective: having been criticised for the inexpressive immobility of his statues, the artist was determined to prove that he could render movement and feeling. The exaggeration of this grimacing face is inspired by the famous work of the romantic sculptor François Rude, *La Marseillaise* on the Arc de Triomphe. Finally, going beyond simple recreation, Gérôme wanted to take advantage of scientific discoveries by applying them to works of art. He considered *Bellona* 'an interesting work from the decorative point of view' (Ackerman), the kind of alliance between the arts and crafts that was in tune with his industrial century; he called on reputed professionals such as the Siot-Decauville foundry for the bronzes, Gautruche for the patinas and electroplating, Moreau-Vauthier and Clovis Delacour for the ivories, and Emile Gallé, then René Lalique for the small glass Medusa's head. By virtue of its extreme preciousness, Simart's *Athena* was designed to be a unique piece, as was Phidias's mythical example. Gérôme, however, was interested in multiples as a way of popularising the fine arts.

The art of the Salon 181

55 Jean-Léon Gérôme
Sarah Bernhardt 1895–97

Marble, painted, 67.7 x 41 x 29 cm, signed on the pedestal at the left: J.-L. Gérome; inscribed: SARAH BERNHARDT
Paris, Musée d'Orsay

This portrait of the great actress (1844–1923) is one of the few Gérôme sculptures to have retained its original coloration. There is a sense of immediacy and presence in the dark-brown uncombed hair, the absent-minded glance and the slightly open mouth. Works such as this certainly caused discomfort in many of the artist's contemporaries, still under the spell of the purity and abstraction of white marble. The unadorned realism is counteracted by the strange combination of assisting figures: to the left, a figurine of Melpomene, the muse of tragedy, lifting the veil from her terrifying mask, and, to the right, the genii crawling up the sitter's shoulder.

We can assume that Gérôme and his model discussed both the attributes and their position in detail. Sarah Bernhardt was herself a sculptor, had exhibited several times at the Salon, and could certainly have given her colleague professional advice.

The art of the Salon

56 Jean-Léon Gérôme

The ball player 1902

Marble, tinted, 63 x 36.5 x 27 cm, signed on the socle at the left: J.L. GEROME

Caen, Musée des Beaux-Arts

57 Jean-Léon Gérôme

Self-portrait painting the masks of *The ball player* c.1902

Oil on canvas, 61 x 50 cm

Vesoul, Musée municipal Georges Garret

This ball player has to throw the balls into the mouths of the masks at her feet without moving them. The rules of the game, invented by Gérôme, are the pretext for a pleasing contortion of the female figure. The *Self-portrait* was painted at the end of the artist's life, circa 1902, the year he presented another life-size version of this sculpture, also rubbed with wax and tinted, at the Salon (present location unknown). This work was the artist's ultimate public statement of his belief in polychrome sculpture. Indeed, so complete was the identification of the artist with this movement that he was given the nickname 'le père Polychrome' by the writer Marcel Schwob.

Two of Gérôme's paintings, *Painting breathes life into sculpture* [45] and *Workshop at Tanagra* (present location unknown), show a coroplast's studio, with a woman in the foreground painting *The hoop dancer* and customers at the window looking at the finished sculptures. These naturally include Gérôme's own works, *Tanagra* [112] and *Corinth* (private collection). The half-humorous, half-doctrinal Latin title invented by Gérôme, 'Sculpturae vitam insufflat pictura,' shows how closely he associated the archaeological truth of the Graeco-Roman world with his own quest to restore colour to sculpture. More even than his apologias, the correspondences between Gérôme's painting and sculpture attest to his proud belief in the renovation of the much-reviled art of polychromatic sculpture. The culmination of Gérôme's historical realism, it also requires a complete practice and mastery of the art, on a par with the line of geniuses from Phidias to Michelangelo, both of whom he greatly admired.

129 Louis-Ernest Barrias, *Nature reveiling herself to science*, 1899, marbles, Paris, Musée d'Orsay

58 Louis-Ernest Barrias
Nature revealing herself to science c.1905
Bronze, partially gilt, ivory, scarab, 58 cm, signed: E. Barrias
Paris, Musée des arts décoratifs

Originally conceived and executed as an over-life-size marble figure for the medical faculty at the university of Bordeaux, Barrias's statue later underwent numerous transformations. The Musée d'Orsay owns a second large version, made of various kinds of marble, exhibited at the Salon of 1899. The Susse foundry, owned by the brothers Albert und Jacques, also produced small bronze versions, marble and bronze combinations, variations in silver and marble, as well as chryselephantine statuettes, all in series and in at least five different sizes. [72] One and the same image could thus exist in classical white marble, in 'natural polychromy' (various types of stone), in bronze, and in compositions of stone and metal.

When first presented to an international public at the Exposition Universelle of 1900, the figure must have been seen as a kind of allegory of the century just past. Breath0taking technical progress seemed to solve all the mysteries of the world, and it appeared only a matter of time before – to use Barrias's visual language – nature revealed its last secrets. That such old-fashioned academic female figures could still be employed at the beginning of the age of electricity is characteristic for the 19th century, with its usual simultaneity of heterogeneous forms of expression.

59 Désiré-Maurice Ferrary 1852–1904
Leda and the swan 1898
Marble, green onyx, bronze, 50.8 cm,
signed: FERRARY
The Board of Trustees of the National
Museums and Galleries on Merseyside,
Port Sunlight, Lady Lever Art Gallery

Ferrary won a gold medal at the Exposition Universelle of 1900 for this group, first exhibited in 1898. It is not certain if the version shown here is actually the same one, since the literature mentions the work variously as made of ivory or marble. The brilliant white figure of Leda makes a powerful contrast to the green-black of the bronze swan, its head resting lovingly on its sweetheart's breast. In triad with the onyx, Ferrary created a sculptural *objet d'art* whose erotic content is underlined by the sensuality and colour of the materials employed.

Lord Leverhulme, a Liverpool entrepreneur who had made his fortune in soap, was the work's first owner. He further indulged his taste for polychrome sculpture with the purchase of Ferrary's life-size *Salammbô* [91], as well as decorative pieces by Onslow Ford, Clovis Delacour and others. The masterly craftsmanship with which the sculptor combined his various substances must have been enormously appealing to him. Works from Leverhulme's collection could, and can, be seen in his museum in Port Sunlight on the Mersey river, an authentic example of the taste of the period and a *gesamtkunstwerk* in its own right.

60 Clovis Delacour 1859–1929

Andromeda c.1900

Ivory, onyx, bronze, granite, 76.8 x 44.4 x 38.1 cm, signed: C. Delacour
The Board of Trustees of the National Museums and Galleries on Merseyside, Port Sunlight, Lady Lever Art Gallery

Delacour had helped Jean-Léon Gérôme in assembling his full-length *Bellona* (Toronto, private collection), being responsible for the parts in ivory. In this independent work – as in Ferrary's *Leda* – the materials are allowed to speak for themselves. Andromeda, threatened and vulnerable, is made of ivory, while the hissing dragon is reproduced in bronze with a black patina. The rocks are made of granite and the waves of onyx. This highly decorative ensemble has something almost baroque, and Andromeda, whose saviour has not yet appeared on the horizon, resembles numerous painted versions. The incomparable bravura must have particularly attracted Lord Leverhulme, who did not hesitate to include it in his collection.

The art of patina

61 Antoine-Louis Barye 1795–1875
Tiger devouring a gavial 1831/1874
Bronze, 41 x 101 cm, signed at the left: BARYE 1831; foundry mark on the base at the back: Syndicat des FABRts de bronze/UNIS FRAN
Amsterdam, Van Gogh Museum

Barye, like Cordier somewhat later approached his subjects from a scientific point of view. The great *animalier* had early on recognised the commercial advantages of small-scale sculpture. He was able to exploit a gap in the market by creating relatively inexpensive and large editions. His animal collection varies not only in size but also in patina. Barye was a master of patination, which he knew how to manipulate with both great skill and the help of chemicals. He created subtle differentiations in shading, from the classic brown-black of the Renaissance to a modern green, a colour which has come to be considered typical for French bronzes. When, at the middle of the century, the first Japanese copper alloy sculptures arrived in Europe, Barye was anxious to learn the new techniques.

Barye produced his bronzes in new editions until late in life. This group, cast in 1874, is based on one of his earliest successes. The intense emotional reaction of the French public to this unideal representation of a life-and-death struggle between to wild animals has been described many times. It is most likely the work was sand-cast, a method which, unlike lost wax, requires a scrupulous chaser to refine the final product. The patination was also a later addition; as in all such cases it is difficult to know whether it was the sculptor himself who carried it out, someone following his instructions, or someone completely independent. The tiger (brown) and the reptile (green) are very subtle differentiated, and the overall effect is not nearly as obtrusive as the gleaming polish employed by some of Barye's contemporaries.

It is not known whether the artist was acquainted with the green marble crocodile in the Canopus of Hadrian's Villa. Whatever the case, Barye was not only able to distinguish the animals through their external appearances, movements and surfaces, but also through the masterful use of colour.

The art of patina 191

62 Marcello 1836–1879
Bianca Capello c.1863
Bronze, 85 x 59 x 32 cm, signed on the base at the left: A. MARCELLO; inscribed at the front: BIANCA CAPELLO; foundry mark at the back: F. BARBEDIENNE.FONDEUR
Paris, Collection Lucile Audouy

63 Marcello
Bianca Capello c.1863
Bronze, 85 x 59 x 32 cm, signed on the base at the left: A. MARCELLO; inscribed at the front: BIANCA CAPELLO; foundry mark at the back: F. BARBEDIENNE.FONDEUR
Paris, Collection Lucile Audouy

'Born into a noble Venetian family, Bianca Capello ran away at the age of 18 in the company of a young Florentine, taking with her the family's jewels. She sought refuge in Florence, where she became the mistress of Francesco de' Medici, feigned pregnancy, rid herself of her accomplices in deceit, and claimed the hand of her lover. Having become the Grand Duchess of Tuscany, she tried to poison her brother-in-law, the Cardinal de' Medici, but when her husband inadvertently ate the dish she had prepared, she resigned herself to dying with him.' So the entry in the catalogue of the 1863 Salon where the first (untraced) marble bust of this tragic heroine was exhibited. This debut by Marcello, the pseudonym of Adèle d'Affry, the Duchess Castiglione-Colonna, was a great success.

In spite of her aristocratic background, Marcello was far from dilettantish about her artistic career. She consolidated her success at the Salon by securing prestigious commissions. She was a modern-minded artist who used new techniques to produce copies in marble and bronze. She sold the reproduction rights for *Bianca Capello* to Ferdinand Barbedienne, retaining ownership of the model herself and keeping a careful eye on the finish of the copies, which, although they had the same dimensions, were sometimes treated very differently. The polychromy of the gilded and silvered bronze draws attention to the precious nature of both object and subject. One of the busts shown here is unique for the way Marcello has reworked the gilded face and neck and embellished the hollows of the hair and coat with nielloed blue enamel. Just as the elaborate hairstyle was inspired by a Michelangelo drawing, so the rich polychromy of the piece evokes the splendour of the Italian Renaissance and the precious statuettes of Antico [111] and Cellini.

64 Emile Hébert 1828–1893

Semiramis c.1878

Bronze, 60 × 32.5 cm, signed on the base: EMILE HEBERT; inscribed at the front: SEMIRAMIS

Paris, Collection Lucile Audouy

A precocious sculptor, Emile Hébert studied with his father, Pierre, and Jean-Jacques Feuchère. Reflecting the aspirations of the age, the sources of his inspiration throughout his career were many and various, from the macabre Romanticism of his early years to Graeco-Roman history and myth, historical and contemporary portraiture and the exotic ancient civilisations then in vogue.

Semiramis, an Assyrian queen of the 13th century B.C., was a figure both historical and legendary. Though her name means dove (Schamiram), this beauty was also the tyrannical founder of Babylon and a bellicose conqueror. According to the legend related by Diodorus Siculus, she was abandoned in the desert by her mother, the goddess Derceto, and fed by doves before being taken in by shepherds. When she disappeared from the earth, she rose heavenwards as a dove. The story of this 'daughter of the doves' inspired tragedies by Crébillon and Voltaire and operas by Gluck and Rossini. Paul-Emile Botta's discovery of the palace of King Sargon at Khorsabad, followed by the opening of an Assyrian department at the Louvre in 1847, revived interest in a civilisation known essentially through antique and biblical texts. In 1873, a paper on *La légende de Semiramis* was delivered at the Académie des Inscriptions. The base of this sculpture refers to the famous Assyrian winged bulls that used to guard the entrances to Sargon's palace, which the artist no doubt saw in the Louvre. The legendary queen is dishevelled and helmeted, but she is also metamorphosing into a dove: two wings frame her half-bared chest. This kind of Baudelairian *femme fatale* with her venomous and heroic charms was much to the taste of fin-de-siècle audiences.

Hébert used patinas to heighten the exoticism of the subject. Unusually, the bust is patinated with three different colours, and the polychromy is heightened by the marble of the base. The green patina of the flesh underscores the *morbidezza* of the subject while the brown helmet and old gold orphrey underline its preciousness.

65 Vincenzo Gemito 1852–1929

The water vendor, a figural fountain c.1886

Bronze, 55.5 x 20 x 28.5 cm, signed on the jar: GEMITO; inscribed on the back: DALL ORIGINALE/PROPTA DEL RE DI NAPOLI/SM FRANCESCO II/NAPOLI GEMITO

Amsterdam, Van Gogh Museum

The Italian sculptor and draughtsman Vincenzo Gemito worked in a classicising but realistic style, combining contemporary and classical elements. When Francesco II, the former king of Naples living in exile in Paris, asked the sculptor to make him a souvenir of his people and of his native land, Gemito chose a water vendor as his subject.

This version of *The water vendor* was designed in 1881. There is another version from 1880 in short trousers, as the *scugnizzi* were seen on the streets. The naked figure recalls Greek and Pompeiian statues, which raises it above mere realism, but it is nonetheless very lively and spontaneous. His dancing pose and broad grin are particularly charming.

Wax and clay were the first materials Gemito employed. Later, he turned to bronze and, at the end of his life, to gold and silver. He then made many small replicas of his early works, among them the *Water vendor*. The sculpture has been given two patinas, a light, almost golden brown for the body and dark brown for the jug, the hair and the fountain. The piece was probably cast by Lagana, who took over the production in 1886 after Gemito's own foundry went bankrupt.

130 Vincenzo Gemito, *Cesare Correnti*, 1880, bronze, Rome, Galleria Nazionale d'Arte Moderna (during restoration)

66 Constantin Meunier 1831–1905
Charlotte 1886

Bronze, 55 x 38 cm, signed: C Meunier/86; inscribed at upper left: CHARLOTTE; foundry mark at bottom right: A PETER-MANN/BRUXELLES

Brussels, Musées royaux des Beaux-Arts de Belgique (Musée Meunier)

Meunier exhibited this relief of his daughter's profile at the Les XX exhibition in Brussels in 1887. The artist's intense emotional attachment to the sitter is palpable in this intimate portrait which, not accidentally, recalls Italian Renaissance examples.

The critic from *L'Indépendance Belge* was, however, only able to ascertain a kind of clumsiness in the work, stemming, he thought, from the artist's lack of experience in the medium. The sculptor, however, patinated the bronze so that the work appears to shimmer in different colours in changing light. It is most likely Meunier intentionally sought to create a clear distinction between this piece and his figures of workers, which demonstrate a love of strong colours. [77 78] Both form and colour serve here to underline the charming nature of the person represented.

67 Raoul Larche 1860–1912

Jesus in the temple c. 1900

Bronze, 36.5 x 40 x 19.5 cm, signed on the left shoulder: RAOUL LARCHE; foundry mark at the back: SIOTDECAUVILLE./FONDEUR/PARIS; and no.: T 808
Kunsthalle Bremen

Jesus in the temple was certainly Larche's most popular work. The life-size standing figure, found in Copenhagen and Bordeaux, bears an inscription which refers directly to Luke 2:46-47. The facial expression and the attentive glance that appears directed at an imaginary listener emphasises both the momentary and, above all, Jesus's humanity. The Messiah is transformed into an historical figure, just as he was presented in Ernest Renan's influential *La vie de Jésus*, which first appeared in 1864 and was later republished in numerous editions. The original plaster is dated 1890.

Versions of this figure exist in marble, porcelain, bronze and pewter, sometimes as a statue, sometimes as a statuette or, as in this case, in bust form. This cast is particularly interesting because of its striking gold and red patina.

131 Raoul Larche, *The young Jesus in the temple*, c. 1900, bronze, Copenhagen, Ny Carlsberg Glyptotek

68 Alfred Gilbert
Head of a girl 1883
Bronze, 38.1 cm
Cardiff, The National Museum of Wales

This bronze study was modelled after Michaelena, the nursemaid of Gilbert's son Francis when the family lived in Rome. An early work, dating to before Gilbert began his exploration of polychromy, its colour is limited to the traces of gilding in the hair. It is, however, replete with that quality known as *couleur*, so important in the early days of the New Sculpture. The bust's fine, lively surface – made possible by lost-wax casting – invites touch and suggests living flesh in a way that Gilbert's contemporaries found highly admirable: the bust, which was Gilbert's debut at the Royal Academy, became the subject of a bidding war, so eager were would-be patrons to own it. Gilbert effectively moved in his career from an early concern with the warm surface qualities of *couleur* to the colour of polychromy, which gave an almost anti-naturalistic, symbolistic interest to his works.

This bust shows the influence of Gilbert's period in Italy, especially in its inspiration from the bronze tradition of masters such as Donatello and Cellini, and, more specifically, in the motif of the turbaned head, likely suggested to the sculptor by the similarly-garbed figures of Sibyls on Michelangelo's Sistine Ceiling.

69 Alfred Gilbert
Charity 1899
Bronze, 38.1 cm
London, The Trustees of the Victoria and Albert Museum

This statuette reflects Gilbert's experimentation with different alloys and patination methods to achieve colouristic effects. By 1888 the artist had met William Chandler Roberts-Austen, a metallurgist who published extensively on different alloys. Of particular interest to Roberts-Austin were certain alloys developed by the Japanese and the different colours that could be produced through their selective patination. One such alloy, *shakudo*, substituted gold for the usual tin found in bronze and could be patinated to a purplish tone by application of a caustic solution. This is the basic effect achieved in the *Charity*, which is a dark blackish bronze except in the areas of flesh, where a pickling solution was applied, supplying the reddish-purple tone. Interestingly, this bronze seems to have been Gilbert's last polychromatic work.

The figure derives from a large bronze candlestick Gilbert finished in 1900 as a memorial to Lord Arthur Russell in his family chapel at Chenies, Buckinghamshire. Near the centre of the vertical support of that candlestick are four figures of Virtues, one of them a *Charity*. As in the Clarence Tomb, some of these figures also exist as independent statuettes, the *Charity* foremost among them.

132 Auguste Rodin, *Bellona*, 1879, bronze, Philadelphia, The Rodin Museum, Bequest of Jules E. Mastbaum

70 Auguste Rodin 1840–1917

The Age of Bronze 1876–77/1906
Bronze, 178 x 59 x 61.5 cm, signed: Rodin
Leeds Museums and Galleries (City Art Gallery)

Rodin's *Age of Bronze* has an interesting and controversial history which makes it significant not only in Rodin's own career but also as a mirror of contemporary French attitudes towards sculpture. Rodin began work on the piece in Brussels and modelled it from a young Flemish soldier. Rodin had told his friends that 'an artist can establish his reputation with a single piece of sculpture' and it is clear that he aimed to make the *Age of Bronze* a deliberate watershed in his career.

Even before it was exhibited there was ensuing rumour that its realism had been achieved by casting from life. Rodin became actively involved in the next months in preparing the defence for his piece and in writing to as many influential figures as possible to defend his craftsmanship. For Rodin, the exhibition of the *Age of Bronze* at the Salon of 1877 was both successful and unsuccessful. Although the professors of the Academy and the critics in the press were not prepared to accept Rodin's word, his reputation had nevertheless been made and the figure received many enthusiastic compliments. The *Age of Bronze* marks the end of Rodin's time as an apprentice and jobbing sculptor for others and the beginning of his concentration on ideal sculpture on his own account.

Rodin's *L'âge d'airain* is well known, but the cast which has recently joined the collections of the Leeds Museums and Galleries has an unusual history. It also has a distinctive appearance and its water-marked patina comes from the fact that the sculpture has stood in the grounds of the family who commissioned it from the artist in 1906. This piece has not previously been documented as one of the many casts at this height (there are 34 currently listed, of which 17 are cast by Rudier, as is this one). Its provenance is nevertheless sufficiently clear to indicate that it should now be added to that listing. Correspondence in the archives of the Rodin Museum shows that Gervase and Mabel Beckett, who made the commission, were in correspondence with the artist between 8 February 1906 and 15 March 1907. A first cast was delivered to London and was deemed in some way unsatisfactory. The patrons asked Rodin if he would take it back, and a second cast was delivered. The statue remained with the Beckett family in Yorkshire until 1995.

Impressionism

71 Auguste Rodin Rose Beuret c.1880
Bronze (green), 29 x 18 x 16 cm, signed: A. Rodin
Lyons, Musée des Beaux-Arts

72 Auguste Rodin Rose Beuret c.1880
Bronze (black), 27 x 18 x 16 cm, signed: A. Rodin
Lyons, Musée des Beaux-Arts

73 Auguste Rodin Rose Beuret 1898
Marble, 51.5 x 43.5 x 44.8 cm, signed: A. Rodin
Paris, Musée Rodin

74 Auguste Rodin and Jean Cros Rose Beuret 1911
Glass paste, 25.8 x 16.6 x 14.2 cm
Paris, Musée Rodin

Rodin's model and mistress from 1864 onwards, the seamstress Rose Beuret was his lifelong companion. Rodin portrayed her in a mask showing her at the age of 36 or 38, its closed eyes giving this highly individualised depiction a strange inward quality. The mask was translated into bronze and was the starting point for a series of later works. In 1898 Rodin showed his assistant Antoine Bourdelle a maquette in which the mask was laid against a plaster-covered canvas that suggested a block of stone, and asked him to produce a marble version. Then, in 1911, Jean Cros transposed it into polychrome *pâte de verre*.

Rodin characteristically reused this model to make a series of different works, just as the same words can be reused to make different sentences. In each instance the colour and material play a particular role. Bronze underlines the severity of the mask, breaking down reflecting light and revealing the uneven modelling; an austere black patina heightens the contrasts between light and shade on a binary chromatic scale, whereas white marble surrounds the face with a luminous glow, an effect strengthened by the difference in handling between the crude block and the smooth mask. This delicate contrast between the *non-finito* and the smooth is one of Rodin's frequently used techniques for setting off the subject, preventing it from standing out abruptly in the empty air. The background is both a receptacle for light and a transition towards the surrounding space. Finally, *pâte de verre* allows for a wider range of colours: Rose Beuret's brown hair contrasts with the delicate pink of her face.

75 Auguste Rodin
Minerva with a helmet c.1896
Marble, bronze, 48 cm, signed on the marble: A. Rodin
The Board of Trustees of the National Museums and Galleries on Merseyside, Liverpool, Walker Art Gallery

The distant relationship between this sculpture and the helmeted *Bellona* [132], an early monumental bronze bust, demonstrates Rodin's continuing interest in militant female figures. While it was Rose Beuret who probably modelled for the earlier work, in this case it was Mariana Russell, wife of the Australian painter.

A photograph was enough to convince the Liverpool wine merchant and collector James Smith to buy Rodin's *Minerve au casque* in 1905. The black and white contrast achieved by the marble head and bronze helmet must have appeared quite striking in the reproduction. By combining bronze and marble in one work, Rodin united the sculptural working methods *porre* and *levare*, that is, the addition of soft material (clay) and the chiselling of hard stone. Rodin, an enemy of polychromy *à la Gérôme*, sought to create painterly effects not only with patina and ceramics but also by combing the classical materials of sculpture. Purists, of course, showed little appreciation for the *Minerva*, and even John Tancock called her 'more bizarre than pleasing.' Rodin's unfinished *Minerva without a helmet* in the National Gallery of Victoria in Melbourne, with its truncated cranium, demonstrates that the headdress is more than a simple attribute. Technical difficulties or a lack of acknowledgment may have been the reason why the Liverpool *Minerva with a helmet* remained an exception in the sculptor's oeuvre.

76 Medardo Rosso 1858–1928
The flesh of others 1883
Wax on plaster, 23.5 x 22.5 x 16 cm
Paris, Galerie de France

After a brief training as a painter, Rosso devoted himself to sculpture from 1882 to 1889, the year he moved from Milan to Paris. Close to the radical Scapigliatura movement in Lombardy, which advocated the fusion of the arts and the analysis of sensations, Rosso practised the fashionable *verismo*, but this had less to do with ideology than with his desire to communicate the impression of real life. *The flesh of others*, or *Carne altrui*, is a melancholy portrait of a prostitute, which marks a turning point in his art. Rosso was abandoning a rough modelling style for the fluid gradations of *sfumato*, moving away from picturesque detail to concentrate on the essence of the subject. Where once it was fragmented, light now slid easily over the smooth, compact wax. Exhibited in Paris alongside one of Rosso's copies of the *Medici Madonna*, *The flesh of others* is the artist's homage to Michelangelo's *non finito*.

'Like a painting, my block must be seen from a specific point, at that optical distance where it recomposes itself with the assistance of the viewer's retina: its value, its quality, its beauty are apparent only if your eye beholds it in its proper light,' explained Rosso. The wax, his favourite material, was modelled directly on the plaster core. Arguing that 'we must overcome matter,' Rosso rejected monumental form, presenting his sculptures without a base in order to integrate them into their environment. The translucency of the often tinted wax means that colour and form interpenetrate in space, creating an effect similar to that of his partially erased pencil drawings.

Though often classified as Impressionist, Rosso's oeuvre is independent of movements. Answering a survey by Edmond Claris on Impressionism in sculpture, he insisted that 'You cannot put painting on one side and sculpture on the other,' and affirmed that 'there are no limits in nature, there can be none in a work of art. That is how one obtains the atmosphere surrounding the figure, the colour that enlivens it, the perspective that defines it.'

77 Constantin Meunier

Puddlers 1893

Bronze, 49.9 x 49.7 x 10.4 cm, signed at the right: C Meunier;
Brussels, Musées royaux des Beaux-Arts de Belgique (Musée Meunier)

78 Constantin Meunier

The soil 1892

Bronze, 44.7 x 46 x 15.6 cm, signed at the right: C Meunier; inscribed at bottom left: LA/GLÈBE
Brussels, Musées royaux des Beaux-Arts de Belgique (Musée Meunier)

Sculptures and paintings depicting the world of Belgian miners have determined Meunier's reputation. Most of the casts of his bronzes seen in museums are in what has come to be considered a characteristic black. This dominance of black has led to the false assumption that Meunier was more or less uninterested in the patina of his works, or that he considered this colour to be particularly appropriate to his working-class subject matter. Both the reliefs shown here, however, demonstrate that the sculptor in fact employed a much broader 'palette' than is generally recognised. One is brown, almost red, while the other is patinated dark green. Even if the surfaces are not treated in the same broken manner as Rodin's, a comparison of the effect of light leads to some interesting observations: whether brown or green, the colour helps to unify the forms of Meunier's relief, while in Rodin, together with the modelling, it serves to differentiate them.

133 Edvard Munch, *Rodin's* Thinker *in the park of Dr Linde in Lübeck*, c. 1907, Paris, Musée Rodin

79 Auguste Rodin and Paul Jeanneney 1861–1920
Colossal head of Balzac c.1905

Stoneware, enamelled, 48 x 44.5 x 37 cm, signed on the neck at the left: RODIN

Paris, Musée du Petit Palais

Exhibited at the 1898 Salon in Paris, Rodin's monumental full-length sculpture of the writer Balzac provoked a violent polemic, causing the Société des gens de lettres, who had commissioned it, to refuse the work. The plaster was kept in Rodin's studio in Meudon (now in Paris, Musée d'Orsay). Not until 1939 was a bronze cast put into place on Boulevard Raspail. Other bronzes were also made, along with over 20 intermediary studies of the head.

Rodin took a passionate interest in technique. His experiments with ceramics started early. Between 1879 and 1882 he worked for short periods with Albert-Ernest Carrier-Belleuse, then director of the national porcelain manufacture at Sèvres, making epergne figurines and vases. Later, he would call on renowned ceramists such as Ernest Chaplet and Edmond Lachenal to transpose his works into other materials. In 1903, Rodin authorised Paul Jeanneney to reproduce in stoneware a life-size model of one of the *Burghers of Calais*, Jean d'Aire, along with several copies of the only bust of Jean d'Aire and a bust of Balzac for the exhibition in St Louis in 1904.

Jeanneney was himself a collector of Japanese stoneware and specialised in this material, which had been rediscovered at the Expositions Universelles in 1878 and 1889 and adapted to contemporary taste. Not only does stoneware allow for a very faithful reproduction of the model, it also enriches it with *flambé* tones and drips of enamel, giving the work a subtle, mobile colouring. At present, we know of four enamelled stoneware versions of the *Colossal head of Balzac* in various shades, ranging from green to brown.

80 Auguste Rodin
Torso of a young woman 1909
Bronze, 86 x 48 x 32.2 cm, signed at the left corner of the base: A Rodin; foundry mark: ALEXIS RUDIER FONDEUR PARIS
Paris, Musée Rodin

Rodin was commissioned to make the *Gates of hell* for the entrance to the Musée des arts décoratifs in 1880. Although the piece was never installed, its Dantean themes served the sculptor as a laboratory of forms until 1888. The original idea for *Torso of a young woman* came from the crouching woman at the top right-hand corner of the lintel. Indeed, Rodin recycled most of the figures he had conceived for this monumental portal. As Rodin reworked his ideas, this model was successively transformed into *Prayer*, *The martyr* and the seated bather in *Icarus*. In the end it became this torso, the plaster enlargement of which was shown at the 1910 Salon (Meudon, Musée Rodin). Without head, arms or legs it is an essential symbol of femininity, stripped of anecdote or superfluity.

The uneven, vibrant green patina underlines the modelling under the light but does not colour it. 'Colour! Try to give your work colour! This is an expression a sculptor should never use!' noted Rodin. 'There are no blotches in sculpture; there are only exact forms; the distribution of light is given by nature herself.' For Rodin, to colour a sculpture was to mistake it for a bas-relief. Echoing his ideas on the need to multiply the profiles in order to obtain truthful representation, he observed that: 'A statue is transformed in the light, like all things that have volume; atmosphere imposes successive transformations. It is important therefore that the work be close to reality, and then the coloration will settle, be distributed and play on truthful models, and consequently on exact profiles. Light separates, disjoins, decomposes and destroys inadequate, rounded or meagre modelling, but when it falls on accurate models, it gives the work the appearance and the character of life.' Like Medardo Rosso, Rodin held that a work was never isolated, that it is acted upon by its environment. Colour and form cohabit in a total fusion, beyond the frontiers of painting and sculpture, in the sole service of truth and life.

81 Auguste Rodin and Jean Cros 1884–1932
Camille Claudel in a bonnet c.1911
Glass paste, 24.9 x 14.9 x 17.9 cm
Paris, Musée Rodin

Camille Claudel remained powerfully present in Rodin's imagination after their separation in 1892. Apart from the 'short-haired' bronze *Head of Camille Claudel* (Paris, Musée Rodin) of 1884, his portraits of her all seem to have been made after they lived together. This first bust served as a reference for subsequent allegorical treatments of the subject. The only other bust portraying Claudel as herself is *Camille Claudel in a bonnet*. This model is not precisely dated: at first thought to be from 1886 or 1889, it may in fact be the bust Rodin gave to the sculptor Peter to translate into marble between 1893 and 1895, or even a later piece since, stylistically, it could have been made in or after 1900.

A student of the school at the Sèvres porcelain manufacture, Jean Cros perpetuated the tradition of *pâte de verre* developed by his father Henry. More a craftsman than an artist, he transposed several works by Antoine Bourdelle and Rodin in the atelier provided by the state right up to his death. Rodin was a declared admirer of Henry Cros, whom he considered one of the most glorious, if underestimated, figures in 19th-century sculpture. According to their correspondence, Rodin entrusted his plasters to Jean at the latter's request. However, he remained precise, vigilant and demanding with regard to their transposition, and was quick to refuse any firings he considered unsatisfactory.

Due to the intentionally unfinished execution, the plaster and terracotta versions of *Camille Claudel in a bonnet* have irregular surfaces (San Francisco, Palace of the Legion of Honor and Paris, Musée Rodin, respectively). Whereas the two bronzes cast by Alexis Rudier also have irregular surfaces, the two *pâte de verre* versions (the other recently auctioned) have smooth skins and their right eyebrows have been redrawn, as if the glass paste could not tolerate the roughness of the unfinished. This smooth, translucent material, with its light and diffuse colouring, softens the portrait, giving its subject a dreamlike quality.

82 Camille Claudel 1864–1943

Lost in thought 1905

Bronze, onyx, lamp, 24 x 22 x 27.5 cm, signed on the pedestal:
C. Claudel; marked: E. Blot; no. 10
Paris, Collection Lucile Audouy

Camille Claudel was the pupil, assistant and mistress of Auguste Rodin. By 1898, however, their separation was definitive and her work was beginning to emerge from his influence. Already in 1893-94, Claudel had begun to find new inspiration in everyday subjects. She exhibited a first bronze version of *La profonde pensée* at the Salon de la Société nationale des Beaux-Arts in Paris in 1898, and another was shown at the Exposition Universelle in 1900 (present location unknown). Eugène Blot acquired the rights to this and other works in 1900 and exhibited it in his gallery in 1905 under the title *Intimité*. Ten copies were sold. The one shown here (no. 10) belonged to his personal collection.

The work was also known as *La bûche de Noël*. According to Reine-Marie Paris, it illustrated the popular belief that the sparks from the Christmas log represented the fecundity of the family and of its cattle over the coming year. However, the title *Lost in thought* gives this depiction a more universal appeal. Claudel's choice of a genre scene is original: the wealth of descriptive detail and accessories characteristic of such pieces is more anecdotal than allegorical, more pictorial than sculptural, and was rarely attempted in three dimensions. In fact, *Lost in thought* is presented like a painting, with the fireplace framing the scene visually as well as contextually. The intimacy of the prayer is underlined by the perpendicular axis defined by the hearth and low pedestal, which demarcate a cubic space from which the viewer is excluded. Instead of a sculpture in the round, Claudel treats the scene as a high relief, relying entirely on the woman's physical attitude to suggest her contemplative state.

Lost in thought was originally edited in white marble and bronze. However, when Blot suggested that she include a lamp, and thus transform the sculpture into a night light, Claudel preferred to use onyx, the translucency of which is set off by the red light bulb evoking the warmth of the hearth. This hidden light source adds intensity to this profane prayer: 'A red lamp in the fireplace turns the woman into a black silhouette. The effect is amusing,' wrote her brother Paul. But, beyond its decorative effect, the light helps suggest the idea of an inner flame.

134 Pierre-Auguste Renoir, *Madame Renoir*, 1885, Philadelphia Museum of Art, W.P. Wilstach Collection

83 Pierre-Auguste Renoir 1841–1919
Madame Renoir 1916
Mortar, painted, 82.4 × 53 × 34.5 cm
Paris, Musée d'Orsay

In 1913, on the recommendation of his dealer Ambroise Vollard, the famous impressionist painter Renoir began to take up sculpture. In fact, apart from the bust and two medallions of his son Claude, or Coco, he did little modelling himself. Since his hands were paralysed, he supervised the work of Richard Guino, a pupil of Aristide Maillol, between 1914 and 1918. Often, as in the case of this bust of his wife, the sculptures were three-dimensional translations of his own paintings.

Aline Chaligot, a young seamstress, met Renoir in 1880, modelled for him and married him in 1889, giving him three children. She died suddenly on 27 June 1915, at the age of 56. In a letter dated 23 July 1916, Renoir asked Guino to come and model a bust of Aline based on a study for his seated woman, to be placed on her tomb. The first model for this sculpture was the painting *L'enfant au sein*, or *Maternity*, which showed Aline giving the breast to their first son, Pierre (St Petersburg, Florida, Museum of Fine Arts). *Mother and child*, which was issued in bronze by Hodebert, is almost an exact replica of this painting: apart from the rattan chair (replaced by a bench), the nurseling holding its foot as it suckles, the unbuttoned blouse and the wide-brimmed straw hat (without flowers) are all similar. It would seem that Renoir disliked this sculpture. After repeated sessions in which he did some of the modelling himself, he decided to keep only the bust, which was enlarged and cast in bronze, then placed on the tomb.

This bust, however, of which there are two known versions in hydraulic lime mortar and 'fresco-style' painted sand (the other being in Cagnes-sur-Mer, Musée des Collettes), although different from the bronze *Mother and child*, is identical to the portrait of Aline painted circa 1885 in which she has the same narrow-brimmed straw hat with roses, the same large-buttoned shirt and the same tousled, curly hair. [134] The pinkish colour of the flesh and the clothing underline this similarity. Whereas Renoir sold *Mother and child* to the dealer Paul Durand-Ruel in 1892, he kept this portrait until his death, preferring its more characterful rendering to the archetypal image of maternity that he returned to in so many later works.

84 Antoine Bourdelle 1861–1924
Head of Apollo 1900–09
Bronze, gold leaf, 67 x 21 x 28 cm, signed:
EMILE ANTOINE BOURDELLE 1900.
Paris, Mme Rhodia Dufet Bourdelle, on loan to the Musée Bourdelle

'In 1900 I tore myself away from Rodin and at the same time attempted to go higher than man, all the way to the God Apollo.' Bourdelle's *Head of Apollo*, which was nine years in gestation, was for many years kept secret. It is intimately bound up with his artistic renaissance. Bourdelle sculpted like an architect, invented a language of disciplined form that is more intellectual than naturalistic. For this head of Apollo, as he explained, 'more than human blood, bone, cartilage and muscle, I gave the form the ambient structure of forces.' Here, the variations in the modelling, on which the light now catches, now slides, reveal both the doubts and new certainties of the artist's quest. Bourdelle's curiosity embraced all forms of art and, according to his biographer Gaston Varenne, this work's delicacy of facture can be explained by his parallel practice of pastel techniques. Whereas in the work of his master light dissolves form in the multiplication of profiles, with Bourdelle it structures and anchors the work in space, resulting in a very different polychromy of light and shade, made of large, contrasting planes and thus in greater unity. Sometimes, as in this *Head of Apollo*, Bourdelle applied gold leaf to the green and black patinas of the bronzes cast for him by Alexis Rudier. As a divine colour and metal, gold symbolised not only the deity, but above all the extreme importance of this work to its creator after so much struggle. This new classicism also reflected a new cultural mood imbued with a nostalgia for a lost and mythical golden age.

85 **Pablo Picasso** 1881–1973

Head of a jester 1905

Bronze, 41.5 × 37 × 22.8 cm, signed: Picasso
Martigny (Switzerland), Collection Fondation
Pierre Gianadda

Picasso once said that 'the best commentary a painter can make on his painting is sculpture.' In the same way, this *Head of a jester*, or *Harlequin*, is a commentary on Picasso's transition from his blue to his rose period in the years 1904-05. It was during this transitional, or *Saltimbanque*, period that Picasso befriended the poets Max Jacob and Guillaume Apollinaire. According to one of his biographers, Roland Penrose, Picasso modelled a portrait of Max Jacob after the two men had spent an evening together at the circus. Going back to the piece the next morning, he added a jester's cap, leaving only the lower part of the face unchanged. The sculpture was then issued in bronze by his dealer Ambroise Vollard. The work is more a moral self-portrait than a likeness of the poet. The young Picasso was fascinated by the world of the circus and the disenchanted solitude of street performers and identified with Harlequin, a figure that reappears throughout his work, particularly at this time. The handling of the material and play of light and shade of the *Head of a jester* has prompted comparisons with Impressionism. The emaciated cheeks, sunken eyes and ambiguous smile reflect the destiny of the *Saltimbanque*, whose melancholy expression is set off by his grotesque outfit. The sad clown is a plastic experiment that is complementary to Picasso's painting. Picasso had freed himself from the influence of Rodin, whose work he had discovered in 1900. Red and green spots on the bronze prove that the Spaniard's ambitions went beyond the Frenchman's more natural patination.

Fin-de-siècle sculpture

86 Jean Carriès 1855–1894
The sleeping faun c.1880–85
Stoneware, applications in gilt and silvered metal, 30 x 28.5 x 21 cm, signed on the base at the front: J.CARRIES
Private collection

Carriès came from a lower-class background and was conscious of this throughout his entire life. That he so often treated outsiders, beggars and outcasts is therefore not merely a whim, and least of all condescension. Contemporary reality, history and mythology merge into one in his art. Even his portraits of artists, from Molière to Frans Hals, demonstrate his love of unrefined characters. The aging faun, of course, does not belong in the series of *déshérités*, *désesperés* and *épaves*, but may be seen as related in spirit to these humble figures. Despite the fact that this creature's appearance mocks all human beauty, the artist has touchingly modelled and refined the head.

In addition to the irregular tinting of the stoneware – beige with some pink areas – Carriès has incorporated gold and silver coloured metals, which emphasise the unique character of the work. Two other, less elaborate versions in stoneware are known; one of these can be found in Paris, Musée du Petit Palais.

135 Harry Bates, *Pandora*, 1891, London, Tate Gallery

87 Fix-Masseau 1869–1937

The secret 1894

Mahogany, partially painted, ivory, 76 x 17.5 x 18 cm, signed on the socle at the right: Fix-Masseau
Paris, Musée d'Orsay

Mysterious women, nude or in archaic garments, were a favourite subject of sculptors around the turn of the century – Fix-Masseau's *Secret*, Lemaire's *Woman from Egypt* [23] or Harry Bates's *Pandora* [135] are but a few among many. Often, these figures were given obscure ivory vessels with an undefined content, which of course did little more than justify the viewer's gazing at a partially-clothed female body. Such figures also allowed the sculptor to combine refined and expensive materials.

The star of David incised on the front of the socle leads to the conclusion that Fix-Masseau meant his female figure to evoke the era of the Old Testament; she is perhaps a sibyl or a vestal virgin. There may also be a reference to Pandora's box. The small ivory chest is, stylistically speaking, indeterminate. The woman seems to be keeping other secrets as well. The strictly hieratic pose forms a strong contrast to her eroticism, a characteristic of Symbolism.

The secret was reproduced by Emile Muller in stoneware and by Siot-Decauville in bronze.

136 View of the display of modern ivories in the Congo exhibition of 1897 in Brussels-Tervuren, photograph, Brussels, Musée royal de l'Afrique centrale

88 Julien Dillens 1849–1904
Allegretto 1894
Ivory, silver, 62 × 24 × 13.5 cm, signed on the socle at the right: Jul. Dillens
Brussels, Musées royaux de l'Art et de l'Histoire

This work in ivory was created for the first large-scale colonial exhibition in Antwerp in 1894 and was also displayed at its successor, which took place in Brussels in 1897. There it was bought by the 'Etat indépendant du Congo,' in fact the private property of King Leopold II of Belgium. These fairs, designed to encourage the export of products from these central African possessions, brought lucrative commissions for a number of sculptors and led to a renaissance of ivory. The stylistic pluralism of the turn of the century is reflected in these works, which include everything from solid neo-classical forms and neo-baroque reminiscences to the flowing lines of Art Nouveau, the soft material being particularly well-suited to the latter.

Dillens's *Allegretto* is a classically proportioned female nude, whose dancing pose is meant to express the playful lightness indicated in the title. The pale ivory certainly conformed to contemporary taste in female skin colour, and it is therefore not surprising that female nudes make up the majority of the production. Ivory's softness and fragility also accommodated the desire for preciousness in these objects.

89 Joseph-Louis Geleyn 1863–1934
Fury 1897
Ivory, silver, 47 × 19 × 17 cm, signed on the base: J. Geleyn
Brussels, Musées royaux de l'Art et de l'Histoire

While in Dillens's *Allegretto* [**88**] the applications in silver are carried out with the utmost discretion and are probably only meant to hide the figure's seams, Geleyn has placed great emphasis on this combination of the two materials in his more lively and temperamental *Fury*. The precious metal is used for the angry figure's attributes, the snakes and weapons. Additions such as these served to further enhance the value of the already precious ivory, turning the statuette into an art object for those refined tastes that rejected mass produced bronzes created merely to fill the need for decorative small-scale sculpture.

90 **Fernand Khnopff** 1858–1921
Mask c.1897
Plaster, painted, 18.5 × 28 × 6.5 cm
Hamburger Kunsthalle

The Belgian Symbolist Khnopff, better known as a painter, gave colour to this *Mask*, as he did to all his other sculptures. A version in ivory, bronze and enamel was shown in 1897 at the Brussels Congo exhibition, and another in 1898 in Vienna at the Secession. Ludwig Hevesi interpreted it as a Medusa. The mask played an important role in the artist's self-presentation. In many of the photographs he took in his villa, most of which included his sister Marguerite, it can be seen either attached to or hanging from a thin fluted column, as it had been exhibited in Brussels. It was given a prominent place in the house as a kind of idol in a chapel-like room. One of the photographs shows Marguerite dressed as a magician and gazing thoughtfully at it, gently covering the mouth with her right thumb, a gesture alluded to by Charles Van der Stappen in his *Secretive sphinx*. [138] Khnopff repeated the composition of the photograph in his pastel *Secret and reflection* of 1902, this time using an English model instead of Marguerite (Bruges, Groeningemuseum). The wings on the head have been seen as a reference to Hermes, but are above all reminiscent of Hypnos, a recurring motif in the Belgian's oeuvre. The wreath of flowers may also point to Flora and the laurel wreath is an Apollonian attribute. Khnopff thus created a creature representative of his own personal mythology, one which allowed him to forget the banal reality of daily life.

137 Fernand Khnopff, Photograph of Marguerite with the first, now lost version of the *Mask*

Fin-de-siècle sculpture

138 Charles Van der Stappen, *Secretive sphinx*, 1897, ivory and silver alloy, Brussels, Musées royaux de l'Art et de l'Histoire

91 George Frampton 1860–1928

Lamia 1899–1900

Bronze, ivory, opals, 61 x 55.3 x 25.4 cm, signed on the back: George Frampton 1899; on the base at the right: George Frampton 1900

London, Royal Academy of Arts

Lamia is particularly striking in its colouristic effect, linking the sculptor to symbolist movements such as the Belgian La Libre Esthétique, in whose first exhibition Frampton participated. The subject derived from Keats's eponymous poem of 1819 in which a snake-woman enchantress attempts to seduce a young man to gain mortality. In contrast to the 1905 painting of *Lamia* by John William Waterhouse (private collection), in which she is depicted in a brightly-coloured, snake-patterned dress, Frampton concentrated on the poem's ending, where a thwarted Lamia pales to a deadly white. He presented her in bust form, partly in homage to the busts of the Italian Renaissance, contrasting the pallor of her ivory skin with darkly-patinated bronze. Opals punctuate both *Lamia*'s scaly headdress and her bodice, the gems traditionally carrying a negative, menacing connotation stretching back at least to Sir Walter Scott, whose novel *Anne of Geierstein* (1829) featured an opal that eventually killed the heroine after having first given her great power. A small sphere of crystal hangs from *Lamia*'s pendant, also providing a sinister effect, given the well-known connection of the 'crystal ball' with divination and witchcraft.

Frampton chose and combined his materials for their symbolic (and decidedly non-naturalistic) qualities. He departed from the earliest paradigms of the New Sculpture, moving from the warm, *couleuriste* surfaces of works such as Gilbert's *Head of a girl* [68], to an expressionistic mode more concerned with inner psychology. Frampton was criticised for the lax quality of his sculptural surfaces, although it is clear that the creation of truly fleshlike skin was not his aim.

Another version of this bust, in painted plaster, was given by Frampton to Walter Bell, brother of his collaborator Robert Anning Bell (Birmingham Museum and Art Gallery).

Fin-de-siècle sculpture

139 Reconstruction of the Fouquet jewellery store by Alphonse Mucha, Paris, Musée Carnavalet

92 Alphonse Mucha 1860–1939
Nature c.1899

Bronze, silvered and gilt, 70 × 28 × 22 cm, signed under the right shoulder: MuchA; foundry mark: PINEDO PARIS
Karlsruhe, Badisches Landesmuseum

The cosmopolitan character of his career, the massive dissemination of his work, and the diversity of his painted, graphic and decorative production put the Czech artist Alphonse Mucha at the centre of the European Jugendstil. Mucha made only a few sculptures. Whereas the others were produced in collaboration with Auguste Seysses, it would seem that the artist delivered the maquette of *Nature* directly to the founder Emile Pinédo. Several versions of the work are known, not all of them bronze-coloured, but all slightly different. One is entirely gilded, another still has a pair of circular earrings with pearls and stars designed by Mucha (private collections). This one is notable for the matt finish of its silver, which sets off the subtlety of the modelling. The stones, too, are varied: green crocidolite with yellow veins, red marble (Richmond, Virginia Museum of Fine Arts) or amethyst. Another version has lost its stone (the last two in private collections). According to Victor Arwas, the egg-shaped stone replaces a light bulb, a device Mucha originally intended to crown the head.

This model was shown at the 1900 Exposition Universelle in Paris and probably in Turin in 1902. At the time it was thought to be a portrait of the actress Sarah Bernhardt or the fashionable beauty Cléo de Mérode, but Mucha probably based it on *Zodiaque*, a lithograph he made in 1896-97 representing an allegorical figure whose long blond hair is held down by a wrought gold diadem surmounted by a crystal oval. In keeping with a tradition that dates back to the Middle Ages, *Nature* wears a diadem symbolising the stars and planets and exudes a fecundity that transcends sensuality.

93 **Maurice Denis** 1870–1943
Audi filia 1889

Wood, painted, 41 x 30 cm, signed with monogram at upper left: MAVD; inscribed at upper right: AVDI FILIA
Saint-Germain-en-Laye, Musée départemental Maurice Denis – Le Prieuré

Jeanne Dufour was a pious and chaste young woman whom the adolescent Maurice Denis met and fell in love with in the church of Saint-Germain-en-Laye. In 1898, Jeanne joined the order of Les Filles de Saint-Vincent-de-Paul and, as a journal entry from 1885 shows, Denis had never doubted her vocation: 'O Jesus, love her, she is worthy of you, number her among your Virgins; and make her hear the *Audi me, filia, Rex concupivit puchritudinem tuam*.' (Psalm 45:10-11). Like the painting from the same period (private collection), this relief shows Jeanne before a crucifix in the church of Saint-Germain-en-Laye. She wears a white veil and her eyes are closed, her appearance contrasting with the two women in hats and town-clothes in the foreground.

At the time, Denis was a member of the Nabis, a group of young artists who advocated a symbolic, synthetic approach to art. It was a time of great experimentation, as demonstrated by this wood relief, a rare example of sculpture by the 'Nabi of the beautiful icons.' Denis was certainly familiar with the wooden reliefs of the Pont-Aven School and particularly admired Gauguin, whose *Yellow Christ* (Buffalo, Albright-Knox Art Gallery) may be echoed in the yellow legs on the crucifix here, and whose *Be in love you will be happy* (1889, Boston Museum of Fine Arts) and *Be mysterious* (1890) [100] were shown at Boussod, Valadon et Cie, a gallery Denis knew well. It may be that these translations of paintings into wooden bas-reliefs inspired Denis to do the same with *Audi filia*. Like Gauguin before him, Denis found that these three-dimensional transpositions allowed him to simplify both content and style. The relief uses fewer colours than the painting, while the tiered planes underline the idea of an ascension towards faith, from pious reading (seated) and inward prayer (kneeling) to the final accomplishment of divine grace (standing). The flecked, multicoloured ground of the canvas is replaced here by a simple backdrop dominated by a sort of stele engraved with the title. This work is more a painting in relief than a painted relief, for Denis's approach is that of a painter, not a sculptor. While in his paintings he sought to flatten colour, here he used volume simply to emphasise outline. The third dimension obliged him to match, or to synthesise, colour and form.

94 Jens Ferdinand Willumsen 1863–1958

Prostitute awaiting her prey in the *Montagnes Russes* 1890

Wood, painted, gilt and silvered, 100 x 60.5 cm, signed at upper right: J F Willumsen/1890
Frederikssund, J.F. Willumsens Museum

Willumsen could have learned about the combination of colour and volume from his teacher Per Severin Krøyer even before he saw Gauguin's *Be in love* in 1890 (Boston, Museum of Fine Arts). This relief is believed to have been of decisive influence on the Dane, although he continually denied any inspiration in other than purely technical matters. It is certain, however, that both artists had worked near each other in the early 1890s. The former exchanged a painting for a polychrome statuette by the Frenchman, *Luxury* (Willumsens Museum). Contacts with Theo van Gogh are also documented, and the *Prostitute* is vaguely reminiscent of Vincent's *Woman at a table in the Café du Tambourin* (Amsterdam, Van Gogh Museum, Vincent van Gogh Foundation). The flat relief certainly conforms to the ideals of the circle around Gauguin and the Nabis, who sought to synthesise the principles of painting and sculpture. The intentionally rough execution was an avant-garde trope, which helped to differentiate this generation from the still relatively refined impressionist masters of the previous decade. The artist painted the wood in contrasting colours, distributing them with great sensitivity towards proportion. Provocative in subject matter, style and execution it is no surprise that the public's response was entirely negative. Willumsen continued to work in various media, particularly in ceramic. His life's work was to become *The great relief*, a multifigured mountain of coloured stones and gilt bronze, which took about 35 years to complete (Willumsens Museum).

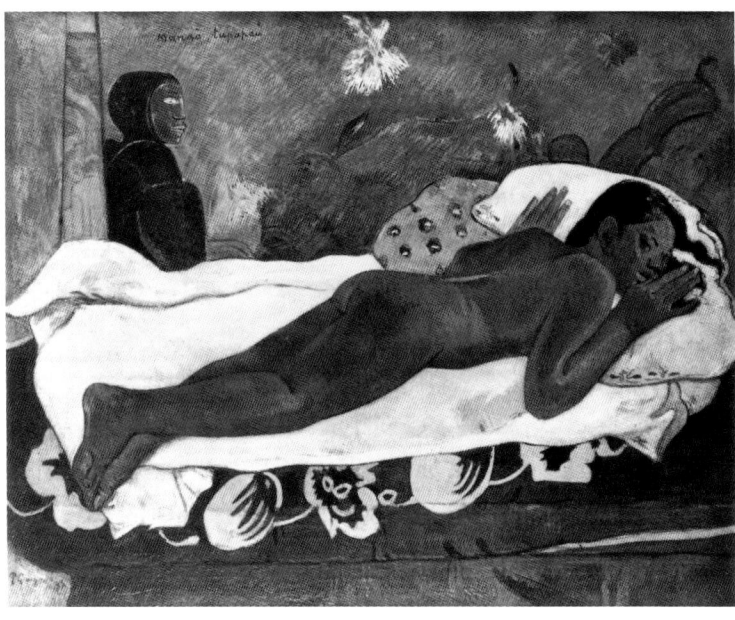

140 Paul Gauguin, *Manao Tupapau (The Spirit of the Dead watches)*, 1892, Buffalo, Albright-Knox Art Gallery, A. Conger Goodyear Collection

95 Paul Gauguin 1848–1903
Oviri 1894

Stoneware, partially glazed, 75 × 19 × 27 cm, signed at bottom right in relief: Pgo; inscribed on the front: OVIRI; dated on the base at the left in relief: 1894
Paris, Musée d'Orsay

Oviri, Tahitian for 'savage,' represents a wild-eyed woman pressing or choking a wolf-cub against her side and a wolf lying in a pool of blood at her feet. This 'strange figure, cruel enigma,' as Gauguin called her, unites the principles of life and death in a hybrid inspired by both the nacreous-eyed mummified skulls of the Marquesas Islands and the fertility symbols at Borobodur. For Gauguin, it was so intimately identified with the 'savage-in-spite-of-myself' that he also represented it in engravings and drawings, and asked to have it set on his tomb (where a bronze version now stands).

Gauguin made the work in the studio of the ceramist Ernest Chaplet in the winter of 1894, between two voyages to Tahiti. This was where he had begun learning the secrets of stoneware in 1886. He particularly appreciated the crude, brutal appearance of this material which had come back into fashion after the discovery of ancient Japanese stoneware. Gauguin was a sculptor more than a ceramist and preferred to model rather than use the wheel. The 100 or so pieces he made were increasingly plastic, becoming veritable *ronde-bosse* sculptures.

Even if Gauguin probably needed Chaplet's help to make this technically complex work, particularly with the enamelling, its polychromy is different from what was usually done on ceramics. Potters who transposed works sculpted by others, men like Emile Muller or Paul Jeanneney, or ceramist-sculptors such as Jean Carriès, tended to glaze or enamel their works more or less evenly, thus creating effects of overall colouring. Here, colour is used only in places and for descriptive purposes: while the matt brown colour of the oxidised stoneware, exposed to the air during firing, figures the flesh tint, white enamel was applied to the base and hair, bluish black to the animals' fur, and red for the blood.

Gauguin's non-conformism, symbolised by *Oviri*, was an important influence on the development of art. In connection with the history of polychromy, one can see this figure as the dawn of modern sculpture.

Fin-de-siècle sculpture

96 **Georges Lacombe** 1868–1916

Mary Magdalene 1896

Plaster, painted, 104 x 42 x 55 cm, signed on the base at the right:
Geo Lacombe/1896

Kunsthalle Bremen

Inspired to take up sculpture by Gauguin, the *Mary Magdalene* is probably Lacombe's most important work. His figures and reliefs are considered to be the most significant contributions to Nabis sculpture. The penitent's meditative state is given expression through a highly modern simplification of the forms. Contour and mass determine the sculpture, whose blocklike character points forward in time to the work of Aristide Maillol, who also exhibited with the Nabis. At the same time, Lacombe has worked the surface with an almost ornamental chasing, creating a pattern of parallel lines on the garment and hair. This, and even more clearly the hands, demonstrate a new interest in the early Romanesque. Lacombe was searching for 'primitivism' in his own culture. It has been suggested that Bretonian folk art served him with direct models.

This painted plaster precedes the version in wood in the Musée des Beaux-Arts in Lille, which was never, however, polychromed.

Fin-de-siècle sculpture

Notes

Andreas Blühm

In living colour

In memory of Peter Bloch.
Translated from the German by Rachel Esner.

1 Quoted in Albert Elsen, exhib. cat. *Pioneers of modern sculpture*, London (Hayward Gallery) 1973, p. 70.
2 Giovanni Dupré, *Pensieri sull'arte e ricordi autobiografici*, Florence 1910, pp. 289-90.
3 Oliver Sacks, 'The case of the colour-blind painter,' in idem, *An anthropologist on mars: seven paradoxical tales*, London 1995, p. 5.
4 Johann Joachim Winckelmann, *Geschichte der Kunst des Altertums* (1763-68), ed. Ludwig Goldscheider, Vienna 1934, p. 61.
5 For example by Anton Friedrich Büsching, *Entwurf einer Geschichte der zeichnenden schönen Künste*, Hamburg 1781, p. 48, quoted in Thomas Brachert and Friedrich Kobler, 'Fassung von Bildwerken,' *Reallexikon der deutschen Kunstgeschichte*, 9 vols. (to date), Munich 1937-, vol. 7 (1981), p. 826.
6 According to, among many others, Theodor Alt, *Die Grenzen der Kunst und die Buntfarbigkeit der Antike*, Berlin 1886, p. 97.
7 See Günter Bandmann, 'Der Wandel der Materialbewertung in der Kunsttheorie des 19. Jahrhunderts,' in Helmut Koopmann and J.A. Schmoll gen. Eisenwerth (eds.), *Beiträge zur Theorie der Künste im 19. Jahrhundert*, 2 vols., Frankfurt am Main 1971, vol. 1, p. 130: '[...] ein Kunstwerk wird verändert, um neue Werte aufzudecken, deren oft kurzphasige Gültigkeit nicht bewußt ist. Die Werte werden als dem Kunstwerk immanent angesehen, in Wirklichkeit aber dem Kunstwerk oktroyiert.'
8 G. Schäfer, 'Die Ausstellung gefärbter und getönter Bildwerke in Berlin,' *Centralblatt der Bauverwaltung* 5 (1885), p. 493.
9 Bandmann, op. cit. (note 7), p. 130.
10 Louis Courajod, *La polychromie dans la statuaire du Moyen Age et de la Renaissance*, Paris 1888, pp. 5-6.
11 Elizabeth S. Darby, 'John Gibson, Queen Victoria, and the idea of sculptural polychromy,' *Art History* 4 (1981), no. 1, pp. 39, 44.
12 Philip Ward-Jackson, 'The French background of royal monuments at Windsor and Frogmore,' *Journal of the Church Monuments Society* 8 (1993), p. 75.
13 Horst W. Janson, 'Rediscovering nineteenth century sculpture,' *The Art Quarterly* 36 (1973), no. 4, p. 411. See Anne Pingeot, 'La sculpture du XIXe siècle: la dernière décennie,' *Revue de l'Art* 104 (1994), no. 2, p. 7.
14 Rainer Michael Mason (ed.), exhib. cat. *Pygmalion photographe: la sculpture devant la camera*, Geneva (Musée d'art et d'histoire) 1985.
15 In the same way, the outline engraving is to blame for the wide-spread belief that Neo-classicism lacks depth; see J.J.L. Whiteley, 'Light and shade in French Neo-classicism,' *The Burlington Magazine* 117 (December 1975), p. 768.
16 Heinrich Wölfflin, *Kunstgeschichtliche Grundbegriffe: Das Problem der Stilentwicklung in der neueren Kunst*, Munich 1915 and idem, 'Wie man Skulpturen aufnehmen soll,' *Zeitschrift für bildende Kunst* 7 (1896), pp. 224-28; 8 (1897), pp. 294-97; and 26 (1914), pp. 237-44.
17 Rudolf Wittkower, *Sculpture: processes and principles*, London 1977. In the mistaken belief that it was a phenomenon that interested only the 'outsiders' among 19th-century sculptors, Eduard Trier discusses the problem of colour only briefly in his *Bildhauertheorien*; see Trier, *Bildhauertheorien im 20. Jahrhundert*, Berlin 1992, p. 134. Albert Elsen, op. cit. (note 1), p. 68, also dealt with the subject in the shortest possible manner.
18 Janson, op. cit. (note 13), p. 412.
19 Monographs have occasionally been dedicated to the pioneers of architectural polychromy, but with only brief mentions of the role of colour in sculpture. An early example of a work in which all the reproductions are in colour is the catalogue of selections from the Berliner Skulpturengalerie: *Staatliche Museen Preußischer Kulturbesitz: Katalog der Skulpturengalerie Berlin*, Stuttgart & Zürich 1980. The large exhibition *La sculpture française au XIXe siècle* (1986) did give coloured sculpture its own category, but only included eight numbers: Antoinette Le Normand-Romain and Jean-Luc Olivié, 'La polychromie,' in Anne Pingeot (ed.), exhib. cat. *La sculpture française au XIXe siècle*, Paris (Galeries nationales du Grand Palais) 1986, pp. 148-59. Although there have only been two publications in the last 25 years which focus exclusively on colour in sculpture, it is finally becoming commonplace to reproduce works in colour. The small exhibition catalogue *Polychromies à travers les âges et les civilisations*, Paris (Musée Bourdelle) 1971, is only sparsely illustrated. The most recent book on the subject, and the first to discuss the 19th century at length if not exclusively, is Karina Türr, *Farbe und Naturalismus in der Skulptur des 19. und 20. Jahrhunderts: Sculpturae vitam insufflat pictura*, Mainz 1994. The present essay owes much to Türr, although our approaches are very different.
20 Johann Gottlieb Herder, 'Plastik: Einige Wahrnehmungen aus Pygmalions bildendem Traume,' (1778), *Herders Sämtliche Werke*, ed. Bernhard Suphan, 32 vols., Berlin 1892, vol. 8, p. 26: 'Warum wird die Bildsäule durch Färbung nach der Natur und ähnliche Entwürfe nicht schön, sondern häßlich? da doch in der Mahlerei Farbe so große Wirkung thut. [...] Weil Farbe nicht Form ist, weil sie also dem verschloßenen Auge und tastenden Sinne nicht merkbar wird, oder merkbar sogleich die schöne Form hindert.'
21 For information on the current state of scholarship on the appearance of monochrome wooden sculptures in the late Middle Ages, see Jürgen Michler, 'Die holzsichtigen Skulpturen auf der Stuttgarter Ausstellung *Meisterwerke massenhaft*,' *Kunstchronik* 47 (August 1994), pp. 412-18, with bibliography.
22 According to the *paragone*, painting could reproduce a work of sculpture, but sculpture itself could never depict a painting. The best analysis of the *paragone* is offered by Leatrice Mendelsohn-Martone, *Benedetto*

Varchi's 'Due lezzioni': 'paragoni' and Cinquecento art theory, 2 vols., (diss., New York University, 1978). Cf. Andreas Blühm, *Pygmalion: Die Ikonographie eines Künstlermythos zwischen 1500 und 1900*, Frankfurt am Main & Bern & New York & Paris 1988.

23 Jennifer Montagu, 'The influence of the Baroque on classical sculpture,' in idem, *Roman Baroque sculpture: the industry of art*, New Haven & London 1989, pp. 152-55. On antique works see Harald Mielsch, *Buntmarmore aus Rom im Antikenmuseum Berlin*, Berlin 1985 and Rolf Michael Schneider, *Bunte Barbaren: Orientalenstatuen aus farbigem Marmor in der römischen Repräsentationskunst*, Worms 1986.

24 See most recently Suzanne L. Stratton (ed.), exhib. cat. *Spanish polychrome sculpture 1500-1800 in United States collections*, New York (The Spanish Institute) 1994, with bibliography.

25 Denis Diderot, 'Salon de 1765,' in idem, *Salons*, ed. Jean Seznec and Jean Adhémar, 4 vols., Oxford 1957-1967, vol. 2, 1960, pp. 211-12. Charles Blanc, *Grammaire des arts du dessin: architecture, sculpture, peinture*, Paris 1867, p. 459, also relied on his arguments. The quote is drawn from Etienne-Maurice Falconet, 'Réflexions sur la sculpture' (1761), in idem, *Œuvres complètes*, 3 vols., Paris 1808, vol. 3, p. 16: 'Chacun des arts a ses moyens d'imitations; la couleur n'est point un pour la sculpture.' See also Blühm, op. cit. (note 22), pp. 85-94.

26 John Stuart and Nicholas Revett, *The antiquities of Athens*, London 1762.

27 The most important publications on antique polychromy and its exploration include: Patrik Reuterswärd, *Studien zur Polychromie der Plastik, Griechenland und Rom: Untersuchungen über die Farbwirkung der Marmor- und Bronzeskulpturen*, Stockholm 1960; M.-Fr. Billot, 'Recherches aux XVIIIe et XIXe siècles sur la polychromie de l'architecture grecque,' exhib. cat. *Paris-Rome-Athènes: le voyage en Grèce des architectes français au XIXe et XXe siècles*, Paris (Ecole des Beaux-Arts) & Athens (National Gallery) & Houston (The Museum of Fine Arts) & New York (IBM Gallery of Science) 1982-83, pp. 61-125; and David Van Zanten, *The architectural polychromy of the 1830s* (diss. New York 1977).

28 Quatremère was probably the first to use the term 'polychromy' in relation to Greek sculpture. See Robin Middleton, 'Hittorff's polychrome campaign,' in Robin Middleton (ed.), *The Beaux-Arts and nineteenth-century French architecture*, London 1982, p. 176.

29 See René Schneider, *Quatremère de Quincy et son intervention dans les arts (1788-1830)*, Paris 1910, p. 127 and Hugh Honour, 'Canova's studio practice II: 1792-1822,' *The Burlington Magazine* 114 (April 1972), p. 219.

30 See Mario Praz (ed.), *L'opera completa del Canova*, Milan 1976, p. 91, no. 14 and Giuseppe Pavanello and Giandomenico Romanelli (eds.), exhib. cat. *Canova*, Venice (Museo Correr) & Possagno (Gipsoteca) 1992, no. 120. Compare also the *Paolina Borghese* in the Galleria Borghese in Rom, the *Penitent Magdalene* (1790) in the Museo Sant'Agostino in Genoa, and the statue of *Napoleon* (1803-06) in London, Wellington Museum, Aspley House.

31 There is a version in, among others, the Nationalgalerie in Berlin; later versions are in the Hermitage in St Petersburg, the Devonshire Collection in Chatsworth and the Pinacoteca Communale in Forlì; exhib. cat. *Canova*, cit. (note 30), p. 272.

32 In a letter to his friend Francesconi, dated 21 September 1800, quoted in Praz, op. cit. (note 30), p. 102.

33 Schneider, op. cit. (note 29), p. 127. On the *Brutus* see Robert L. Herbert, *David, Voltaire, Brutus and the French Revolution: an essay in art and politics*, New York 1973.

34 Van Zanten, op. cit. (note 27), pp. 8-9.

35 The relief was broken in 1813. Johann Gottfried Schadow, *Kunstwerke und Kunstansichten: Ein Quellenwerk zur Berliner Kunst- und Kulturgeschichte zwischen 1780 und 1845* (1849), ed. Götz Eckardt, 3 vols., Berlin 1987, vol. 1, p. 95 and vol. 2, p. 529: 'Wills bemalen lassen u. soll das Gantze antikisch gotisch barbarisch aussehen. Ist jetzt *grand mode*!'

36 Antoine-Chrysostome Quatremère de Quincy, *Le Jupiter Olympien, ou l'art de la sculpture antique consideré sous un nouveau point de vue: ouvrage qui comprend un essai sur le goût de la sculpture polychrome, etc.*, Paris 1814.

37 Johann Martin von Wagner, *Bericht über die Aeginetischen Bildwerke im Besitz Seiner Königlichen Hoheit des Kronprinzen von Bayern. Mit kunstgeschichtlichen Anmerkungen von F.W.J. Schelling*, Stuttgart & Tübingen 1817, p. 599: 'Wir wundern uns über diesen scheinbar bizarren Geschmack, und beurtheilen ihn als eine barbarische Sitte und ein Überbleibsel aus frühren, rohen Zeiten. Allein, wie mir scheint, geht es uns nicht anders als jenem im Evangelium, der mit dem Balken im eignen Auge dem andern den Splitter herausziehen wollte. Hätten wir vorerst unsere Augen rein und vorurtheilsfrei und das Glück zugleich, einen dieser griechischen Tempel in seiner ursprünglichen Vollkommenheit zu sehen, ich wette [daß wir] unser voreiliges Urteil gern wieder zurücknehmen, und preisen, was wir jetzt zu verdammen uns herausgenommen.'

38 Schelling was not only a propagator of the *gesamtkunstwerk*, he also considered it of great importance to society: Odo Marquard, 'Gesamtkunstwerk und Identitätssystem: Überlegungen im Anschluß an Hegels Schellingkritik,' exhib. cat. *Der Hang zum Gesamtkunstwerk: Europäische Utopien seit 1800*, Zürich (Kunsthaus), 2nd ed. Aarau & Frankfurt am Main 1983, pp. 40-49. Cf. Adrian von Buttlar, 'Klenzes Beitrag zur Polychromie-Frage,' exhib. cat. *Ein griechischer Traum: Leo von Klenze, der Archäologe*, Munich (Glyptothek) 1985-86, p. 214.

39 Ian Jenkins and A. Middleton, 'Paint on the Parthenon sculptures,' *The Annual of the British School of Archaeology at Athens* 83 (1988), pp. 183-207.

40 Middleton, op. cit. (note 28), p. 185.

41 The excavation sites themselves occasionally became a – verbal – battleground. When Klenze met Hittorff in Selinunt in 1853, he behaved so narrowmindedly that his contribution to the polychrome debate (in contrast to Hittorff's) has remained controversial until today; see Buttlar, op. cit. (note 38), passim.

42 Ibid., p. 214.

43 Frank Otten, *Ludwig Michael Schwanthaler 1802-1848: Ein Bildhauer unter König Ludwig I. von Bayern, Monographie und Werkverzeichnis*, Munich 1970. Otten makes little mention of the issue of colour. Klenze himself had developed the colour scheme; see Leo von Klenze, *Walhalla in artistischer und technischer Beziehung*, Munich 1842, p. 6.

44 Buttlar, op. cit. (note 38), p. 223.

45 Jakob Ignaz Hittorff, *Restitution du temple d'Empédocle à Sélinonte, ou l'architecture polychrôme chez les Grecs*, Paris 1851, quoted in Hans Georg Niemeyer, 'Der Bauforscher und Archäologe Hittorff,' exhib. cat. *Jakob Ignaz Hittorff: Ein Architekt aus Köln im Paris des 19. Jahrhunderts*, Cologne (Wallraf-Richartz-Museum) 1987, p. 49: '[...] Elemente zu suchen, die geeignet waren, mir mit Nutzen in der praktischen Karriere des Architekten zu dienen.' The catalogue includes a bibliography on Hittorff.

46 Reuterswärd, op. cit. (note 27), pp. 29-30.

47 Franz Kugler, *Über die Polychromie der griechischen Architektur und Sculptur und ihre Grenzen*, Berlin 1835.

48 Gottfried Semper, *Die vier Elemente der Baukunst*, Braunschweig 1851, pp. 13-29.

49 Ibid., p. 5, note.

50 Ibid., pp. 7-8.

51 Ibid., p. 99.

52 The term 'polychromania' is borrowed from Ian Jenkins's informative book *Archeologists and aesthetes in the sculpture galleries of the British Museum 1800-1939*, London 1992, p. 49.

53 Van Zanten, op. cit. (note 27), p. 34: 'What began as a picturesque visualization of ancient Greek architectural polychromy with von Klenze, von Wagner, Kugler, von Stackelberg and Hittorff, became a dematerialized symphonic and universal vision in the minds of Semper and Jones.'

54 Blühm, op. cit. (note 22), pp. 128-36, 246-51; Schneider, op. cit. (note 29), p. 385.

55 Exhib. cat. *Charles Gleyre ou les illusions perdues*, Winterthur (Kunstmuseum) 1974, pp. 36-38; Jörg Zutter (ed.), exhib. cat. *Charles Gleyre: La danse des Bacchantes*, Lausanne (Musée cantonal des Beaux-Arts) 1995.

56 Meredith Shedd, 'Phidias at the Universal Exposition of 1855: the Duc de Luynes and the *Athena Parthenos*,' *Gazette des Beaux-Arts* (October 1986), pp. 123-34.

57 Charles-Ernest Beulé, 'La statuaire d'or et d'ivoire: la Minerve de M. Simart,' *Revue des Deux-Mondes* (1856), pp. 565-66: 'M. Simart est un conservateur que l'on charge d'une révolution.'

58 Théophile Gautier, *Les beaux-arts en Europe 1855*, Paris 1856, pp. 171-79.

59 Türr, op. cit. (note 19), p. 170. On Pradier: exhib. cat. *Statues de chair: sculptures de James Pradier*, Geneva

(Musée d'art et d'histoire) 1985-86, nos. 10 and 11.
60 Ibid., no. 84; Claude Lapaire, 'Léda et le cygne de James Pradier,' *Genava* 35 (1987), pp. 55-61; Marcel G. Roethlisberger, 'La Léda de Pradier,' ibid., pp. 63-64. 19th-century polychrome works before Pradier are known only through written descriptions, for example those by Augustin Dumont and Emile Seurre; see Le Normand-Romain and Olivié, op. cit. (note 19), p. 153 and Darby, op. cit. (note 11), p. 49, note 47.
61 Quoted in Lapaire, op. cit. (note 60), p. 56: 'C'est alors que les bouches s'ouvriront et resteront en extase. C'est malheureux que ces travaux ne me rapporteront que la jalousie de mes confrères.'
63 Gibson to Mrs. Sandbach, 17 December 1846. National Library of Wales, Mss. 20, 566-7 E, quoted in Darby, op. cit. (note 11), p. 39.
64 Darby, op. cit. (note 11), passim. See also Lady Eastlake (ed.), *Life of John Gibson, R.A., sculptor*, London 1870; T. Matthews, *The biography of John Gibson, R.A., sculptor, Rome*, London 1911; Jörgen B. Hartmann, 'Canova, Thorwaldsen and Gibson,' *English Miscellany* 6 (1955)', pp. 205-36; Jeremy Cooper, 'John Gibson and his "Tinted Venus",' *Connoisseur* (October 1971), pp. 84-92; and Hans Fletcher, 'John Gibson's polychromy and Lord Londonderry's "Bacchus",' *Connoisseur* (September 1974), pp. 2-5.
65 Darby, op. cit. (note 11), p. 41: '[...] while contemplating his statue of Cupid tormenting the Soul, exhibited at the Royal Academy in 1839, he dreamt that the ancient god appeared before him and begged him to paint the figure as Praxiteles had done his statue of Cupid centuries before.'
66 Gibson to Crouchley, 23 June 1846, National Library of Wales, 4914, quoted in Darby, op. cit. (note 11), p. 41. See Eva-Maria Wasem, *Die Münchener Residenz unter Ludwig I.: Bildprogramme und Bildausstattungen in den Neubauten*, Munich 1981, pp. 170-72; she attributes the plaster caryatids to Ernst Mayer. Schwanthaler also created nine polychrome reliefs representing antique dances (after designs by Klenze).
67 Ibid., p. 39. Gibsons plan (1853) to paint the group *Queen Victoria between Justice and Clemency* (London, Palace of Westminster, Prince's Chamber) was never carried out. Ibid., p. 49, note 47: 'The only 19th century British example of a work painted in imitation of Greek practice to predate Gibson's *Queen Victoria*, seems to have been a figure of *A dancing girl* exhibited at the Royal Academy in 1845 by Joseph Gott (1786-1860), another English sculptor resident in Rome. In this the girl holds a gilded triangle above her head, but *The Literary Gazette*, 3 July 1847, p. 493 stated that other parts of the statue had been painted, and that these had been whitewashed by the Academy because "coloured marbles were contrary to regulations".'
68 On the different versions see Fletcher, op. cit. (note 64), pp. 2-3.
69 Eastlake, op. cit. (note 64), p. 211.
70 Ibid., p. 128.
71 Newspaper clipping reprinted in Darby, op. cit. (note 11), p. 46.

72 Fletcher, op. cit. (note 64), p. 5, note 8.
73 Paul Mantz, 'Exposition de Londres: peinture et sculpture,' *Gazette des Beaux-Arts* (October 1862), p. 374. The American author Nathaniel Hawthorne, like many others, felt uncomfortable when confronted with a coloured nude; see Dolly Sherwood, *Harriet Hosmer: American sculptor 1830-1908*, Columbia, Missouri & London 1991, p. 172.
74 Beulé, op. cit. (note 57), p. 576.
75 Ibid., p. 586.
76 Richard Westmacott, 'On colouring statues,' *Archaeological Journal* 12 (1855), pp. 22-46.
77 Ibid., p. 28.
78 Ibid., pp. 41-42.
79 Charles Lock Eastlake, *Contributions to the literature of fine arts*, London 1848, p. 62.
80 Ibid., p. 93.
81 Westmacott, op. cit. (note 76), p. 43.
82 Ludovic Vitet, 'Les monuments historiques du Nord-Ouest de la France' (1831), in idem, *Etudes sur l'histoire de l'art, Deuxième série: Moyen Age*, Paris 1864, p. 355.
83 Beulé, op. cit. (note 57), pp. 584-85: '[...] la statuaire polychrome [...] existe, elle n'a jamais cessé d'exister.'
84 Ibid., p. 585.
85 Heinrich Hübsch, *In welchem Style sollen wir bauen?*, Karlsruhe 1828, p. 1.
86 Hartmut Boockmann, *Die Marienburg im 19. Jahrhundert*, Frankfurt am Main & Berlin & Vienna 1982.
87 Fritz Buchenrieder, *Gefaßte Bildwerke: Untersuchung und Beschreibung von Skulpturenfassungen mit Beispielen aus der praktischen Arbeit der Restaurierungswerkstätten des Bayerischen Landesamtes für Denkmalpflege*, Munich 1990, pp. 92-94.
88 For an overview see exhib. cat. *Viollet-le-Duc*, Paris (Galeries nationales du Grand Palais) 1980 and Penelope Farrant (ed.), *Eugène Emmanuel Viollet-le-Duc 1814-1879*, London 1980.
89 Decloux and Doury, *Histoire archéologique, déscriptive et graphique de la Sainte-Chapelle du Palais*, Paris 1857; Jean-Michel Leniaud, *Jean-Baptiste Lassus (1807-1857) ou le temps retrouvé des cathédrales*, Geneva 1980; and Jean-Michel Leniaud and Françoise Perrot, *La Sainte Chapelle*, Paris 1991.
90 *Réaction de l'Académie contre l'art gothique*; see Leniaud op. cit. (note 89), p. 41.
91 Here, as elsewhere, comparisons of polychrome statues with wax figures were made regularly, so, for example in an anonymous essay in the *Deutsches Kunstblatt* 48 (26 November 1853), pp. 420-21; see Eduard Trier, 'Bildwerke für Kultus und Andacht,' in Eduard Trier and Willy Weyres (eds.), *Kunst des 19. Jahrhunderts im Rheinland*, 5 vols., Düsseldorf 1980, vol. 4, p. 66.
92 Anselm Feuerbach, 'Geschichte der griechischen Plastik,' in idem, *Nachgelassene Schriften*, 2 vols., Braunschweig 1853, vol. 2, p. 59: 'Das ehrwürdige graue Haar des Alters wird durch die blonde Perücke eines alten Gecken oder durch eine buntscheckige

Narrenkappe verhüllt.' This remark relates to the efforts of the partisans of both Neo-classicism and the Neo-gothic. See also Friedrich Theodor Vischer, *Aesthetik*, Stuttgart 1853, pp. 378-84.
93 See Buchenrieder, op. cit. (note 87), p. 95; Thomas Brachert, *Patina: Vom Nutzen und Nachteil der Restaurierung*, Munich 1985, p. 72; and Bandmann, op. cit. (note 7), p. 129.
94 See J.M. Wilson, 'Was the effigy of King John originally coloured or gilt?,' *Reports and Papers of the Associated Architectural Societies* 32 (1914), pp. 485-86 and R.B. Lockett, 'The Victorian restoration of Worcester Cathedral,' *Medieval art and architecture of Worcester Cathedral* (The British Archaeological Association Conference Transactions 1975), London 1978, pp. 161-85.
95 Gustave Le Vavasseur, *Notice biographique sur M. Le Harivel-Durocher, sculpteur*, Caen 1879, p. 32.
96 Schäfer, op. cit. (note 8), pp. 477-78.
97 There was no 'Nazarene' sculpture of any importance, and if there had been it certainly would not have been in colour: the German Romantics were simply too impressed by the numerous versions and casts of Bertel Thorvaldsen's marble *Christ* (1821). One of the few exceptions is Konrad Eberhard's delicately tinted stone *Madonna* from circa 1830 in the church of Maria Eich near Munich (with special thanks to Stephan Seeliger). Little has been written on neo-gothic sculpture, generally only in relationship to architecture: in addition to Kenneth Clark's classic *The Gothic Revival: an essay in the history of taste*, London 1928, see Georg Germann, *Neugotik: Geschichte ihrer Architekturtheorie*, Stuttgart 1974, and more recently Megan Aldrich, *Gothic Revival*, London 1994; Jean Van Cleven (ed.), exhib. cat. *Neogotiek in België*, Ghent (Oudheidkundig Museum van de Bijloke) 1994; and Paul Atterbury and Clive Wainwright (eds.), exhib. cat. *Pugin: a gothic passion*, London (Victoria and Albert Museum) 1994.
98 The changing history of taste still means many, anonymous, monuments of the 19th century are allowed to fall into decay. Even when scholarship succeeds in re-establishing a forgotten name, this does not automatically mean that a work is saved: the life-size polychrome *Madonna* by Francisque-Joseph Duret (1845) in the Chapelle Potocka in the cemetery on Montmartre, for example, has not yet been protected from the rigours of the weather; see Antoinette Le Normand-Romain, 'La chapelle Potocka,' *Les Appels d'Orphée (Association pour la défense des cimetières)* 3 (September 1991), pp. 6-9.
99 It is no accident that Luc Benoist, author of the standard work on romantic sculpture, calls neo-gothic sculpture 'sculpture décorative': Luc Benoist, *La sculpture romantique*, Paris 1928, pp. 127-47.
100 I only know of one article on the artist: Juliette Barbotte, 'La dague de Félicie de Fauveau,' *Revue du Louvre et des Musées de France* 33 (1983), no. 2, pp. 122-25. See also exhib. cat. *Touraine néo-gothique*, Tours (Musée des Beaux-Arts) 1978, no. 207; Gert

Schiff, 'The sculpture of the *style troubadour*,' *Arts Magazine* 58 (June 1984), pp. 102-10.

101 As is the case with Benoist, op. cit. (note 99) and his followers in the catalogue *La sculpture française*, cit. (note 19).

102 One example is Claude Vignon's (i.e. Noémie Rouvier) terracotta version of her *Daphne* of 1866, whose Della-Robbia-colours were remarked upon by the visitors to the Salon of 1875 (Marseilles, Musée des Beaux-Arts), vgl. Le Normand-Romain and Olivié, op. cit. (note 19), p. 157. Interesting in this context is also the Bernard Palissy-revival, cf. Anne-Marie Lecoq, 'Morts et résurrections de Bernard Palissy,' *Revue de l'Art* 78 (1987), no. 4, pp. 26-32; Marshall P. Katz, 'Nineteenth century French followers of Bernard Palissy,' *Magazine Antiques* 145 (April 1994), pp. 582-89. Emmanuelle Héran pointed out to me a life-size statue in polychrome faience representing Palissy in Guebwiller, Alsace.

103 Still in *Katalog der Skulpturengalerie Berlin*, cit. (note 19), no. 31, it is listed as 'Umkreis des Leonardo da Vinci.' For a summary and discussion of the *Flora* case see Hans Ost, *Falsche Frauen: Zur Flora im Berliner und zur Klytia im British Museum*, Cologne 1984; see also Peter Bloch and A. Kratz in Mark Jones (ed.), exhib. cat. *Fake? The art of deception*, London (The British Museum) 1990, pp. 303-07. The attribution history of the wax bust of a young girl, the famous *Tête Wicar* in the Musée des Beaux-Arts in Lille, is also interesting: in the 19th century it was ascribed to Raphael and is now thought to be by François Duquesnoy.

104 *Die Lionardische Flora: Eine Fälschung aus dem 19. Jahrhundert*, Leipzig 1910.

105 Darby, op. cit. (note 11), p. 48, note 31 and Shedd, op. cit. (note 56), fig. 5, p. 125.

106 Looking at coloured sculpture, David d'Angers was reminded of the models displayed in the windows of barber shops: 'Elles ont la couleur de la vie, une chevelure naturelle, des prunelles qui regardent sans voir; cela fait horreur'; see Henry Jouin, *David d'Angers: sa vie, son œuvre, ses écrits et ses contemporains*, 2 vols., Paris 1878, vol. 2, pp. 95-96 and Türr, op. cit. (note 19), pp. 170-71. Despite this, the coloured reliefs on the facade of the theatre in Béziers have been attributed to him; if this is the case the sculptor, like many of his colleagues, was later unwilling to admit that he had committed such a 'sin' against good taste.

107 Beulé, op. cit. (note 57), p. 579 and Charles Baudelaire, quoted in Wolfgang Drost, 'L'évolution du concept Baudelairien de la sculpture,' *Gazette des Beaux-Arts* (September 1994), p. 45.

108 Julius von Schlosser, 'Geschichte der Porträtbildnerei in Wachs: Ein Versuch,' *Jahrbuch der kunsthistorischen Sammlungen des allerhöchsten Kaiserhauses* 29 (1910-11), pp. 171-258 and E.J. Pyke, *Biographical dictionary of wax modellers*, Oxford 1973.

109 Arthur Schopenhauer, 'Parerga und Paralipomena: Kleine philosophische Schriften,' in idem, *Sämtliche Werke*, ed. Wolfgang Freiherr von Löhneysen, 5 vols., Darmstadt 1976, vol. 5/2, p. 498: 'Es ist also dem Kunstwerke *wesentlich*, die Form allein ohne die Materie zu geben, und zwar dies offenbar und augenfällig zu tun. Hier liegt nun eigentlich der Grund, warum Wachsfiguren keinen ästhetischen Eindruck machen und daher keine Kunstwerke (im ästhetischen Sinne) sind; obgleich sie, wenn gut gemacht, hundertmal mehr Täuschung hervorbringen als das beste Bild oder Statue es vermag, und daher, wenn täuschende Nachahmung des Wirklichen der Zweck der Kunst wäre, den ersten Rang einnehmen müßten.'

110 Paul Mantz, 'Le Salon de 1859,' *Gazette des Beaux-Arts* (June 1859), p. 371 (on Clésinger).

111 Blanc, op. cit. (note 25), pp. 450-60.

112 Anselm Feuerbach, *Der Vaticanische Apollo: Eine Reihe archäologisch-ästhetischer Betrachtungen*, 2nd. ed., Stuttgart & Augsburg 1855, p. 190: '[...] so mancher Grieche oder an den Griechen herangebildete Römer nicht halb so viel für die Reinheit seines Geschmackes besorgt war, als wir es nun in ihrem Namen sind. Man betrachte nur z.B. die Schauspielerfigürchen im vaticanischen Museum. Welcher Kunstfreund würde heut zu Tage noch jene Schäfer und Dudelsackpfeifer aus Elfenbein und Holz in seiner Nähe dulden [...]?' For a more thorough discussion on 'high and low' in 19th-century sculpture see the essay by Alison Yarrington in this book.

113 Jeanne L. Wasserman, exhib. cat. *Daumier sculpture: a critical and comparative study*, Cambridge, Massachusetts (Fogg Art Museum, Harvard University) 1969 and, more recently, Antoinette Le Normand-Romain (ed.), *Daumier: les parlementaires, portraits des célébrités du Juste-Milieu*, Paris 1993.

114 The literature on Marochetti was meagre until quite recently when Philip Ward-Jackson rediscovered the importance of the artist. The long silence may have been a result not of his status but rather of the fact that none of the nations for whom he worked seems to think of him as one of their own; see Marco Calderini, *Carlo Marochetti: monografia con ritratti, fac-simile e riproduzioni di opere dell'artista*, Turin & Milan & Florence 1928.

115 See Edward W. Said, *Orientalism*, New York 1978; Hugh Honour, *The image of the black in western art: from the American Revolution to World War I*, 2 vols. Cambridge, Massachusetts & London 1989; Linda Nochlin, 'The imaginary Orient,' in idem, *The politics of vision*, New York 1989, pp. 33-59; and Albert Boime, *The art of exclusion: representing blacks in the nineteenth century*, London 1990.

116 Letter to Lord Houghton, c. 16 June 1877, *Selected letters of Oscar Wilde*, ed. Rupert Hart-Davis, London 1962, pp. 16-17. I would like to thank Gerlof Janzen for this information. Marochetti's polychrome model for a seated statue of Queen Victoria very nearly changed the opinions of Charles Blanc: see idem, 'La Reine de la Paix par M. le baron Marochetti,' *Gazette des Beaux-Arts* (June 1864), pp. 566-67 and Philip Ward-Jackson, 'Carlo Marochetti et les photographes,' *Revue de l'Art* 104 (1994), no. 2, pp. 43-48.

117 Jeannine Durand-Revillon, 'Un promoteur de la sculpture polychrome sous le Second Empire: Charles-Henri-Joseph Cordier (1827-1905),' *Bulletin de la Société d'Histoire de l'Art Français* (1982), pp. 181-98 and Antoinette Le Normand-Romain (ed.), exhib. cat. *La sculpture ethnographique: de la Vénus hottentote à la Tehura de Gauguin*, Paris (Musée d'Orsay) 1994.

118 For bibliography see note 23.

119 Hugh Honour has pointed out that between Jean-Antoine Houdon's *Négresse* of 1781 and the year 1848 only 'two sculptured images of blacks [were] shown in the Salons in Paris'; Honour, op. cit. (note 115), vol. 2, p. 100. Although Winckelmann believed that 'moors' could be beautiful, he felt their skin colour stood in the way of true appreciation; op. cit. (note 4), p. 148.

120 Bénédicte Ottinger, 'La sculpture exposée,' exhib. cat. *Marseille au XIXème: rêves et triomphes*, Marseilles (Musées de Marseille) 1991-92, p. 235.

121 Honour, op. cit. (note 115), vol. 2, p. 101.

122 Durand-Revillon, op. cit. (note 117), p. 182.

123 Charles Cordier, *Sculptures ethnographique: marbres et bronzes d'après divers types de races humaines, 19 photographies par Marville*, Paris 1858 and Marc Trapadoux, *L'œuvre de M. Cordier: galerie anthropologique et ethnographique pour servir à l'histoire des races. Types des anciennes races*, etc., Paris 1860.

124 Present location unknown; see Albert Boime, *Hollow icons: the politics of sculpture in nineteenth century France*, Kent, Ohio & London 1987, p. 94.

125 Dupré, op. cit. (note 2), pp. 298-99.

126 Léon Lagrange, 'Le Salon de 1864,' *Gazette des Beaux-Arts* (July 1864), p. 32. See also Paul Mantz, 'Le Salon de 1863,' *Gazette des Beaux-Arts* (July 1863), p. 59: 'Si le progrès de la polychromie consiste à multiplier les matières précieuses, M. Cordier est en progrès.' Cordier had many followers, among them his compatriots Henri-Emile Allouard and Paul Loiseau-Rousseau. The Italian sculptor Pietro Calvi was the first to create a portrait of a black actor, namely Ira Aldridge in his role as *Othello* (1868). The Swiss sculptress Adèle d'Affry, Duchesse de Castiglione Colonna, who worked under the name Marcello, also began to make orientalising polychrome busts after a visit to Algiers with the painter Henri Regnault; see exhib. cat. *Marcello 1836-1879, Adèle d'Affry, Duchesse de Castiglione Colonna*, Fribourg (Musée d'Art et d'Histoire) 1980, pp. 152-57. The descendants of these works are the figurines produced by Goldscheider-Keramik in Vienna and the genre scenes found in Europe's colonial museums.

127 Reutersvärd, op. cit. (note 27), p. 30.

128 Edmond and Jules de Goncourt, *Journal: mémoires de la vie littéraire*, ed. Robert Picatte, 21 vols., Monaco 1956, vol. 7, p. 27 (31 May 1867).

129 Mantz, op. cit. (note 110), p. 370.

130 Billot, op. cit. (note 27), pp. 214-15.

131 Charles Garnier, *Le nouvel opéra de Paris*, 2 vols., Paris 1878, vol. 1, pp. 358-60: '[...] j'avais compris la porte centrale de l'escalier comme une espèce de joyau qui, par ses matières colorées, devait former un point brillant au milieu du brillant ensemble dans lequel il se trouvait. [...] Mais ce brave Thomas, cet artiste de haute conscience et de talent si pur, fut un peu effrayé de cette violation faite à la tradition du grand art, et il chercha à me convaincre de faire les cariatides en marbre blanc. Je fus à mon tour aussi effrayé que lui en pansant que, si belles que fussent le figures qu'il modèlerait, elles auraient toujours l'air de deux fantômes glacés, et que ma fameuse invention polychrome allait mourir avant que de naître.'

132 Monika Steinhauser, *Die Architektur der Pariser Oper: Studien zu ihrer Entstehungsgeschichte und ihrer architekturgeschichtlichen Stellung*, Munich 1969, p. 310.

133 Exhib. cat. *Das Albertinum vor 100 Jahren: Die Skulpturensammlung Georg Treus*, Dresden (Staatliche Kunstsammlungen Dresden, Skulpturensammlung) 1994-95, passim.

134 Georg Treu, *Sollen wir unsere Statuen bemalen? Ein Vortrag*, Berlin 1884.

135 Exhib. cat. *Ausstellung farbiger und getönter Bildwerke in der Königlichen Nationalgalerie zu Berlin*, Berlin (Nationalgalerie) 1885.

136 Treu, op. cit. (note 134), p. 40: 'Die meisten von uns sind auf dem Gebiete der Plastik nicht anders wie Jemand, der sein ganzes Leben lang nichts als Cartons und Kupferstiche gesehen, und nun plötzlich in seinem sechzigsten Jahre zum ersten Mal ein Oelgemälde erblickt, vor dessen frevelhafter Naturwahrheit erschrickt und Zeter schreit.' In other countries as well, whether inspired by Treu or not, museums began to make coloured reconstructions to help educate the public. In 1892 Edmond Pottier mentions a 'conservateur du Musée de Boston, M. Edward Robinson, [qui] vient, avec l'aide d'un sculpteur, M.J. Lindon Smith, de reconstituer au moyen de moulages peints deux chefs-d'œuvre de l'époque classique: l'*Hermès d'Olympie* et la *Vénus Genitrix* du Louvre'; Edmond Pottier, 'Les Salons de 1892,' *Gazette des Beaux-Arts* (July 1892), p. 27. Even today, the Metropolitan Museum of Art's coloured model of the Parthenon stands in the entrance foyer to the education department; the model was made by Adolphe Jolly in 1889 according to plans by Charles Chipiez. As the Philadelphia Museum of Art, which was given a coloured tympanum in the 1920s, the Parthenon in Nashville, Tennessee, and the reconstruction by Neda Leipen from the 1970s (*Athena Parthenos: a reconstruction*, Toronto 1971) demonstrate, this tradition is still very much alive.

137 Schäfer, op. cit. (note 8), p. 493.

138 Alfred Lichtwark, 'Farbige Skulptur' (1885), in idem, *Studien*, 2 vols., Hamburg 1896, vol. 1, p. 90.

139 Max Schasler, 'Polychrome Plastik und moderne Panoramen,' *Die Gegenwart* 27 (1885), no. 18, pp. 277-81.

140 Schäfer, op. cit. (note 8), p. 550.

141 This, however, never came to pass; Jules Laforgue, 'Correspondance de Berlin: exposition de sculpture polychrome à la National-Galerie' (1886), in idem, *Texte de critique d'art*, ed. Mireille Dottin, Lille 1988, p. 79.

142 Ibid., p. 80.

143 Ibid., pp. 95-96.

144 Treu, op. cit. (note 134), p. 7: 'Im allgemeinen wird es ja immer wahr bleiben, daß wir in unserem unwirtlichen Klima keinen farbigen Süden sollen erheucheln wollen. Aber im Inneren unserer Wohnungen, unserer Festräume, wo das Farbenbedürfniß unseres Auges sich ungestraft genug thun kann, wo es sich erquicken und erholen will von der grauen Außenwelt, was sollte uns hier wohl hindern, auch unsere Plastik mit Farbe zu sättigen?'

145 Martin Feddersen, 'Ueber polychrome Plastik,' *Kunstchronik* 2 (1891), p. 200: 'Wie der reiche Mann seine Wohnung dekorirt, davon hat das Volk herzlich wenig, weil es diese Räume doch nicht zu sehen bekommt.'

146 Treu, op. cit. (note 134), p. 9: 'Eine wahrhaft populäre Kunst, wie sie es im Altertum und Mittelalter war, kann unsrer Ueberzeugung nach die Bildhauerei erst wieder werden, wenn sie dem Drang der Neuzeit nach Wahrheit, Leben und Farbe, voll nachgiebt und es von neuem mit der Polychromie versucht.'

147 Ibid., p. 10: 'Und diese werden doch hoffentlich nicht mehr gegen eine künstlerische Verwendung der Farbe bei plastischen Werken beweisen wollen, als ein beliebiges Wirtshausschild gegen die Oelmalerei.' Schäfer was of the same opinion: op. cit. (note 8), p. 523, and Feddersen, op. cit. (note 145), p. 196.

148 Catherine Chevillot, 'Réalisme optique et progrès esthétique: la fin d'un rêve,' *Revue de l'Art* 104 (1994), no. 2, pp. 25-28.

149 The most important literature on Degas's sculptures is summarised in Roger J. Crum, 'Degas bronzes?,' *Art Journal* 54 (Spring 1994), pp. 93-98. See also the number dedicated to Degas of *Apollo* 142 (August 1995), no. 42.

150 Joris-Karl Huysmans, 'L'exposition des indépendans en 1881,' in idem, *L'art moderne*, Paris 1911, p. 250: 'La terrible réalité de cette statuette lui produit un évident malaise; toutes ces idées sur la sculpture, sur ces froides blancheurs inanimées, sur ces mémorables poncifs recopiés depuis des siècles, se bouleversent.'

151 Marcel Dieulafoy, *La statuaire polychrome en Espagne*, Paris 1908. Bibliography available in Stratton, op. cit. (note 24).

152 Samuel Butler, *Ex voto: an account of the Sacro Monte or New Jerusalem at Varallo-Sesia*, London 1888, p. 78. I would like to thank Philip Ward-Jackson for pointing this work out to me.

153 Huysmans, op. cit. (note 150), p. 252. On the *Little dancer*, see the essay by June Hargrove in this book.

154 Kugler, op. cit. (note 47) and Mantz, op. cit. (note 110), p. 371.

155 Schäfer, op. cit. (note 8), p. 478 and Alt, op. cit. (note 6), p. 97: 'Von "weissen Damen" hat man schon sehr viel, von farbigen Gespenstern noch nie etwas gehört.'

156 Matthew Webb, 'On colouring sculpture,' *The Studio* 3 (1894), p. 80.

157 Heiner Protzmann, 'Salome: Zur Polychromie in der Skulptur. Aus der Korrespondenz Max Klingers mit Georg Treu,' *Jahrbuch der Staatlichen Kunstsammlungen Dresden* 14 (1984), pp. 61-72 and Ekkehard Mai, 'Polychromie und Gesamtkunstwerk: Von der Synästhesie zur Synthese im bildnerischen Schaffen Max Klingers,' in Manfred Boetzkes (ed.), exhib. cat. *Max Klinger: Wege zum Gesamtkunstwerk*, Hildesheim (Roemer- und Pelizaeus-Museum) 1984, pp. 25-48. See also, more recently, exhib. cat. *Max Klinger, 1857-1920*, Frankfurt am Main (Städtische Galerie im Städelschen Kunstinstitut) 1992 and Herwig Guratzsch (ed.), *Max Klinger: Bestandskatalog der Bildwerke: Gemälde und Zeichnungen im Museum der bildenden Künste Leipzig*, Leipzig 1995.

158 Max Klinger, *Malerei und Zeichnung: Tagebuchaufzeichnungen und Briefe*, Leipzig 1985, p. 29: 'Hier, bei der Raumkunst, ist es, wo die farbige Skulptur einzusetzen hat, der wir so merkwürdig zaudernd gegenüberstehen. Wir haben bei jedem Monumentalraum das Bedürfnis, an den rein architektonischen unteren Gliederungen plastische Werke zu suchen, die in Gestalt bekräftigender Charaktere, stimmender Gruppen die Vermittlung bilden zu den Phantasiewerken der höheren Raumteile. Da nun in solchen Räumen der erste Gesamteindruck zweifellos in der farbigen Erscheinung besteht, dürfen jene keinesfalls in einfarbigen Werken bestehen, die durch den Kontrast silhouettenartig wirken müßten, ihrer Bestimmung und ihrem Wesen zuwiderlaufend.'

159 Ibid., pp. 29-30: 'Die Farbe muß hier zu ihrem Recht kommen, muß gliedern, stimmen, sprechen. Und ganz mit Unrecht fürchtet man in dieser farbigen Plastik das Übergreifen des Realismus. Gewiß wird man diesem oder einer zwecklosen Farbenspielerei in die Hände fallen, wenn solche Werke nicht farbig für farbige Räume gedacht sind. Wo von der farbigen Erscheinung ausgegangen, mit den entsprechenden Materialien gearbeitet wird, da würde, ganz im Gegensatz zur allgemeinen Befürchtung, die Rückkehr zur Einfachheit, zum strengen Festhalten des plastisch Wesentlichen, zum schärfsten Abwägen der Kompositionsteile nur immer notwendiger sich herausstellen, und damit würde der Weg zur Stilbildung, d.h. das Ablassen vom Unwesentlichen, von Naturkünstelei sich eröffnen. Nichts verleitet mehr zum Zuviel, zur Übertreibung der Technik, als das schrille Weiß eines Materials.'

160 Ibid., pp. 47-48: 'Wir haben nun Baukunst und Bildhauerkunst, Malerei und reproduzierende Kunst, dazu noch dekorative und Fachkünste. Der große, gesammelte Ausdruck unserer Lebensanschauung fehlt uns. Wir haben Künste, keine Kunst.'

161 Henry Weekes, *Lectures on art*, London 1880, pp. 155-78. See also Francis Haskell, 'The Shelley Memorial,' *Oxford Art Journal* 1 (1978), pp. 3-6.

162 It was Pottier who opened up the *Gazette des Beaux-Arts* to more progressive ideas. In 1892 he praised the coloured sculptures exhibited in the Salon, with specific reference to Treu; Pottier, op. cit. (note 136), p. 28. Collignon illustrated his book *La polychromie dans la sculpture grecque* (Paris 1898) with the *Antinous* relief (pl. X), a work painted under Treu's supervision.

163 Alain Daguerre de Hureaux, 'Salammbô: entre l'Orient des romantiques et l'orientalisme fin-de-siècle?,' exhib. cat. *Carthage: l'histoire, sa trace et son écho*, Paris (Musée du Petit Palais) 1995, pp. 133-34.
164 Reinhard Kekulé von Stradonitz, *Griechische Thonfiguren aus Tanagra*, Stuttgart 1878. The plates were executed by Ludwig Otto, who later worked for Georg Treu painting antique casts. See also Reynolds Higgins, *Tanagra and the figurines*, London 1986 and exhib. cat. *Bürgerwelten: Hellenistische Tonfiguren und Nachschöpfungen im 19. Jahrhundert*, Berlin (Staatliche Museen zu Berlin, Preußischer Kulturbesitz, Antikensammlung) 1994.
165 Chevillot, op. cit. (note 148), p. 23.
166 Gerald M. Ackerman, *The life and work of Jean-Léon Gérôme*, New York 1986, pp. 110-12, with illustrations and commentary of all the works discussed here.
167 A version of this painting was recently auctioned in New York (Sotheby's), 1 November 1995, lot 83.
168 Blühm, op. cit. (note 22), pp. 148-50 (Gérôme) and pp. 128-36 (Girodet).
169 Ibid., pp. 151-53.
170 John L. Tancock, *The sculpture of Auguste Rodin: the collection of the Rodin Museum Philadelphia*, Philadelphia 1976, pp. 585-88.
171 Ackerman, op. cit. (note 166), p. 318, no. S 26.
172 Pliny the Elder, *Naturalis historia* XXXIV, 140. For a general discussion on patination see Brachert, op. cit. (note 93) and Richard Hughes, 'Artificial patination,' in Susan La Niece and Paul Craddock (eds.), *Metal plating and patination: cultural, technical and historical developments*, Oxford 1993, pp. 1-18.
173 Vasari on technique, ed. G. Baldwin Brown, New York 1960, pp. 165-66, no. 68.
174 Peter Bloch and Waldemar Grzimek, *Das klassische Berlin: Die Berliner Bildhauerschule im 19. Jahrhundert*, Frankfurt am Main & Berlin 1978, p. 438.
175 See Michael Forrest, *Art bronzes*, West Chester, Pennsylvania 1988, p. 227 and Victor Harris, exhib. cat. *Japanese imperial craftsmen: Meiji art from the Khalili collection*, London (British Museum) 1994, p. 15.
176 Richard Dorment, exhib. cat. *Alfred Gilbert: sculptor and goldsmith*, London (Royal Academy of Arts) 1986, pp. 176-81.
177 Catherine Chevillot, 'Les stands industriels d'édition de sculptures à l'Exposition universelle de 1889: l'exemple de Barbedienne,' *Revue de l'Art* 95 (1992), no. 1, pp. 61-67.
178 See also the article by Philip Ward-Jackson and the catalogue entries by Donald Myers in this book.
179 Alt, op. cit. (note 6), p. 98: 'Möchte die Nation sich einen so wichtigen ökonomischen Wert schnell genug sichern, um auf dem Weltmarkt in das Vortreffen zu treten und mit dem eigenen Schmuck höheren Wohlstand zu erringen. Die Einführung der Farbe wird sich für die Plastik selbst als fruchtbar erweisen, und von ihr wird eine neue Blüte derselben und ein wirtschaftlicher Sieg abhängen.'
180 Stuart Pivar, *The Barye bronzes: a catalogue raisonné*, 2nd ed., Woodbridge 1990 and Glenn F. Benge, *Antoine-Louis Barye: sculptor of romantic Realism*, University Park & London 1984, esp. pp. 167-84.
181 Ernest Chesneau's reaction to this phenomenon is discussed in Drost, op. cit. (note 107), p. 42, and in Patricia Mainardi, 'French sculpture, English morals: Clesinger's *Bacchante* at the Crystal Palace, 1851,' *Gazette des Beaux-Arts* (December 1983), p. 216.
182 Laforgue, op. cit. (note 141), p. 81: 'On n'imagine pas les entrepôts que ce public achalande: meubles fabriqués à la grosse, bronze et bibelots passés au rifloir de la banalité mécanique, entre autres quatre vastes magasins qui ne vivraient pas à Paris et qui étalent ici toute une industrie de copies, non en plâtre franc, mais en terre cuite rose et en "pâte d'ivoire" insipide et douceâtre, des plus banals antiques, des mièvreries de Canova et de tous les sculpteurs modernes qui travaillent dans le *gemüth*.'
183 Bloch and Grzimek, op. cit. (note 174), p. 436.
184 Henri Charles Etienne Dujardin-Beaumetz, *Entretiens avec Rodin* (1913), Paris 1992, p. 36: 'La couleur! Chercher à donner de la couleur! Voilà une expression qu'un statuaire ne devrait jamais employer!'
185 Anne Pingeot in Françoise Cachin (ed.), *L'art du XIXe siècle: 1850-1905*, Paris 1990, p. 222.
186 See Brachert, op. cit. (note 93), p. 147.
187 See Tancock, op. cit. (note 170), pp. 480-87 and J.A. Schmoll gen. Eisenwerth, *Rodin-Studien*, Munich 1983, pp. 24-25, 78.
188 Henry Hawley, 'Sculptures by Jules Dalou, Henry Cros and Medardo Rosso,' *Bulletin of the Cleveland Museum of Art* 58 (September 1971), p. 205.
189 Edmond Claris, *De l'impressionisme en sculpture: Auguste Rodin et Medardo Rosso*, Paris 1902, quoted in Luciano Caramel, exhib. cat. *L'impressionismo nella scultura*, Lugano (Galleria Pieter Coray) 1989, pp. 79-91.
190 Christopher Gray, *Sculpture and ceramics of Paul Gauguin*, Baltimore 1963, no. 3 and exhib. cat. *The art of Paul Gauguin*, Washington, D.C. (National Gallery of Art) & Chicago (The Art Institute) & Paris (Galerie nationales du Grand Palais) 1988-89, pp. 23-24.
191 The black patina found on so many of his works is by no means his trademark, as a visit to the Musée Meunier in Brussels makes clear.
192 Judith Cladel, *Aristide Maillol: sa vie, son œuvre, ses idées*, Paris 1937, p. 151.
193 The latter, for example, has clear tonal variations, but unfortunately, the work has never been reproduced in colour; see exhib. cat. *Nabis*, Paris (Galeries nationales du Grand Palais), 1993-94, no. 68d.
194 Werner Spies, *Picasso: Das plastische Werk*, Stuttgart 1983, pp. 20-23, although with no mention of polychromy, and Elizabeth Cowling and John Golding, exhib. cat. *Picasso: sculptor/painter*, London (Tate Gallery) 1994.
195 Cited in Brachert, op. cit. (note 93), p. 143.
196 William Ritter, 'La céramique moderne de Meissen,' *Art et Décoration* 5 (January 1899), pp. 22-27, esp. p. 25.
197 With thanks to Jean-Luc Olivié. See also Bloch and Grzimek, op. cit. (note 174), p. 19.
198 On Cros in general: Jean-Luc Olivié, 'All of Antiquity in a new soul,' *New Work* (Fall 1987), no. 31, pp. 10-15, with bibliography.
199 See Katharine Morrison McClinton, 'The renaissance of pâte-de-verre,' *Connoisseur* (November 1979), p. 172 and Noël Daum, *La pâte de verre*, Paris 1984, pp. 29-43.
200 Jules Laforgue must have recognised a connection between Treu and Cros, since he had planned to dedicate his translation of the German archaeologist's treatise to him; Laforgue, op. cit. (note 141), p. 79.
201 On Carriès see, most recently, Thérèse Burollet, 'Deux grands fonds de sculpture du musée du Petit Palais: Dalou et Carriès,' *La sculpture du XIXe siècle: une mémoire retrouvée*, Rencontres de l'Ecole du Louvre, Paris 1986, pp. 107-14. I would like to thank Daniel Imbert for valuable information. The question should be examined whether Carriès had come into contact with the polychrome efforts of his teacher, Augustin Dumont, while a student at the Ecole des Beaux-Arts.
202 J.L. de Rudder, 'Sculpteur, patineur puis potier: Jean Carriès planta l'Art Nouveau en pleine terre,' *L'Estampille* 32 (May 1972), p. 63.
203 Gerhard Dietrich, 'Alexandre Bigot: Steinzeug in der Architekturdekoration,' *Keramos* 97 (1982), p. 103.
204 Hannelore Künzl, *Der Einfluß des alten Orients auf die europäische Kunst besonders im 19. und 20. Jahrhundert*, (diss., Cologne University 1973), p. 119.
205 There was no – polychrome – Pre-Raphaelite sculpture *per se*. Only Edward Burne-Jones turned his attention occasionally to coloured reliefs: Benedict Read and Joanna Barnes (eds.), *Pre-Raphaelite sculpture: nature and imagination in British sculpture, 1848-1914*, London 1991, p. 84. See also Benedict Read, 'Was there Pre-Raphaelite sculpture?,' in Leslie Perris (ed.), *Pre-Raphaelite papers*, London 1984, pp. 97-110.
206 See, most recently, Debra N. Mancoff, *The return of King Arthur: the legend through Victorian eyes*, New York 1995, which, unfortunately, mentions almost no sculptural examples.
207 Walter Crane, 'Notes on gesso work,' *The Studio* 1 (1893), p. 45.
208 *The Studio* 13 (1898), pp. 46-47.
209 Webb, op. cit. (note 156), p. 82.
210 Aside from Crane's own article, op. cit. (note 207), the most important essays are: Robert Anning Bell, 'Coloured relief,' *Architectural Review* 3 (1897-98), pp. 206-211; idem, 'Painted relief,' *Journal of the Royal Institute of British Architects* 18 (1910-11), pp. 485-99; and George Frampton, 'On colouring sculpture,' *The Studio* 3 (1893), pp. 78-80.
211 Regine Pernoud (ed.), exhib. cat. *Les images de Jeanne d'Arc*, Paris (Hôtel de la Monnaie) 1979; Marina Warner, *Joan of Arc: the image of female history*, New York 1981; and Gerd Krumeich, *Jeanne d'Arc in der Geschichte: Historiographie-Politik-Kultur*, Sigmaringen 1989.
212 The most important example is Prosper d'Epinay's *Joan of Arc* in the cathedral at Rheims; it was executed in 1902 in marble, ivory and lapis lazuli. The Musée

Historique in Orléans owns a coloured sandstone bust from the 15th century believed to be a portrait of Jeanne d'Arc; it probably served as the sculptor's model. With thanks to Wolfgang Drost.

213 Alfred Maskell, *Ivories*, London 1905, pp. 395-96. See further M. Luwel and M. Bruneel-Hye de Crom, exhib. cat. *'Tervueren 1897': studie en catalogus van de commemoratieve tentoonstelling*, Brussels-Tervuren (Musée royal de l'Afrique Centrale) 1967. Tom Flynn, who is preparing a study of Belgian ivories, kindly allowed me access to his manuscript.
214 Zana Aziza Etambala, 'Antwerpen en de kolonie: van 1885 tot ca. 1920,' exhib. cat. *De panoramische droom: Antwerpen en de wereldtentoonstellingen 1885-1894-1930*, Antwerp (Bouwcentrum) 1993, p. 179.
215 Heide Eilert, 'Die Vorliebe für kostbar-erlesene Materialien und ihre Funktion in der Lyrik des Fin de Siècle,' in Roger Bauer et al., *Fin de Siècle: Zur Literatur und Kunst der Jahrhundertwende*, Frankfurt am Main 1977, pp. 421-41. On this subject and Symbolism in general see the essay by Emmanuelle Héran in this book.
216 Fernand Khnopff, 'The revival of ivory carving in Belgium,' *The Studio* 4 (1894), pp. 150-51.
217 Werner Hofmann (ed.), exhib. cat. *Zauber der Medusa: Europäische Manierismen*, Vienna (Wiener Künstlerhaus) 1987, p. 484.
218 There is varying information about the materials used for this bust. On Khnopff see Robert L. Delevoy, Catherine De Croës and Gisèle Ollinger-Zinque, *Fernand Khnopff*, 2nd ed., Brussels 1987 and Michel Draguet, *Khnopff ou l'ambigu poétique, 1858-1921*, Paris 1995.
219 Draguet, op. cit. (note 218), p. 109.
220 Susan Beattie, *The New Sculpture*, New Haven & London 1983, p. 160.
221 Quoted in ibid., p. 161.
222 Sue Taylor, 'Oviri: Gauguin's savage woman,' *Konsthistorisk Tidskrift* 62 (1993), Häfte 3-4, pp. 197-220.
223 Ibid., p. 199. See also the article by June Hargrove in this book.
224 Taylor, op. cit. (note 222), p. 218.
225 Exhib. cat. *Maurice Denis*, Lyons (Musée des Beaux-Arts) & Cologne (Wallraf-Richartz-Museum) & Liverpool (Walker Art Gallery) & Amsterdam (Van Gogh Museum) 1994-95, no. 13; Derek Lionel Paul, 'Willumsen and Gauguin in the 1890s,' *Apollo* 111 (January 1980), pp. 36-45; and Leila Krogh, *Katalogbog J.F. Willumsens Museum*, Copenhagen 1986.
226 Ursula Heiderich also mentions Bretonian folk-art as a possible source: *Katalog der Skulpturen in der Kunsthalle Bremen*, Bremen 1993, p. 286.
227 Lipchitz quoted in Elsen, op. cit. (note 1), p. 70.
228 Klee quoted in Will Grohmann, *Paul Klee*, Stuttgart 1954, p. 46.
229 Quentin Bell, interview in *The Observer Magazine*, 1979, quoted in Ian Crofton, *A dictionary of art quotations*, New York 1989.
230 27 December 1809, quoted in Jörg Traeger, *Philipp Otto Runge und sein Werk: Monographie und kritischer Katalog*, Munich 1975, p. 135: '[...] daß man am Ende glaubt, daß keiner sich um den anderen zu bekümmern braucht, und es also unmöglich geworden ist, daß mehrere tüchtige Leute eine große Arbeit zusammen ausführen können, die ihrer Natur nach die Kräfte eines einzelnen übersteigt, und liegt die Vereinzelung aller Praxis und aller praktischen Kenntnis wirklich wie ein Chaos vor uns.'
231 Lichtwark, op. cit. (note 138), p. 97.
232 This phrase was used by Louis Courajod; in 1888, fueled by current debates, he pleaded for an end to the prejudice against the realism of Spanish sculpture: Courajod, op. cit. (note 10), p. 10.
233 Vern G. Swanson, *The biography and catalogue raisonné of the paintings of Sir Lawrence Alma-Tadema*, London 1990, no. 419.
234 See Lisa Florman, 'Gustav Klimt and the precedent of ancient Greece,' *Art Bulletin* 72 (June 1990), pp. 310-26.
235 Mai, op. cit. (note 157), p. 47. See also Ilse Dolinschek, *Die Bildhauerwerke in den Ausstellungen der Wiener Sezession von 1898-1910*, Munich 1989, p. 83.
236 Bandmann, op. cit. (note 7), pp. 132-34.
237 Quoted in Brachert and Kobler, op. cit. (note 5), p. 814. Gustav Pazaurek, *Guter und schlechter Geschmack im Kunstgewerbe*, Stuttgart 1912 and John Ruskin, *The seven lamps of architecture* (1880), London 1907, p. 249.
238 Adolf von Hildebrand, *Gesammelte Schriften zur Kunst*, ed. Henning Bock, Cologne & Opladen 1965, pp. 233-34.
239 Cf. August Schmarsow, *Plastik, Malerei und Reliefkunst in ihrem gegenseitigen Verhältnis*, Leipzig 1899. Already in 1922, Alfred Kuhn retrospectively recognised in Klinger's works a 'baroque sensibility,' which he felt was also at the heart of Georg Treu's art-historical rehabilitation of polychrome sculpture: Alfred Kuhn, *Die neuere Plastik von 1800 bis zur Gegenwart*, 2nd ed., Munich 1922, pp. 68-69. This proves once again that scholarship cannot distance itself from the 'spirit of the times.' See also Gillo Dorfles, *Kitsch: an anthology of bad taste*, London 1969, p. 105 and Maurice Rheims, *Nineteenth century sculpture*, London 1972, pp. 379-80.

Wolfgang Drost

Colour, sculpture, mimesis

Translated from the German by Rachel Esner.

1 André Michel, 'Exposition Universelle de 1889: la sculpture,' *Gazette des Beaux-Arts* (September 1889), p. 309.
2 Paul Mantz, 'Le Salon de 1859,' *Gazette des Beaux-Arts* (June 1859), p. 371: 'L'idée de joindre la couleur à la forme est ancienne comme le monde: elle durera autant que lui.'
3 For an overview, see Patrik Reuterswärd, *Studien zur Polychromie der Plastik: Griechenland und Rom*, Stockholm 1960.
4 Mantz, op. cit. (note 2), p. 371.
5 See Thomas Lersch, 'Farbenlehre II: Antike,' *Reallexikon zur deutschen Kunstgeschichte*, 9 vols. (to date), Munich 1937-, vol. 7 (1981), pp. 158-66.
6 Plato, *The statesman*, 277B.
7 Lersch, op. cit. (note 5), p. 163.
8 Ibid., p. 192, as well as Justus Brinckmann (ed.), *Abhandlungen über die Goldschmiedekunst und die Skulptur von Benvenuto Cellini*, Osnabrück 1978.
9 Francisco de Hollanda, *Diálogos de Roma: da pintura antiga*, ed. Manuel Mendes, Lisbon 1955; see particularly the fourth dialogue.
10 See *Aretino oder Dialog über die Malerei*, ed. Cajetan Cerri, Osnabrück 1970, pp. 64-65.
11 The author would here like to gratefully acknowledge the work of Karina Türr, *Farbe und Naturalismus in der Skulptur des 19. und 20. Jahrhunderts: Sculpturae vitam insufflat pictura*, Mainz 1994, without which the following observations would not have been possible. It is thanks to the stimulating nature of her work, that different accents could be set here, particularly in relation to her thesis on Naturalism. On colour theory and its relationship to sculpture see: Giulio Carlo Argan, 'Scultura e plastica,' in *Enciclopedia universale dell'arte*, 15 vols., Venice & Rome 1964, vol. 12, pp. 343-65.
12 Johann Joachim Winckelmann, *Geschichte der Kunst des Altertums*, Baden-Baden & Strasbourg 1966, p. 148.
13 Quatremère de Quincy's book was published in Paris and includes the following subtitle: *Ouvrage qui comprend un essai sur le goût de la sculpture polychrome, l'analyse explicative de la toreutique et l'histoire de la statuaire en or et ivoire chez les Grecs et les Romains avec la restitution des principaux monuments de cet art.*
14 Ibid., p. 28.
15 Ibid., p. 31: 'Les anciens en effet séparèrent beaucoup moins qu'on ne se le figure, dans leurs travaux, le plaisir des yeux de celui de l'esprit; c'est-à-dire que la richesse, la variété et la beauté des matières [...] furent chez eux bien plus intimément réunies qu'on ne le pense, au beau intrinsèque.'

16 William Gell, *Pompeiana: the topography, edifices and ornaments of Pompeii,* London 1817-19, p. 160; quoted in John Gage, *Colour and culture,* London 1993, p. 11.

17 Etienne-Maurice Falconet, 'Réflexions sur la sculpture (7 June 1760),' in *Œuvres complètes,* 3d ed. (1808), Geneva 1970, p. 10.

18 Ibid., p. 5.

19 Ibid., pp. 20-21.

20 Ibid., p. 9.

21 Johann Gottfried Herder, *Herders Werke,* ed. Theodor Matthias, 5 vols., Leipzig & Vienna 1903, vol. 3, pp. 99, 106, 100-01.

22 See Wolfgang Drost, 'Le regard intérieur: du modèle idéal chez Diderot,' in Michel Delon and Wolfgang Drost (eds.), *Le regard et l'objet: Diderot critique d'art,* Heidelberg 1989, pp. 69-90.

23 Denis Diderot, *Salon de 1765,* ed. Else Marie Bukdahl and Annette Lorenceau, Paris 1984, p. 285: 'il n'y a rien de si déplaisant que le contraste du vrai mis à côté du faux, et jamais la vérité de la couleur ne répondra à la vérité de la chose; la chose, c'est la statue seule, isolée, solide, prête à se mouvoir.'

24 Falconet, op. cit. (note 17), p. 10: 'Le brillant de la dorure, la rencontre brusque des couleurs discordantes de différents marbres, éblouira l'œil d'une populace toujours subjuguée par le clinquant, et l'homme de goût sera révolté.'

25 *Goethes Werke: Hamburger Ausgabe,* 14 vols., Hamburg 1967, vol. 12, p. 32: '[...] ruht der Stil auf den tiefsten Grundfesten der Erkenntnis, auf dem Wesen der Dinge, insofern uns erlaubt ist, es in sichtbaren und greiflichen Gestalten zu erkennen.'

26 Friedrich Hegel, *Ästhetik,* ed. Fr. Bassenge, 2 vols., Frankfurt am Main n.d., vol. 2, p. 94: '[Die] Skulptur die eigentliche Kunst des klassischen Ideals als solchem.' The following quotations are drawn from the third part: 'Das System der einzelnen Künste: 2. Abschnitt: die Skulptur.'

27 Ibid., pp. 89-90.

28 Ibid., p. 90: 'Dies ist aber kein zufälliger Mangel, sondern eine durch den Begriff der Kunst selbst gesetzte Beschränkung des Materials und der Darstellungsweise. Denn die Kunst ist ein Produkt des Geistes, und zwar des höheren, denkenden Geistes, und solch ein Werk macht sich einen bestimmten Inhalt und deshalb auch eine von anderen Seiten abstrahierende Weise der künstlerischen Realisierung zu ihrem Vorwurf.'

29 Ibid., p. 91; original emphasis.

30 Ibid., p. 92.

31 See Wolfgang Drost, 'Materialgerechtigkeit und absolute Kunst: Zu Charles Blancs Ästhetik der Vasenmalerei. Die Absage an die Tradition von Luca della Robbia und Bernard Palissy,' *Wallraf-Richartz-Jahrbuch* 44 (1983), pp. 367-74.

32 Charles Blanc, *La sculpture,* Paris n.d., p. 166.

33 The 5th edition of *Du vrai, du beau et du bien* was published in Paris in 1855.

34 Blanc, op. cit. (note 32), p. 170.

35 Théophile Gautier, *Salon de 1847,* Paris 1847, p. 198.

36 Henri Jouin, *La sculpture en Europe, 1878: précédé d'une conférence sur le génie dans l'art plastique,* Paris 1879, p. 19.

37 Eugène Véron, *Supériorité des arts modernes sur les arts anciens: poésie, sculpture, peinture, musique,* Paris 1862, p. 477: 'On ne peut nier en effet que leurs peintures aient quelque chose de plus physique et de plus sensuel que de celles de leurs rivaux.'

38 Louis Courajod, *Leçons professées à l'Ecole du Louvre 1887-1896,* ed. Henry Lemonnier and André Michel, 3 vols., Paris 1899-1903, vol. 3 (Année 1894-95), p. 220.

39 See Anne Pingeot, 'Néo-baroque et orientalisme,' in idem (ed.), exhib. cat. *La sculpture française aux XIXe siècle,* Paris (Galeries nationales du Grand Palais) 1986, p. 335.

40 The problem of colour and form in 'exotic' countries like Tunisia, India, Egypt and Turkey was also a subject of interest; see Owen Jones, 'Gleanings from the Great Exhibition of 1851: on the distribution of form and colour developed in the articles exhibitions in the Indian, Egyptian, Turkish, and Tunisian department,' *The Journal of Design and Manufactures* 28 (June 1851), pp. 89-93.

41 From the myriad contributions here a selection: Charles Lock Eastlake, *Sculpture: contributions to the literature of the fine arts,* London 1848, pp. 61-94; J.B. Waring, 'Polychromy,' *The Builder* 10 (6 March 1852), pp. 150-51; Anonymous, 'Colour in sculpture,' *The Athenaeum* (24 December 1853), no. 1365, pp. 1559-60 and (31 December 1853), p. 1597; R.A.S., 'Colour in sculpture,' *The Athenaeum* (18 February 1854), no. 1373, pp. 219-20; Richard Westmacott, 'On colouring statues,' *The Archeological Journal* 12 (March 1855), pp. 22-46; John Bell, 'Colouring statues,' *The Art Journal* (1858), pp. 18-20, 69-70, 179, 230-32; and Anonymous, 'Tinted sculpture,' *The Art Journal* (July 1862), pp. 161-62.

42 See G. Scharf and C.O. Müller, *On the polychromy of sculpture: being recollections of remarks on this subject,* London 1851, pp. 228-46. Semper emphasised the importance of the research done by the English, particularly by a certain Professor Donaldson, who had demonstrated as early as 1830 that the entire marble surface of Greek temples had been painted (p. 232). Particularly important as well had been the discoveries in Assyria, which had led to a better knowledge of Persepolis and Egypt in general, and thus to a deeper understanding of antique polychromy. In England itself, however, decisive impulses had come first with the work of Gowny and Jones on the Alhambra (p. 233).

43 Jones, op. cit. (note 40), p. 91.

44 London, Crystal Palace Library, 1854, as part of the series *The fine arts' courts in the Crystal Palace, first series.* See also Donata Levi, 'Ercole tatuato come un indigeno: il dibattito sulla policromia nel mondo classico nella Gran Bretagna di metà Ottocento,' *Ricerche di storia dell'arte* 38 (1990), pp. 22-43.

45 Gage, op. cit. (note 16), p. 11.

46 See T. Matthews, *The biography of John Gibson R.A., sculptor, Rome,* London 1911, which includes Gibson's own comments.

47 Anonymous, 'Notabilia of the International Exhibition,' *The Art Journal* (July 1862), p. 161.

48 Ibid.

49 John Bell, 'The late John Gibson, R.A., of Rome, the colouring of statues and the Venus of Cnidos,' *The Builder* 38 (29 November 1879), p. 1310.

50 Paul Mantz, 'Exposition de Londres,' *Gazette des Beaux-Arts* (October 1862) p. 374.

51 Ibid., pp. 374-75: 'L'échec est définitif, et il n'est plus possible aujourd'hui de faire de la sculpture coloriée.'

52 Théophile Gautier, *Exposition de 1859,* ed. Wolfgang Drost and U. Henninges, Heidelberg 1992, p. 204: 'M. Clésinger s'est passé le caprice de faire une statue polychrome comme un sculpteur athénien. Nous n'y voyons pas grand mal, et nous avouons que la Sappho peinte nous séduit tout à fait.'

53 Ibid., p. 205: 'Si la polychromie vous gêne, faites évanouir ces teintes légères appliquées avec une sobriété intelligente, il vous restera une statue charmante d'une délicatesse et d'une pureté parfaites.'

54 Nonetheless, Gautier's position is already a progressive one. Two decades earlier, in the name of idealism in sculpture, David d'Angers had condemned polychromy as the product of a realist aesthetic: the special quality of white marble did not allow for any association with physical reality, and this is what made the material so suited to idealised representation: 'La statuaire est la représentation de l'âme. Cette couleur uniforme l'éloigne de l'idée de la réalité physique.' From *Les carnets de David d'Angers,* ed. André Bruel, 2 vols., Paris 1958, vol. 2, p. 32; quoted in Antoinette Le Normand-Romain and Jean-Luc Olivié, 'La polychromie,' in Anne Pingeot (ed.), op. cit. (note 39), p. 148.

55 Théophile Gautier, *Les beaux-arts en Europe 1855,* 2 vols., Paris 1855-56, vol. 2, p. 178.

56 Charles Lévêque, *Le spiritualisme dans l'art,* Paris 1864, p. 76. The treatise was written in 1857.

57 Ibid., pp. 79-80: 'Je tiens que l'œuvre de M. de Luynes et de Simart a été utile; non-seulement elle nous a donné une idée des magnificences de l'art grec en son plus beau temps, mais elle a fait plus; elle a rappellé à nos artistes que le plus grand sculpteur qui fût jamais mit sa gloire à exprimer ce qu'il y a de plus invisible au monde: la pure pensée divine.'

58 Falconet, op. cit. (note 17) p. 10: 'Sans doute que des matériaux de diverses couleurs, employés avec intelligence, produiraient quelques effets pittoresques.'

59 Blanc, op. cit. (note 32), p. 166.

60 Charles Blanc, *Grammaire des arts du dessin,* Paris 1867, p. 469: 'Ce fut surtout sous le règne des empereurs que la sculpture, dégénérée usa et abusa de la polychromie.'

61 René de Saint-Marceaux, 'La sculpture aux Salons de 1897,' *Gazette des Beaux-Arts* (June 1897), p. 488.

62 See Le Normand-Romain and Olivié, op. cit. (note 54), p. 150.

63 Gautier, op. cit. (note 52), p. 485: '[...] remplacer

un idéal épuisé [par] des natures vierges, des types purs, des modèles étranges et superbes.'
64 Paul Desjardins, 'Les Salons de 1899: sculpture,' *Gazette des Beaux-Arts* (October 1899), p. 288.
65 Ibid.: 'C'est une coquette qui provoque en souriant.'
66 See Maxime Collignon, 'Une statue polychrome de M. Ernest Barrias,' *La Revue de l'Art Ancien et Moderne* 6 (1899), p. 197.
67 Ibid., p. 192: 'Elle a toute la valeur d'une théorie d'art [....] elle plaide éloquemment la cause de la statuaire polychrome.'
68 Illustrated in Nicholas Penny, *The materials of sculpture*, New Haven & London 1993, p. 193.
69 Spire Blondel, 'Les modeleurs en cire,' *Gazette des Beaux-Arts* (November 1882), pp. 438-39: 'le public vit avec plaisir cette résurrection d'un art si justement goûté de nos ancêtres.' The first article appeared in *Gazette des Beaux-Arts* (May 1882), pp. 493-504; the second was published in September 1882, pp. 259-72 and the third in November 1882, pp. 429-39.
70 Henri Bouchot, 'Le Salon de 1893: la sculpture,' *Gazette des Beaux-Arts* (August 1893), p. 114.
71 Philippe Burty, 'Exposition des beaux-arts à Lille,' *Gazette des Beaux-Arts* (October 1866), p. 390.
72 See Michael Pantazzi, 'La petite danseuse de quatorze ans,' exhib. cat. *Degas*, Paris (Galeries nationales du Grand Palais) 1988, p. 343: 'On ne saurait guère exagérer l'importance de la célébrité de la tête de Lille dans la seconde moitié du XIXe siècle.'
73 Eugène Guillaume, 'L'art et la nature: Salon de 1879,' in idem, *Etudes d'art antique et de moderne*, Paris 1888, p. 181. The article appeared originally in the *Revue des Deux-Mondes*.
74 Blondel, op. cit. (note 69), p. 438.
75 Türr, op. cit. (note 11), pp. 34-35.
76 Guillaume, op. cit. (note 73), p. 181: 'ce qui semble résulter de cette tentative, c'est que dans la statuaire, la couleur ne peut s'allier qu'à des formes idéales ou de grand caractère et au portrait. Venant s'ajouter à la simple réalité, elle lui donne nous ne savons quoi de fade ou de morbide, et, dans ce cas, une association d'idées involontaire reporte la pensée aux galeries anatomiques.'
77 Ibid, p. 182: 'Au fond, n'est-ce pas là en grande partie l'attrait de cet art complexe: avoir sous la main des cires diversement colorées comme un peintre a sa palette, les pétrir, obtenir en les mélangeant les tons que l'on souhaite, sentir naître à la fois sous ses doigts la forme et la couleur!'
78 Charles Ephrussi, 'Exposition des artistes indépendants,' *Chronique des Arts* (18 April 1881); quoted in Anthea Callen, 'Anatomie et physiognomie: *La petite danseuse de quatorze ans* de Degas,' exhib. cat. *L'âme au corps: arts et science 1793-1993*, Paris (Galeries nationales du Grand Palais) 1994, pp. 360-73, here p. 360.
79 Quoted in Michael Pantazzi and Douglas W. Druick, 'Le réalisme scientifique,' exhib. cat. *Degas*, cit. (note 72), p. 197. Abadies trial had been the cause of much public excitement a short time before; Degas had made sketches of the proceedings: see Douglas Druick, 'La petite danseuse et les criminels: Degas moraliste,' *Degas inédit* (Actes du colloque Degas, 18-21 avril 1988), Paris 1989, pp. 225-50.
80 See exhib. cat. *Degas*, cit. (note 72), p. 210.
81 Ibid.
82 A mannequin of this type, wearing a pink dress and a large straw hat, is included in the foreground of Degas's *The artist in his studio* (c. 1873, Lisbon, Fondation Calouste Gulbenkian).
83 Blondel, op. cit. (note 69), p. 434.
84 Ibid., p. 439.
85 Degas owned a number of Neapolitan nativity figures.
86 Herder, op. cit. (note 21), vol. 3, pp. 99-100.
87 Bell, op. cit. (note 41), p. 18.
88 Georg Treu, *Sollen wir unsere Statuen bemalen? Ein Vortrag*, Berlin 1884.
89 Edmond Pottier, 'Les Salons de 1892,' *Gazette des Beaux-Arts* (July 1892), p. 27 cites Treu and was actually in contact with him.
90 Treu, op. cit. (note 88), p. 39: 'Daß die farblose Skulptur seit den Zeiten der Renaissance Großes, Unsterbliches geleistet hat, wer zweifelt daran? Folgt daraus, daß auch unsere plastische Kunst nichts Großes und Gutes auf Gebieten leisten dürfe, die jene Epoche und doch auch nur zum Teil, aus einem theoretischen Mißverständnis beiseite gelassen hat?'
91 Ibid., pp. 12, 8, 10, 39, 9.
92 Wilhelm von Bode (ed.), *Sammlung von Bildwerken und Abgüssen des christlichen Zeitalters: Italienische Portraitskulpturen des 15. Jahrhunderts in den Königlichen Museen zu Berlin*, Berlin 1883.
93 Treu, op. cit. (note 88), pp. 38-39.
94 Türr, op. cit. (note 11), p. 78, note 71.
95 Jules Laforgue, 'Correspondance de Berlin: exposition de sculpture polychrome à la National-Galerie' (1886), in idem, *Textes de critique d'art*, ed. Mireille Dottin, Lille 1988, pp. 85-86.
96 Ibid., p. 86: 'Quoi qu'il en soit, la voie est ouverte: le public et les artistes y viendront.'
97 Jules Buisson, 'Salon de 1881: la sculpture,' *Gazette des Beaux-Arts* (September 1881), p. 231.
98 Umberto Boccioni, *Manifesto tecnico della scultura futurista*; reprinted in Pontus Hulten (ed.), exhib. cat. *Futurismo & futurismi*, Venice (Palazzo Grassi) 1986, pp. 433-34. For their untiring assistance I would like to thank Petra Scheiffgen, Gabriele Stettner-Ayani and Armin Junker, as well as Kordelia Knoll (Staatliche Kunstsammlungen Dresden).

Philip Ward-Jackson

Sculpture colouring and the industries of art in the 19th century

1 Richard Dorment, *Alfred Gilbert*, New Haven & London 1985.
2 'Nous avons hésité à parler des deux bustes de M. Cordier, parce que selon nous ils appartiennent plutôt à l'industrie qu'aux beaux arts. A part quelques bijoutiers et quelques ouvriers en marqueterie qui se sont extasiés devant cet assemblage discordant de marbres de couleurs, tout le monde s'est récrié contre ce mauvais gout [...].' Louis Auvray, *Exposition des beaux arts: Salon de 1863*, Paris 1863, p. 97.
3 Gustave Planche, 'L'orfèvrerie et l'ébénisterie à l'Exposition universelle de 1855,' *Revue des Deux-Mondes* 12 (15 November 1855), pp. 728-45; Paul Meurice, letter with signatures of artists, 'Correspondance,' *Revue des Deux-Mondes* 12 (1 December 1855), pp. 1164-68.
4 Victor Champier, 'A propos de la Gallia de M.L. Falize,' *Revue des Arts Décoratifs* 16 (1896), pp. 65-68; E. Robert and L. Falize, 'La collaboration dans les œuvres d'art: encore la Gallia,' *Revue des Arts Décoratifs* 16 (1896), pp. 357-59. See also Marc Bascou, 'Le sculpteur, l'orfèvre, le fondeur-editeur,' *L'orfèvrerie au XIXe siecle, Rencontres de l'Ecole du Louvre* (November 1944), pp. 39-50.
5 Paul Bellot, 'La Chapelle du Champ de Mars,' *L'Exposition de 1867 Illustrée* (28 August 1867), pp. 327-30.
6 Pugin 'a resuscité le moyen âge entier, corps et ame [...] tout est couvert d'ornements peints et dorés; c'est un effet réellement magique.' A.N. Didron, 'Promenade en Angleterre,' *Annales Archéologiques* 5 (1846), pp. 284-308.
7 On the Sainterie de Vendeuvre and its founder Léon Moynet, see: 'Les sculpteurs du XIXe siècle dans le département de l'Aube,' *La Vie en Champagne*, special number 324 (September 1982); Jean Francois Dhuys, 'Un paradis perdu: l'histoire exemplaire de Léon Moynet,' *Feuilles* (Paris, Musée-galérie de la Seïta) 8 (Spring 1984), pp. 71-75; Sylvie Forestier, 'Art industriel et l'industrialisation de l'art: l'exemple de la statuaire réligieuse de Vendeuvre-sur-Barse,' *Revue d'Ethnologie Francaise* 8 (March-September 1978), pp. 191-210.
8 'Non content d'améliorer l'industrie de la peinture réligieuse, M. Chovet applique la même reforme à la statuaire et à la sculpture d'eglise.' H.C., 'Exposition des art industriels,' *L'Illustration* (10 October 1863), p. 253. See also *Le Monde Illustré* (2e semaine 1863).
9 Eugène Emmanuel Viollet-le-Duc, 'L'art chrétien,' *Bien Public* (18 December 1876).
10 Joris-Karl Huysmans, *L'art moderne*, Paris 1883, pp. 226-31.
11 'Des Madones sérieuses et bonnes à mettre en

niche, des Christs, grandeur nature, avec des lilas sur le ventre et du carmin aux doigts, des Jesus bénisseurs, frisottés et blonds, les bras en avant, accueillants et bien vêtus [...].' Joris-Karl Huysmans, *Les sœurs Vatard* (1879), Paris 1953, p. 18.

12 G. Debouliez and F. Malepeyre, *Encyclopédie Roret: bronzage des métaux et du plâtre, nouvelle édition, classée et augmentée par M. S. Lacombe*, Paris 1887.

13 *Almanach de Messieurs les fabricans de bronzes réunis de la ville de Paris pour l'année 1844*, pp. 76-77.

14 For an assessment of the merits of *fonte brute*, see *Rapport des délégations ouvrières: Exposition de 1867 à Paris (Rapport adressé à la commission d'encouragement par la délégation des fondeurs en cuivre)*, Paris 1867, p. 6.

15 *Rapport de la delegation ouvrière à l'Exposition de Vienne, 1878*, n.p. n.d. (Paris 1878-79), p. 32 (Maisons Pautrot et Valon), p. 33 (Maison Peyrol); *Rapports du jury mixte internationales: Exposition universelle de 1855*, Paris 1855, pp. 919-20, 922.

16 *Encyclopédie Roret*, cit. (note 12), p. 32.

17 *Journal des Beaux-Arts et de la Littérature* 9 (13 March 1836), p. 136.

18 Jules Janin, *Notice sur J. Feuchère*, Paris 1853, p. 10.

19 'celle [...] de viser au charlatanisme d'effet en colorant de teintes diverses un bronze qui devrait n'en avoir qu'une seule.' *Journal des Beaux-Arts et de la Littérature* 11 (2 April 1838), p. 199.

20 Isabelle Leroy-Jay Lemaistre, 'La renaissance de l'ivoire,' exhib. cat. *Un âge d'or des arts décoratifs*, Paris (Galeries nationales du Grand Palais) 1991, pp. 423-25.

21 Philippe Burty, 'F.-D. Froment-Meurice, argentier de la ville de Paris 1802-1855,' *Revue des Arts Décoratifs* 4 (1882), pp. 193-200, 225-35.

22 'Exposition d'Algérie: matières premières,' *L'Exposition Universelle de 1867 Illustrée* (8 June 1867), p. 184.

23 Bruno Fornari, 'La sculpture chryséléphantine,' in Jacques Van Lennep (ed.), exhib. cat. *La sculpture belge au XIXe siècle*, 2 vols., Brussels (La Générale de Banque) 1990, vol. 1, pp. 136-39.

24 Léonce Bénédite, 'Exposition de l'Union centrale: les industries de l'art (suite), IV. Le cuivre et le bronze,' *Revue des Arts Décoratifs* 1 (1880), p. 388.

25 Dorment, op. cit. (note 1).

26 Pierre Cadet, *Susse Frères: 150 years of sculpture 1837-1987*, Paris 1992, pp. 190-302, facsimiles of Susse catalogues of 1905 and 1910. Siot Decauville, *Catalogue des bronzes d'art*, Paris c. 1900.

27 'il y a *le vert Barye*, jeune ou vieux, suivant les transparences de marron des pleins modelés, et les notes claires, qui courent en gouttes de lumières sur les extremités; il y a la *patine fleurie*, ou sont semées les taches rouges, comme des coquelicots chantant dans la blondeur des moissons roussies; il y a la *patine giroflée* qui donne une admirable intensité de rouge sur un fond vert; il y a le *vert antique* il y a la *patine vieil or*, la *patine herbeuse*, la *patine d'argent*, et d'autres encore [...]. J'ai vu dans les ateliers un bronze destiné au Musée de Vienne, *L'Abel* de Carlès [...] jamais on n'a obtenu des patines semblables; il y a des parties ou l'on croit voir le sang à fleur de peau; l'oxydation a donné là des gammes d'une surprenante harmonie [...].' René Mauglas, 'Siot Decauville fondeur,' *Bulletin de l'Art dans l'Industrie (supplement à la Gazette des Beaux-Arts*, June 1894), pp. 1-8.

28 Catherine Chevillot, 'Les stands industriels d'édition de sculptures à l'Exposition universelle de 1889: l'exemple de Barbedienne,' *Revue de l'Art* 95 (1992), no. 1, pp. 61-67.

29 '[...] qui permet aux dames, à l'aide d'un vernis magique et de feuilles imprimées en couleur, de décorer instantanément le bois, la soie, la bougie, les porcelaines.' 'Revue de l'industrie: Maison Susse,' *L'Illustration* (14 December 1861), p. 383.

30 Paul Atterbury (ed.), *The Parian phenomenon: a survey of Victorian Parian porcelain statuary and busts*, Shepton Beauchamp 1989.

31 Léon Arnoux, 'On ceramic manufactures, porcelain and pottery,' *Lectures on the results of the Great Exhibition of 1851: delivered before the Society of Arts, Manufactures and Commerce*, 2nd series, London 1853, lecture XXIII; Elizabeth Aslin and Paul Atterbury, exhib. cat. *Minton 1798-1910*, London (Victoria and Albert Museum) 1976; Victoria Cecil, exhib. cat. *Minton Majolica*, London (Jeremy Cooper Ltd.) 1982.

32 Exhib. cat. *Un âge d'or des arts décoratifs*, cit. (note 20), pp. 265-67, 492.

33 Giuseppe Liverani, 'Il Museo delle Porcellane di Doccia,' *Societa Ceramica Italiana Richard Ginori*, n.p. 1967, p. 44; A. de Gubernatis, *Dizionario degli artisti italiani viventi*, Florence 1889.

34 Emile de la Bedollière, 'Le monument céramique,' *L'Exposition Universelle de 1867 Illustrée* (13 June 1867), p. 202.

35 Henry Havard, 'La céramique architecturale,' *L'art et l'industrie de tous les peuples à l'Exposition universelle de 1878*, Paris 1879, pp. 279-82; Louis de Fourcaud, 'Rapport general: 8e Exposition de l'Union centrale des arts décoratifs,' *Revue des Arts Décoratifs* 4 (1884-85), pp. 231-61.

36 Paul Atterbury and Louise Irvine, exhib. cat. *The Doulton story*, London (Victoria and Albert Museum) 1979.

37 Berthold Daun, *Siemering*, Bielefeld & Leipzig 1906, pp. 53-54.

38 *The Illustrated London News* (20 October 1894), p. 508.

Alison Yarrington

Under the spell of Madame Tussaud

1 Henry Weekes, *Lectures on art, delivered at the Royal Academy*, London 1880, p. 169.

2 Olivier G. Destrée, *The renaissance of sculpture in Belgium*, London 1895, p. 26.

3 Weekes discusses the different methods of colouring sculpture, op. cit. (note 1), pp. 163-67. For a discussion of Dampt's works in the context of fin-de-siècle decorative arts, see Debora L. Silverman, *Art Nouveau in fin-de-siècle France: politics, psychology and style*, London & Los Angeles 1989, pp. 222-24, 295.

4 Marion H. Spielmann, *British sculpture and sculptors of to-day*, London 1901, p. 139.

5 Warren De La Rue and A.W. Hofman, 'Class XXIX: report on miscellaneous manufactures and small wares,' *Exhibition of the Works of Industry of All Nations 1851: reports by the juries on the subjects in the thirty classes into which the exhibition was divided*, London 1852, p. 680.

6 Translated and cited by Friona E. Wissman, 'Realists among the Impressionists,' in Charles S. Moffett (ed.), exhib. cat. *The new painting: Impressionism 1874-1886*, San Francisco (The Fine Arts Museum of San Francisco) & Washington, D.C. (National Gallery of Art) 1986, pp. 342, 351, note 42.

7 Claudine Mitchell, 'Spectacular fears and popular arts: a view from the nineteenth century,' in Alison Yarrington and Kelvin D. Everest (eds.), *Reflections of revolution: images of Romanticism*, London 1993, p. 160.

8 Antoinette Le Normand-Romain, 'La polychromie,' in Anne Pingeot (ed.), exhib. cat. *La sculpture française au XIXe siècle*, Paris (Galeries nationales du Grand Palais) 1986, p. 155. For a survey of polychromy in the context of British late 19th-century sculpture, see Benedict Read, 'Sailing to Byzantium?,' in John Christian (ed.), exhib. cat. *The last Romantics: the romantic tradition in British art, Burne-Jones to Stanley Spencer*, London (Barbican Art Gallery) 1989, pp. 55-61.

9 With August Kiss, James Pradier, Richard Wyatt and Carlo Marochetti, Gibson was recommended for a Council Medal for his marble group of *The hunter and dog* (exhibited by Lord Yarborough) but he turned this down on the grounds that it would be improper for a juror to be given such a prize, see A. Panizzi, 'Class XXX: report on sculpture, models and plastic art,' *Exhibition of the Works*, cit. (note 5), p. 684.

10 *The Illustrated Exhibitor: a tribute to the world's industrial jubilee; comprising sketches, by pen and pencil, of the principal objects in the Great Exhibition of the Industry of All Nations 1851* 16 (20 September 1851), p. 291. These works were the property of Captain John Leyland.

11 C. Waagen, 'Class XXX: supplementary report,' *Exhibition of the Works*, cit. (note 5), p. 704.

12 *The Illustrated Exhibitor*, cit. (note 10), pp. 288-89.

13 De La Rue and Hofman, op. cit. (note 5), p. 649.
14 Ibid.
15 Peter Fusco and Horst W. Janson (eds.), exhib. cat. *The Romantics to Rodin: French nineteenth-century sculpture from North American collections*, Los Angeles (Los Angeles County Museum of Art) & Minneapolis (The Minneapolis Museum of Art) & Detroit (The Detroit Institute of Arts) & Indianapolis (Indianapolis Museum of Arts) 1980-81, p. 180. See also Horst W. Janson, *Nineteenth-century sculpture*, London 1985, p. 136. For a discussion of Cordier's busts in the context of 19th-century polychromed sculpture, see Antoinette Le Normand-Romain (ed.), exhib. cat. *La sculpture ethnographique: de la Vénus hottentote à la Tehura de Gauguin*, Paris (Musée d'Orsay) 1994.
16 A. Andrei, 'Galerie anthropologique et ethnographique de M. Cordier,' *L'Art au Dix-neuvième Siècle* 5 (1860), pp. 188-89. Cordier exhibited a *Head of a Negro* in bronze at the 1851 Great Exhibition which was given an Honourable Mention as 'a true example of characteristic portraiture.'
17 De La Rue and Hofman, op. cit. (note 5), p. 604.
18 Panizzi, op. cit. (note 9), p. 684.
19 Joseph Henry Green, 'Class Xc: report on surgical instruments,' *Exhibition of the Works*, cit. (note 5), p. 345. For a history of anatomical waxworks on public display in London see Richard D. Altick, *The shows of London*, Cambridge, Massachusetts & London 1978, pp. 54-55. Altick also notes that by the 19th century, the word 'Florentine' was used as a 'shorthand allusion' to the Instituto di Anatomia Patologica in Florence with its 20 rooms full of anatomical wax models. 'Thus for show purposes the word "Florentine" was a convenient synonym for "anatomical".' (Ibid., p. 339). For a discussion of wax anatomical models of female bodies and the relationship between body image and sex roles see Ludmilla Jordanova, *Sexual visions: images of gender in science and medicine between the 18th and 20th centuries*, Hemel Hempstead 1989, pp. 42-65.
20 Green, op. cit. (note 19), pp. 345-46. The American sculptor, William Rush, was noted for his polychromed anatomical models made from pine, leather, papier-mâché, some of which are preserved at the Wistar Institute of Anatomy and Biology, Philadelphia; see exhib. cat. *William Rush: American sculptor*, Philadelphia (Pennsylvania Academy of Fine Arts) 1982, no. 33. Auzoux's models included a life-size human body composed of 130 parts 'which may be detached, exhibiting upwards of 1,700 objects,' *Great Exhibition of the Works of Industry of All Nations: official descriptive and illustrated catalogue*, London 1851, vol. 3, p. 1170.
21 Waagen, op. cit. (note 11), p. 700.
22 Fusco and Janson, op. cit. (note 15), p. 319.
23 T. Matthews, *The biography of John Gibson, R.A., sculptor, Rome*, London 1911, pp. 137-38. For a full account of the statue and Gibson's experiments in polychromy, see Elizabeth S. Darby, 'John Gibson, Queen Victoria, and the idea of sculptural polychromy,' *Art History* 4 (March 1981), pp. 32-53.
24 Cited by Rupert Gunnis, *Dictionary of British sculptors 1660-1851*, London, n.d. For a full account of the dissemination of this article in the English press, and the generally adverse response to the statue in England, see Darby, op. cit. (note 23), pp. 41-42, 48, note 27.
25 Mitchell, op. cit. (note 7), p. 161.
26 *Biographical and descriptive sketches of the distinguished characters which compose the unrivalled exhibition of Madame Tussaud and Sons*, London 1844, p. 20, no. 89.
27 This figure had been made by Dr Curtius whose waxwork collection Madame Tussaud inherited and by whom she was trained. The work is still on display at Madame Tussaud's in London.
28 *Biographical and descriptive sketches*, cit. (note 26), no. 88.
29 Madame Tussaud, *Memoirs and reminiscences of France forming an abridged history of the French Revolution*, ed. Francis Hervé, London 1838. For a discussion of the history of waxworks in Paris during the Revolutionary period see Carol Ockman, *Ingres's eroticized bodies retracing the serpentine line*, New Haven & London 1995, pp. 100-108.
30 *Biographical and descriptive sketches*, cit. (note 26), p. 28.
31 Ibid., no. 79.
32 Ibid., no. 81.
33 Ibid., nos. 69, 70.
34 Ibid., no. 1.
35 Matthews, op. cit. (note 23), p. 182.
36 Altick, op. cit. (note 19), p. 531, note 30.
37 Ibid., pp. 341, 531, note 44. See also Jordanova, op. cit. (note 19), pp. 44-45, and Ockman, op. cit. (note 29), p. 100. The latter cites the wax bodies on display at the Musée Dupuytren in the Ecole de Médecine, Paris, which opened in 1835.
38 See Frederick Rehberg, *Drawings faithfully copied from nature at Naples and with permission dedicated to the Right Honourable Sir William Hamilton His Britannic Majesty's Envoy Extraordinary and Plenipotentiary at the court of Naples*, 1794. The copy held at the Paul Mellon Center for British Art, Yale University, New Haven, has Gillray cartoons (ca. 1800) of Lady Hamilton's attitudes pasted in opposite those of Rehberg: 'the fair original has so *grown* in grace and *encreased* in loveliness, that it would be injustice in the highest degree not to portray her *as she really is*.'
39 Altick, op. cit. (note 19), pp. 347, 531, note 73.
40 John Stokes, *In the nineties*, London 1989, p. 79.
41 For a detailed study of these wax votives, see Gislind M. Ritz, *Die lebensgroßen angekleideten Kinder-Wachsvotive in Franken*, Volkach 1981.
42 Richard Mortimer, 'the history of the collection,' in Anthony Harvey and Richard Mortimer (eds.), *The funeral effigies of Westminster Abbey*, Woodbridge 1994, p. 27. For the decline in popularity of these effigies see Phillip Lindley's entry for Lord Nelson, pp. 176-77.
43 Allan Cunningham, *The lives of the most eminent British sculptors*, London 1830, pp. 154-55. See also Phillip Lindley's entry for Lord Nelson, in Harvey and Mortimer, op. cit. (note 42), p. 176, note 14 where a version of this quotation is cited.
44 Matthews, op. cit. (note 23), p. 183.
45 J. Beavington Atkinson, 'Modern sculpture and sculpture of all nations in the International Exhibition,' *Art Journal illustrated catalogue of the International Exhibition of 1862*, London 1862, pp. 313-24. This reference cited by Dorothy Sherwood, *Harriet Hosmer: American sculptor, 1830-1908*, Columbia, Missouri & London 1991, pp. 217, 354, note 15. For the reaction to the statue's polychromy in England, see Benedict Read, *Victorian sculpture*, New Haven & London 1982, pp. 25-26, 388, note 5, which cites the myth of Pygmalion 'retold' by Frank Anstey as *The Tinted Venus: a farcical romance*, London 1885.
46 Sherwood, op. cit. (note 45), pp. 216, 354, note 12. Here Sherwood cites an article from the *Missouri Republican*, St Louis (April 1862).
47 Spielmann, op. cit. (note 4), p. 4.
48 Ibid.
49 Ibid.
50 For a summary of the critical responses to *Angelica*, see Fusco and Janson, op. cit. (note 15), p. 163.
51 Gustave Flaubert, *Salammbô*, translated with an introduction by A.J. Krailsheimer, London 1977, p. 173.
52 Charles Avery, Edward Morris and Mark Evans, *Lady Lever Art Gallery Port Sunlight: catalogue of foreign paintings, drawings, miniatures, tapestries, postclassical sculpture and prints*, Liverpool 1983, nos. LL 205, LL 206. For a discussion of the polychromy of Ferrary's *Salammbô* see Le Normand-Romain, op. cit. (note 8), p. 154.
53 Weekes, op. cit. (note 1), p. 130.
54 Ibid., p. 131.

Emmanuelle Héran

Art for the sake of the soul

Translated from the French by Charles Penwarden.
1 Mme Celnart, *Manuel des dames ou l'art de l'élégance*, 2nd ed., Paris 1883, p. 31. This and the following references were suggested by the excellent study by Philippe Perrot, *Le travail des apparences: le corps féminin, XVIIIe - XIXe siècle*, Paris 1984.
2 Honoré de Balzac, *César Birotteau* (1838), Paris 1978, p. 44 (*La comédie humaine*, vol. 4).
3 A. Debay, *Hygiène vestimentaire*, Paris 1857, pp. 159-60.
4 J.-G. Bourke, *Les rites scatologiques* (1913), Paris 1981, pp. 262-63.
5 '[...] ce que notre temps appelle vulgairement maquillage, qui ne voit que l'usage de la poudre de riz, si niaisement anathématisé par les philosophes candides, a pour but et pour résultat de faire disparaître du teint toutes les taches que la nature y a outrageusement semées, et de créer une unité abstraite dans le grain et la couleur de la peau, laquelle unité, comme celle produite par le maillot, rapproche immédiatement l'être humain de la statue, c'est-à-dire d'un être divin et supérieur.' Charles Baudelaire, 'Éloge du maquillage,' in idem, *Le peintre de la vie moderne* (1863), in idem, *Œuvres complètes*, 2 vols., Paris 1976, vol. 2, p. 717.
6 'Lutte avec le carrare/Avec le paros dur/Et rare,/Gardiens du contour pur.' Théophile Gautier, 'L'art,' in idem, *Emaux et camées* (1852, definitive ed. 1872), Paris 1981, p. 148. Translation from E. Canfield (ed.), *Selections from French poetry*, New York 1965, pp. 96-97.
7 '[...] une unité de ton préférable à ces martelages de blanc, de jaune et de rose qu'offrent les teints les plus purs. Peut-être même un vague frisson de pudeur engage-t-il les femmes à poser sur leur col, leurs épaules, leurs seins et leurs bras ce léger voile de poussière blanche qui atténue la nudité en lui retirant les chaudes et provocantes couleurs de la vie. La forme se rapproche ainsi de la statuaire, elle se spiritualise et se purifie.' Théophile Gautier, *La mode* (1858), Le Méjean 1993, pp. 35-36.
8 Gautier, *Emaux et camées*, cit. (note 6).
9 Translated from the French edition: Friedrich Hegel, *Esthétique*, trans. S. Jankélévitch, Paris 1979, vol. 1, pp. 9-10.
10 'Je laisse à Gavarni, poëte des chloroses/Son troupeau gazouillant de beautés d'hôpital/Car je ne puis trouver parmi ces pâles roses/Une fleur qui ressemble à mon rouge idéal' Charles Baudelaire, 'Idéal,' in idem, *Les fleurs du mal*, trans. Richard Howard, London 1987, p. 25.
11 Emile Zola, *Nana*, trans. George Holden, London 1972, p. 470.
12 Jules Bois, *L'éternelle poupée*, Paris 1894, p. 338.

13 Published in *La Revue de Paris* (January 1900).
14 'A mesure que la femme avance dans la vie, elle augmente la richesse de son costume. Elle croit que la richesse supplée à la beauté qui lui échappe. Combien est touchante et belle la jeune fille ornée des grâces que la nature lui a départies. Elle n'a point besoin des parures de l'art. Et ne peut-on pas dire ainsi de l'art moderne, qui est obligé de colorier des statues? N'est-ce pas l'absence du sentiment du beau?' Cited in *Les carnets de David d'Angers*, ed. André Bruel, 2 vols., Paris 1958, vol. 2, p. 245.
15 'Ceux qui mettent la forme avant la couleur ont bien raison. N'est-ce pas la forme qui vous initie dans les rapports les plus secrets de l'âme d'une jeune fille. La couleur peint la santé d'un être: c'est l'égoïsme de la nature, c'est l'expression matérielle de la vie.' Ibid., p. 56.
16 Paul Mantz, 'Salon de 1859,' *Gazette des Beaux-Arts* (June 1859), pp. 363-71.
17 'Nous donc, sculptons avec le ciseau des Pensées/Le bloc vierge du Beau, Paros immaculé...' Paul Verlaine, 'Epilogue,' in idem, *Poèmes saturniens* (1866), Paris 1973, p. 93.
18 Mantz, op. cit. (note 16).
19 'La terrible réalité de cette statuette [...] produit un évident malaise; toutes ses idées sur la sculpture; sur ces froides blancheurs inanimées, sur ces mémorables poncifs recopiés depuis des siècles, se bouleversent.' Joris-Karl Huysmans, 'L'exposition des Indépendants en 1881,' in idem *L'art moderne: certains*, Paris 1975, pp. 49-50.
20 'Type éternel et insipide du Beau, parfaite Vénus, dite de Milo, quel audacieux brisera tes reins célèbres qui inspirent depuis si longtemps touts les gratteurs de marbre pâle...? Tu fus sublime, sans doute, mais tu n'es plus la femme d'aujourd'hui, comme le marbre rigide n'est plus la matière que veulent nos yeux avides de couleur, de mouvement et de vie. Brisons les marbres, les moules et les admirations antiques. Cherchez, imaginez, trouvez. Fouillez le bois, pétrissez la terre, modelez la cire!... Et la couleur s'alliant à la forme, nous verrons peut-être bientôt des statues peintes.' Guy de Maupassant, 'Notes d'un démolisseur,' *Gil Blas* (17 May 1882), reprinted as *Au Salon: chroniques sur la peinture*, Paris 1993, pp. 49-50.
21 'Je ne puis aimer les femmes réelles:/L'idéal entre nous ouvre ses profondeurs/[...]/Il faudrait avoir sa vierge sculptée/Comme Pygmalion...' Louis Ménard, 'L'idéal,' in idem, *Rêveries d'un païen mystique*, Paris 1876.
22 Sander Pierron, 'Philippe Wolfers,' *Revue des Arts Décoratifs* (May 1900), p. 156.
23 The long list of polychrome Medusas includes those by Arnold Böcklin, Wilhelm von Cranach, Henry Cros, Franz von Stuck and George Frederick Watts.
24 'Sur ses doigts de rubis, le saphir, l'améthyste/Font resplendir leurs feux charmants: dans un plat d'or/Elle porte le chef sanglante de Jean-Baptiste' Théodore de Banville, 'Les princesses,' 'Hérodiade,' (1854), in idem, *Les exilés* (1857), Paris 1991, p. 76.

25 'Ses yeux polis sont faits de minéraux charmants' Baudelaire, op. cit. (note 10), p. 38.
26 Joris-Karl Huysmans, *A rebours* (1884), Paris 1978, chapter IV.
27 Jean Lorrain, *Monsieur de Phocas* (1901), Paris 1992, p. 24.
28 Jules Laforgue, 'Salomé,' in idem, *Moralités légendaires* (1887), Paris 1977.
29 Lorrain, op. cit. (note 27), p. 92.
30 Jean Lorrain, *Monsieur de Bougrelon* (1897), Paris 1993, p. 37.
31 Octave Mirbeau, *Le jardin des supplices* (1899), Paris 1991, pp. 145-46.
32 See Ernest Raynaud, *La mêlée symboliste* (n.d.), Paris 1971, p. 317. The author describes how Oscar Wilde used to take him to look at the jewellers' shops, with the words: 'I am mad about jewels. [...] It was from looking at them that I got the idea of writing a Salome. Her image appeared to me with a gold helmet, glittering with jewels.'
33 Charles Baudelaire, 'Jewels,' in idem, op. cit. (note 10), p. 26.
34 See for example the recent study by Rae Beth Gordon, *Ornament, fantasy and desire in nineteenth century French literature*, Princeton, New Jersey 1992.
35 'La reine Nicosis, portant des pierreries,/A pour parure un calme et merveilleux concert/D'étoffes, où l'éclair d'un flot d'astres se perd/Dans les lacs de lumière et les flammes fleuries./Son vêtement tremblant chargé d'orfèvreries/Est fait d'un tissu rare et sur la pourpre ouvert,/Où l'or éblouissant, tour à tour rouge et vert,/Sert de fond méprisable aux riches broderies./Elle a de lourds pendants d'oreilles, copiés/Sur les feux des soleils du ciel, et sur ses pieds/Mille escarboucles font pâlir le jour livide./Et fière sous l'éclat vermeil de ses habits,/Sur les genoux du roi Salomon elle vide/Un vase de saphir d'où tombent des rubis.' Théodore de Banville, 'Les princesses,' 'La Reine de Saba,' (1865), in idem, op. cit. (note 24), p. 74.
36 See Jean Pierrot, *L'imaginaire décadent (1880-1900)*, Paris 1977, pp. 265-71.
37 Translated from: Heinrich Mann, *Professor Unrat* (1905). French trans. *L'ange bleu*, Paris 1974, p. 128.
38 Max Beerbohm, 'A defence of cosmetics,' *The Yellow Book* (April 1894), p. 73.
39 Jean Lorrain offers the most conspicuous example in his books *Ames d'automne*, *Histoires de masques* ('La dame aux portraits'), *Monsieur de Phocas* and *Le crime des riches*.
40 'Pendue auprès du lit, la tête aux lèvres peintes.../Il baisa longuement cette bouche rosâtre.' Jean Lorrain, 'Réclamation posthume,' in idem, *Contes d'un buveur d'éther* (1895), reprinted as *Histoires de masques*, Saint-Cyr-sur-Loire 1987, p. 179.
41 Maurizioni Bettini, 'Loving statues,' exhib. cat. *Identity and alterity: figures of the body 1895-1995*, Venice (Biennale) 1995, pp. 18-25.
42 Robert L. Delevoy, Catherine De Croës and Gisèle Ollinger-Zinque, *Fernand Khnopff*, 2nd ed., Brussels 1987, no. 363. The proposed date of 1900 seems

illogical. The work was probably made before 1891.

43 Ibid., no. 239.

44 Ibid., no. 365.

45 Cf. Michel Draguet, *Khnopff ou l'ambigu poétique*, Paris 1995, p. 366. The work is known as *La recluse* or *La belle au bois dormant*.

46 Wilhelm Jensen, *Gradiva: ein pompejanisches Phantasiestück*, Dresden & Leipzig 1903. From the French translation by Roger Ollivier (1903): *Pompéi: le rêve sous les ruines*, Paris 1992. See also Sigmund Freud, 'Delusion and dreams in Jensen's Gradiva' (1907), in *The Pelican Freud Library*, vol. 14 (Art and literature), London 1988, pp. 33-118. Note the scene in the poppy field: 'The dream flowers that grow on the banks of the Lethe, filled the entire space, and Hypnos was lying amidst them, Hypnos, that god who, uses the juices collected in the night in the red calyxes of the poppies, then distributes sleep and dulls the senses. Norbert [...] felt a pleasant dreamlike softness coming over his thoughts...' Writing in 1903, is not Jensen using the same mythological reference as Khnopff did in 1891?

47 Jensen's novella does not immediately state that the bas-relief is not polychrome, which suggests that this is taken for granted. In the middle of the story, he mentions a 'reproduction in stone, uniform and without colour.' It is indeed in white marble.

48 We could also have cited the story of George Frederick Watts, who found an ancient bust of Sappho in the store rooms of the Ashmolean Museum, Oxford. The work was in two parts, which the artist set about putting back together. The result was three different works: the bust itself (it was later discovered that the two halves were unrelated), painted or rather patinated by Watts, a cast, which he put in his studio, and even a painting with the revealing title *The wife of Pygmalion* (c. 1868, Buscot Park, Oxfordshire, The Faringdon Collection Trust).

49 'je mets au-dessus d'un buste en marbre ou en bronze, ce buste, en cire par exemple, avec les yeux bleus ou noirs, des lèvres rouges ou exsangues, les cheveux et la parure, etc.' Jules Laforgue, 'Notes d'esthétique,' *Revue Blanche* 9 (1 December 1896), pp. 481-88.

50 Rachilde, *Monsieur Vénus* (1884), Paris 1977.

51 'Digne de la Vénus Callipyge, cette chute de reins où la ligne de l'épine dorsale fuyait dans un méplat voluptueux et se redressait, ferme, grasse en deux contours adorables, avait l'aspect d'une sphère de Paros aux transparences d'ambre.' The heroine of another Rachilde novel, *La Marquise de Sade*, frequents 'the boulevard wax museums' (1887), Paris 1981, p. 85.

52 'Je regardais tourner le mannequin/Et j'admirais sa taille, sa poitrine,/Ses cheveux d'or et son minois taquin,/Lorsque j'ai vu palpiter sa narine/Et son cou mince à forme vipérine./"Elle vit donc!" me dis-je épouvanté,/Et depuis lors, à toute heure hanté/Par un amour que rien ne peut occire,/J'ai peur et la curiosité/De voir entrer chez moi la dame en cire.' Maurice Rollinat, *Les névroses* (1883), Paris 1923, p. 328.

53 'une tête d'adolescent au nez brusque, le menton creusé d'un coup de pouce, avec une saisissante expression d'énergie dans le bombement du front et de la proéminence des arcades sourcilières au-dessus des yeux enfoncés: une face douloureuse et souffrante d'enfant tragique, une tête de mutisme et de défi, belle par le silence de lèvres minces et renflées. La pâleur verdâtre de la face amaigrie et demeurée pourtant carrée accentuait encore l'amertume de la bouche. Au-dessous, dans un blason, larmaient encore trois perles: les trois pilules des Médicis.' Jean Lorrain, op. cit. (note 27), pp. 85-87. Also of interest is 'La dame aux lèvres rouges,' a tale he published in *L'Echo de Paris* (March 1888).

54 Jules Laforgue, 'Bibliographie: l'encaustique de H. Cros et Ch. Henry,' *Chronique des Arts et de la Curiosité* (6 September 1884), pp. 238-39 (cited in idem, *Textes de critique d'art*, ed. Mireille Dottin, Lille 1988, pp. 137-39). The book reviewed by Laforgue is: Henry Cros and Charles Henry, *L'encaustique et les autres procédés de peinture chez les anciens, histoire et technique*, Paris 1884.

55 Laforgue, op. cit. (note 54), p. 154.

56 Joris-Karl Huysmans, 'L'étiage,' in idem, *Croquis parisiens* (1880), Paris 1981. On the theme of the wax dummies and 'sidonies' (female busts) shown in the windows of wig-makers' shops, see Mireille Dottin-Orsini, *Cette femme qu'ils disent fatale*, Paris 1993, pp. 102-09.

57 'C'est un garçon tout maigre, tout noir, tout barbu, avec une inquiétante fixité dans ses yeux caves. Et cette lampe allumée, et ces petits morceaux de cire qui semblent, en leur boîte à cigares, de petits morceaux de chair [...] me jettent, à la longue, dans une espèce de peur de cette vie magique, que cuisine dans cette cave ce pâle garçon.' Edmond and Jules de Goncourt, *Journal: mémoires de la vie littéraire*, Paris 1989, vol. 2, p. 534 (10 December 1872).

58 Cf. Andreas Blühm, *Pygmalion: Die Ikonographie eines Künstlermythos zwischen 1500 und 1900*, Frankfurt am Main & Bern & New York & Paris 1988.

59 '[...] son corps offre un ensemble de lignes à surprendre les plus grands statuaires [...] C'est, en vérité, la splendeur de la *Venus victrix* humanisée [...] ses pieds ont cette même élégance des marbres grecs [...] Prodigieux!... C'est, en effet, la fameuse VENUS du sculpteur inconnu! [...] – c'est plus que prodigieux... c'est stupéfiant, en vérité! [...] Lorsque Alicia cessait de parler, son visage [...], son marbre, resté divin, démentait le langage évanoui. [...] la *non-correspondance* du physique et de l'intellectuel s'accusait constamment et dans les proportions paradoxales [...] A l'extérieur – et du front aux pieds – une sorte de Vénus Anadyomène: au-dedans, une personnalité tout à fait ETRANGERE à ce corps. [...] Si elle était privée de toute pensée, je pourrais la comprendre. La *Venus* de marbre, en effet, *n'a que faire de la Pensée*. La déesse est voilée de minéral et de silence. Il sort de son aspect de Verbe-ci: "Moi, je suis seulement la Beauté même. Je ne pense que par l'esprit de qui me contemple." [...] "Ah! qui m'ôtera l'âme de ce corps!" [...] un bras humain posé sur un coussin de soie violâtre... C'était le bras et la main gauche d'une jeune femme... Les chairs étaient d'un ton demeuré si vivant, le derme si pur et si satiné que l'aspect en était aussi cruel que fantastique.' Auguste de Villiers de L'Isle-Adam, *L'Eve future* (1886), Paris 1993, p. 56.

60 'Cette chair, qui se prête à la pénétration du tiède calorique [...], donne au toucher l'impression prestigieuse, le bondissement, l'onctueuse élasticité de la Vie... Comme elle doit transparaître, adoucie d'éclat par l'épiderme, sa nuance est celle d'une neige teintée d'une fumée d'ambre et de roses pâles, et d'un brillant vague, que le mica d'une faible dose d'amiante pulvérisée sait lui donner. L'action photochromique saturera du ton définitif.' Ibid. p. 247.

61 It should be noted that Villiers began meeting the Cros brothers at the salon of Nina de Villard in around 1872. He was particularly close to Charles Cros, who claimed to have invented the phonograph before Edison, and attention has been drawn to the similarities between their writing. It is highly likely that Villiers knew of Cros's work on wax (see below).

62 'Dieu fit l'homme avec un peu de boue. Avec un peu de boue, on peut faire du métal, des pierres précieuses, avec un peu de boue et aussi un peu de génie! N'est-ce donc point là une matière intéressante?' Paul Gauguin, 'Notes sur l'art: l'Exposition universelle,' *Le Modernisme Illustré* (11 July 1889).

63 Jules Henrivaux, 'Au Musée Galliera: les verreries de Gallé,' *Le Verre* (August 1910), n.p.

64 Roger Marx, 'Emile Gallé: psychologie de l'artiste et synthèse de l'œuvre,' *Art et Décoration* 30 (August 1911), p. 243.

65 'La couleur ajoute au mystère et spiritualise la matière... La transmutation qu'obtint en ses creusets l'alchimiste, l'esthète ne la considère qu'un cément à son idéal, qu'un moyen précieux de représenter ses rêves; il éthérise le tangible et tangibilise l'immatériel.' Alphonse Germain, 'Henri Cros et la sculpture polychrome,' *La Plume* 56 (15 August 1891), pp. 280-81.

June Hargrove

Painter-sculptors and polychromy in the evolution of modernism

1 Generously supported by the Graduate School of the University of Maryland, the research for this essay is part of a larger project on the topic. I am most grateful to the staff of the Service de Documentation and of the Département de Sculpture of the Musée d'Orsay for their assistance.
2 The medieval practices, such as that around Hans Multscher, present another set of issues, which I am leaving aside here.
3 Karina Türr, *Farbe und Naturalismus in der Skulptur des 19. und 20. Jahrhunderts: Sculpturae vitam insufflat pictura*, Mainz 1994, makes many correlations between the two centuries, noting, p. 14, that polychromy touches upon many issues including the *gesamtkunstwerk*.
4 Rosalind Krauss, 'Changing the work of David Smith,' *Art in America* 62 (September-October 1974), pp. 31-34.
5 The legendary *Theater Piece #1* is described in Daniel Wheeler, *Art since mid-century*, New York 1991, p. 129.
6 'Gerome,' *Journal of Decorative Art* 24 (1904), pp. 221-23, p. 222.
7 The best survey of this remains Stephan Madsen, *Sources of Art Nouveau*, New York 1955.
8 See Ekkehard Mai, 'Abstraction and synthesis,' exhib. cat. *Maurice Denis 1870-1943*, Lyons (Musée des Beaux-Arts) & Cologne (Wallraf-Richartz-Museum) & Liverpool (Walker Art Gallery) & Amsterdam (Van Gogh Museum) 1994-95, pp. 31-48, pp. 43-44.
9 John Christian, 'Burne-Jones and sculpture,' in Benedict Read and Joanna Barnes (eds.), *Pre-Raphaelite sculpture: nature and imagination in British sculpture 1848-1914*, London 1991, pp. 77-91.
10 Léonce Bénédite, 'Henry Cros,' exhib. cat. *Salon d'Automne*, Paris 1922, pp. 369-81, p. 371. Cros studied with the genre painter Jules Valadon.
11 Maurice Testard, 'Henry Cros,' *L'Art Décoratif* 18 (January-June 1908), pp. 149-55, p. 152.
12 Jean-Luc Olivié, entry on Cros in Jean-René Gaborit and Jack Ligot (eds.), *Sculptures en cire de l'ancienne Egypte à l'art abstrait* (Notes et documents des Musées de France 18), Paris 1987, pp. 213-17, p. 215.
13 Jacques Brenner, *Charles Cros*, Paris 1963, p. 52.
14 Ibid., pp. 54 and 68.
15 Charles Henry, 'Introduction à une esthétique scientifique,' *Revue Contemporaine* 2 (August 1885), pp. 443-44.
16 Henry Hawley, 'Sculptures by Jules Dalou, Henry Cros and Medardo Rosso,' *Bulletin of the Cleveland Museum of Art* 58 (September 1971), pp. 199-209, p. 202.

17 Antoinette Le Normand-Romain, '*Le voyageur* de Meissonier,' *Revue du Louvre* 35 (1985), no. 2, p. 135.
18 Aimée Brown Price confirmed in conversation 8 March 1996 that Puvis achieved matte effects by mixing wax with his pigments. I believe that Cros played an important role in promoting encaustic among his acquaintances, such as Degas and Puvis.
19 Douglas Druick and Peter Zegers, 'La petite danseuse et les criminels: Degas moraliste?' *Degas inédit* (Actes du colloque Degas, 18-21 avril 1988), Paris 1989, pp. 225-50. See also Theodore Reff, *Degas: the artist's mind*, New York 1976, p. 241.
20 According to Charles Millard, *The sculpture of Edgar Degas*, Princeton, New Jersey 1976, p. 63, if Degas heightened the innate polychromy of the materials through tinting the wax, no traces of the colour remain. He cites the distinguished conservator Arthur Beale.
21 Reff, op. cit. (note 19), pp. 270-91.
22 Türr, op. cit. (note 3), pp. 125-30.
23 David Gariff, *Giuseppe Grandi (1843-1894) and the Milanese Scapigliatura*, (diss. University of Maryland at College Park 1991), p. 36.
24 Musée d'Orsay, Service de Documentation, review by Louis Vauxelle [sic], 'Salon d'Automne,' *Gil Blas* (c. 1904), pp. 22-25, p. 23.
25 Luciano Caramel, exhib. cat. *Medardo Rosso*, London (Whitechapel Art Gallery) 1994, p. 12.
26 Ibid., p. 16. Hawley, op. cit. (note 16), p. 205, speculates that Cros and Rosso had met by 1889, noting, p. 202, that a portrait by Cros of the 'sculpteur Rossi' may have been Rosso. See also Reff, op. cit. (note 19), pp. 261-62.
27 Hawley, op. cit. (note 16), p. 205. Edmond Claris, *De l'impressionisme en sculpture: Auguste Rodin et Medardo Rosso*, Paris 1902, p. 57.
28 Caramel, op. cit. (note 25), pp. 11-12, and Claris, op. cit. (note 27), pp. 1-2.
29 Claris, op. cit. (note 27), p. 58. Colourist effects here means the accentuation of light and shadow on the sculptural surface through modulations of texture, an approach in vogue among the neo-baroque artists.
30 Caramel, op. cit. (note 25), pp. 14-16, 37, and 39, note 23.
31 Rosso returned to Italy in 1897. Ibid., p. 30.
32 Gerhard Winkler, *Max Klinger*, Leipzig 1984, pp. 19 and 209. I would like to thank Marcia Morton for sharing her bibliography on polychromy with me.
33 Susan Graage, *Max Klinger's monument to Beethoven* (Master's thesis, University of Maryland 1991), p. 23, quoting Max Klinger, *Malerei und Zeichnung*, reprinted in Manfred Boetzkes (ed.), exhib. cat. *Max Klinger: Wege zum Gesamtkunstwerk*, Hildesheim (Roemer- und Pelizaeus-Museum) 1984, pp. 208-52, p. 243. Winkler, op. cit. (note 32), p. 181, quotes a letter of 21 June 1886 to Albers (see also p. 265).
34 Boetzkes, op. cit. (note 33), p. 252, states that the first publication was in 1891; however, the National Gallery of Art, Washington, D.C., owns a copy dated 1885.

35 Klinger, op. cit. (note 33), p. 213, and Graage, op. cit. (note 33), pp. 4, 23-25, 45, 55-57. Klinger's debt to Wagner's ideas are analysed by Ekkehard Mai and Ulrike Planner-Steiner, in Boetzkes, op. cit. (note 33), pp. 25-65. Türr, op. cit. (note 3), pp. 70-71.
36 Graage, op. cit. (note 33), pp. 23-24, 62. See Klinger, op. cit. (note 33), pp. 213, 243-47, on verisimilitude and the function of colour, specifically leading up to his definition of *raumkunst*.
37 Jean-Paul Bouillon, *La promenade du critique influent*, Paris 1990, p. 238. For more on the relationship between the two men, see the essay by Andreas Blühm in this book.
38 Winkler, op. cit. (note 32), p. 19, citing a letter to Dr. H.H. Meier of 9 February 1885.
39 Brandes, professor at Berlin University, brought Klinger to the public eye in his *Moderne Geister*, Frankfurt am Main 1882.
40 Winkler, op. cit. (note 32), p. 205, quotes Willy Pastor, *Max Klinger*, Berlin 1919, p. 168, where Klinger makes this claim many years after the fact.
41 Winkler, op. cit. (note 32), pp. 19, 181-82, quoting a letter to Albers of 21 June 1886.
42 Marie Busco in Robert Kashey (ed.), exhib. cat. *Viewpoints: European sculpture 1875-1925*, New York (Shepherd Gallery) 1991, no. 30, notes that Klinger may have influenced Barrias and Gérôme.
43 See Blühm's essay for additional comments and the article by Joseph Lux, 'Klingers Beethoven und die moderne Raumkunst,' *Deutsche Kunst und Dekoration* 10 (1902), pp. 475-93.
44 For a full account, see Graage, op. cit. (note 33), pp. 44-69.
45 Ibid., pp. 61, 67. Winkler, op. cit. (note 32), pp. 205-06. Türr, op. cit. (note 3), p. 74, also discusses the use of colour as not naturalistic.
46 Heinrich Voss, *Franz von Stuck 1863-1928*, Munich 1973, p. 59, describes the 1897-98 villa in terms of a *gesamtkunstwerk* and provides, note 250, bibliographical references. See also Franz Meissner, *Franz Stuck*, Munich 1897, pp. 11-13. Edwin Becker, exhib. cat. *Franz von Stuck: eros & pathos*, Amsterdam (Van Gogh Museum) 1995.
47 Michel Draguet, *Khnopff ou l'ambigu poétique*, Paris 1995, p. 136, note 134. The *Sibyl*'s present location is unknown.
48 Ibid., p. 138, articulates this at length, concluding that 'Khnopff cherche l'ambiguïté en liant peinture et sculpture.' Türr, op. cit. (note 3), p. 91, examines the unnaturalistic qualities of Khnopff's colour.
49 Draguet, op. cit. (note 47), figs. 216-20, illustrates examples in oil, in chalk, and in photographs.
50 Draguet, op. cit. (note 47), p. 330, laments that the link between Khnopff and Stuck has never been studied.
51 Ibid., p. 142.
52 Ibid., fig. 334. A bronze cast of the *Amazon* by Stuck stood on a tall pedestal in front of the bassin opposite the Hypnos altar.
53 Reff, op. cit. (note 19), p. 262. Françoise Cachin,

'Degas et Gauguin,' in *Degas inédit*, cit. (note 19), p. 117, describes the bust of *Clovis*, combining 'le bois, la cire peinte et le tissu collé' as 'un hommage à Degas.'

54 Reff, op. cit. (note 19), pp. 267-68.

55 Vojtech Jirat-Wasiutyński, *Paul Gauguin in the context of Symbolism*, New York 1978, p. 17, suggests the date of 1884-85 for the *Notes synthétiques*, available in a facsimile of the text in *Carnet de croquis*, Paris 1962, pp. 2-12.

56 See Henri Dorra, 'Le "Texte Wagner" de Gauguin,' *Bulletin de la Société de l'Histoire de l'Art Français* (1984), pp. 281-88.

57 See Christopher Gray, *Sculpture and ceramics of Paul Gauguin*, Baltimore 1963, no. 5. Gray, p. 79, maintains that Gauguin had no influence on modern sculpture.

58 It resembles a 'coffre du Loango,' from the Congo, in the Musée national des Arts océaniens et africains, Paris, inv. no. 963-508. See also Gray, op. cit. (note 57), pp. 4-5.

59 Exhib. cat. *The art of Paul Gauguin*, Washington, D.C. (National Gallery of Art) & Chicago (The Art Institute of Chicago) & Paris (Galeries nationales du Grand Palais) 1988-89, no. 96.

60 Merete Bodelsen, *Gauguin's ceramics: a study in the development*, London 1964, pp. 11-13.

61 Ibid., p. 191. Elsewhere, pp. 46, 50, 165, 184, Merete Bodelsen comments further on how the ceramics affected Gauguin's painting style.

62 Ibid., p. 135, among many possible examples.

63 Haruko Hirota, 'La sculpture en céramique de Gauguin: sources et significations,' *Histoire de l'Art* 15 (September 1991), pp. 43-60, p. 43, discusses this.

64 Jirat-Wasiutyński, op. cit. (note 55), pp. 177-83.

65 Albert Elsen, exhib. cat. *Pioneers of modern sculpture*, London (Hayward Gallery) 1973, pp. 69, 86.

66 Joëlle Ansieu, 'Deux sculptures de Georges Lacombe, *Isis et le Christ*,' *Revue du Louvre* 33 (1983), no. 4, pp. 287-95.

67 The opposition to the Caillebotte bequest is the most famous instance of Gérôme's conservativism; see Gerald M. Ackerman, *The life and work of Jean-Léon Gérôme*, New York 1986, p. 192.

68 Ibid., p. 141. Gérôme invented this inscription, combining ancient and medieval Latin.

69 For more details about the *Tanagra*, see the essay by Blühm. Given that the piece was in progress by 1888, one must wonder if Gérôme knew Klinger.

70 Georges Jeanniot, 'Souvenirs sur Degas,' *La Revue Universelle* (15 October 1933), pp. 152-74, p. 171, states that the two friends discussed their sculpture.

71 Millard, op. cit. (note 20), pp. 56-57, note 9.

72 The colour has faded badly. Ackerman, op. cit. (note 67), pp. 136-38, quotes Gérôme, commenting on his technique to Germaine Bapst.

73 Exhib. cat. *The art of Paul Gauguin*, cit. (note 59), p. 274, quotes *Lettres de Paul Gauguin à Georges-Daniel de Monfreid*, ed. A. Joly-Segalen, Paris 1918 (revised ed. 1950), no. XIII.

74 Gauguin based his text of the *Ancien culte Mahorie* (manuscript begun 1893, facsimile ed. René Huyghe, Paris 1951) on J.A. Moerenhout, *Voyage aux îles du Grand Océan*. Jehanne Teilhet-Fisk, *Paradise reviewed: an interpretation of Gauguin's Polynesian Symbolism*, Ann Arbor, Michigan 1983, pp. 54-56, provides a detailed analysis of the specific non-western religious and visual references in the Idol. She elaborates on the additional figures carved around the back. For further comments on syncretic combinations, see Ziva Amishai-Maisels, *Gauguin's religious themes*, New York 1985, pp. 358-62. This author concludes, p. 484, that, despite the multiplicity of Gauguin's 'naive' sources, they are all 'assimilated into the style, colors, and iconography of a Frenchman of the end of the 19th century.'

75 Hirota, op. cit. (note 63), p. 51, assesses Gauguin's ceramics, notably the *Oviri*, in the context of the grotesque.

76 Gauguin's witty article vilifying Sèvres, 25 April 1895, reprinted in *Oviri: écrits d'un sauvage*, Paris 1974, pp. 135-37, should be seen as a riposte to his rejection by the Société National des Beaux-Arts for the Salon of 1895.

77 Vojtech Jirat-Wasiutyński, 'Paul Gauguin's self-portraits and the *Oviri*: the image of the artist, Eve, and the fatal woman,' *Art Quarterly* 2 (Spring 1979), pp. 172-90, p. 186. See also Barbara Landy, 'The meaning of Gauguin's *Oviri* ceramic,' *The Burlington Magazine* 109 (April 1967), pp. 242-46. The *Oviri* image recurs in numerous graphics and at least two paintings, and the word itself was inscribed on a self-portrait relief, not to mention the textual references in his writings.

78 Amy Day, *Gauguin's Noa Noa: aspects of narrative in text and image* (Master's thesis, University of Maryland at College Park 1991). Koji Takahashi, 'The superficial paradise: a study on Gauguin's sculpture and ceramics,' exhib. cat. *Paul Gauguin*, Tokyo (National Museum of Modern Art) 1987, pp. 37-42, p. 40, writes in this same spirit when he states the 'metamorphosis of materials [...] is [...] the myth of creation.'

79 Richard Bretell in exhib. cat. *The art of Paul Gauguin*, cit. (note 59), p. 395, describes the house as a 'total work of art' without elaborating. He also cites, p. 392, Gauguin's exhibition at Vollard's in 1898 as a total work of art. Amishai-Maisels, op. cit. (note 74), pp. 405-06, comments on the influence of Wagner's *credo* on ideas that Gauguin espoused in the 1892 *Cahier pour Aline* (ed. Suzanne Damiron, Paris 1963).

80 Bengt Danielsson, *Gauguin in the South Seas*, transl. by Reginald Spink, New York 1966, p. 254.

81 Tuliza Fleming connected the polychrome Micronesian panels with these reliefs in her report for my seminar in spring, 1995. The Musée national des Arts océaniens et africains, Paris, has examples from the Men's Houses of New Guinea (e.g. inv. no. 85.1.2). Typically the artist conflates his sources, so this observation does not preclude the panels widely-recognised relationship to the Maori Council house. Gray, op. cit. (note 57). pp. 66-67, fig. 23, presents the photograph of a Maori house that Gauguin bought while in Auckland, New Zealand, on his return to Tahiti in 1895. Gray, p. 77, accepts that the Maori carvings influenced the Atuona panels. He connects the title *Maison du jour*, but not the decoration, with the Polynesian 'fare popi, [...] that was used by the unmarried young people as a sort of club where they gathered to play and sing, and to sleep and have intercourse.'

82 These phrases are translated from the French, 'Soyez amoureuses vous serez heureuses' and 'Soyez mystérieuses.'

83 Danielsson, op. cit. (note 80), p. 254, and Brettell in exhib. cat. *The art of Paul Gauguin*, cit. (note 59), pp. 464, 428-43.

84 Paul Gauguin, *Avant et après* (manuscript begun 1903, facsimile published Paris 1923), p. 46, and Amishai-Maisels, op. cit. (note 74), p. 459, locates them persuasively in her interpretation of the Temptation theme.

85 Amishai-Maisels, op. cit. (note 74), pp. 260-69, relates the five panels to Adam and Eve, with the iconography, which includes the fox, the snake, and fruit.

Select bibliography

Frequently cited sources and literature to 1910

Alt, Theodor, *Die Grenzen der Kunst und die Buntfarbigkeit der Antike*, Berlin 1886

Anonymous, 'Colour in sculpture,' *The Athenaeum* (24 December 1853), pp. 1559-60; (31 December 1853), p. 1597

Anonymous, 'Tinted sculpture,' *The Art Journal* (July 1862), pp. 161-62

Bapst, Germain, 'La sculpture chryséléphantine: Phidias, le duc de Luynes, M. Gérôme,' *La Revue de Famille* 2 (1892), pp. 334-42

Bell, John, 'Colouring statues,' *The Art Journal* (1858), pp. 18-20, 69-70, 179, 230-32

Bell, John, 'Colouring of sculpture,' *The Society of Arts Journal* (26 April 1861), pp. 420-31

Bell, Robert Anning, 'Coloured relief,' *Architectural Review* 3 (1897-98), pp. 206-11

Bell, Robert Anning, 'Painted relief,' *Journal of the Royal Institute of British Architects* 18 (1910-11), pp. 485-99

Blanc, Charles, *Grammaire des arts du dessin: architecture, sculpture, peinture*, Paris 1867

Buchner, Georg, *Die Metallfärbung und deren Ausfärbung mit besonderer Berücksichtigung der chemischen Metallfärbung*, Berlin 1891

Chennevières, Philippe de, *Notes d'un compilateur sur les sculpteurs et les sculptures en ivoire*, Paris 1857

Claris, Edmond, *De l'impressionisme en sculpture: Auguste Rodin et Medardo Rosso*, Paris 1902, reprinted in Luciano Caramel, exhib. cat. *L'impressionismo nella scultura*, Lugano (Galleria Pieter Coray) 1989, pp. 79-91

Collignon, Maxime, *La polychromie dans la sculpture grecque*, Paris 1898

Courajod, Louis, *La polychromie dans la statuaire du Moyen Age et de la Renaissance*, Paris 1888

Crane, Walter, 'Notes on gesso work,' *The Studio* 1 (1893), pp. 44-49

Cros, Henry and Charles Henry, *L'encaustique et les autres procédés de peinture chez les anciens: technique et histoire*, Paris 1884

Destrée, Olivier Georges, *The renaissance of sculpture in Belgium*, London 1895

Dieulafoy, Marcel, *La statuaire polychrome en Espagne*, Paris 1908

Dujardin-Beaumetz, Henri-Charles-Etienne, *Entretiens avec Rodin* (1913), Paris 1992

Dumersan, Theophile Marion, *Empreintes polychromes, ou camées coloriées, imitant les pierres gravées*, Paris 1825

Eastlake, Charles Lock, *Contributions to the literature of fine arts*, London 1848

Falkener, Edward, *Daedalus, or the causes and principles of the excellence of Greek sculpture*, London 1860

Feddersen, Martin, 'Ueber polychrome Plastik,' *Kunstchronik* 2 (1891), pp. 193-202

Floerke, Gustav, *Zehn Jahre mit Böcklin: Aufzeichnungen und Entwürfe*, Munich 1901

Frampton, George, 'On colouring sculpture,' *The Studio* 3 (1893), pp. 78-80

Garnier, Charles, *Le nouvel opéra de Paris*, 2 vols., Paris 1878

Herder, Johann Gottlieb, 'Plastik: Einige Wahrnehmungen aus Pygmalions bildendem Traume' (1778), *Herders Sämtliche Werke*, ed. Bernhard Suphan, 32 vols., Berlin 1892, vol. 8, pp. 1-87

Hessling, Egon, *La sculpture belge contemporaine*, Berlin 1903

Hildebrand, Adolf von, *Gesammelte Schriften zur Kunst*, ed. Henning Bock, Cologne & Opladen 1965

Hittorff, Jakob Ignaz, *Restitution du temple d'Empédocle à Sélinonte, ou l'architecture polychrôme chez les Grecs*, Paris 1851

Jones, Owen, *On the true and false in decorative arts*, London 1852

Jones, Owen, *The Alhambra Court in the Crystal Palace*, London 1854

Jones, Owen, *An apology for the colouring of the Greek Court in the Crystal Palace*, London 1854

Kekulé von Stradonitz, Reinhard, *Griechische Thonfiguren aus Tanagra*, Stuttgart 1878

Khnopff, Fernand, 'The revival of ivory carving in Belgium,' *The Studio* 4 (1894), pp. 150-51

Klenze, Leo von, *Der Tempel des olympischen Jupiters zu Agrigent, nach den neusten Ausgrabungen dargestellt*, Stuttgart & Tübingen 1821

Klenze, Leo von, *Walhalla in artistischer und technischer Beziehung*, Munich 1842

Klinger, Max, *Malerei und Zeichnung: Tagebuchaufzeichnungen und Briefe*, ed. Anneliese Hübscher, Leipzig 1985

Kugler, Franz, *Über die Polychromie der griechischen Architektur und Sculptur und ihre Grenzen*, Berlin 1835 (also in idem, *Kleine Schriften und Studien zur Kunstgeschichte*, 3 vols., Stuttgart 1853, vol. 1, pp. 265-361)

Laforgue, Jules, 'Correspondance de Berlin: exposition de sculpture polychrome à la National-Galerie' (1886), in idem, *Textes de critique d'art*, ed. Mireille Dottin, Lille 1988, pp. 79-86

Lichtwark, Alfred, 'Eine Ausstellung farbiger Skulptur,' *Die Gegenwart* 28 (1885), pp. 234-36

Lichtwark, Alfred, 'Farbige Skulptur' (1885), in idem, *Studien*, 2 vols., Hamburg 1896, vol. 1, pp. 87-131

Magnus, Eduard, *Ueber die Polychromie vom künstlerischen Standpunkte: Ein Vortrag für eine Anzahl befreundeter Künstler und Kunstverständiger*, Bonn 1872

Maus, Octave, 'La sculpture en ivoire à l'Exposition de Bruxelles,' *Art et Décoration* 2 (1897), pp. 129-33

Montalembert, Charles de, 'De l'état actuel de l'art religieux en France' (1837), in idem, *Du vandalisme et du Catholicisme dans l'art (fragmens)*, Paris 1839, pp. 159-204

Nageotte, E., *La polychromie dans l'art antique*, Besançon 1883

Offermann, Friedrich, 'Bunt oder einfarbig?' *Kunstwart* 4 (1890), pp. 65-67

Pazaurek, Gustav, *Guter und schlechter Geschmack im Kunstgewerbe*, Stuttgart 1912

Quatremère de Quincy, Antoine Chrysostome, *Le Jupiter Olympien, ou l'art de la sculpture antique considéré sous un nouveau point de vue; ouvrage qui comprend un essai sur le goût de la sculpture polychrome, etc.*, Paris 1814

R.A.S., 'Colour in sculpture,' *The Athenaeum* (18 February 1854), pp. 219-20

Rosenberg, Adolf, 'Ausstellung farbiger und getönter Bildwerke in der Berliner Nationalgalerie,' *Kunstchronik* 21 (1885-86), no. 9, pp. 166-70 and no. 11, pp. 193-97

Rosso, Medardo, *La sculpture impressioniste*, ed. Giovanni Lista, Paris 1994

Ruskin, John, *The seven lamps of architecture* (1880), London 1907

Schadow, Johann Gottfried, *Kunstwerke und Kunstansichten: Ein Quellenwerk zur Berliner Kunst- und Kulturgeschichte zwischen 1780 und 1845*, ed. Götz Eckardt, 3 vols., Berlin 1987

Schäfer, G., 'Die Ausstellung gefärbter und getönter Bildwerke in Berlin,' *Centralblatt der Bauverwaltung* 5 (1885), pp. 477-78, 493-94, 522-23, 550-51

Scharf, George, 'On the polychromy of sculpture: being recollections of remarks on this subject by C.O. Müller, at Athens, in 1840,' *The Museum of Classical Antiquities* 1 (1851), pp. 247-55

Schasler, Max, 'Polychrome Plastik und moderne Panoramen,' *Die Gegenwart* 27 (1885), no. 18, pp. 277-81

Schelling, Friedrich Wilhelm Joseph, 'Kunstgeschichtliche Anmerkungen zu Johann Martin Wagners Bericht über die Aeginetischen Bildwerke' (1817), in *Schellings Werke*, ed. Manfred Schröter, 13 vols., Munich 1946-62, 3rd supplementary vol. (1959), pp. 515-610

Scherer, Christian, *Elfenbeinplastik seit der Renaissance*, Leipzig 1903

Schmarsow, August, *Plastik, Malerei und Reliefkunst in ihrem gegenseitigen Verhältnis*, Leipzig 1899

Schumann, Paul, 'Farbige Bildnerei,' *Die Kunst für Alle* 4 (1889), pp. 362-64

Semper, Gottfried, 'Vorläufige Bemerkungen über bemalte Architektur und Plastik bei den Alten' (1834), in idem, *Kleine Schriften*, ed. Manfred and Hans Semper, Berlin & Stuttgart 1884, pp. 215-58

Semper, Gottfried, 'On the study of polychromy and its revival,' *The Museum of Classical Antiquities* 1 (1851), pp. 228-46

Semper, Gottfried, *Die vier Elemente der Baukunst*, Braunschweig 1851

Semper, Gottfried, *Der Stil in den technischen und tektonischen Künsten oder Praktische Aesthetik: Ein Handbuch für Techniker, Künstler und Kunstfreunde*, 2 vols., Frankfurt am Main 1860

Spielmann, Marion H., *British sculpture and sculptors of to-day*, London 1901

Springer, Anton, 'Sollen wir unsere Statuen bemalen?' *Beiblatt zur Zeitschrift für bildende Kunst* 19 (1884), no. 21, pp. 341-46

Treu, Georg, *Sollen wir unsere Statuen bemalen? Ein Vortrag*, Berlin 1884

Treu, Georg, *Hellenistische Stimmungen in der Bildhauerei von einst und jetzt*, Leipzig 1910

Tschudi, Hugo von, 'Ausstellung farbiger und getönter Bildwerke in der National-Galerie,' *Der Kunstfreund* 1 (1885), pp. 371-76

Volkmann, Artur, *Vom Sehen und Gestalten: Ein Beitrag zur Geschichte der jüngsten deutschen Kunst*, Jena 1912

Volkmann, Ludwig, *Grenzen der Künste: Auch eine Stillehre*, Dresden 1903

Voß, Georg, 'Farbige Bildhauerarbeiten in der Berliner Nationalgalerie,' *Die Kunst für Alle* 1 (1885), pp. 72-73

Wagner, Johann Martin von, *Bericht über die Aeginetischen Bildwerke im Besitz Seiner Königlichen Hoheit des Kronprinzen von Bayern: Mit kunstgeschichtlichen Anmerkungen von F.W.J. Schelling*, Stuttgart & Tübingen 1817

Walz, Christian, *Über die Polychromie der antiken Skulptur*, Tübingen 1853

J.B. Waring, 'Polychromy,' *The Builder* 10 (6 March 1852), pp. 150-51

Webb, Matthew, 'On colouring sculpture,' *The Studio* 3 (1894), pp. 80-82

Weekes, Henry, *Lectures on art*, London 1880

Westmacott, Richard, 'On colouring statues,' *The Archaeological Journal* 12 (March 1855), pp. 22-46

Westmacott, Richard, *Handbook of sculpture ancient and modern*, Edinburgh 1864

Winckelmann, Johann Joachim, *Geschichte der Kunst des Altertums* (1763-68), ed. Ludwig Goldscheider, Vienna 1934

Secondary literature: monographs and essays written after 1910

Adhémar, Jean, 'Les musées de cire en France, Curtius, le "Banquet royal", les têtes coupées,' *Gazette des Beaux-Arts* (December 1978), pp. 203-14

Aerts, Willem (ed.), *De restauratie van de Onze-Lieve-Vrouwekathedraal van Antwerpen*, Antwerp 1993

Aldrich, Megan, *Gothic Revival*, London 1994

Ames, Winslow, *Prince Albert and Victorian taste*, London 1967

Applegate, Judith, 'A Sarah Bernhardt inkwell and a Louis Ernest Barrias bronze,' *Boston Museum Bulletin* 73 (1975), pp. 36-39

Atterbury, Paul (ed.), *The Parian phenomenon: a survey of Victorian Parian porcelain statuary and busts*, Shepton Beauchamp 1989

Bandmann, Günter, 'Der Wandel der Materialbewertung in der Kunsttheorie des 19. Jahrhunderts,' in Helmut Koopmann and J. Adolf Schmoll gen. Eisenwerth (eds.), *Beiträge zur Theorie der Künste im 19. Jahrhundert*, 2 vols., Frankfurt am Main 1971, vol. 1, pp. 129-57

Baschet, Roger, *Le monde fantastique du musée Grevin*, Paris 1982

Baudry, Marie-Thérèse (ed.), *La sculpture: méthode et vocabulaire*, Paris 1978

Beattie, Susan, *The New Sculpture*, New Haven & London 1983

Beattie, Susan, 'The New Sculpture: aspects of a nineteenth-century English renaissance,' *Bulletin of the Detroit Institute of Arts* 62 (1987), no. 4, pp. 21-29

Belrose-Huyghues, Vincent, 'Impressionisme en sculpture,' *Connaissance des Arts* (December 1974), pp. 84-91

Benoist, Luc, *La sculpture romantique*, Paris 1928

Berman, Harold, *Bronzes: sculptors and founders 1800-1930*, 4 vols., Chicago 1974-80

Beutler, Christian, 'Marmorbilder,' in idem, Peter-Klaus Schuster and Martin Warnke (eds.), *Kunst um 1800 und die Folgen: Werner Hofmann zu Ehren*, Munich 1988, pp. 98-107

Billot, M.-Fr., 'Recherches aux XVIIIe et XIXe siècles sur la polychromie de l'architecture grecque,' exhib. cat. *Paris - Rome - Athènes: le voyage en Grèce des architectes français au XIXe et XXe siècles*, Paris (Ecole des Beaux-Arts) & Athens (National Gallery) & Houston (The Museum of Fine Arts) & New York (IBM Gallery of Science) 1982-84, pp. 61-125

Bloch, Peter and Waldemar Grzimek, *Das klassische Berlin: Die Berliner Bildhauerschule im 19. Jahrhundert*, Frankfurt am Main & Berlin 1978

Bloch, Peter, *Skulpturen des 19. Jahrhunderts im Rheinland*, Düsseldorf 1980

Blühm, Andreas, *Pygmalion: Die Ikonographie eines Künstlermythos zwischen 1500 und 1900*, Frankfurt am Main & Bern & New York & Paris 1988

Select bibliography: monographs and essays

Boime, Albert, *Hollow icons: the politics of sculpture in nineteenth century France*, Kent, Ohio & London 1987

Boime, Albert, *The art of exclusion: representing blacks in the nineteenth century*, London 1990

Borghini, Gabriele (ed.), *Marmi antichi*, Rome 1989

Brachert, Thomas, *Patina: Vom Nutzen und Nachteil der Restaurierung*, 2nd ed., Munich 1995

Brachert, Thomas and Friedrich Kobler, 'Fassung von Bildwerken,' *Reallexikon der deutschen Kunstgeschichte*, 9 vols. (to date), Munich 1937-, vol. 7 (1981), pp. 743-826

Buchenrieder, Fritz, *Gefaßte Bildwerke: Untersuchung und Beschreibung von Skulpturenfassungen mit Beispielen aus der praktischen Arbeit der Restaurierungswerkstätten des Bayerischen Landesamtes für Denkmalpflege*, Munich 1990

Buttlar, Adrian von, 'Klenzes Beitrag zur Polychromie-Frage,' exhib. cat. *Ein griechischer Traum: Leo von Klenze, der Archäologe*, Munich (Glyptothek) 1985-86, pp. 213-25

Cachin, Françoise (ed.), *L'art du XIXe siècle: 1850-1905*, Paris 1990

Cadet, Pierre, *Susse Frères: 150 years of sculpture, 1837-1987*, Paris 1994

Cézan, Claude, *Le musée Grevin*, Paris 1947

Chevillot, Catherine, 'Les stands industriels d'édition de sculptures à l'Exposition universelle de 1889: l'exemple de Barbedienne,' *Revue de l'Art* 95 (1992), no. 1, pp. 61-67

Chevillot, Catherine, 'Réalisme optique et progrès esthétique: la fin d'un rêve,' *Revue de l'Art* 104 (1994), no. 2, pp. 22-29

Clark, Kenneth, *The Gothic Revival: an essay in the history of taste*, London 1928

Collins, Judith, 'The *Tinted Venus* and beyond: painted stone sculpture from 1850-1930,' in Jackie Heuman (ed.), *From marble to chocolate: the conservation of modern sculpture* (Tate Gallery Conference, 18-20 September 1995), London 1995, pp. 9-14

Cooper, Jeremy, *Nineteenth century romantic bronzes: French, English and American bronzes 1830-1913*, Boston 1975

Cornell, Henrik, *Svensk skulptur från Sergel til 1900-talets början*, Stockholm 1952

Crook, Joseph Mordaunt, *William Burges and the High Victorian dream*, London 1981

Curtis, Penelope, *Sculpture on Merseyside*, Liverpool 1988

Curtis, Penelope (ed.), *Patronage and practice: sculpture on Merseyside*, Liverpool 1989

Daalen, P.K. van, *Nederlandse beeldhouwers in de negentiende eeuw*, Den Haag 1957

Darby, Elizabeth and Nicola Smith, *The cult of the Prince Consort*, New Haven & London 1983

Daum, Noël, *La pâte de verre*, Paris 1984

Devaux, Yves, *L'univers des bronzes et des fontes ornementales*, Paris 1978

Dietrich, Gerhard, 'Alexandre Bigot: Steinzeug in der Architekturdekoration,' *Keramos* 97 (1982), pp. 1-137

Dimitriou, P., *The polychromy of Greek sculpture: to the beginning of the Hellenistic period* (diss., New York 1947), Ann Arbor 1989

Dolinschek, Ilse, *Die Bildhauerwerke in den Ausstellungen der Wiener Sezession von 1898-1910* (diss.), Munich 1989

Dorfles, Gillo, *Kitsch: an anthology of bad taste*, London 1969

Dorival, Bernard, 'La sculpture des peintres en France de Géricault à nos jours,' *Journal de Psychologie Normale et Pathologique* 75 (1978), no. 1, pp. 27-62

Drost, Wolfgang, 'L'inspiration plastique chez Baudelaire,' *Gazette des Beaux-Arts* (January-July 1957), pp. 321-36

Drost, Wolfgang, 'Kriterien der Kunstkritik Baudelaires: Versuch einer Analyse,' in Helmut Koopmann and J. Adolf Schmoll gen. Eisenwerth (eds.), *Beiträge zur Theorie der Künste im 19. Jahrhundert*, 2 vols., Frankfurt am Main 1971, vol. 1, pp. 257-85

Drost, Wolfgang, 'La photosculpture entre art industriel et artisanat: la réussite de François Willème (1830-1905),' *Gazette des Beaux-Arts* (October 1985), pp. 113-29

Drost, Wolfgang, 'L'évolution du concept Baudelairien de la sculpture,' *Gazette des Beaux-Arts* (September 1994), pp. 39-52

Duncan, Alastair, *Art Nouveau sculpture*, London 1978

Eilert, Heide, 'Die Vorliebe für kostbar-erlesene Materialien und ihre Funktion in der Lyrik des Fin de Siècle,' in Roger Bauer et al., *Fin de Siècle: Zur Literatur und Kunst der Jahrhundertwende*, Frankfurt am Main 1977, pp. 421-41

Elsen, Albert, *Origins of modern sculpture: pioneers and premises*, New York 1974

Farrant, Penelope et al., *Eugène Emmanuel Viollet-le-Duc 1814-1879*, London 1980

Finn, David, *How to look at sculpture*, New York 1989

Florman, Lisa, 'Gustav Klimt and the precedent of Ancient Greece,' *Art Bulletin* 72 (June 1990), pp. 310-26

Forestier, Sylvie, 'Art industriel et l'industrialisation de l'art: l'exemple de la statuaire réligieuse de Vendeuvre-sur-Barse,' *Revue d'Ethnologie Française* 8 (March-September 1978), pp. 191-210

Forrest, Michael, *Art bronzes*, West Chester 1988

Gaborit, Jean-René and Jack Ligot (eds.), *Sculptures en cire de l'ancienne Egypte à l'art abstrait* (Notes et documents des Musées de France 18), Paris 1987

Gage, John, *Colour and culture: practice and meaning from antiquity to abstraction*, London 1993

Gardner, Albert Ten Eyck, 'Arabesques in bronze,' *The Metropolitan Museum of Art Bulletin* 4 (January 1946), pp. 131-35

Gonzales-Palacios, Alvar, 'Jacques-Louis David: le décor de l'antiquité,' in Regis Michel (ed.), *David contre David* (Actes du colloque organisé au musée du Louvre par le service culturel du 6 au 10 décembre 1989), 2 vols., Paris 1993, vol. 2, pp. 927-36

González, Juan José Martin, *Escultura Barroca en España 1600-1770*, Madrid 1983

Gorden, Rae Beth, *Ornament, fantasy, and desire in nineteenth century French literature*, Princeton, New Jersey 1992

Hammer, Karl, *Jakob Ignaz Hittorff: Ein Pariser Baumeister 1792-1867*, Stuttgart 1968

Hanotelle, Micheline, *Paris et Bruxelles: Rodin et Meunier, relations des sculpteurs français et belges à la fin du XIXe siècle*, Paris 1982

Harvey, Anthony and Richard Mortimer (eds.), *The funeral effigies of Westminster Abbey*, Woodbridge 1994

Haskell, Francis and Nicholas Penny, *Taste and the Antique: the lure of classical sculpture 1500-1900*, New Haven & London 1981

Hawley, Henry, 'Sculptures by Jules Dalou, Henry Cros and Medardo Rosso,' *Bulletin of the Cleveland Museum of Art* 58 (September 1971), pp. 199-209

Hentzen, Alfred, 'Gedanken über das Verhältnis von Plastik und Malerei im 19. und 20. Jahrhundert,' *Eduard von der Heydt zum 70. Geburtstag*, Zurich 1952, pp. 72-78

Heuman, Jackie (ed.), *From marble to chocolate: the conservation of modern sculpture* (Tate Gallery Conference, 18-20 September 1995), London 1995

Higgins, Reynolds, *Tanagra and the figurines*, London 1986

Honour, Hugh, *The image of the black in western art: from the American Revolution to World War I*, 2 vols., Cambridge, Massachusetts & London 1989

Humbert, Jean-Marcel, *L'egyptomanie dans l'art occidental*, Paris 1989

Janson, Horst W., 'Rediscovering nineteenth century sculpture,' *The Art Quarterly* 36 (1973), no. 4, pp. 411-14

Janson, Horst W. (ed.), *La scultura nel XIX secolo* (Atti del XXIV Congresso Internazionale di Storia dell'Arte, Bologna 1979), Bologna 1984

Janson, Horst W., *Nineteenth-century sculpture*, London 1985

Jenkins, Ian, *Archeologists and aesthetes in the sculpture galleries of the British Museum 1800-1939*, London 1992

Jenkins, Ian and A. Middleton, 'Paint on the Parthenon sculptures,' *The Annual of the British School of Archaeology at Athens* 83 (1988), pp. 183-207

Kaltenbrunner, Gerda, *Polychromierte Skulpturen und Altäre des späten 19. und beginnenden 20. Jahrhunderts im Rheinland: Vorläufige Untersuchungsergebnisse zur Technologie, Raum und Ausstattung rheinischer Kirchen 1860-1914*, Düsseldorf 1981

Katz, Marshall P., 'Nineteenth century French followers of Bernard Palissy,' *Magazine Antiques* 145 (April 1994), pp. 582-89

Kjellberg, Pierre, *Les bronzes du XIXe siècle: dictionnaire des sculpteurs*, Saint-Amand-Montrond 1989

Knoch, M.M., *Farbige Plastik*, Cologne 1975

Knoll, Kordelia, 'Treus Versuche zur antiken Polychromie und Ankäufe farbiger Plastik,' exhib. cat. *Das Albertinum vor 100 Jahren: Die Skulpturensammlung Georg Treus*, Dresden (Staatliche Kunstsammlungen Dresden, Skulpturensammlung) 1994-95, pp. 164-68

Krause, Walter, *Die Plastik der Wiener Ringstraße: Von der Spätromantik bis zur Wende um 1900*, Wiesbaden 1980

Künzl, Hannelore, *Der Einfluß des alten Orients auf die europäische Kunst besonders im 19. und 20. Jahrhundert* (diss. Cologne 1973)

Kuhn, Alfred, *Die neuere Plastik von 1800 bis zur Gegenwart*, 2nd ed., Munich 1922

Lami, Stanislas, *Dictionnaire des sculpteurs de l'école française au dix-neuvième siècle*, 4 vols., Paris 1914-21

La Niece, Susan and Paul Craddock (eds.), *Metal plating and patination: cultural, technical and historical developments*, Oxford 1993

Lecoq, Anne-Marie, 'Morts et résurrections de Bernard Palissy,' *Revue de l'Art* 78 (1981), no. 4, pp. 26-32

Leeuwen, A.J.C. van, *De maakbaarheid van het verleden: P.J.H. Cuypers als restauratiearchitect*, Zwolle 1995

Leipen, Neda, *Athena Parthenos: a reconstruction*, Toronto 1971

Leniaud, Jean-Michel, *Jean-Baptiste Lassus (1807-1857) ou le temps retrouvé des cathédrales*, Geneva 1980

Leniaud, Jean-Michel and Françoise Perrot, *La Sainte Chapelle*, Paris 1991

Le Normand-Romain, Antoinette and Jean-Luc Olivié, 'La polychromie,' in Anne Pingeot (ed.), exhib. cat. *La sculpture française au XIXe siècle*, Paris (Galeries nationales du Grand Palais) 1986, pp. 148-59

Le Normand-Romain, Antoinette et al., *Sculpture: the adventure of modern sculpture in the 19th and 20th centuries*, London 1987

Levi, Donata 'Ercole tatuato come un indigeno: il dibattito sulla policromia nel mondo classico nella Gran Bretagna di metà Ottocento,' *Ricerche di storia dell'arte* 38 (1990), pp. 22-43

Licht, Fred, *Sculpture: nineteenth and twentieth centuries*, London 1967

McClinton, Katharine Morrison, 'The renaissance of pâte-de-verre,' *Connoisseur* (November 1979), pp. 170-75

Mackay, James, *The dictionnary of western sculptors in bronze*, Woodbridge 1977

Mackay, James, *Dictionary of sculptors in bronze*, Woodbury 1995

Merkel, Ursula, *Das plastische Porträt im 19. und frühen 20. Jahrhundert: Ein Beitrag zur Geschichte der Bildhauerei in Frankreich und Deutschland* (diss. Heidelberg), Berlin 1995

Metman, Bernard, 'La petite sculpture au XIXe siècle: les éditeurs, documents sur la sculpture française du XIXe siècle et répertoire des fondeurs du XIXe siècle,' *Archives de l'Art Français* 30 (1989), pp. 175-228

Myers, Donald, '"Couleur" and colour in the New Sculpture,' *Apollo* 143 (June 1996), pp. 23-31

Micheli, Mario de, *La scultura dell'Ottocento*, Turin 1992

Middleton, Robin, 'Hittorff's polychrome campaign,' in idem (ed.), *The Beaux-Arts and nineteenth-century French architecture*, London 1982, pp. 175-95

Mielsch, Harald, *Buntmarmore aus Rom im Antikenmuseum Berlin*, Berlin 1985

Millard, Charles W., 'Sculpture and theory in nineteenth century France,' *The Journal of Aesthetics and Art Criticism* 34 (1975), no. 1, pp. 15-20

Mills, J.S. and Perry Smith (eds.), *Cleaning, retouching and coatings: technology and practice for easel paintings and polychrome sculpture* (Preprints of the contributions to the Brussels Conference, 3-7 September 1990), London 1990

Montagu, Jennifer, *Roman baroque sculpture: the industry of art*, New Haven & London 1989

Neuwirth, Waltraud, *Österreichische Keramik des Jugendstils: Sammlung des Österreichischen Museums für angewandte Kunst*, Vienna & Munich 1974

Neuwirth, Waltraud, *Wiener Keramik: Historismus, Jugendstil, Art Déco*, Braunschweig 1974

Novotny, Fritz, *Painting and sculpture in Europe 1780-1880*, Harmondsworth 1971

Panzetta, Alfonso, *Dizionario degli scultori italiani dell'Ottocento e del primo Novecento*, Turin 1994

Penny, Nicholas, *The materials of sculpture*, New Haven & London 1993

Pingeot, Anne, '80 ans de *Jeanne d'Arc* sculptées,' in Regine Pernoud (ed.), exhib. cat. *Les images de Jeanne d'Arc*, Paris (Hôtel de la Monnaie) 1979, pp. 185-295

Pingeot, Anne, 'La sculpture du XIXe siècle: la dernière décennie,' *Revue de l'Art* 104 (1994), no. 2, pp. 5-7

Pötzl-Malikowa, Maria, *Die Plastik der Ringstraße: Künstlerische Entwicklung 1890-1918*, Wiesbaden 1976

Prevost-Marcilhacy, Pauline, *Les Rothschild: bâtisseurs et mécènes*, Paris 1995

Preyß, Adolf, 'Athena Hope und Winckelmanns Pallas,' *Jahrbuch des Deutschen Archäologischen Instituts* 28 (1913), pp. 244-65

Protzmann, Heiner, 'Polychromie und Dresdner Antikensammlung,' exhib. cat. *Gottfried Semper 1803-1879*, Dresden (Staatliche Museen, Skulpturengalerie) 1979, pp. 101-07

Pyke, E.J., *Biographical dictionary of wax modellers*, Oxford 1973

Raff, Thomas, *Die Sprache der Materialien: Prolegomena zu einer Ikonologie der Werkstoffe*, Munich 1994

Rama, Jean-Pierre, *Le bronze d'art et ses techniques*, Dourdan 1988

Read, Benedict, *Victorian sculpture*, New Haven & London 1982

Read, Benedict, 'Was there Pre-Raphaelite sculpture?' in Leslie Perris (ed.), *Pre-Raphaelite papers*, London 1984, pp. 97-110

Read, Benedict, 'Sailing to Byzantium?' in John Christian (ed.), exhib. cat. *The last Romantics: the romantic tradition in British art, Burne-Jones to Stanley Spencer*, London (Barbican Art Gallery) 1989, pp. 55-61

Read, Herbert, *The art of sculpture*, London 1956

Reinle, Adolf, *Das stellvertretende Bildnis: Plastiken und Gemälde von der Antike bis ins 19. Jahrhundert*, Zurich & Munich 1984

Reuterswärd, Patrik, *Studien zur Polychromie der Plastik, Griechenland und Rom: Untersuchungen über die Farbwirkung der Marmor- und Bronzeskulpturen*, Stockholm 1960

Rheims, Maurice, *Nineteenth century sculpture*, London 1972

Richemond, Stephanie, 'Terres cuites orientalistes des XIXe et XXe siècles,' *L'Objet d'Art/Estampille* 290 (April 1995), pp. 54-65

Schiessl, Ulrich, *Rokokofassung und Materialillusion: Untersuchungen zur Polychromie sakraler Bildwerke im süddeutschen Rokoko*, Mittenwald 1979

Schiff, Gert, 'The sculpture of the *style troubadour*,' *Arts Magazine* 58 (June 1984), pp. 102-10

Schivelbusch, Wolfgang, *Lichtblicke: Zur Geschichte der künstlichen Helligkeit im 19. Jahrhundert*, Frankfurt am Main 1986

Schlosser, Julius von, 'Geschichte der Porträtbildnerei in Wachs: Ein Versuch,' *Jahrbuch der kunsthistorischen Sammlungen des allerhöchsten Kaiserhauses* 29 (1910-11), pp. 171-258

Schneider, Donald, *The works and doctrine of Jacques Ignace Hittorff, 1792-1867*, New York 1977

Schneider, René, *Quatremère de Quincy et son intervention dans les arts (1788-1830)*, Paris 1910

Schneider, Rolf Michael, *Bunte Barbaren: Orientalenstatuen aus farbigem Marmor in der römischen Repräsentationskunst*, Worms 1986

Sculpter-photographier, photographie-sculpture (Actes du colloque organisé au Musée du Louvre par le service culturel les 22 et 23 novembre 1991), Paris 1993

La sculpture du XIXe siècle: une mémoire retrouvée (Rencontres de l'Ecole du Louvre), Paris 1986

Settis, Salvatore (ed.), *Il colore dell'antico*, Rome 1989

Silverman, Deborah L., *Art Nouveau in fin-de-siècle France: politics, psychology, and style*, 2nd. ed., Berkeley & Los Angeles & Oxford 1992

Steinhauser, Monika, *Die Architektur der Pariser Oper: Studien zu ihrer Entstehungsgeschichte und ihrer architekturgeschichtlichen Stellung*, Munich 1969

Taubert, Johannes, *Farbige Skulpturen: Bedeutung, Fassung, Restaurierung*, Munich 1978

Traeger, Jörg, *Der Weg nach Walhalla: Denkmallandschaft und Bildungsreise im 19. Jahrhundert*, Regensburg 1987

Trier, Eduard and Willy Weyres (eds.), *Kunst des 19. Jahrhunderts im Rheinland*, 5 vols., Düsseldorf 1980, vol. 4: Plastik

Trier, Eduard, *Bildhauertheorien im 20. Jahrhundert*, 2nd ed., Berlin 1992

Türr, Karina, *Zur Antikenrezeption in der französischen Skulptur des 19. und frühen 20. Jahrhunderts*, Berlin 1979

Türr, Karina, *Farbe und Naturalismus in der Skulptur des 19. und 20. Jahrhunderts: Sculpturae vitam insufflat pictura*, Mainz 1994

Van Zanten, David, *The architectural polychromy of the 1830's* (diss. New York 1977)

Wagner-Rieger, Renate and Maria Reissberger, *Theophil von Hansen*, Wiesbaden 1976

Wittkower, Rudolf, *Sculpture: processes and principles*, London 1977

Exhibition catalogues (in chronological order)

Ausstellung farbiger und getönter Bildwerke in der Königlichen Nationalgalerie zu Berlin, Berlin (Nationalgalerie) 1885

Le décor de la vie sous la IIIe République de 1870 à 1900, Paris (Musée des arts décoratifs) 1933

'Tervueren 1897': studie en catalogus van de commemoratieve tentoonstelling, M. Luwel and M. Bruneel-Hye de Crom, Brussels-Tervuren (Musée royal de l'Afrique centrale) 1967

British Sculpture 1850-1914, introduction by Lavinia Handley-Read, London (Fine Art Society) 1968

Nineteenth century French sculpture: monuments for the middle class, Jane Van Nimmen and Ruth Mirolli (eds.), Louisville, Kentucky (J.B. Speed Art Museum) 1971

Polychromies à travers les âges et les civilisations, Paris (Musée Bourdelle) 1971

Victorian and Edwardian art: the Handley Read collection, London (Royal Academy of Arts) 1972

Pioneers of modern sculpture, Albert Elsen, London (Hayward Gallery) 1973

Western European bronzes of the nineteenth century: a survey, Robert Kashey and Martin L.H. Reymert, New York (Shepherd Gallery) 1973

Metamorphoses in nineteenth-century sculpture, Jeanne L. Wasserman (ed.), Cambridge, Massachusetts (Fogg Art Museum) 1975

Aspects of nineteenth century sculpture, foreword by Horst W. Janson, Cleveland (Cleveland Museum of Art) 1975-76

Art Nouveau Belgium, France, Houston (Institute for the Arts, Rice University) 1976

Leo von Klenze als Maler und Zeichner 1784-1864, Inge Feuchtmayr (ed.), Munich (Bayerische Akademie der Schönen Künste, Münchner Residenz) 1977-78

The other nineteenth century: paintings and sculpture in the collection of Mr. and Mrs. Joseph M. Tanenbaum, Louise d'Argencourt and Douglas Druick, Ottawa (The National Gallery of Canada) 1978

Victorian High Renaissance, Manchester (City Art Gallery) & Minneapolis (The Minneapolis Museum of Art) & Brooklyn (Brooklyn Museum) 1978-79

Les images de Jeanne d'Arc, Regine Pernoud (ed.), Paris (Hôtel de la Monnaie) 1979

The Second Empire: art in France under Napoleon III, Philadelphia (Philadelphia Museum of Art) & Detroit (Detroit Institute of Arts) & Paris (Galeries nationales du Grand Palais) 1979

Gottfried Semper 1803-1879: Baumeister zwischen Revolution und Historismus, Dresden (Staatliche Museen, Skulpturengalerie) 1979

Viollet-le-Duc, Paris (Grand Palais) 1980

Art Nouveau Belgique, Brussels (Palais des Beaux-Arts) 1980-81

The Romantics to Rodin: French nineteenth-century sculpture from North American collections, Peter Fusco and Horst W. Janson (eds.), Los Angeles (Los Angeles County Museum of Art) & Minneapolis (The Minneapolis Museum of Art) & Detroit (The Detroit Institute of Arts) & Indianapolis (Indianapolis Museum of Arts) 1980-81

Gauguin to Moore: primitivism in modern sculpture, Alan G. Wilkinson, Toronto (Art Gallery of Ontario) 1981-82

De Carpeaux à Matisse: la sculpture française de 1850 à 1914 dans les musées et les collections publiques du Nord de la France, Calais (Musée des Beaux-Arts) & Lille (Musée des Beaux-Arts) & Boulogne-sur-Mer (Musée des Beaux-Arts et d'Archéologie) & Paris (Musée Rodin) 1982-83

Paris - Rome - Athènes: le voyage en Grèce des architectes français au XIXe et XXe siècles, Paris (Ecole des Beaux-Arts) & Athens (National Gallery) & Houston (The Museum of Fine Arts) & New York (IBM Gallery of Science) 1982-84

Czech sculpture 1800-1938, Peter Cannon-Brookes, Cardiff (The National Museum of Wales) 1983

Ex aere solido: Bronzen von der Antike bis zur Gegenwart, Peter Bloch (ed.), Berlin (Staatliche Museen Preußischer Kulturbesitz, Skulpturengalerie) 1983

German expressionist sculpture, Stephanie Barron (ed.), Los Angeles (County Museum of Art) 1983

Der Hang zum Gesamtkunstwerk: Europäische Utopien seit 1800, Harald Szeemann (ed.), Zurich (Kunsthaus) & Düsseldorf (Städtische Kunsthalle) & Vienna (Museum moderner Kunst) 1983

'Primitivism' in 20th century art, William Rubin (ed.), New York (The Museum of Modern Art) 1984

Ein griechischer Traum: Leo von Klenze, der Archäologe, Munich (Glyptothek) 1985

Nineteenth century French and western sculpture in bronze and other media, New York (Shepherd Gallery) 1985

Pygmalion photographe, Geneva (Musée de l'art de l'histoire) 1985

Goldscheider Keramik: Historismus, Jugendstil, Art déco, Susanne Walther, Vienna (Historisches Museum der Stadt Wien) 1985-86

In tandem: the painter-sculptor in the 20th century, Lynne Cooke (ed.), London (Whitechapel Art Gallery) 1986

La sculpture française au XIXe siècle, Anne Pingeot (ed.), Paris (Galeries nationales du Grand Palais) 1986

Académie royale des Beaux-Arts de Bruxelles: 275 ans d'enseignement, Brussels (Musées royaux des Beaux-Arts de Belgique) 1987

Jakob Ignaz Hittorff: Ein Architekt aus Köln im Paris des 19. Jahrhunderts, Cologne (Wallraf-Richartz-Museum) 1987

Zauber der Medusa: Europäische Manierismen, Werner Hofmann (ed.), Vienna (Wiener Künstlerhaus) 1987

A qui ressemblons-nous? Les portraits dans les musées de Strasbourg, Strasbourg (Musées de la ville de Strasbourg) 1988

L'impressionismo nella scultura, Luciano Caramel, Lugano (Galleria Pieter Coray) 1989

Ethos und Pathos: Die Berliner Bildhauerschule 1786-1914, Peter Bloch (ed.), Berlin (Staatliche Museen Preußischer Kulturbesitz, Skulpturengalerie) 1990

Fake? The art of deception, Mark Jones (ed.), London (The British Museum) 1990

La sculpture belge au XIXe siècle, Jacques Van Lennep (ed.), 2 vols., Brussels (La Générale de Banque) 1990

Un âge d'or des arts décoratifs 1814-1848, Paris (Galeries nationales du Grand Palais) 1991

Viewpoints: European sculpture 1875-1925, Robert Kashey (ed.), New York (Shepherd Gallery) 1991

Photographie/sculpture, Paris (Palais de Tokyo) 1991-92

Pre-Raphaelite sculpture: nature and imagination in British sculpture 1848-1914, Benedict Read and Joanna Barnes (eds.), London (The Matthiesen Gallery) & Birmingham (Birmingham Museum and Art Gallery) 1991-92

Gibson to Gilbert: British sculpture 1840-1914, London (Fine Art Society) 1992

Reverie, myth, sensuality: sculpture in Britain 1880-1910, Stoke on Trent (City Museum and Art Gallery) 1992

European drawings and sculpture: nineteenth and twentieth century, Elisabeth Kashey and Robert Kashey, New York (Shepherd Gallery) 1993

De panoramische droom: Antwerpen en de wereldtentoonstellingen 1885-1894-1930, Antwerp (Bouwcentrum) 1993

Nabis, Zürich (Kunsthaus) & Paris (Galeries nationales du Grand Palais) 1993-94

L'âme au corps: arts et science 1793-1993, Jean Clair (ed.), Paris (Grand Palais) 1994

Bürgerwelten: Hellenistische Tonfiguren und Nachschöpfungen im 19. Jahrhundert, Berlin (Staatliche Museen zu Berlin, Preußischer Kulturbesitz, Antikensammlung) 1994

Carvings, casts and replicas: nineteenth-century sculpture from Europe and America in New England collections, John Hunisak, Middlebury (College Museum of Art) 1994

Chiseled with a brush: Italian sculpture 1860-1925 from the Gilgore collections, Chicago (The Art Institute of Chicago) 1994

Egyptomania: l'Egypte dans l'art occidental 1730-1930, Paris (Musée du Louvre) 1994

Goethe und die Kunst, Sabine Schulze (ed.), Frankfurt am Main (Schirn Kunsthalle) 1994

Japanese imperial craftsmen: Meiji art from the Khalili collection, Victor Harris, London (British Museum) 1994

Neogotiek in België, Jean Van Cleven (ed.), Ghent (Oudheidkundig Museum van de Bijloke) 1994

Pugin: a gothic passion, Paul Atterbury and Clive Wainwright (eds.), London (Victoria and Albert Museum) 1994

La sculpture ethnographique: de la Vénus hottentote à la Tehura de Gauguin, Antoinette Le Normand-Romain (ed.), Paris (Musée d'Orsay) 1994

Spanish polychrome sculpture 1500-1800 in United States collections, Suzanne L. Stratton, New York (The Spanish Institute) 1994

Das Albertinum vor 100 Jahren: Die Skulpturensammlung Georg Treus, Dresden (Staatliche Kunstsammlungen Dresden, Skulpturensammlung) 1994-95

Carthage: l'histoire, sa trace et son écho, Paris (Musée du Petit Palais) 1995

Paradise lost: symbolist Europe, Montreal (The Montreal Museum of Fine Arts) 1995

Félix Duban: les couleurs de l'architecte, Blois (Château) 1996

Literature on individual artists

Louis-Ernest Barrias

Max Collignon, 'Une statue polychrome de M. Ernest Barrias,' *Revue de l'Art Ancien et Moderne* 6 (10 September 1899), pp. 191-98

Georges Lafenestre, *L'œuvre de Ernest Barrias statuaire 1841-1903*, Paris 1908

Antoine-Louis Barye

Glenn F. Benge, *Antoine-Louis Barye: sculptor of romantic Realism*, University Park & London 1984

Martin Sonnabend, *Antoine-Louis Barye (1795-1875): Studien zum plastischen Werk* (diss.), Munich 1988

Stuart Pivar, *The Barye bronzes: a catalogue raisonné*, 2nd ed., Woodbridge 1990

Robert Anning Bell

Anonymous, 'A new treatment of bas-reliefs in coloured plaster,' *The Studio* 1 (1893), pp. 53-55

Peter Rose, 'The coloured relief decoration of Robert Anning Bell,' *Decorative Arts Society Journal* 14 (1990), pp. 16-23

Martin Barnes, *Robert Anning Bell (1863-1933): aspects in the career of a designer associated with the Arts and Crafts Movement* (undergraduate thesis, University of Leicester 1993)

Arnold Böcklin

Gustav Floerke, *Zehn Jahre mit Böcklin: Aufzeichnungen und Entwürfe*, Munich 1901

Alain Moirandat, 'Der Plastiker Böcklin,' exhib. cat. *Arnold Böcklin 1827-1901*, Basel (Oeffentliche Kunstsammlungen Basel & Basler Kunstverein) 1977, pp. 81-84

Cristina Nuzzi (ed.), exhib. cat. *Böcklin e la cultura artistica in Toscana*, Fiesole (Palazzo Mangani) 1980

Andrea Linnebach, *Arnold Böcklin und die Antike: Mythos, Geschichte, Gegenwart*, Munich 1991

Antoine Bourdelle

Antoinette Le Normand-Romain, '*La tête d'Apollon*: la "cause de divorce" entre Rodin et Bourdelle,' *Revue du Louvre et des Musées de France* 40 (June 1990), pp. 212-20

Jean-Baptiste Carpeaux

Anne Middleton Wagner, *Jean-Baptiste Carpeaux: sculptor of the Second Empire*, New Haven & London 1986

Albert-Ernest Carrier-Belleuse

June Hargrove, *The life and work of Albert Carrier-Belleuse* (diss.), New York & London 1977

Barbara Lepper, 'Werke von Albert Carrier-Belleuse in Berlin,' *Jahrbuch der Berliner Museen* 22 (1980), pp. 178-225

Select bibliography: individual artists

Jean Carriès

Comte Robert de Montesquiou Fezensac, 'Jean Carriès,' *Gazette des Beaux-Arts* (September 1894), pp. 202-12

Arsène Alexandre, *Jean Carriès, imagier et potier: etude d'une œuvre et d'une vie*, Paris 1895

Armand Dayot, 'Notes sur Carriès,' *Art et Décoration* 7 (1900), no. 1, pp. 65-73

J.L. de Rudder, 'Sculpteur, patineur puis potier: Jean Carriès planta l'Art Nouveau en pleine terre,' *L'Estampille* 32 (May 1972), pp. 56-57

Thérèse Burollet, 'Deux grands fonds de sculpture du musée du Petit Palais: Dalou et Carriès,' *La sculpture du XIXe siècle: une mémoire retrouvée* (Rencontres de l'Ecole du Louvre), Paris 1986, pp. 107-14

Camille Claudel

Reine-Marie Paris and Arnaud de la Chapelle, *L'œuvre de Camille Claudel: catalogue raisonné*, 2nd ed., Paris 1991

Exhib. cat. *Camille Claudel*, Martigny (Fondation Pierre Giannadda) & Paris (Musée Rodin) 1991

Auguste Clésinger

A. Estignard, *Clésinger: sa vie, ses œuvres*, Paris 1900

Clésinger (1814-1883): notice biographique, catalogue des œuvres, foreword by Remy de Gourmont, 2nd ed., Paris 1903

Charles-Henri-Joseph Cordier

Charles Cordier, *Sculptures ethnographiques, marbres et bronzes d'après divers types de races humaines, 19 photographies par Marville*, Paris 1858

A. Andrei, 'Galerie anthropologique et ethnographique de M. Cordier,' *L'Art au Dix-neuvième Siècle* 5 (1860), pp. 188-89

Marc Trapadoux, *L'œuvre de M. Cordier: galerie anthropologique et ethnographique, pour servir à l'histoire des races, types des anciennes races, statues, statuettes, bustes, médaillons, groupes, bas-reliefs, marbres, bronzes, émaux, sculpture polychrome etc., catalogue descriptif*, Paris 1860

Charles Cordier, 'Types ethniques représentés par la sculpture,' *Bulletin de la Société d'Anthropologie de Paris* (6 February 1862), pp. 64-66

Jeannine Durand-Revillon, 'Un promoteur de la sculpture polychrome sous le Second Empire: Charles-Henri-Joseph Cordier (1827-1905),' *Bulletin de la Société d'Histoire de l'Art Français* (1982), pp. 180-98

Henry Cros

Alphonse Germain, 'Henri Cros et la sculpture polychrome,' *La Plume* 56 (15 August 1891), pp. 280-81

Anne-Marie Belfort, 'Pâtes de verre d'Henry Cros,' *Cahier de la Céramique* 39 (1967), pp. 182-85

François Duret-Robert, 'Le sculpteur qui a redécouvert la pâte de verre: Henry Cros,' *Connaissance des Arts* (December 1974), n.p. (Encyclopédie)

Jean-Luc Olivié, 'Henry Cros: pourquoi et comment restituer les antiques pâtes de verre,' *Annales du IXe Congrès de l'Association Internationale pour l'Histoire du Verre* (Nancy, 22-28 Mai 1983), Liège 1985, pp. 385-99

Jean-Luc Olivié, 'Un atelier et des recherches subventionnés par l'état: Henry Cros à Sèvres,' *La sculpture du XIXe siècle, une mémoire retrouvée* (Rencontres de l'Ecole du Louvre), Paris 1986, pp. 193-99

Jean-Luc Olivié, 'All of antiquity in a new soul,' *New Work* 31 (Fall 1987), pp. 10-15

Jean Dampt

Gustave Soulier, 'Jean Dampt,' *Art et Décoration* 1 (1897), pp. 72-74

Alphonse Germain, 'Jean Dampt,' *Gazette des Beaux-Arts* (September 1912), pp. 173-94

André Michel, 'Jean Dampt,' *Revue de l'Art* 36 (1914), pp. 161-76

Laure Murat, 'L'appel des chimères,' *L'Objet d'Art* 5 (March 1988), pp. 52-61

Honoré Daumier

Jeanne L. Wasserman, exhib. cat. *Daumier sculpture: a critical and comparative study*, Cambridge, Massachusetts (Fogg Art Museum) 1969

Pierre Cabanne et al., *Les bustes des parlementaires par Honoré Daumier*, Lausanne 1980

Antoinette Le Normand-Romain, *Daumier: les parlementaires, portraits des célébrités du Juste-Milieu*, Paris 1993

Edgar Degas

Theodore Reff, 'Degas' sculpture 1880-1884,' *Art Quarterly* 33 (1970), no. 3, pp. 277-98

Charles W. Millard, *The sculpture of Degas*, Princeton, New Jersey 1976

Douglas Druick and Peter Zegers, 'La petite danseuse et les criminels: Degas moraliste?' *Degas inédit* (Actes du colloque Degas, 18-21 avril 1988), Paris 1989, pp. 225-50

John Rewald, *Degas's complete sculpture: a catalogue raisonné*, San Francisco 1990

Anne Pingeot, *Degas: sculptures*, Paris 1991

Roger J. Crum, 'Degas bronzes?,' *Art Journal* 54 (Spring 1994), pp. 93-98

Sara Campbell, 'Degas' bronzes: introduction and a catalogue of Degas' bronzes,' *Apollo* 142 (August 1995), pp. 6-48

Jean-Baptiste-Gustave Deloye

Emile Cardon, 'Gustave Deloye,' *Moniteur des Arts* 39 (16 August 1895), pp. 218-22

Godefroid Devreese

Denise Cluytens-Dons in Jacques Van Lennep (ed.), exhib. cat. *La sculpture belge au XIXe siècle*, 2 vols., Brussels (La Générale de Banque) 1990, vol. 2, pp. 364-66

Exhib. cat. *Godefroid Devreese (1861-1941)*, Brussels-Schaerbeek (Hôtel Communal de Schaerbeek) 1993

Julien Dillens

Arnold Goffin, 'Juliaan Dillens,' *Onze Kunst* 4 (1906), no. 1, pp. 149-69

Jules Potvin, *Julien Dillens, statuaire*, Brussels 1913

Hugo Lettens in Jacques Van Lennep (ed.), exhib. cat. *La sculpture belge au XIXe siècle*, 2 vols., Brussels (La Générale de Banque) 1990, vol. 2, pp. 367-72

Conrad Dressler

Robert Prescott Walker, 'Conrad Dressler and the Medmenham Pottery,' *Omnium Gatherum* 18 (1994), pp. 50-60

Marjorie Trusted, 'Dressler's terracotta bust of his wife at the V & A,' *Apollo* 143 (January 1996), p. 50

Paul Du Bois

Judith Ogonovsky in Jacques Van Lennep (ed.), exhib. cat. *La sculpture belge au XIXe siècle*, 2 vols., Brussels (La Générale de Banque) 1990, vol. 2, pp. 375-78

Prosper d'Epinay

Thiebault-Sisson, 'L'art élégant: Prosper d'Epinay,' *La Nouvelle Revue* 49 (November-December 1887), pp. 830-49

Félicie de Fauveau

Baron de Coubertin, 'Mademoiselle de Fauveau,' *Gazette des Beaux-Arts* (June 1887), pp. 512-21

Juliette Barbotte, 'La dague de Félicie de Fauveau,' *Revue du Louvre* 33 (1983), no. 2, pp. 122-25

Fix-Masseau

C.B., 'Fix Masseau: a French sculptor,' *The Artist* (July 1897), pp. 347-50

Henri Frantz, 'Fix-Masseau, sculpteur,' *L'Art Décoratif* 18 (March 1900), pp. 229-35

Edward Onslow Ford

Francis Haskell, 'The Shelley Memorial,' *Oxford Art Journal* 1 (1978), pp. 3-6

Phillipa Laurenson, 'Case study of a nineteenth-century bronze with a decorative resin inlay,' in Jackie Heuman (ed.), *From marble to chocolate: the conservation of modern sculpture* (Tate Gallery Conference, 18-20 September 1995), London 1995, pp. 15-22

Select bibliography: individual artists

George Frampton
Timothy Stevens, 'George Frampton,' in Penelope Curtis (ed.), *Patronage and practice: sculpture on Merseyside*, Liverpool 1989, pp. 74-85

Emmanuel Fremiet
Bruno Foucart, 'Emmanuel Fremiet: le réalisme clinique,' *Beaux-Arts Magazine* (March 1988), pp. 39-43

Catherine Chevillot, exhib. cat. *Emmanuel Fremiet: la main et le multiple*, Dijon (Musée des Beaux-Arts) & Grenoble (Musée de Grenoble) 1988-89

Catherine Chevillot, 'A propos de l'*Orang-outang* (1893) de Fremiet au musée de Dijon: le marbre seul? L'expérience de la peinture,' *Revue du Louvre* 39 (1989), no. 1, pp. 53-58

Paul Gauguin
Christopher Gray, *Sculpture and ceramics of Paul Gauguin*, Baltimore 1963

Merete Bodelsen, *Gauguin's ceramics: a study in the development of his art*, London 1964

Barbara Landy, 'The meaning of Gauguin's "Oviri" ceramic,' *The Burlington Magazine* 109 (April 1967), pp. 242-46

Vojtech Jirat-Wasiutyński, 'Paul Gauguin's self-portraits and the *Oviri*: the image of the artist, Eve, and the fatal woman,' *Art Quarterly* 2 (Spring 1979), pp. 172-90

Koji Takahashi, 'The superficial paradise: a study on Gauguin's sculpture and ceramics,' exhib. cat. *Paul Gauguin*, Tokyo (National Museum of Modern Art) 1987, pp. 37-42

Exhib. cat. *The art of Paul Gauguin*, Washington, D.C. (National Gallery of Art) & Chicago (The Art Institute of Chicago) & Paris (Galeries nationales du Grand Palais) 1988-89

Haruko Hirota, 'La sculpture en céramique de Gauguin: sources et significations,' *Histoire de l'Art* 15 (September 1991), pp. 43-60

Sue Taylor, 'Oviri: Gauguin's savage woman,' *Konsthistorisk Tidskrift* 62 (1993), Häfte 3-4, pp. 197-220

Jean-Léon Gérôme
Ch. Moreau-Vauthier, *Gérôme: peintre et sculpteur, l'homme et l'artiste, d'après sa correspondance, ses notes, les souvenirs de ses élèves et de ses amis*, Paris 1906

Exhib. cat. *Jean-Léon Gérôme (1824-1904)*, Dayton (The Dayton Art Institute) & Minneapolis (The Minneapolis Institute of Arts) & Baltimore (The Walters Art Gallery) 1972-73

Exhib. cat. *Jean-Léon Gérôme 1824-1904: peintre, sculpteur et graveur*, Vesoul (Musée Garret) 1981

Gerald M. Ackerman, *The life and work of Jean-Léon Gérôme: with a catalogue raisonné*, New York 1986

John Gibson
Lady Eastlake (ed.), *Life of John Gibson, R.A., sculptor*, London 1870

T. Matthews, *The biography of John Gibson, R.A., sculptor, Rome*, London 1911

Jörgen B. Hartmann, 'Canova, Thorwaldsen and Gibson,' *English Miscellany* 6 (1955), pp. 205-36

Jeremy Cooper, 'John Gibson and his *Tinted Venus*,' *Connoisseur* (October 1971), pp. 84-92

Hans Fletcher, 'John Gibson's polychromy and Lord Londonderry's *Bacchus*,' *Connoisseur* (September 1974), pp. 2-5

Elizabeth S. Darby, 'John Gibson, Queen Victoria, and the idea of sculptural polychromy,' *Art History* 4 (March 1981), pp. 32-53

Alfred Gilbert
Richard Dorment, *Alfred Gilbert*, New Haven & London 1985

Richard Dorment, exhib. cat. *Alfred Gilbert: sculptor and goldsmith*, London (Royal Academy of Arts) 1986

Emile Hébert
Jeanne Stump, 'The sculpture of Emile Hébert: themes and variations,' *The Register of the Spencer Museum of Art* 5 (Spring 1982), pp. 28-61

Adolf von Hildebrand
Angela Hass, *Adolf von Hildebrand: Das plastische Porträt*, Munich 1984

Sigrid Esche-Braunfels, *Adolf von Hildebrand (1847-1921)*, Berlin 1993

Fernand Khnopff
Robert L. Delevoy, Catherine De Croës and Gisèle Ollinger-Zinque, *Fernand Khnopff*, 2nd ed., Brussels 1987

Michel Draguet, *Khnopff ou l'ambigu poétique*, Paris 1995

Max Klinger
Ekkehard Mai, 'Polychromie und Gesamtkunstwerk: Von der Synästhesie zur Synthese im bildnerischen Schaffen Max Klingers,' in Manfred Boetzkes (ed.), exhib. cat. *Max Klinger*, Hildesheim (Roemer- und Pelizaeus-Museum) 1984, pp. 25-48

Heiner Protzmann, 'Salome: Zur Polychromie in der Skulptur. Aus der Korrespondenz Max Klingers mit Georg Treu,' *Jahrbuch der Staatlichen Kunstsammlungen Dresden* 14 (1984), pp. 61-72

Exhib. cat. *Max Klinger 1857-1920*, Frankfurt am Main (Städelsches Kunstinstitut) 1992

Herwig Guratzsch (ed.), *Max Klinger: Bestandskatalog der Bildwerke, Gemälde und Zeichnungen im Museum der bildenden Künste Leipzig*, Leipzig 1995

Ursula Kral and Heiner Protzmann, 'Das restaurierte Modell der Neuen Salome von Max Klinger,' *Dresdener Kunstblätter* 40 (1996), no. 1, pp. 2-7

Georges Lacombe
Joëlle Ansieu, 'Deux sculptures de Georges Lacombe, *Isis* et le *Christ*,' *Revue du Louvre* 33 (1983), no. 4, pp. 287-95

Blandine Salmon and Olivier Meslay, *Georges Lacombe: sculptures, peintures, dessins*, Paris 1991

Raoul Larche
Dominique Renoux, 'Raoul Larche, statuaire (1860-1912),' *Bulletin de la Société de l'Histoire de l'Art Français* (1989), pp. 243-76

Richard Luksch/Elsa Luksch-Makowsky
Heinz Spielmann, *Bildhauer in Hamburg 1900-1972: Zum 100. Geburtstag von Richard Luksch am 31.1.1972*, Hamburg 1972

Joachim Heusinger von Waldegg and Helmut R. Leppien, *Richard Luksch und Elsa Luksch-Makowsky*, Hamburg 1979

Aristide Maillol
Judith Cladel, *Aristide Maillol: sa vie, son œuvre, ses idées*, Paris 1937

Waldemar George, *Aristide Maillol et l'âme de la sculpture: avec une biographie établie par Dina Vierny*, Neuchatel 1964

Rudolf Maison
Dietrich Schubert, 'Hinweis auf Rudolf Maison (1854-1904),' *Jahrbuch Preußischer Kulturbesitz* 14 (1977), pp. 281-91

Marcello
Comtesse d'Alcantara, *Marcello: Adèle d'Affry, Duchesse Castiglione Colonna, 1836-1879, sa vie, son œuvre, sa pensée et ses amis*, Geneva 1961

Exhib. cat. *Marcello 1836-1879, Adèle d'Affry, duchesse de Castiglione Colonna*, Fribourg (Musée d'Art et d'Histoire) 1980

Henriette Bessis, *Marcello sculpteur*, Fribourg 1980

Henriette Bessis, 'Pourquoi une telle résonance de la *Bianca Capello* de Marcello dans les dernières années du XIXe siècle?,' *Gazette des Beaux-Arts* (November 1982), pp. 183-87

Carlo Marochetti
Charles Blanc, 'La Reine de la Paix par M. le baron Marochetti,' *Gazette des Beaux-Arts* (June 1864), pp. 566-67

Marco Calderini, *Carlo Marochetti: monografia con ritratti, fac-simile e riproduzioni di opere dell'artista*, Turin & Milan & Florence 1928

Anna Bovero, 'L'opera di Carlo Marochetti in Italia,' *Emporium* 95 (1945), pp. 185-99

Philip Ward-Jackson, 'Carlo Marochetti et les photographes,' *Revue de l'Art* 104 (1994), no. 2, pp. 43-48

Select bibliography: individual artists

Ernest Meissonier

Antoinette Le Normand-Romain, 'Le voyageur de Meissonier,' *Revue du Louvre* 35 (1985), no. 2, pp. 129-35

Exhib. cat. *Ernest Meissonier: rétrospective*, Lyons (Musée des Beaux-Arts) 1993

Joseph Mendes da Costa

A.M. Hammacher, *Mendes da Costa: de geestelijke boodschap der beeldhouwkunst*, Rotterdam 1941

Constantin Meunier

A. Thiery and E. Van Dievoet, *Catalogue complet des œuvres dessinées, peintes et sculptées de Constantin Meunier*, Louvain n.d. (1909)

Alphonse Mucha

Exhib. cat. *Alfons Mucha 1860-1939*, Darmstadt (Mathildenhöhe) 1980

Arthur Ellridge, *Mucha*, Paris 1992

Pablo Picasso

Werner Spies, *Picasso: Das plastische Werk*, Stuttgart 1983

Elizabeth Cowling and John Golding, exhib. cat. *Picasso: sculptor/painter*, London (Tate Gallery) 1994

Michael Powolny

Elisabeth Frottier, *Michael Powolny: Keramik und Glas aus Wien 1900-1950, Monografie und Werkverzeichnis*, Vienna & Cologne 1990

James Pradier

Exhib. cat. *Statues de chair: sculptures de James Pradier*, Geneva (Musée d'art et d'histoire) & Paris (Musée du Luxembourg) 1985-86

Claude Lapaire, 'Léda et le cygne de James Pradier,' *Genava* 35 (1987), pp. 55-61

Marcel G. Roethlisberger, 'La Léda de Pradier,' *Genava* 35 (1987), pp. 63-64

Denys Puech

Catherine Gaich and Catherine Chevillot, *Denys Puech*, Rodez 1993

Pierre-Auguste Renoir

Paul Haesaerts, *Renoir sculpteur*, Brussels n.d.

Théodore-Louis-Auguste Rivière

Loys Delteil, 'Théodore Rivière,' *Revue des Arts Décoratifs* 19 (January 1899), pp. 305-20

Edouard Sarradin, 'Théodore Rivière,' *Arts Décoratifs* (1899), no. 2, pp. 65-73

Louis Rochet

André Rochet, *Louis Rochet: sculpteur, sinologe, 1813-1878*, Paris 1978

Auguste Rodin

Henri Charles Etienne Dujardin-Beaumetz, *Entretiens avec Rodin* (1913), Paris 1992

John L. Tancock, *The sculpture of Auguste Rodin: the collection of the Rodin Museum Philadelphia*, Philadelphia 1976

J.A. Schmoll gen. Eisenwerth, *Rodin-Studien*, Munich 1983

Cécile Goldscheider, *Rodin: catalogue raisonné de l'œuvre sculpté, 1840-1886*, Lausanne & Paris 1989

Medardo Rosso

Margaret Scolari Barr, exhib. cat. *Medardo Rosso*, New York (The Museum of Modern Art) 1972

Luciano Caramel, *Medardo Rosso: impressions in wax and bronze, 1882-1906*, New York 1988

Luciano Caramel (ed.), exhib. cat. *Medardo Rosso*, London (Whitechapel Art Gallery) 1994

Augustus Saint-Gaudens

John H. Dryfhout, *The work of Augustus Saint-Gaudens*, Hanover & London 1982

Kathryn Greenthal, exhib. cat. *Augustus Saint-Gaudens master sculptor*, New York (The Metropolitan Museum of Art) 1985

Charles Simart

Charles-Ernest Beulé, 'La statuaire d'or et d'ivoire: la Minerve de M. Simart,' *Revue des Deux-Mondes* (1 February 1856), pp. 564-86

Léon Lagrange, 'Simart,' *Gazette des Beaux-Arts* (February 1863), pp. 97-123

Meredith Shedd, 'Phidias at the Universal Exposition of 1855: the duc de Luynes and the Athena Parthenos,' *Gazette des Beaux-Arts* (October 1986), pp. 123-34

Hélène Maraus, 'Simart et le tombeau de Napoléon Ier aux Invalides: bas-reliefs (1846-1852) et effigie de l'Empereur (1850-1853),' *Revue de la Société des Amis du Musée de l'Armée* 101 (June 1991), pp. 50-59

Arthur Strasser

Ludwig Hevesi, 'Arthur Strasser,' *Kunst und Kunsthandwerk* 1 (1898), pp. 349-66

Franz von Stuck

Heinrich Voss, *Franz von Stuck 1863-1928*, Munich 1973

Angela Heilmann, *Die Plastik Franz von Stucks: Studien zur Monographie und Formentwicklung* (diss., Technische Universität Munich 1985)

Exhib. cat. *Franz von Stuck: Gemälde, Zeichnung, Plastik aus Privatbesitz*, Passau (Museum Moderner Kunst, Stiftung Wörlen) 1993-94

Edwin Becker, exhib. cat. *Franz von Stuck: eros & pathos*, Amsterdam (Van Gogh Museum) 1995

Viktor Tilgner

Ludwig Hevesi, *Viktor Tilgner*, Vienna 1910

Charles Van der Stappen

Octave Maus, 'Charles van der Stappen,' *Art et Décoration* 4 (1898), pp. 51-59

Arnold Goffin, 'Karel van der Stappen,' *Onze Kunst* 10 (June 1911), pp. 191-200; (July 1911), pp. 1-13; (Augustus 1911), pp. 41-52

Arnold Goffin, *Charles Van der Stappen*, Paris 1912

Arnold Goffin, 'Charles Van der Stappen,' *Annuaire de l'Académie Royale des Sciences, des Lettres et des Beaux-Arts de Belgique*, Brussels 1926, pp. 1-41

Jacques Van Lennep in exhib. cat. *Académie royale des Beaux-Arts de Bruxelles: 275 ans d'enseignement*, Brussels (Musées royaux des Beaux-Arts de Belgique) 1987, pp. 380-85

Hugo Lettens in Jacques Van Lennep (ed.), exhib. cat. *La sculpture belge au XIXe siècle*, 2 vols., Brussels (La Générale de Banque) 1990, vol. 2, pp. 574-82

Artur Volkmann

Woldemar von Wasielewski, *Artur Volkmann: Eine Einführung in sein Werk*, Munich & Leipzig 1908

Jens Ferdinand Willumsen

V. Jastrau, *J.F. Willumsen: malererier, skulpturer, keramik*, Copenhagen 1928

Merete Bodelsen, *Willumsen i halvfemsernes Paris*, Copenhagen 1957

Derek Lionel Paul, 'Willumsen and Gauguin in the 1890s,' *Apollo* 111 (January 1980), pp. 36-45

Leila Krogh, exhib. cat. *J.F. Willumsens keramiske vaerker 1891-1900*, Frederikssund (J.F. Willumsens Museum) 1986

Leila Krogh, *Katalogbog J.F. Willumsens Museum Frederikssund*, Copenhagen 1986

Eva Braemer-Jensen, 'Fra barvaeg til museumsstykke - J.F. Willumsen: det store relief,' *Cras, Tidsskrift for Kunst og Kultur* 51 (1987), pp. 4-31

Philippe Wolfers

Exhib. cat. *Philippe und Marcel Wolfers: Art Nouveau und Art Déco aus Brüssel*, Zurich (Museum Bellerive) 1993-94

Literature on the works exhibited

1

Medusa early 19th century

Detlev Kreikenboom in Sabine Schulze (ed.), exhib. cat. *Goethe und die Kunst*, Frankfurt am Main (Schirn Kunsthalle) 1994, pp. 33-34 and no. 12

2

The 'Psyche of Capua' cast of c.1893

Heiner Protzmann in exhib. cat. *Das Albertinum vor 100 Jahren: Die Skulpturensammlung Georg Treus*, Dresden (Staatliche Kunstsammlungen Dresden, Skulpturensammlung) 1994-95, no. 154

3

The 'Antinous Albani' cast of 1893

Kordelia Knoll in exhib. cat. *Das Albertinum vor 100 Jahren: Die Skulpturensammlung Georg Treus*, Dresden (Staatliche Kunstsammlungen Dresden, Skulpturensammlung) 1994-95, no. 155

4 5

Masks of a satyr casts of 1883 and 1893

Ingeborg Raumschüssel in exhib. cat. *Das Albertinum vor 100 Jahren: Die Skulpturensammlung Georg Treus*, Dresden (Staatliche Kunstsammlungen Dresden, Skulpturensammlung) 1994-95, nos. 156, 157

6

James Pradier

The birth of Cupid c.1840

(other version) Exhib. cat. *Statues de chair: sculptures de James Pradier*, Geneva (Musée d'art et d'histoire) & Paris (Musée du Luxembourg) 1985-86, no. 86

7

John Gibson

Tinted Venus c.1851–56

Jeremy Cooper, 'John Gibson and his *Tinted Venus*,' *Connoisseur* (October 1971), pp. 84-92

Hans Fletcher, 'John Gibson's polychromy and Lord Londonderry's *Bacchus*,' *Connoisseur* (September 1974), pp. 2-5

Elizabeth S. Darby, 'John Gibson, Queen Victoria, and the idea of sculptural polychromy,' *Art History* 4 (1981), no. 1, pp. 32-53

Benedict Read, *Victorian sculpture*, New Haven & London 1982, p. 26

The Walker Art Gallery Liverpool, Liverpool 1994, p. 65

8

Prosper d'Epinay

Medusa c.1865–70

19th and 20th century sculpture: the Joey and Toby Tanenbaum collection, New York (Sotheby's), 26 May 1994, lot 1

Andreas Blühm, 'Une beauté sauvage: Prosper d'Epinay's Medusa,' *Van Gogh Museum Journal* 2 (1996) (forthcoming)

9

Prosper d'Epinay

The golden belt c.1874

Thiebault-Sisson, 'L'art élégant: Prosper d'Epinay,' *La Nouvelle Revue* 49 (November-December 1887), pp. 845-46

10

Auguste Clésinger

Helen 1860

A. Estignard, *Clésinger: sa vie, ses œuvres*, Paris 1900, pp. 84-85

12

Henry Cros

Incantation 2 1891

François Duret-Robert, 'Le sculpteur qui a rédecouvert la pâte de verre: Henry Cros,' *Connaissance des Arts* (December 1974), n.p. (Encyclopédie)

17

Arnold Böcklin

Shield with the head of Medusa 1887

(other casts) Exhib. cat. *Arnold Böcklin 1827-1901*, Basel (Oeffentliche Kunstsammlungen Basel & Basler Kunstverein) 1977, no. P 3

Werner Hofmann (ed.), exhib. cat. *Zauber der Medusa: Europäische Manierismen*, Vienna (Wiener Künstlerhaus) 1987, no. XII/15

18 19

Max Klinger

Busts of Cassandra c.1895 and c.1903

Georg Syamken, *Die dritte Dimension: Plastiken, Konstruktionen, Objekte. Bestandskatalog der Skulpturenabteilung der Hamburger Kunsthalle*, Hamburg 1988, pp. 238-41

Renate Hartleb in exhib. cat. *Max Klinger 1857-1920*, Frankfurt am Main (Städtische Galerie im Städelschen Kunstinstitut) 1992, p. 284

Dietulf Sander in Herwig Guratzsch (ed.), *Max Klinger: Bestandskatalog der Bildwerke, Gemälde und Zeichnungen im Museum der bildenden Künste Leipzig*, Leipzig 1995, pp. 54-55

20

Richard König

Bust of a muse 1901

Barbara Stephan in exhib. cat. *Das Albertinum vor 100 Jahren: Die Skulpturensammlung Georg Treus*, Dresden (Staatliche Kunstsammlungen Dresden, Skulpturensammlung) 1994-95, no. 168

21

Franz von Stuck

Fighting fauns 1903–04

Edwin Becker, exhib. cat. *Franz von Stuck 1863-1928: eros & pathos*, Amsterdam (Van Gogh Museum) 1995-96, no. 39

22

Edward Onslow Ford

The singer c.1889

Exhib. cat. *Reverie, myth, sensuality: sculpture in Britain 1880-1910*, Stoke on Trent (City Museum and Art Gallery) 1992, no. 11

Phillipa Laurenson, 'Case study of a 19th-century bronze with a decorative resin inlay,' in Jackie Heuman (ed.), *From marble to chocolate: the conservation of modern sculpture* (Tate Gallery Conference, 18-20 September 1995), London 1995, pp. 15-22

23

George–Henri Lemaire

An Egyptian woman c.1890

Marie-José Salmon and Josette Galiègue, *De Thomas Couture à Maurice Denis: vingt ans d'acquisitions du Conseil Général de l'Oise*, 2 vols., Beauvais 1994, vol. 2: Les collections du XXe siècle du Musée départemental de l'Oise, p. 64

24

Félicie de Fauveau

St Louis c.1840

Exhib. cat. *Touraine néo-gothique*, Tours (Musée des Beaux-Arts) 1978, no. 208

25

Anonymous

The Four Evangelists c.1895–1900

A.J.C. van Leeuwen, *De maakbaarheid van het verleden: P.J.H. Cuypers als restauratiearchitect*, Zwolle 1995, p. 52

26

Anonymous

St Gregory c.1895–1900

Rijksdienst Beeldende Kunst: bestandcatalogus oude beeldhouwkunst 1300-1900, The Hague 1995, no. 113

Select bibliography: works exhibited

27
Félix Bauer
A lesson in illumination 1892
Marie-José Salmon, *Revue du Louvre* 43 (June 1995), p. 84

28 29
Emmanuel Fremiet
Chimeras c.1878
This catalogue entry is based on information provided by the owners with the help of Tamara Préaud.

30
Albert-Ernest Carrier-Belleuse
The reader c.1880
(other version) Barbara Lepper, 'Werke von Albert Carrier-Belleuse in Berlin,' *Jahrbuch der Berliner Museen* 22 (1980), pp. 178-225

31
Emmanuel Fremiet
Credo 1885
Anne Pingeot, Antoinette Le Normand-Romain and Laure de Margerie, *Musée d'Orsay: catalogue sommaire illustré des sculptures*, Paris 1986, p. 158
Catherine Chevillot, exhib. cat. *Emmanuel Fremiet: la main et le multiple*, Dijon (Musée des Beaux-Arts) & Grenoble (Musée de Grenoble) 1988-89, no. S 264

32
Jean-Baptiste Hugues
Ravenna c.1885
Exhib. cat. *De Carpeaux à Matisse: la sculpture française de 1850 à 1914 dans les musées et les collections publiques du Nord de la France*, Calais (Musée des Beaux-Arts) & Lille (Musée des Beaux-Arts) & Boulogne-sur-Mer (Musée des Beaux-Arts et d'Archéologie) & Paris (Musée Rodin) 1982-83, no. 115

34
Jean-Baptiste-Gustave Deloye
The captain's share 1898
Stanislas Lami, *Dictionnaire des sculpteurs de l'école française au XIXe siècle*, 4 vols., Paris 1914-21, vol. 2, p. 162

35 36
Alfred Gilbert
St Elizabeth of Hungary and The Virgin 1899
Exhib. cat. *Victorian High Renaissance*, Manchester (City Art Gallery) & Minneapolis (The Minneapolis Museum of Art) & Brooklyn (Brooklyn Museum) 1978-79, nos. 108-09
Exhib. cat. *British sculpture 1850-1914*, introduction Lavinia Handley-Read, London (Fine Art Society) 1968, nos. 75-76
Richard Dorment, exhib. cat. *Alfred Gilbert: sculptor and goldsmith*, London (Royal Academy of Arts) 1986, nos. 75-76

37 38
William Ernest Reynolds-Stephens
Sir Lancelot and the nestling 1899
Guinevere and the nestling 1900
Benedict Read and Joanna Barnes (eds.), exhib. cat. *Pre-Raphaelite sculpture: nature and imagination in British sculpture 1848-1914*, London (The Matthiesen Gallery) & Birmingham (Birmingham Museum and Art Gallery) 1991-92, nos. 44 a, b

39
Gilbert Bayes
St George c.1900
Exhib. cat. *Gibson to Gilbert: British sculpture 1840-1914*, London (Fine Art Society) 1992, no. 3
Exhib. cat. *Reverie, myth, sensuality: sculpture in Britain 1880-1910*, Stoke on Trent (City Museum and Art Gallery) 1992, no. 5

41
Adolf von Hildebrand
Elisabeth von Herzogenberg as St Cecilia 1893-97
Sigrid Esche-Braunfels, *Adolf von Hildebrand (1847-1921)*, Berlin 1993, pp. 182, 372

42
Artur Volkmann
Eve c.1890-93
Bärbel Stephan, 'Die Erwerbung der Bildwerke des 19. Jahrhunderts,' *Vom Klassizismus bis zum Jugendstil: Staatliche Kunstsammlungen Dresden, Gemäldegalerie Neue Meister, Skulpturensammlung*, Dresden 1993, p. 13
Heiner Protzmann in exhib. cat. *Das Albertinum vor 100 Jahren: Die Skulpturensammlung Georg Treus*, Dresden (Staatliche Kunstsammlungen Dresden, Skulpturensammlung) 1994-95, no. 164

43 44
Robert Anning Bell
Mermaid 1900
Mother and children 1906
Benedict Read and Joanna Barnes (eds.), exhib. cat. *Pre-Raphaelite sculpture: nature and imagination in British sculpture 1848-1914*, London (The Matthiesen Gallery) & Birmingham (Birmingham Museum and Art Gallery) 1991-92, nos. 1, 2

45 46
Carlo Marochetti
Princess Gauramma of Coorg c.1856
Dalip Singh c.1856
Marco Calderini, *Carlo Marochetti: monografia con ritratti, fac-simile e riproduzioni di opere dell'artista*, Turin & Milan & Florence 1928, pl. LII
Benedict Read, *Victorian sculpture*, New Haven & London 1982, p. 174

49
Charles-Henri-Joseph Cordier
Jewess from Algiers c.1862
(other versions]) Jeannine Durand-Revillon, 'Un promoteur de la sculpture polychrome sous le Second Empire: Charles-Henri-Joseph Cordier (1827-1905),' *Bulletin de la Société d'Histoire de l'Art Français* (1982), pp. 187, 195
Michael Forrest, *Art bronzes*, West Chester, Pennsylvania 1988, p. 429

50
Louis-Ernest Barrias
Girl from Bou-Saada 1890
(other versions) Georges Lafenestre, *L'œuvre de Ernest Barrias statuaire 1841-1903*, Paris 1908, p. 104, no. 25
Robert Kashey and Martin L.H. Reymert, exhib. cat. *Western European bronzes of the 19th century: a survey*, New York (Shepherd Gallery) 1973, no. 59
Pierre Kjellberg, *Les bronzes du XIXe siècle: dictionnaire des sculpteurs*, Saint-Amand-Montrond 1989, pp. 49-51

51
Emmanuel Fremiet
Orang-utan and the savage from Borneo 1895
Catherine Chevillot, 'A propos de l'*Orang-outang* (1893) de Frémiet du musée de Dijon: Le marbre seul? L'expérience de la peinture,' *Revue du Louvre* 39 (1989), no. 1, pp. 53-58
Catherine Chevillot, exhib. cat. *Emmanuel Fremiet: la main et le multiple*, Dijon (Musée des Beaux-Arts) & Grenoble (Musée de Grenoble) 1988-89, no. S 146

53
Henri Gréber
Emmanuel Fremiet 1908
Anne Pingeot (ed.), exhib. cat. *La sculpture française au XIXe siècle*, Paris (Galeries nationales du Grand Palais) 1986, no. 25
Exhib. cat. *Les Gréber: une dynastie d'artistes*, Bregenz (Vorarlberger Landesmuseum) & Beauvais (Musée départemental de l'Oise) 1994, no. 201
Marie-José Salmon, *De Thomas Couture à Maurice Denis: vingt ans d'acquisitions du Conseil Général de l'Oise*, 2 vols., Beauvais 1994, vol. 1: Les collections du XIXe siècle du Musée départemental de l'Oise, p. 241

54
Jean-Léon Gérôme
Bust of Bellona 1892
Anne Pingeot (ed.), exhib. cat. *La sculpture française au XIXe siècle*, Paris (Galeries nationales du Grand Palais) 1986, no. 86
Gerald M. Ackerman, *The life and work of Jean-Léon Gérôme*, New York 1986, p. 318, no. S. 27

55
Jean-Léon Gérôme
Sarah Bernhardt 1895–97
Gerald M. Ackerman, *The life and work of Jean-Léon Gérôme*, New York 1986, pp. 149, 320, no. S.33
Anne Pingeot, Antoinette Le Normand-Romain and Laure de Margerie, *Musée d'Orsay: catalogue sommaire illustré des sculptures*, Paris 1986, p. 165

56 57
Jean-Léon Gérôme
The ball player 1902
Self-portrait painting the masks of *The ball player* c.1902
Gerald M. Ackerman, *The life and work of Jean-Léon Gérôme*, New York 1986, p. 287, no. 474, p. 326, no. S. 57

58
Louis-Ernest Barrias
Nature revealing herself to science c.1905
Werner Hofmann (ed.), exhib. cat. *Zauber der Medusa: Europäische Manierismen*, Vienna (Wiener Künstlerhaus) 1987, no. XIII/39
Exhib. cat. *La science pour tous*, Paris (Musée d'Orsay) 1994, no. 1
(other versions) Max Collignon, 'Une statue polychrome de M. Ernest Barrias,' *Revue de l'Art Ancien et Moderne* 6 (10 September 1899), pp. 191-98
Marie Busco and Peter Fusco in Peter Fusco and Horst W. Janson (eds.), exhib. cat. *The Romantics to Rodin: French 19th-century sculpture from North American collections*, Los Angeles (Los Angeles County Museum of Art) & Minneapolis (The Minneapolis Museum of Art) & Detroit (The Detroit Institute of Arts) & Indianapolis (Indianapolis Museum of Arts) 1980-81, no. 10
Elisabeth Kashey and Robert Kashey, exhib. cat. *European drawings and sculpture: 19th and 20th century*, New York (Shepherd Gallery) 1993, no. 32

59
Désiré-Maurice Ferrary
Leda and the swan 1898
Exhib. cat. *Lord Leverhulme*, London (Royal Academy of Arts) 1980, no. 9
Charles Avery, Edward Morris and Mark Evans, *Lady Lever Art Gallery Port Sunlight: catalogue of foreign paintings, drawings, miniatures, tapestries, post-classical sculpture and prints*, Liverpool 1983, pp. 114-15
Penelope Curtis, *Sculpture on Merseyside*, Liverpool 1988, p. 48

60
Clovis Delacour
Andromeda c.1900
Charles Avery, Edward Morris and Mark Evans, *Lady Lever Art Gallery Port Sunlight: catalogue of foreign paintings, drawings, miniatures, tapestries, post-classical sculpture and prints*, Liverpool 1983, p. 110

61
Antoine-Louis Barye
Tiger devouring a gavial 1831/1874
(other casts) Glenn Benge in Peter Fusco and Horst W. Janson (eds.), exhib. cat. *The Romantics to Rodin: French 19th-century sculpture from North American collections*, Los Angeles (Los Angeles County Museum of Art) & Minneapolis (The Minneapolis Museum of Art) & Detroit (The Detroit Institute of Arts) & Indianapolis (Indianapolis Museum of Arts) 1980-81, no. 16
Glenn F. Benge, *Antoine-Louis Barye: sculptor of romantic Realism*, University Park & London 1984, pp. 167-84
Martin Sonnabend, *Antoine-Louis Barye (1795-1875): Studien zum plastischen Werk* (diss.), Munich 1988, passim
Stuart Pivar, *The Barye bronzes: a catalogue raisonné*, 2nd ed., Woodbridge 1990, no. A 61

62 63
Marcello
Bianca Capello c.1863
(other versions) Henriette Bessis, *Marcello sculpteur*, Fribourg 1980, pp. 82-90
Henriette Bessis, 'Pourquoi une telle résonance de la Bianca Capello de Marcello dans les dernières années du XIXe siècle?,' *Gazette des Beaux-Arts* (November 1982), pp. 183-87

65
Vincenzo Gemito
The water vendor, a figural fountain c.1886
(other versions) Gianna Piantoni and Fred Leeman (ed.), exhib. cat. *Ottocento/Novecento: Italiaanse kunst 1870-1910*, Amsterdam (Van Gogh Museum) 1988, pp. 20, 49
Ian Warddropper and Fred Licht, exhib. cat. *Chiseled with a brush: Italian sculpture 1860-1925 from the Gilgore collections*, Chicago (Art Institute of Chicago) 1994, no. 19

66
Constantin Meunier
Charlotte 1886
Exhib. cat. *Les XX – La Libre Esthétique: cent ans après*, Brussels (Musées royaux des Beaux-Arts de Belgique) 1993, no. 143

67
Raoul Larche
Jesus in the temple c.1900
Dominique Renoux, 'Raoul Larche, statuaire (1860-1912),' *Bulletin de la Société de l'Histoire de l'Art Français* (1989), p. 257
Ursula Heiderich, *Katalog der Skulpturen in der Kunsthalle Bremen*, Bremen 1993, p. 289

Select bibliography: works exhibited

68
Alfred Gilbert
Head of a girl 1883
Exhib. cat. *Victorian High Renaissance*, Manchester (City Art Gallery) & Minneapolis (The Minneapolis Museum of Art) & Brooklyn (Brooklyn Museum) 1978-79, no. 92
Richard Dorment, exhib. cat. *Alfred Gilbert: sculptor and goldsmith*, London (Royal Academy of Arts) 1986, no. 12

69
Alfred Gilbert
Charity 1899
Exhib. cat. *Victorian and Edwardian art: the Handley Read collection*, London (Royal Academy of Arts) 1972, no. F 29
Exhib. cat. *Victorian High Renaissance*, Manchester (City Art Gallery) & Minneapolis (The Minneapolis Museum of Art) & Brooklyn (Brooklyn Museum) 1978-79, no. 104
Richard Dorment, exhib. cat. *Alfred Gilbert: sculptor and goldsmith*, London (Royal Academy of Arts) 1986, no. 90

70
Auguste Rodin
The Age of Bronze 1876–77/1906
(other casts) John L. Tancock, *The sculpture of Auguste Rodin: the collection of the Rodin Museum Philadelphia*, Philadelphia 1976, no. 64
Cécile Goldscheider, *Rodin: catalogue raisonné de l'œuvre sculpté, 1840-1886*, Lausanne & Paris 1989, no. 95

71-74
Auguste Rodin
Rose Beuret c. 1880-1911
John L. Tancock, *The sculpture of Auguste Rodin: the collection of the Rodin Museum Philadelphia*, Philadelphia 1976, no. 81
J.A. Schmoll gen. Eisenwerth, *Rodin-Studien*, Munich 1983, p. 25

75
Auguste Rodin
Minerva with a helmet c.1896
John L. Tancock, *The sculpture of Auguste Rodin: the collection of the Rodin Museum Philadelphia*, Philadelphia 1976, pp. 595-98
Edward Morris, 'James Smith of Liverpool and Auguste Rodin,' in Penelope Curtis (ed.), *Patronage and practice: sculpture on Merseyside*, Liverpool 1989, pp. 68-69
The Walker Art Gallery Liverpool, Liverpool 1994, p. 84

76
Medardo Rosso
The flesh of others 1883
Luciano Caramel (ed.), exhib. cat. *Medardo Rosso*, London (Whitechapel Art Gallery) 1994, no. 11

79
Auguste Rodin and Paul Jeanneney
Colossal head of Balzac c.1905
Exhib. cat. *Polychromies à travers les âges et les civilisations*, Paris (Musée Bourdelle) 1971, no. 143
John L. Tancock, *The sculpture of Auguste Rodin: the collection of the Rodin Museum Philadelphia*, Philadelphia 1976, p. 457

81
Auguste Rodin and Jean Cros
Camille Claudel in a bonnet c. 1911
Exhib. cat. *Camille Claudel*, Martigny (Fondation Pierre Giannadda) & Paris (Musée Rodin) 1990-91, p. 20

82
Camille Claudel
Lost in thought 1905
Reine-Marie Paris and Arnaud de la Chapelle, *L'œuvre de Camille Claudel: catalogue raisonné*, 2nd ed., Paris 1991, no. 55
Exhib. cat. *Camille Claudel*, Martigny (Fondation Pierre Gianadda) & Paris (Musée Rodin) 1990-91, no. 81

83
Pierre–Auguste Renoir
Madame Renoir 1916
Anne Pingeot, Antoinette Le Normand-Romain and Laure de Margerie, *Musée d'Orsay: catalogue sommaire illustré des sculptures*, Paris 1986, p. 228

84
Antoine Bourdelle
Head of Apollo 1900–09
Ionel Jianou and Michel Dufet, *Bourdelle: catalogue des sculptures complété et numéroté*, Paris 1975, no. 259
Antoinette Le Normand-Romain, 'La tête d'Apollon: la "cause de divorce" entre Rodin et Bourdelle,' *Revue du Louvre et des Musées de France* 40 (June 1990), pp. 212-20
Antoinette Le Normand-Romain, 'Devenir Bourdelle,' *Revue de l'Art* 104 (1994), no.3, pp. 30-39

85
Pablo Picasso
Head of a jester 1905
Werner Spies, *Picasso: Das plastische Werk*, Stuttgart 1983, no. 4
Luciano Caramel, exhib. cat. *L'impressionismo nella scultura*, Lugano (Galleria Pieter Coray) 1989, no. 46
Exhib. cat. *Picasso 1905-1906*, Barcelona (Museu Picasso) & Berne (Kunstmuseum) 1992, no. 73

87
Fix-Masseau
The secret 1894
Anne Pingeot (ed.), exhib. cat. *La sculpture française au XIXe siècle*, Paris (Galeries nationales du Grand Palais) 1986, no. 242
Anne Pingeot, Antoinette Le Normand-Romain and Laure de Margerie, *Musée d'Orsay: catalogue sommaire illustré des sculptures*, Paris 1986, p. 154
Jürgen Schultze (ed.), exhib. cat. *Paris – Belle Epoque: Faszination einer Weltstadt*, Essen (Kulturstiftung Ruhr, Villa Hügel) 1994, no. 590

88
Julien Dillens
Allegretto 1894
M. Luwel and M. Bruneel-Hye de Crom, exhib. cat. *'Tervueren 1897': studie en catalogus van de commemoratieve tentoonstelling*, Brussels-Tervuren (Musée royal de l'Afrique centrale) 1967, no. 16
Exhib. cat. *Symbolisme en Belgique*, Tokyo (National Museum of Modern Art) 1982-83, no. 21

89
Joseph-Louis Geleyn
Fury 1897
M. Luwel and M. Bruneel-Hye de Crom, exhib. cat. *'Tervueren 1897': studie en catalogus van de commemoratieve tentoonstelling*, Brussels-Tervuren (Musée royal de l'Afrique centrale) 1967, no. 20

90
Fernand Khnopff
Mask c.1897
Robert L. Delevoy, Catherine De Croës and Gisèle Ollinger-Zinque, *Fernand Khnopff*, 2nd ed., Brussels 1987, pp. 306, 449, no. 299
Werner Hofmann in idem (ed.), exhib. cat. *Zauber der Medusa: Europäische Manierismen*, Vienna (Wiener Künstlerhaus) 1987, no. XIII/21
Georg Syamken, *Die dritte Dimension: Plastiken, Konstruktionen, Objekte, Bestandskatalog der Skulpturenabteilung der Hamburger Kunsthalle*, Hamburg 1988, p. 231
Michel Draguet, *Khnopff ou l'ambigu poétique*, Paris 1995, pp. 127-33

91

George Frampton

Lamia 1899–1900

Susan Beattie, *The New Sculpture*, New Haven & London 1983, pp. 160-62

John Christian (ed.), exhib. cat. *The last Romantics: the romantic tradition in British art, Burne-Jones to Stanley Spencer*, London (Barbican Art Gallery) 1989, no. 193

Exhib. cat. *Reverie, myth, sensuality: sculpture in Britain 1880-1910*, Stoke on Trent (City Museum and Art Gallery) 1992, no. 14

92

Alphonse Mucha

Nature c.1899

Exhib. cat. *Alfons Mucha 1860-1939*, Darmstadt (Mathildenhöhe) 1980, no. 149

Werner Hofmann (ed.), exhib. cat. *Zauber der Medusa: Europäische Manierismen*, Vienna (Wiener Künstlerhaus) 1987, no. XIII/31

Irmela Franzke, *Jugendstil: Glas, Graphik, Keramik, Metall, Möbel, Skulpturen und Textilien von 1880 bis 1915, Bestandskatalog, Badisches Landesmuseum Karlsruhe*, Karlsruhe 1987, no. 6

93

Maurice Denis

Audi filia 1889

Exhib. cat. *Maurice Denis 1870-1943*, Lyons (Musée des Beaux-Arts) & Cologne (Wallraf-Richartz-Museum) & Liverpool (Walker Art Gallery) & Amsterdam (Van Gogh Museum) 1994-95, no. 13

94

Jens Ferdinand Willumsen

Prostitute awaiting her prey in the *Montagnes Russes* 1890

Derek Lionel Paul, 'Willumsen and Gauguin in the 1890s,' *Apollo* 111 (January 1980), p. 39

Alan G. Wilkinson, exhib. cat. *Gauguin to Moore: primitivism in modern sculpture*, Toronto (Art Gallery of Ontario) 1981-82, p. 30

Leila Krogh, *Katalogbog J.F. Willumsens Museum Frederikssund*, Copenhagen 1986, p. 86

95

Paul Gauguin

Oviri 1894

Christopher Gray, *Sculpture and ceramics of Paul Gauguin*, Baltimore 1963, no. 113

Merete Bodelsen, *Gauguin's ceramics: a study in the development of his art*, London 1964, pp. 146-49

Barbara Landy, 'The meaning of Gauguin's "Oviri" ceramic,' *The Burlington Magazine* 109 (April 1967), pp. 242-46

Vojtech Jirat-Wasiutyński, 'Paul Gauguin's self-portraits and the *Oviri*: the image of the artist, Eve, and the fatal woman,' *Art Quarterly* 2 (Spring 1979), pp. 172-90

Exhib. cat. *The art of Paul Gauguin*, Washington, D.C. (National Gallery of Art) & Chicago (The Art Institute of Chicago) & Paris (Galeries nationales du Grand Palais) 1988-89, no. 211

Sue Taylor, '*Oviri*: Gauguin's savage woman,' *Konsthistorisk Tidskrift* 62 (1993), nos. 3-4, pp. 197-220

96

Georges Lacombe

Mary Magdalene 1896

Blandine Salmon and Olivier Meslay, *Georges Lacombe: sculptures, peintures, dessins*, Paris 1991, p. 25

Ursula Heiderich, *Katalog der Skulpturen in der Kunsthalle Bremen*, Bremen 1993, p. 286

Index

19th-century artists who created polychrome sculpture

Adams, Herbert 1858–1945
Alaphilippe, Camille 1874–after 1934
Allouard, Henri-Emile 1844–1929
Arnaud, Charles-Auguste 1825–1883

Bareau, Georges 1866–1931
Barlach, Ernst 1870–1938
Barrau, Théophile-Eugène-Victor 1848–1913
Barre, Jean-Auguste 1811–1896
Barrias, Louis-Ernest 1841–1905
Bartholomé, Albert 1848–1928
Barye, Antoine-Louis 1795–1875
Basset, Urbain 1842–1924
Bates, Harry 1850–1899
Baumbach, Max 1859–1915
Bayes, Gilbert 1872–1953
Bell, John 1811–1895
Bell, Robert Anning 1863–1933
Benk, Johannes 1844–1914
Bilek, Frantisek 1872–1941
Bistolfi, Leonardo 1859–1933
Böcklin, Arnold 1827–1901
Bône, Léon called Bohn 1837–1899
Bottée, Louis-Alexandre 1852–1941
Boucher, Alfred 1850–1934
Bourdelle, Antoine 1861–1924
Brancusi, Constantin 1876–1957
Breymann, Adolf 1839–1878
Broad, John active 1873–1919
Broggi, Giovanni 1853–1919
Brown, Henry Kirke 1814–1886
Bruckmann, Peter 1850–1925

Cabet, Jean-Baptiste-Paul 1815–1876
Calvi, Pietro 1833–1884
Cantini, Jules 1826–1916
Cappiello, Leonetto 1875–1942
Carlier, Emile-Joseph 1849–1927
Caron, Alexandre-Auguste 1857–1932
Carpeaux, Jean-Baptiste 1827–1875
Carrier-Belleuse, Albert-Ernest 1824–1887
Carriès, Jean 1855–1894
Cauer, Carl 1828–1885
Cauer, Ludwig 1866–1947
Charpentier, Alexandre 1856–1909
Chartrousse, Emile 1829–1896
Claudel, Camille 1864–1943
Claudet, Max 1840–1893
Clésinger, Auguste 1814–1883
Clodt von Jürgensburg, Peter Jakob 1805–1867
Colton, William Robert 1867–1921
Convers, Louis 1860–1919
Cordier, Charles-Henri-Joseph 1827–1905
Costenoble, Karl 1837–1907
Craco, Arthur 1869–1955
Cros, Henry 1840–1907
Cros, Jean 1884–1932
Cumberworth, Charles 1811–1852

Dalou, Aimé-Jules 1838–1902
Dampt, Jean 1853–1946
Dantan, Antoine-Laurent 1798–1878
Daumier, Honoré 1808–1879
David, Adolphe 1828–1895
David, Pierre-Jean called David d'Angers 1788–1856
Degas, Edgar 1834–1917
Delacour, Clovis 1859–1929
Delagrange, Leon-Noël 1872–1910
Deloye, Jean-Baptiste-Gustave 1848–1899
Denis, Maurice 1870–1945
De Rudder, Isidore 1855–1943
Devreese, Godefroid 1861–1941
Diez, Robert 1844–1922
Dillens, Julien 1849–1904
Dressler, Conrad 1856–1940
Drury, Alfred 1856–1944
Dubois, Alphée 1831–1905
Dubois, Paul 1829–1905
Du Bois, Paul 1859–1938
Dumont, Augustin 1801–1884
Dumontet, Gabrielle active 1891–1912
Dupon, Josuë 1864–1935
Duret, Francisque-Joseph 1804–1865
Du Seigneur, Jean-Bernard 1808–1866

Epinay, Prosper d' 1836–1914

Fauginet, Jacques-Auguste 1809–1847
Fauveau, Félicie de 1802–1868
Fehr, Charles Henry 1867–1940
Fehr, Konrad 1854–after 1892
Ferrary, Désiré-Maurice 1852–1904
Feuchère, Jean-Jacques 1807–1852
Fisher, Alexander 1864–1936
Fix-Masseau, Pierre-Félix Masseau 1869–1937
Ford, Edward Onslow 1852–1901
Frampton, George 1860–1928
Fremiet, Emmanuel 1824–1910
Froment-Meurice, Emile 1837–1913
Fuchs, Peter 1829–1898

Galbrunner, Paul-Charles 1823–1905
Gallian, Octave-Lazare-George-Victor active 1878–1896
Gardet, Georges 1863–1939
Gasteiger, Mathias 1871–after 1916
Gauguin, Paul 1848–1903
Geleyn, Joseph-Louis 1863–1934
Gemito, Vincenzo 1852–1929
Gérôme, Jean-Léon 1824–1904
Gibson, John 1790–1866
Gilbert, Alfred 1854–1934
Göllner, Kurt Eberhard 1880–?
Gott, Joseph 1786–1860
Graillon, Félix-Adrien-Henri 1833–1893
Graillon, Pierre-Adrien 1809–1873
Gréber, Henri 1854–1941
Gregory, John 1879–after 1916
Greiner, Daniel 1872–1943

Index

Hahn, Hermann 1868–1942
Haller, Hermann 1880–1950
Halou, Alfred-Jean-Baptiste-Paul 1829–1891
Hanak, Anton 1875–1934
Hannaux, Emmanuel 1855–1934
Hansen-Jacobsen, Niels 1861–1941
Hébert, Emile 1828–1893
Herkomer, Hubert von 1849–1914
Herter, Ernst 1846–1917
Hildebrand, Adolf von 1847–1921
Hiolle, Ernest-Eugène 1834–1886
Hoetger, Bernhard 1874–1949
Hosmer, Harriet 1830–1908
Hottot, Louis 1829–1905
Hugues, Jean-Baptiste 1849–1917

Idrac, Jean-Antoine-Marie 1849–1884
Injalbert, Jean-Antoine 1845–1933
Iselin, Henri-Frédéric 1825–1905
Jacobs, Henri active turn of the century
Jacquot, Georges 1794–1874
Jeanneney, Paul 1861–1920
Jenkins, Frank Lynn 1870–?
John, William Goscombe 1860–1952

Kaffsack, Joseph 1850–1890
Kahle, Anna von 1853–1920
Kastner, Johann ?–1912
Kaufmann, Hugo 1868–1919
Khnopff, Fernand 1858–1921
Kirchner, Ernst Ludwig 1880–1938
Kiss, August Karl Eduard 1802–1865
Klein, Max 1847–1908
Klinger, Max 1857–1920
Klotz, Hermann 1850–1932
Koch, Gottlieb von 1849–1914
Koch, Max 1859–1930
Kocian, Quido 1874–1928
König, Richard 1863–after 1920
Kopf, Joseph 1827–1903
Korschann, Charles 1872–after 1900
Krøyer, Per Severin 1857–1909
Kundmann, Carl 1838–1919
Kurz, Erwin 1857–1931
Küsthardt, Friedrich 1870–1905

Lacombe, Georges 1868–1916
Landsberg, Max 1850–1906
Larche, Raoul 1860–1912
Larrivé, Jean 1875–1928
Lee, Thomas Stirling 1856–1916
Le Harivel-Durocher, Victor-Edouard 1816–1878
Lemaire, Georges-Henri 1853–1914
Léonard, Agathon called Van Weydeveldt 1841–1923
Loiseau-Rousseau, Paul 1861–1927
Lombard, Henri 1855–1929
Lucas, Richard Cockle 1800–1883
Lucchesi, Andrea Carlo 1860–1924
Luksch, Richard 1872–1936
Luksch-Makowski, Elena 1878–1967

Madrassi, Luca 1848–1919
Maillol, Aristide 1861–1944
Maison, Rudolf 1854–1904
Marcello Adèle d'Affry, Comtesse de Castiglione Colonna, 1836–1879
Marochetti, Carlo 1805–1867
Masini, Girolamo 1840–c. 1893
Meissonier, Jean-Louis-Ernest 1815–1891
Mendes da Costa, Joseph 1863–1939
Mengelberg, Friedrich Wilhelm 1837–1919
Mercié, Antonin 1845–1916
Meunier, Constantin 1831–1905
Michel, Gustave-Frédéric 1851–1924
Milles, Carl 1875–1955
Minghetti, Angelo 1821–1885
Missfeldt, Heinrich 1872–1945
Moine, Antonin-Marie 1796–1849
Moira, Gerald 1867–1959
Moncel, Alphonse-Emmanuel 1866–after 1932
Monti, Raffaello 1818–1881
Montini, Igino 1877–1954
Moreau, Mathurin 1822–1912
Moreau-Vauthier, Augustin-Jean 1831–1893
Moser, Julius 1832–1916
Mucha, Alphonse 1860–1939

Nichols, Thomas c. 1820–c. 1895
Nocq, Henri 1868–after 1927

Pagliaccetti, Raffaello 1839–1900
Palmer, Erastus Dow 1817–1904
Pereda, Raimondo 1840–1915
Pfeifer, Felix Georg 1871–1945
Pfuhl, Johannes 1846–1914
Piccirilli, Attilio 1866–1945
Powolny, Michael 1871–1954
Pradier, James 1790–1852
Protat, Hugues active 1843–1850
Puech, Denys 1854–1942

Renoir, Pierre-Auguste 1841–1919
Reynolds-Stephens, William Ernest 1862–1943
Ringel d'Illzach, Jean-Desiré 1847–1916
Rivière, Théodore-Louis-Auguste 1857–1912
Robert, Luc active end of the 19th century
Rochet, Louis 1813–1878
Rodin, Auguste 1840–1917
Rombaux, Egide 1865–1942
Römer, Bernhard Wilhelm Erdmann 1852–1891
Rosso, Medardo 1858–1928
Rouault, Georges 1871–1958
Roulleau, Jules Pierre 1855–1895

Saint-Marceaux, Charles-René de Paul de 1845–1915
Samuel, Charles 1862–1938
Savine, Léopold-Pierre-Antoine 1861–after 1920
Scailliet, Emile-Philippe 1846–1911
Schaper, Fritz 1841–1919
Schauss, Martin 1867–1927
Schlüter, Carl 1846–1884

Schneider, Franz active c. 1870–1880
Schneider, Sascha Alexander 1870–1927
Schreitmüller, Johannes Daniel 1842–1885
Schroeder, Jean-Louis-Désiré 1828–1898
Schwanthaler, Ludwig von 1802–1848
Schweinitz, Rudolf 1839–1896
Seger, Ernst 1868–1839
Seurre, Charles-Emile-Marie 1798–1858
Seydlitz, Reinhart Freiherr von 1850–after 1903
Siemering, Rudolf 1814–1895
Simart, Charles 1806–1857
Sintenis, Walter 1867–1911
Skovgaard, Niels 1858–1938
Somme, Théophile 1871–1952
Steiner, Clément-Léopold 1853–1899
Strasser, Arthur 1854–1927
Strymans, Alfons Joseph 1866–1959
Stuck, Franz von 1863–1928
Swynnerton, Joseph William 1848–1910

Tantardini, Antonio 1829–1879
Thomas, Gabriel-Jules 1824–1905
Thomas, John 1813–1862
Thornycroft, Mary 1814–1895
Tilgner, Viktor 1844–1986
Tombay, Alexandre de active 1842–1854
Tombay, Alphonse de 1843–1918
Torelli, Jafet active 19th century
Toussaint, François-Christophe-Armand 1806–1862
Toussaint, Gaston 1872–1946
Triqueti, Henri-Joseph-François Baron de 1804–1874
Troubetzkoy, Paul 1866–1938
Tuaillon, Louis 1862–1919

Üchtritz-Steinkirch, Cuno von 1856–1908

Valère-Bernard 1860–1936
Vallgren, Ville 1855–1940
Van der Stappen, Charles 1843–1910
Vernhes, Henri-Edouard 1854–1926
Vever, Henri 1854–1942
Vignon, Claude i.e. Noëmi Rouvier 1832–1888
Volkmann, Arthur 1851–1941
Vrubel, Mikhail Alexandrovich 1856–1910

Walker, Arthur George 1861–1939
Ward, Herbert 1863–1919
Weigele, Henry 1858–1927
Wiertz, Antoine 1806–1865
Wiese, Max 1846–1925
Willumsen, Jens Ferdinand 1863–1958
Wolfers, Philippe 1858–1929
Wolff, Albert 1814–1892
Wouw, Antoon van 1862–1945
Wrba, Georg 1872–1939

Index of proper names

Abadie (murderer) 69
Abdalla, Saïd 35
Abel 36, 78, 250
Ackerman, Gerald M. 180
Adam 114, 255
Affry, Adèle d', Duchess Castiglione-Colonna
    see Marcello
Aire, Jean d' 210
Alaphilippe, Camille 53, 81
Alari-Bonacolsi, Jacopo 126, 192
Albani (family) 119
Albers (family) 43-44, 107, 254
Albert, Prince 13, 65
Alberti, Leone Battista 14
Alcock, Rutherford 48
Aldridge, Ira 244
Alexander I (tsar of Russia) 67
Alexandre, Arsène 98
Allebé, August 13
Allix, A.J. 83
Allouard, Henri-Emile 244
Alma-Tadema, Lawrence 59, 62-63
Alt, Theodor 40, 42, 48
Andromeda 189, 268
Angelica 92, 251
Anstey, Frank 251
Antico see Alari-Bonacolsi
Antinous 95, 99, 119, 141, 266
Antiochus 22
Aphrodite 25 (see also Venus)
Apollinaire, Guillaume 221
Apollo 16, 26, 98, 220, 228, 269
Arago, François 13
Aragon, Isabella d' 32
Archipenko, Alexander 11, 58
Aristonidas 48
Aristotle 61
Arnoux, Léon 78
Arp, Hans 58
Arthur, King 54, 158
Artois-Bourbon, Henri Charles d', duc de Bordeaux 142
Arwas, Victor 232
Athena 15, 22, 25, 27, 34, 59, 66, 76, 110, 180
    (see also Minerva)
Aubry (founder) 74
Auersperg (family) 155
Augustus, Emperor 39
Aurier, Albert 93
Auvray, Louis 73, 76
Auzoux, Louis 86, 251
Avisseau (potter) 78

Bacchus 22
Ballu, Théodore 13
Balzac, Honoré de 50, 76, 93, 210, 269
Banville, Théodore de 95
Bapst, Germaine 255

Barbedienne, Ferdinand 77-78, 125-26, 192
Barbey d'Aurevilly, Jules 97
Barbezat (founder) 74
Barlach, Ernst 53
Barrau, Théophile-Eugène-Victor 97
Barrias, Louis-Ernest 45, 51, 67, 73, 75, 78, 174, 186, 254, 262, 267-68
Barye, Antoine-Louis 48, 75, 77-78, 190, 250, 262, 268
Bastanier (majolica glazer) 81
Bates, Harry 224
Baudelaire, Charles 8, 34, 68, 93-95, 97, 106, 194
Baudot, Anatole de 81
Bauer, Félix 146, 267
Bayes, A.W. 160
Bayes, Gilbert, 79-80, 82, 158, 160, 267
Bayes, Walter 160
Beale, Arthur 254
Beattie, Susan 57
Beauchamp, Countess 13
Bébé (dwarf of Stanislas Leczinski) 69
Beckett, Gervase and Mabel 200
Beerbohm, Max 97
Beethoven, Ludwig van 59-60, 107, 109
Begas, Reinhold 70
Bell, John 66, 70, 79
Bell, Quentin 59
Bell, Robert Anning 34, 54, 166, 230, 262, 267
Bell, Walter 230
Bellona 47, 49, 180, 189, 200, 204, 268
Benoist, Luc 243
Benzoni, Giovanni Maria 85
Bernard, Claude 69
Bernhardt, Sarah 152, 182, 232, 268
Bernini, Gianlorenzo 40, 65, 103, 124
Bethune, Jean-Baptiste 32
Beulé, Charles-Ernest 22, 26-27, 34
Beuret, Rose 49-50, 202, 269
Beuys, Joseph 7
Bigot, Alexandre 81, 148
Birotteau, César 93
Blanc, Charles 34, 58, 64, 67, 150, 244
Blondel, Spire 67-69
Blot, Eugène 216
Boccaccio, Giovanni 15
Boccioni, Umberto 72
Böcklin, Arnold 109, 134, 252, 262, 266
Bode, Wilhelm von 33, 70
Boermans, chaplain 145
Bois, Jules 94
Bonheur, Isidore 76
Bonny, J.L. 141
Borghese, Paolina 242
Bosio, François-Joseph 32
Botta, Paul-Emile 194
Botticelli, Sandro 165
Bouchot, Henri 67
Boulanger, General Georges 151
Bourdelle, Antoine 49, 128, 202, 214, 220, 262, 269

Boussod et Valadon (dealers) 234
Brahms, Johannes 107, 164
Brancusi, Constantin 58
Brandes, Georg 107, 254
Brentano, Clemens 59
Broad, John 79
Bruckmann, Peter 134
Brutus 16-17
Buddha 112
Burke (murderer) 88
Burne-Jones, Edward 54, 101, 104, 109, 246
Burty, Philippe 67, 76
Butler, Samuel 42
Byron, Lord 88

Cage, John 103
Caillebotte, Gustave 255
Calamai, L. 86
Callen, Anthea 69
Calvi, Pietro 170, 244
Camper, Petrus 69
Camus (patinator) 75
Canova, Antonio 16-17, 19, 22, 25, 49, 85, 88-89, 122, 125, 246
Cantini, Jules 35-36
Capello, Bianca 192, 268
Caravaggio 155
Carlès, Antonin-Jean-Paul 78, 250
Carpeaux, Jean-Baptiste 262
Carrier-Belleuse, Albert-Ernest 39-40, 51, 77-79, 92, 150, 210, 262, 267
Carriès, Jean 52-53, 81, 148, 222, 236, 246, 263
Cassandra 44, 95, 110, 136, 266
Cassin, Madame de 125
Cecilia, St 164, 267
Cellini, Benvenuto 62, 120, 192, 198
Chactas 76
Chaligot, Aline (later Aline Renoir) 218, 269
Champdivers, Odette de 154
Chaplain, Jules-Clément 67
Chaplet, Ernest 110, 210, 236
Charles VI (king of France) 154
Charles X (king of France) 142
Charpentier, Alexandre 53, 57
Chaudet, Antoine-Denis 16, 126
Chavassieu d'Audebert, Adèle 19
Chénavard, Aimé 78
Chesneau, Ernest 246
Chipiez, Charles 245
Chovet (editor of religious art) 74, 249
Christofle (founder and electroplater) 77
Chuttraputti, Rajaram, Maharajah of Kolhapur 35, 168
Cicero 62
Clarence, Duke of 73, 158, 199
Claris, Edmond 51, 206
Claudel, Camille 49, 214, 216, 263, 269
Claudel, Paul 216
Cleopatra 126
Clésinger, Auguste 34, 66, 94, 126, 248, 263, 266
Clodion 112

Index

Cockerell, C.R. 85
Colleoni, Bartolommeo 36
Collignon, Maxime 44, 67, 245
Coorg, Princess Gauramma of 35, 168, 267
Coppée, François 101
Cordier, Charles-Henri-Joseph 35-36, 39-40, 44-45, 51, 66, 73, 75, 77, 85, 170, 174, 190, 244, 249, 251, 263, 267
Cordier, Nicolas 170
Cormon, Fernand 180
Correnti, Cesare 195
Courajod, Louis 13, 65, 247
Cousin, Victor 64
Cranach, Wilhelm von 56, 252
Crane, Walter 54
Crébillon, Prosper-Jolyot de 194
Cremona, Tranquillo 106
Cros, Charles 101, 104-05, 110, 253
Cros, Henry 40, 50, 52-53, 67, 70, 101-02, 104-07, 110, 112, 128, 130, 132, 162, 214, 246, 252, 253, 254, 263, 266
Cros, Jean 49-51, 202, 214, 269
Cumberworth, Charles 76
Cunningham, Allan 90
Cupid 120, 243, 266
Curtius, Dr 251
Cuypers, Pierre 145

Daedalus 16
Dampt, Jean 57, 83, 250, 263
Dantan, Edouard 146
Dante 212
Daphne 244
Darby, Elizabeth 25
Darwin, Charles 105
Daumier, Honoré 34-35, 263
David 34, 224
David, Jacques-Louis 16-17
David d'Angers 94, 244, 248
Degas, Edgar 42, 51, 68-71, 74, 84-85, 94, 104-07, 110, 112, 114, 151, 245, 249, 254, 255, 263
Delacour, Clovis 47, 180, 188-89, 268
Delécluze, Etienne 66
Deloye, Jean-Baptiste-Gustave 155, 263, 267
Denière (founder) 75
Denis, Maurice 58, 234, 270
Derceto 194
De Rudder, Isidore 53, 56
Desjardins, Paul 67
De Vigne, Paul 83
Devreese, Godefroid 263
Diderot, Denis 15, 64
Didron, A.N. 74
Dillens, Julien 56, 226, 263, 269
Diodorus Siculus 194
Dolce, Lodovico 62, 65
Donaldson, Professor (archeologist) 248
Donatello 14, 33-34, 36, 62, 97, 99, 160, 162, 164-65, 198
Dorothea 79

Doulton (ceramicists) 79-80, 82, 160
Draguet, Michel 57
Drake, Friedrich 48
Duban, Félix 25, 28
Dubois, Paul 33-34
Du Bois, Paul 263
Du Bos, Abbé 64
Ducel (founder) 74
Duchamp, Marcel 7
Dufour, Jeanne 234
Dumas fils, Alexandre 67, 101
Dumont, Albert 67
Dumont, Augustin 243, 246
Dupon, Josuë 56
Duponchel (goldsmith) 76
Dupré, Giovanni 11, 36
Duquesnoy, François 68, 244
Durand-Ruel, Paul 218
Duranty, Edmond 104
Durenne (founder) 74
Duret, Francisque-Joseph 76, 243
Dutert, Ferdinand 178

Eastlake, Charles Lock 26
Eberhard, Konrad 243
Ebhardt, Bodo 145
Elgin, Lord 65
Elizabeth of Hungary, St 158, 267
Ephrussi, Charles 68
Epinay, Prosper d' 31, 124-25, 246, 263, 266
Eros 57
Eschmoun 92
Estignard, A. 126
Etex, Antoine 128
Eve 70, 101, 113-14, 165, 255, 267

Falconet, Etienne-Maurice 15, 52, 63, 67
Falguière, Alexandre 46
Falize, Lucien 73-74
Falkener, E. 65
Fauginet, Jacques-Auguste 76
Fauveau, Félicie de 33, 142, 263, 266
Fawcett, Henry 140, 158
Feddersen, Martin 42
Fehr, Charles Henry 54-55, 83
Ferrari, Gaudenzio 42
Ferrary, Désiré-Maurice 44, 92, 96-97, 188-89, 268
Feuchère, Jean-Jacques 76, 194
Feuerbach, Anselm (archeologist) 29, 34
Fix-Masseau 224, 263, 269
Flaubert, Gustave 45, 92
Flaxman, John 89
Flora 32-33, 228
Ford, Edward Onslow 44, 140, 188, 263, 266
Fouquet, Georges 57, 232
Fox, Charles James 88
Frampton, George 54, 57, 109, 158, 160, 165, 230, 264, 270
Francesco II (king of Naples) 195
Fremiet, Emmanuel 48, 148, 151, 178, 264, 267-68

Freud, Sigmund 98-99
Froc-Robert (founders) 74
Froment-Meurice, Emile 25, 39, 76
Froment-Meurice, François-Désiré 73
Fuller, Charles Francis 35, 168

Gage, John 65
Galatea 79
Galbrunner, Paul-Charles 36
Gallé, Emile 47, 102, 180
Garnier, Charles 39-40
Gattamelata (Erasmo da Narni) 36
Gau, Franz Christian 13
Gaudí, Antonio 82
Gauguin, Clovis 110, 255
Gauguin, Paul 50-51, 53, 58, 102, 107, 109-14, 234, 236, 238, 255, 264, 270
Gauricus, Pomponius 48
Gautier, Théophile 22, 62, 64, 66-67, 93-94, 170, 248
Gavarni, Paul 94
Geleyn, Joseph-Louis 226, 269
Gell, William 63
Gemito, Vincenzo 195, 268
George, St 79, 83, 158, 160, 267
George III (king of England) 87
George IV (king of England) 88
Géricault, Théodore 67
Germain, Alphonse de 102, 162
Gérôme, Jean-Léon 13, 45-47, 49, 59, 73, 84, 91, 101, 103, 107, 111-12, 114, 128, 155, 180, 182, 184, 189, 204, 254, 255, 264, 268
Ghiberti, Lorenzo 36
Gibson, John 13, 18, 25-26, 33, 42, 65-66, 85-86, 88, 90-91, 122, 168, 174, 243, 250, 264, 266
Gilbert, Alfred 48, 73, 78, 81, 140, 158, 198-99, 230, 264, 267, 269
Gilbert, Francis 198
Gillray, James 251
Gilly, Friedrich 27
Gilot, Françoise 52
Giotto 146
Girodet, Anne-Louis 19, 22, 47
Gladenbeck (founders) 136
Gleyre, Charles 22
Gluck, Christoph Willibald 194
Gobineau, Arthur de 36
Goethe, Johann Wolfgang 64, 117
Gogh, Theo van 235
Gogh, Vincent van 51, 148, 235
Goldscheider (ceramicists) 244
Goncourt, Edmond and Jules 39, 78, 101
Gonse, Louis 125
Gorden, J. 86
Gott, Joseph 243
Graefe, Albrecht von 81
Gréber (ceramicists) 81
Gréber, Henri 151, 178, 268
Gregory I (pope), St Gregory 145, 266
Grévin, Alfred 84-85, 87

Index

Gropius, Martin 81
Guillaume, Eugène 68, 70
Guillaumet, Achille 174
Guimard, Hector 81
Guinevere 158, 267
Guino, Richard 218

Hadrian, Emperor 190
Halou, Alfred-Jean-Baptiste 81
Hals, Frans 222
Hamilton, Lady 83-84, 89, 251
Hansen, Theophil 40
Hansen Jacobsen, Niels 53
Hanson, Duane 106
Hare (murderer) 88
Hawthorne, Nathaniel 243
Hebe 16-17, 88
Hébert, Emile 194, 264
Hébert, Pierre 194
Hébrard (dealer) 50
Hegel, Georg Friedrich Wilhelm 64, 94
Helen 126, 266
Henkel von Donnersmarck, Guido 39
Henri IV (king of France) 32, 69
Henry, Charles 105, 107, 128, 253
Herder, Johann Gottfried 14, 63, 70-71
Heredia, José-Maria de 101
Hermes 228, 245
Herzogenberg, Elisabeth von 164, 267
Hevesi, Ludwig 228
Hildebrand, Adolf von 34, 60, 164-65, 264, 267
Hittorff, Jakob Ignaz 18-19, 22, 27, 39, 65, 242
Hodebert, Léon-Auguste-César 218
Hoffmann, Josef 59
Hofmann, Werner 57
Hollanda, Francisco 62
Honour, Hugh 35
Hosmer, Harriet 85, 91
Houghton, Lord 244
Hugo, Victor 28
Hugues, Jean-Baptiste 152, 267
Huysmans, Joris-Karl 42, 74-75, 84, 94
Hypnos 97, 110, 228, 253, 254

Icarus 16, 158, 212
Ingres, Jean-Auguste-Dominique 22, 54, 66
Injalbert, Jean-Antoine 81
Isabella of Bavaria 101, 154
Iselin, Henri-Frédéric 36
Isis 58, 110

Jacob, Max 221
Janin, Jules 76
Janson, Horst W. 13-14
Jeanneney, Paul 49, 51, 210, 236, 269
Jenkins, Frank Lynn 54
Jensen, Wilhelm 98-99
Jesus 197, 268
Joan of Arc 31-32, 54, 246-47
John, King 29

John the Baptist, St 85, 95
John the Evangelist, St 145
Jolly, Adolphe 245
Jones, Owen 19, 25, 65, 70, 122, 248
Joseph II (emperor of Austria) 60
Jouffroy, François 132
Jouin, Henri 64
Jupiter 16, 18, 19, 62 (see also Zeus)

Kaffsack, Joseph 70
Kandinsky, Wassily 58
Kändler, Johann Joachim 16
Keats, John 35, 57, 230
Kekulé, Reinhard 46
Khnopff, Fernand 54, 57, 70, 97-98, 109-10, 228, 247, 253, 254, 264, 269
Khnopff, Marguerite 98, 228
Kiessling, Paul 119
Kinsky (family) 155
Kirchner, Ernst Ludwig 58, 113
Kiss, August 250
Klee, Paul 58
Klenze, Leo von 17-19, 25-26, 242, 243
Klimt, Gustav 59, 109, 152
Klinger, Max 42-45, 51, 57, 59-60, 70, 95, 106-07, 109-10, 136, 165, 247, 254, 255, 264, 266
Kokoschka, Oskar 58
König, Richard 71, 138, 266
Konrad von Wettin, Margrave 30
Kostka, Stanislaus 65
Krøyer, Per Severin 235
Kugler, Franz 18, 25, 42, 242
Kühnscherf (founder) 138
Kundmann, Carl 59

Lachenal, Edmond 210
Lacombe, Georges 58, 111, 238, 264, 270
Lafleur (patinator) 75
Laforgue, Jules 40-41, 43-44, 48, 51, 70-71, 95, 99, 101, 107, 246
Lagae, Jules 82
Lagana (founder) 195
Lalique, René 47, 56, 180
Lambeaux, Jef 82
Lamia 57, 230, 270
Lancelot 158, 267
Languet de Gergy, Jean-Baptiste-Joseph 65
Larche, Raoul 197, 264, 268
L'Arrivé, Jean-Baptiste 81
Lassus, Jean-Baptiste 28
Laurana, Francesco 32, 164
Laurens, Henri 58
Lavirotte, Jules-Aimé 81
Lawrence, Thomas 88
Leczinski, Stanislas 69
Leda 22, 25, 44, 76, 92, 188-89, 268
Leeuw, Henri 145
Le Harivel-Durocher, Victor-Edouard 32
Leipen, Neda 245
Lemaire, Georges-Henri 97, 141, 224, 266

Lenoir, Alexandre 27
Le Normand-Romain, Antoinette 85
Leonardo da Vinci 14, 33, 48, 146
Leontes 87
Leopold II (king of Belgium) 56, 77, 226
Lesbia 128
Lévêque, Charles 66
Leverhulme, Lord 188-89
Leyland, John 250
Lichtwark, Alfred 40
Liebig, Justus 82
Linde, Max 210
Linssen, H. 145
Lipchitz, Jacques 58
Lockroy, Edouard 150
Loiseau-Rousseau, Paul 244
Lorenzen von Tangermünde 32
Lorrain, Jean 95, 97-99, 101, 252
Louis IX (king of France), St Louis 142, 266
Louis XIII (king of France) 16
Louis XIV (king of France) 16
Louis XV (king of France) 94
Louis XVI (king of France) 87
Loviot, Benoit 41
Lucas, Richard Cockle 32-33
Ludwig I (king of Bavaria) 17-18
Luke, St 145, 197
Luksch, Richard 53, 264
Luksch-Makowsky, Elsa 264
Luynes, Honoré-Théoderic-Paul-Joseph d'Albert, duc de 22, 66, 76, 248

Mai, Ekkehard 59
Maillol, Aristide 51, 53, 218, 238
Maison, Rudolf 264
Makart, Hans 59
Malet, M. 165
Mallarmé, Stephane 93
Manet, Edouard 68, 104
Mann, Heinrich 97
Mansfield (civil servant of the East India Company) 85
Mantz, Paul 26, 39, 42, 61, 66, 94, 174
Marat, Jean-Paul 88-89
Marcello 192, 244, 264, 268
Marcus Aurelius 36
Marées, Hans von 165
Margaret of Scotland, St 31
Marie Antoinette 87
Mark, St 145
Marochetti, Carlo 13, 34-35, 66, 168, 244, 250, 264, 267
Martin, St 146
Mary Magdalene, St 58, 68, 83-84, 238, 242, 270
Masselotte (patinator) 75
Massin, Mme (patinator) 75
Mathô 44, 96-97
Matisse, Henri 51-52
Matthew, St 145
Mauglas, René 78
Maupassant, Guy de 94

Mayer (fabricator of religious art) 74
Mayer, Ernst 243
Medici (family) 99, 101
Medici, Francesco de' 192
Medusa 47, 58, 95, 117, 124, 134, 180, 228, 252, 266
Meissonier, Ernest 105, 151, 265
Melpomene 182
Mélusine 83
Mena, Pedro de 68
Ménard, Louis 95
Mendes da Costa, Joseph 265
Mêne, Pierre-Jules 67, 76
Mercié, Antonin 34, 46
Mérode, Cléo de 232
Metternich (family) 155
Metzner, Franz 53
Meunier, Charlotte 51, 196, 265, 268
Meunier, Constantin 51, 57, 196, 208, 246, 268
Michel, André 61
Michelangelo 62, 103, 184, 192, 198, 206
Midas 110
Millais, John Everett 168
Millais, William 168
Millet, Jean-François 68
Minerva 12, 204, 269 (see also Athena)
Mino da Fiesole 162
Minton (ceramicists) 78-79, 150
Mirbeau, Octave 95
Mitchell, Claudine 87
Moine, Antonin 76, 78
Moira, Gerald 54
Molière, Jean-Baptiste 222
Montalembert, Charles de 27-28, 32
Montanari, Napoleon 69, 85-86
Monti, Raffaelle 168
Moréas, Jean 93
Moreau-Vauthier, Augustin-Jean 47, 74, 180
Morison, David 83
Morris, William 104
Moynet, Léon 74, 249
Mucha, Alphonse 57, 146, 232, 265, 270
Muller, Emile 148, 178, 224, 236
Multscher, Hans 254
Munch, Edvard 210
Myron 70

Nana 58, 69, 94
Napoleon I 34, 242
Napoleon III 7, 36, 39, 148
Neeld, Joseph 122
Nelson, Lord 251
Nicosis, Queen 95
Nieuwerkerke, Comte de 39
Nike 59
Nollekens, Joseph 90

Olivié, Jean-Luc 52
Orléans, Marie d' 32
Othello 170, 244

Otto, Ludwig 246
Ovidius 57

Pacioli, Fra Luca 62
Pagliaccetti, Raffaello 78
Païva, Marquise de 39
Palissy, Bernard 78, 244
Pandora 13, 26, 66, 141, 224
Paris 106-07, 126
Paris, Reine-Marie 216
Parrhasius 62
Pazaurek, Gustav 60
Peachey, Emma 73
Penrose, Roland 221
Percier, Charles 16
Percy, Samuel 83
Perseus 189
Peter (collaborator of Rodin) 214
Petermann (founder) 196
Phidias 12, 15-16, 22, 62-63, 66, 180, 184
Philipon, Charles 34-35
Phryne 22, 86
Picasso, Pablo 51-52, 58, 114, 221, 265, 269
Pilon, Germain 162
Pinédo, Emile 232
Pitt, William 88
Planche, Gustave 73-74
Plato 61-62, 71
Pliny 48
Plutarch 62
Pohle, Leon 41
Polixenes 87
Pontavice de Heussey, Robert du 102
Potocka (family) 243
Pottier, Edmond 44, 245
Poussielgue-Rusand (goldsmith) 74
Poussin, Nicolas 64
Powolny, Michael 53, 265
Pradier, James 22, 25, 33, 35, 45, 76, 85-86, 120, 125, 243, 250, 265-66
Praxiteles 243
Prell, Herrmann 70, 165
Preston, Robert Berthon 65, 122
Protât, Hugues 78
Psyche 25, 118-19, 266
Puech, Denys 45, 265
Pugin, A.W.N. 53, 74, 85, 145, 249
Puvis de Chavannes, Pierre 52-53, 128, 254
Pygmalion 13, 15, 19, 26, 46-47, 54, 57-58, 83, 88, 90, 95, 101, 251, 253

Quatremère de Quincy, Antoine-Chrysostome 15-19, 22, 40, 62, 242

Rachilde 99
Ranzoni, Daniele 106
Raoul-Rochette 18
Raoux, Jean 15
Raphael 244
Rauch, Christian Daniel 32, 49

Rauschenberg, Robert 103
Rauschner, Johann Christoph 83-84
Raymondin 83
Regnault, Henri 244
Régnier, Henri de 94
Rehberg, Friedrich 251
Reichensperger, August 32
Rembrandt 155
Renan, Ernest 197
Renoir, Claude 218
Renoir, Pierre 218
Renoir, Pierre-Auguste 51, 218, 265, 269
Reuterswärd, Patrik 18
Revett, Nicholas 15
Reyer, Ernest 45
Reynolds-Stephens, William Ernest 158, 267
Riemenschneider, Tilman 27
Rimmel, Eugene 79
Ringel d'Illzach, Jean-Désiré 40, 42, 68, 70, 85, 99, 101-02
Rivière, Théodore-Louis-Auguste 44-45, 96-97, 154, 265
Robbia, della (family) 14, 33-34, 54, 62, 78, 165, 244
Robbia, Luca della 79, 155
Roberts-Austen, William Chandler 78, 199
Robinson, Edward 245
Roche, Pierre 81
Rochejacquelein, Comtesse de la 142
Rodenbach, George 57
Rodin, Auguste 47-52, 103, 114, 200, 202, 204, 208, 210, 212, 214, 216, 220-21, 265, 269
Rollinat, Maurice 99
Roma 16
Rossini, Gioacchino 194
Rosso, Medardo 42, 106-07, 206, 212, 254, 265, 269
Rothschild (family) 39
Rouault, Georges 58
Roumi, Valérie 50-51
Rousseau, Jean-Jacques 63
Rouvier, Noémie 244
Rubens, Peter Paul 64
Rude, François 47, 180
Rudier, Alexis 200, 212, 214, 220
Ruella, Dambrosio and Assunta della 124
Runge, Philipp Otto 59
Rush, William 251
Ruskin, John 60, 91, 104, 110
Russell, Arthur 199
Russell, John Peter 204
Russell, Mariana 204

Saba, Queen of 95
St Amaranthe, Madame de 87
Saint-Gaudens, Augustus 48, 265
Saint-Marceaux, René de 67, 81
Salammbô 44, 58, 92, 96-97, 188
Salmon, Mrs 90
Salome 43-44, 70, 95, 107, 136

Index

Sand, George 93
Sansovino 162
Sappé, Madame 88
Sappho 34, 39, 66, 94, 248, 253
Sardou, Victorien 152
Sargon, King 194
Sattler, Ernst 118-19
Schadow, Gottfried 16
Schäfer, G. 42
Schasler, Max 40
Schauss, Martin 33
Schelling, Friedrich 17
Schinkel, Karl Friedrich 16
Schlemmer, Oskar 58
Schmieden, Heino 81
Schneider, Franz 30
Schopenhauer, Arthur 34, 42
Schwanthaler, Ludwig von 18, 20, 25, 243
Schwob, Marcel 184
Scopas 97
Scott, Walter 230
Semiramis 194
Semper, Gottfried 18-19, 42, 65, 134, 248
Seneca 170
Seurre, Emile 243
Seysses, Auguste 232
Shakespeare, William 87, 92
Shearman, William Tecumseh 48
Shelley, Percey Bysshe 44
Shipton, Mother 90
Siemering, Rudolf 81
Simart, Charles 22, 25, 27, 33-35, 66, 76, 180, 242, 248, 265
Simpson, G. 86
Singh, Dalip 13, 35, 168, 267
Siot, Madame 128
Siot-Decauville (founders) 73, 78, 180, 224
Slaughter, Mary 83
Slodtz, Michel-Ange 65
Smirke, Robert 27
Smith, David 103
Smith, James 204
Smith, J. Lindon 245
Solomon, King 97
Sommariva, Count 19
Sophocles 22
Spielmann, Marion 83, 91
Stackelberg, Otto Magnus Freiherr von 242
Stafford, Marquis of 76
Strasser, Arthur 265
Stratonice 22
Stuart, John 15
Stuck, Franz von 57, 97, 108-10, 138, 252, 254, 265-66
Susse, Albert and Jacques 73, 75, 78, 174, 186
Symons, Arthur 89

Ta'aroa 112
Talbot, William Henry Fox 13
Tancock, John 204
Tanit 92
Taylor, Susan 58
Tennyson, Alfred 57
Theodora, Empress 152
Theseus 26
Thomas, Gabriel-Jules 39-40, 53, 244
Thomas, John 29, 79
Thorvaldsen, Bertel 243
Tiffany 77
Tilgner, Viktor 265
Torelli, Jafet 78
Townley, Charles 12
Treu, Georg 40-44, 51, 53, 70, 118-19, 134, 136, 138, 245, 246, 246, 247
Triqueti, Henri de 13, 35, 76
Tussaud, Madame 42, 69, 84-85, 87-89, 251

Ulysses 26

Valadon, Jules 234, 254
Vallgren, Ville 57
Van der Stappen, Charles 56-57, 228, 230, 265
Van Goethem, Marie 69
Varenne, Gaston 220
Vasari, Giorgio 48, 70
Vecchietta (Lorenzo di Pietro) 162
Venus 25-26, 65-66, 76, 88-91, 94-95, 98-99, 101-02, 120, 122, 174, 245, 266 (see also Aphrodite)
Verlaine, Paul 94
Véron, Eugène 64
Verrochio, Andrea del 36
Victoria, Queen 13, 25, 73, 83, 86, 168, 243, 244
Vignon, Claude 244
Villard, Nina de 69, 253
Villiers de l'Isle-Adam, Auguste de 101-02, 253
Viollet-le-Duc, Eugène-Emmanuel 27-28, 74, 104, 110, 145, 148
Virebent (ceramicists) 79
Virgil 162
Vischer, Friedrich Theodor 29
Vitet, Ludovic 27
Vivien 57, 70, 109-10
Volkmann, Artur 43, 70, 165, 265, 267
Vollard, Ambroise 114, 218, 221
Voltaire 83, 194
Vrubel, Mikhail 152

Waagen, Dr (Gustav Friedrich?) 85
Wagner, Martin von 17, 242
Wagner, Richard 42, 104, 106-07, 110, 114, 254, 255
Washington, George 88
Wasserman, Jeanne 34
Waterhouse, John William 230
Watts, George Frederick 252, 253
Webb, Matthew 42, 165
Weekes, Henry 44, 83, 92, 250
Weitsch, Friedrich Georg 16
Wellington, Duke of 11, 26, 87
Westmacott, Richard 26
Wharton, Madame 89
Wicar (collector) 67, 244
Wilde, Oscar 35, 252
Willumsen, Jens Ferdinand 58, 235, 265, 270
Winckelmann, Johann Joachim 12, 14-15, 17, 26, 60, 62, 244
Wittkower, Rudolf 13
Wolfers, Philippe 56, 95, 265
Wolff, Albert (critic) 32
Wolff, Albert (sculptor) 70
Wölfflin, Heinrich 13
Wyatt, Richard 250

Yarborough, Lord 250

Zadkine, Ossip 58
Zenobia 91
Zeus 15, 19 (see also Jupiter)
Zeuxis 62
Zoffany, Johann 12
Zola, Emile 69, 71, 94

Photography

All photographs have been provided by the museums or owners of the works unless otherwise stated:
B. Acloque/CNHMS/SPADEM 24, 118 · Jörg P. Anders/Staatliche Museen zu Berlin, Preußischer Kulturbesitz 32 111 · James Austin **12-16**, **30**, **32**, **35-39**, **43-46**, **53**, **70**, **86**, 30, 57, 76 · Studio Basset/Musée des Beaux-Arts de Lyon **71–72** · Bildarchiv Foto Marburg 41 · Bildarchiv Preußischer Kulturbesitz 44 · Andreas Blühm 49, 79, 132 · Jean Boucher/Musée royaux de l'Art et de l'Histoire, Brussels 138 · Verlag Christian Brandstätter, Vienna 88 · Carlo Catenazzi/Art Gallery of Ontario 45 · Christie's Images 74 · Conway Library, University of London 73, 77, 78, 80, 81, 82, 123 · Dubroca by Spadem/Photothèque des Musées de la Ville de Paris 139 · Repro Gerstenberger after E.A. Seemann Kunstmappe/Museum der bildenden Künste Leipzig 63 · Photothèque Giraudon 17 · Béatrice Hatala/Musée Rodin 73 · Béatrice Hatala/Réunion des musées nationaux 23 · Ole Haupt/Ny Carlsberg Glyptotek 50 · Erik and Petra Hesmerg Front cover, **48-49**, **61**, **80-81**, 108 · R. Ignatiadis/Réunion des musées nationaux 36 · Bruno Jarret/Musée Rodin 133 · Frédéric Jaulmes 6 · Jürgen Karpinski/Staatliche Kunstsammlungen Dresden 8 · Wim van Keulen (repro) 4, 109 · Kluge/Museum der bildenden Künste Leipzig 43 · Hans-Peter Klut/Staatliche Kunstsammlungen Dresden **2-5**, **42**, 42, 113 · Koninklijke Bibliotheek, The Hague 71 · Lessing, Wien/Museum der bildenden Künste Leipzig 62 · H. Lewandowski/Réunion des musées nationaux **31**, 33, 90, 102, 112 · Ursula Lichtlein/Kunsthalle Bremen **67**, **96** · Giorgio Liverani/Skira 10 · Photo Meyer/Kunsthistorisches Museum Vienna 107 · Musée de la Ville de Strasbourg 93 · National Monuments Records, Royal Commission on the Historical Monuments of England, Crown copyright 26 · R.G. Ojeda/Réunion des musées nationaux **83**, 122 · Fotostudio Otto/Österreichische Galerie Belvedere 99, 121 · Pierrain by Spadem/Photothèque des Musées de la Ville de Paris **79**, 54 · Réunion des musées nationaux **19**, **55**, **87**, **94**, 11, 20, 34, 53, 94, 95, 100, 101, 104, 110, 124, 129 · E. Revault/CNHMS/SPADEM 22 · Roger-Viollet 35 · Caroline Rose/CNHMS/SPADEM 38 · Adam Rzepka/Musée Rodin **74** · Katrin Schilling/Museum Villa Stuck 97 · Verlag Schnell & Steiner, Regensburg 27 · Martine Seyve/Musée des Beaux-Arts de Caen 56 · Skira 37 · Sotheby's Photographic Services 125 · Speltdoorn et fils/Musée royaux des Beaux-Arts de Belgique **66**, **77-78** · L. Sully-Jaulmes/Musée des arts décoratifs, Paris **33-34**, **40**, **50**, **58** · Zoltán Szalay 27 · Didier Tragin and Cathérine Lancien/Musée des Beaux-Arts Rouen 126 · Elke Walford/Hamburger Kunsthalle **18**, **90** · Christoph Walter and Karin Maucotel/Musée Bourdelle 84 · Wellcome Institute Library, London 89 · Peter Willi/Skira 19 · Ole Woldbye/J.F. Willumsens Museum **94** · Walter Ziegler, Institut für Kunstgeschichte, Universität Regensburg 16

Colophon

This book is published to coincide with the exhibition *The Colour of Sculpture 1840-1910* at the Van Gogh Museum in Amsterdam (26 July – 17 November 1996) and the Henry Moore Institute in Leeds (13 December 1996 – 6 April 1997).

Conception
Andreas Blühm

Executive committee
Ronald de Leeuw, Andreas Blühm (Van Gogh Museum)
Robert Hopper, Penelope Curtis (Henry Moore Institute)

Authors
Andreas Blühm is Head of Exhibitions at the Van Gogh Museum, Amsterdam.
Wolfgang Drost is Professor emeritus of the Universität Gesamthochschule Siegen.
June Hargrove is Professor of Art History at the University of Maryland.
Emmanuelle Héran is Curator in the Department of Sculpture at the Musée d'Orsay, Paris.
Philip Ward-Jackson is Deputy Conway Librarian at the Courtauld Institute of Art, University of London.
Alison Yarrington is Professor of Art History at Leicester University.

Entries by
Nienke Blom **65**
Andreas Blühm **1-8, 17-21, 24-29, 31, 33-34, 40-42, 48-50, 55, 58-61, 66-67, 75, 77-78, 86-90, 94, 96**
Nathalie Bondil **9-16, 23, 30, 32, 40, 47, 51-54, 56-57, 62-64, 71-74, 76, 79-85, 92-93, 95**
Penelope Curtis **70**
Donald Myers **22, 35-39, 43-44, 68-69, 91**
Philip Ward-Jackson **45-46**

Editors
Andreas Blühm
Penelope Curtis

Translation
Rachel Esner (from the German)
Charles Penwarden (from the French)

Coordination
Aly Noordermeer (Van Gogh Museum)
Stephen Feeke and Helen Pearson (Henry Moore Institute)

Conservation
Jackie Heuman

© Copyright 1996 Van Gogh Museum, Amsterdam / Uitgeverij Waanders bv, Zwolle. All rights reserved. No part of this publication may be reproduced or transmitted in any form or by any means, electronic or mechanical, including photography, recording or any other information storage and retrieval system, without prior permission in writing from the publisher.

Design
Pieter Roozen, Amsterdam

Printer
Waanders Printers, Zwolle

Front cover
Charles-Henri-Joseph Cordier
Jewess from Algiers, c. 1862
Amsterdam, Van Gogh Museum

ISBN 90-400-9847-6 (bound)
ISBN 90-400-9846-8 (paperback; only available at the Van Gogh Museum)
NUGI 921/911